Allies yet Rivals

Allies yet Rivals

INTERNATIONAL POLITICS IN 18TH CENTURY EUROPE

Marco Cesa

Translated by Patrick John Barr

STANFORD UNIVERSITY PRESS
STANFORD, CALIFORNIA

To the memory of Mario Stoppino

Stanford University Press
Stanford, California

Allies yet Rivals was originally published in Italian in 2007 under the title *Alleati ma rivali. Teoria delle alleanze e politica estera settecentesca* © 2007, Società editrice il Mulino, Bologna.

Printed in the United States of America on acid-free, archival-quality paper

Library of Congress Cataloging-in-Publication Data

Cesa, Marco, 1958-
[Alleati ma rivali. English]
Allies yet rivals : international politics in 18th century Europe / Marco Cesa ; [translated by] Patrick John Barr.
p. cm.
Includes bibliographical references and index.
ISBN 978-0-8047-6295-3 (cloth : alk. paper)
1. Europe—Foreign relations. 2. Europe—Politics and government—1648-1789. 3. Alliances—History—18th century. I. Title.
D287.C47 2010
327.4009'033—dc22
2009048524

Typeset by Bruce Lundquist in 10.5/14 Adobe Garamond

Contents

PART TWO | FOUR CASE STUDIES

Tables

Acknowledgments

In submitting the present work for publication in English, I would like to thank both the Facoltà di Scienze Politiche Roberto Ruffilli, University of Bologna at Forlì, and Alenia Aeronautica for their generous financial support covering translation costs. The staff of the Roberto Ruffilli Library, University of Bologna at Forlì, and the Robert H. Evans Library, the Paul H. Nitze School of Advanced International Studies (SAIS), Johns Hopkins University, Bologna Center, have constantly and kindly assisted me during my research work. In 1993 and 1997 I took advantage of a Fulbright Scholarship, and of CNR and NATO funding, to spend two periods at the Minda de Gunzburg Center for European Studies at Harvard University (Cambridge, Massachusetts), to whose director at that time, Stanley H. Hoffmann, I am most grateful. The final pages of the book were written at SAIS, Washington, D.C., where I taught a course on alliances and international relations during the fall semester 2005; this series of lessons enabled me to examine certain ideas in greater depth, and to make a number of improvements to the present work. Finally, over the course of time I have been very fortunate to have benefited from the helpful suggestions of Charles F. Doran, Joseph M. Grieco, Glenn H. Snyder, and Kenneth N. Waltz. Angelo Panebianco read the first part of the book, and his suggestions were, as always, extremely helpful, for which I would like to warmly thank him. My greatest intellectual debt is to Mario Stoppino, who profoundly influenced my initial thoughts on the subject at hand; I would thus like to dedicate the present volume to the memory of Mario.

Allies yet Rivals

Introduction

> Having been advised to suspend the shelling not to risk firing on friendly forces as well, Alphonsus replied, with a severe face, "Go on shooting all around and fear nothing, my gunners; you can't go wrong, for they are all enemies."
>
> —PAOLO GIOVIO, *La Vita di Alfonso da Este*

It is generally accepted that the members of an alliance do not necessarily have to be friends, and that cooperation between allies may well conceal a certain degree of competition. Nevertheless, the majority of international relations scholars tend to perceive allies simply as states working closely together in order to achieve a shared objective; as such, they virtually take it for granted that allies act as one body. Alliances are commonly seen as a union of separate forces, a policy-coordination organization, the taker of joint action against some third party. Even if some observers and scholars point out that such cooperative enterprise and the ensuing relations are often of a rather fragile, contradictory nature, both everyday language and specialized analyses invariably place the stress on the cooperative features of alliances and on their "external" functions, that is, on those aspects of the alliance designed to deal with what is usually described as the "common enemy."

However, even the briefest examination of diplomatic history will reveal a number of other aspects of alliances. First of all, the events associated with each phase of all alliances invariably show that the common cause is not the only dimension of allies' relations; nor does it clearly circumscribe their functional space. In fact, allies are generally involved in more ambiguous and complex maneuvers, by means of which one ally tries to condition and control the other; and even when the common cause is clearly evident, each member pursues the cause while at the same time closely observing the behavior of the other, and trying to limit its freedom of movement to some degree. Second, there is a striking variety of types of alliance, as can be seen not only in the degree to which the various members condition the behavior of the others but also in the tone of their relations, which may vary from tense to cordial, and from a position of reciprocal support to one of substantial diffidence toward, and reluctance to adopt, the other's aims. The most common generalizations—which also happen to be the oldest and most deeply rooted ones—are incapable of encompassing this and other differences. As in a Hegelian night when all cows are perceived as being gray, scholars of alliance politics tend to see one alliance as similar to all others, which to be quite honest is extremely debatable. To conclude then, an alliance can be said to possess an internal dimension that, as well as casting a rather sinister shadow over relations between the partners, is equally as important as the external dimension, if not more so. Furthermore, the notion of alliance conceals such a great variety of phenomena and behavior that it becomes difficult to encapsulate them within a single framework. The present study is going to examine both the "darker side" of alliances and the various forms such alliances may take. The work is subdivided into two main parts, one theoretical, the other historical.

The realist school, with its insistence on the balance of power, has contributed most to developing and spreading the view that alliances are essentially instruments by which states aggregate their power against a common enemy, thus assigning a secondary role to relations between allies (to such an extent as to lose sight of these relations altogether) and to how allies interact with third parties. Traditional theory is naturally not without foundation, but it allows light to be shed on only a small number of alliances, that is, those that are almost exclusively a reflection of an imbalance of power; or on one aspect of most alliances, that is, their "external" orientation against an enemy. Moving from here, we first of all provide an outline of contemporary theoretical debate on alliances (balancing versus bandwagoning, external versus domestic causes), illustrate its limitations, and propose an alternative conception of alliances, at the core of which is the study of inter-allied relations, with all their ambivalence.

This preliminary work serves, in turn, as the basis for a review of the broader theoretical perspective from which alliances are generally analyzed. Claiming that alliances are a manifestation of the principle of the balance of power amounts to inferring that states' ideal objective is the pursuit of security, and adopting, implicitly or otherwise, a systemic-structural approach similar to that of the neorealist school of thought. However, such a position may be accepted as only an initial approximation, given that many alliances cannot be conceived in such terms. Moreover, neorealism was designed to give account of international macro phenomena, and thus it comes as no surprise that such an approach is incapable of grasping the multifaceted nature of alliances. Given our present concern with the regular, recurrent features of international politics, we have decided to remain within a systemic context and focus not so much only on the international structure but rather on how each state is positioned in relation to both allies and enemies. The interpretation of alliances offered within such a framework places considerable importance on the role played by inter-ally exchange and power relations. The implications of such an approach are quite simple: by focusing on how each ally tries to control the behavior of its partner, the emphasis is not so much on pursuit of security in the face of some external threat as on pursuit of the "conformity" of others, in particular the conformity of the same ally. In fact, it will not be possible to focus on the pursuit of other objectives, such as security, until the ally has been bound—in other words, until the ally's freedom of movement has been circumscribed, and its behavior rendered more readily foreseeable, by the alliance itself. The resulting picture is completely in keeping with the realist tradition—with the struggle for power continuing within the alliance itself—although it is one that the realist school overall has itself failed to produce.

We therefore focus on both analytical levels—the internal and the external—at which each and every alliance may be studied. Together with the famous "alliance security dilemma" clearly expounded by Glenn H. Snyder, and based on the twin fears of "abandonment" and "entrapment," the present study focuses on the "alliance power dilemma," which once again has been formulated on the basis of two opposing fears: that one's ally may become too strong, and thus be capable of escaping one's control, or even of exercising control; and that it may be too weak, and as such incapable of making any significant contribution to the alliance. Furthermore, an examination is made of the more common forms of behavior that allies adopt toward their enemies, together with the potential interaction between different levels. Thus the impact on inter-ally relations of a policy of firmness (or of flexibility) toward the enemy (or enemies) is discussed, as are the repercussions on the alliance of a conciliatory (or aggressive) stance adopted by the enemy (or enemies). The fears associated with the two previously mentioned dilemmas, together with the policies adopted to deal with these fears, take various forms depending on the case at hand; similarly, the stance adopted in relation to the enemy may have a variety of consequences. The problem is thus one of distinguishing between forms of alliance. In other words, despite the presence of a common cause, the nature of this cause, the context in which it emerges, the existence of other national causes, and the relations of power between allies all affect the performance and workings of the alliance to a certain degree. These and other differences can be accounted for only if we distinguish between types of alliance, which is yet another matter that previous studies have failed to deal with satisfactorily. This operation is even more important, given the vague, inconclusive nature of the majority of generalizations currently available.

The two criteria we have chosen for characterization of the types of alliance closely reflect the conceptualization of alliances proposed herein: the relation of forces between allies, and their respective systemic positions. What emerges from employment of these two criteria is identification of two general classifications of alliance. The first includes symmetrical and asymmetrical alliances, depending on whether the power relationship between the allies is a balanced one (symmetrical) or is stacked in favor of one of them (asymmetrical). The second classification leads to a subdivision of alliances into homogeneous and heterogeneous varieties, depending on whether the members conform to convergent constraints or grasp compatible opportunities in the former case, or obey divergent constraints or exploit contradictory opportunities in the latter case. The systemic position of allies enables us to understand the degree to which they are prepared to cooperate, and thus the kind of negotiations they are likely to hold—accommodative in the case of homogeneous alliances, or coercive in the case of heterogeneous coalitions. The power relations between allies throw light on the dynamics of exchange, in the case of symmetrical alliances, or on the dynamics of dominion and dependence, in an asymmetrical nature. The two "dilemmas of alliances" take on their own forms in each class. However, the most important factor is the compositional effect produced when the categories intersect to give the various types of alliance described in this book.

This largely deductive operation defines four basic alliance types. First there is the symmetrical, homogeneous type, which we call the *aggregation* alliance, whose members cooperate in a mutually beneficial way subject to commonly agreed conditions. The second type, asymmetrical and homogeneous, which we call the *guarantee* alliance, is also characterized by a substantial degree of cooperation among members, which benefits all of them; however, the terms of this cooperation are basically established by one of the allies, the stronger of the two. The third type, asymmetrical and heterogeneous, is called the *hegemonic* alliance; here the two members adopt different stances, but the imbalance in the power relations between the two is such that it enables the less dependent of the two to drag the other along with it, imposing certain conditions on this weaker party that are at least partly detrimental to it. Finally, the fourth type is the symmetrical, heterogeneous model, which we call the *deadlocked* alliance; this type differs from the others in that its members possess equal bargaining power, but each member has adopted a position that cannot be easily reconciled with that of the other member; the net result is a situation of paralysis. Each type of alliance thus possesses certain general characteristics; within each type, more specific hypotheses are developed regarding the policies adopted by the allies and the results of their interaction. It is at this point that the various forms adopted by the two dilemmas of alliances are further specified and given an initial explanation.

The theoretical propositions formulated for each type of alliance are next illustrated using four case studies taken from the diplomatic history of 18th century Europe, for two reasons. First, given that this period in history has been largely ignored by the specialists until now, we would like to broaden the scope offered by current international studies, to take in what is generally considered one of the most interesting periods in the history of European diplomacy. The four cases in question are presented here in chronological order, starting from the War of Spanish Succession and ending on the eve of the French Revolution, thus offering the reader an overview of almost the entire century. Second, 18th century international politics and diplomacy were played out within a context that is ideal for our purposes. The absence of any ideological conflict makes it fairly easy to isolate the impact of interest and power that we wish to stress here; the existence of a number of great powers gives the international system a certain fluidity and enables us to immediately identify the reactions of states to the smallest change in their situational context. Finally, the absence of any hegemonic actor clears the field of further "noise" capable of conditioning the logic of alliances to the point where it overshadows some of the dynamics we are most interested in here.

During the first half of the 18th century, Britain and the United Provinces clearly represented a case of a guarantee alliance; the two nations joined forces to combat the French, subject to the terms and conditions established by government in London. At the same time, the United Provinces, protected by their major ally and induced in other ways to follow its leadership, over the years progressively attempted to reduce their engagement, dedicating themselves prevalently to trade; Britain, for its part, systematically influenced its minor ally's foreign policy (and sometimes even internal policy). The Dutch were thus absorbed into the various diplomatic mechanisms designed by Britain; yet more often than not they benefited from British leadership.

During the decade after the Peace of Utrecht, Britain laid the foundations for its future "preponderance" thanks in part to a hegemonic alliance with France. By taking advantage of the momentary decline in power and prestige of the latter, Britain managed to closely ally France to itself and use that nation as a means of strengthening its own foreign influence, from the Baltic to the Mediterranean. The pursuit of a common cause—in this case, preservation of peace—cost France dearly, since as Britain's ally it found itself forced to surrender certain important interests.

The Anglo-Prussian alliance during the Seven Years' War enables us to study the mechanisms that characterize the aggregation alliance, which is the one closest to the traditional idea of an alliance often to be found in international studies. In this specific case, we have two powers that closely cooperated in a mutually beneficial manner, in circumstances that reduced any potential sources of conflict between the two to a bare minimum. Their mutual dependence and shared enemies led Britain and Prussia to reach agreements both countries were happy with, without either party being in a position to manipulate the other.

Finally, a fine example of the deadlocked alliance is that of Austro-French relations during the latter half of the century. Far from affording one another mutual support, Austria and France remained united almost against their will, following the end of the Seven Years' War. Each needed the other, but given their diverse positions in the international chessboard neither wished to lend support to the other's policies. Austria thus found itself hindered by France's veto on numerous occasions, while France chose to renounce certain substantial benefits in order not to favor Austria's designs.

The last chapter then offers an assessment of our analysis by reviewing some of the initial hypotheses, by identifying more precisely the conditions under which the causal connections mentioned are more or less likely to hold, and by proposing a series of ideas regarding the transformation and decline of alliances that are in keeping with the overall theoretical framework.

PART ONE

Alliance Theory

ONE

Alliances in the Theory of International Relations

THE NATURE OF THE PROBLEM

According to Niccolò Machiavelli, remaining neutral is almost never a good idea in time of war; dangerous for the weak, and of little benefit to the strong, neutrality is one of those compromises that Machiavelli frequently condemned for the false sense of security they so easily instill.[1] One therefore needs to make a stand, one way or the other. After all, as Giovanni Botero pointed out, alliances can be of substantial benefit to those involved. They tend to increase a state's power, if for no other reason than "there are many things [a ruler] could not and would not dare to attempt on his own which he will consider possible and will undertake in concert with others."[2]

Whether they are the result of harsh political necessity or more simply the means by which states pursue a range of aims, alliances are a frequently present phenomenon in the field of international politics. From the very earliest available historical records, right up to the present day, states have constantly and regularly formed alliances, regardless of the international system in place or the historical period in question. Alliances are often associated with war—another constant on the international political scene—and often with the attempt to impose and maintain a certain international order. Even the form that such alliances take, in terms of the wording thereof, reveals a surprising degree of continuity. Comparing the treaty of alliance stipulated by the ancient Egyptians and Hittites in the 13th century B.C. with modern-day treaties may at first sight appear a rather extravagant exercise, yet there are certain extraordinary similarities between the two: an introductory preamble, clauses of nonaggression and mutual aid in the event of attack by other states, and the promise of intervention in case of internal subversion.[3] While focusing on the degree of historical continuity in international alliances, we should of course take care not to lose sight of how they have changed over the course of time. In particular, it has been pointed out that in the last few centuries alliances have taken on a more defensive purpose than was previously the case; that they have become more multilateral than purely bilateral; that they are increasingly based on the principle of mutual aid, and less on that of the unilateral guarantee; that a growing number of alliances are formed during peacetime than was previously the case; and finally that alliances in this modern age are highly institutionalized (Osgood 1968, 25–31). Nevertheless, it should also be said that they still remain alliances, and as such the regularity with which they accompany international politics and the characteristic dilemmas states are faced with when becoming allies still need to be taken into consideration.[4]

Even if the origins and workings of alliances, together with their effects and their duration, have been studied from various points of view, with the aid of a whole range of approaches in international relations theory, it is the realist tradition that has made the most significant contribution to this field of research.[5] The realist approach, and the various forms it has taken over the course of time, is essentially a state-centric perspective that looks to the power relations between states for an explanation of their respective behavior in the international arena. The multitude of national interests in play and the constant pursuit of national power and security mean that competition and conflict are the most characteristic traits of international politics. Having established these points, realism then examines the various forms taken by such dynamics, together with the means that states employ in order to manage their relations.[6]

This is the context within which realist analyses of alliances should be placed. Realists generally perceive alliances as a union of forces between diverse parties faced with a common enemy, and as such one of the very few cases in which interstate rivalry is set aside in the name of cooperation. The most familiar definitions of *alliance* (submitted by realists but also by exponents of other schools of thought) all focus on three basic elements (albeit using different terms and accentuations): an alliance is a *cooperative* enterprise; it is of a *formal* nature; and its purpose is to guarantee the *security* of the parties involved, in particular their military security.[7] Overall, this definition is a correct one, albeit of a rather limited nature. Although the cooperative aspect of alliances is undoubtedly of fundamental importance, it should not be allowed to conceal the rivalry, and at times the antagonism, between allies in many cases. In other words, the definition of an alliance as a formal agreement on cooperation does not mean that relations between allies are exclusively of a cooperative nature. Furthermore, placing the emphasis on aggregation of forces in view of an external objective—security in the face of a common enemy—is certainly useful, but only as an initial approximation; there are various other aspects, related to the formation and working of alliances, that cannot be interpreted in this manner and that point to a series of more complex dynamics among allies. This notwithstanding, the traditional approach has proven extremely popular, to the point where it influences the majority of studies. Here, it is a good idea to carefully examine the more salient aspects of the question.

ALLIANCES AND THE BALANCE OF POWER

It is an axiom of the realist school of thought that underlying all alliances are the convergent interests of the individual states in question. According to Martin Wight (1978, 122), for example, the function of alliances is to "advance the interests [of the allies] against the outer world." George Liska (1962, 26), for his part, observed that "the decision to align, in what form, and with whom [...] is made with reference to national interests." Hans J. Morgenthau, in his usual vigorous manner, points out that "an alliance requires of necessity a community of interests for its foundation" (1959, 186). What interests are we talking about here? Nearly all realist scholars believe that the interests in question are directly linked to the question of *security*, broadly defined as protection against a common *threat*. Thus an alliance is simply—or mostly—the union of forces of those who, fearing they are incapable of dealing with the enemy on their own, decide to cooperate with other states in the same situation, to present a united front against the external threat. This is the essence of what is usually called the "power aggregation" model, which is probably the most common interpretation of alliances in general, and of the nature of their origins in particular.[8]

It should be pointed out that balance of power theory and alliance theory clearly overlap. Alliances are nothing more than a means for states to maintain an approximately equal distribution of power for security purposes.[9] Since the 16th century, a multitude of historians, philosophers, and politicians have reconstructed the events underlying the creation and persistence of the European states system by attributing fundamental importance to the role played by the balance of power, and by the policy of alliances adopted in order to establish or maintain that balance of power. Indeed, creation of an alliance has been the most commonly recommended, as well as implemented, method of dealing with an impelling threat, and of creating a system of checks and balances guaranteeing fundamental security and stability, and thus a modicum of international order.

According to Francesco Guicciardini, in Italy at the end of the 15th century Ferdinand II of Aragon "realized that it was necessary for him to unite with the others, and especially with the states of Milan and Florence, in order to create a counterbalance against the power of the Venetians."[10] Giovanni Botero wrote that "the ordinary method of counterpoising suspect forces that threaten one's own interests, is the formation of leagues, whereby one force is set against another."[11] Fénelon believed that "defensive alliances are [...] just and necessary, when they are in reality intended to prevent an exorbitant power, such as might be in a condition to subdue all."[12] Daniel Defoe mentioned the importance of "potent Confederacies among the weaker Powers by Joint Assistance to reduce the encroaching growing Part to such Terms of Reason, and preserve and secure the Tranquillity of the rest."[13] Emmerich de Vattel, when enquiring as to the safest means of preserving the balance of power, concluded that "it is simpler, easier and more just [...] to form [...] alliances in order to make a stand against a very powerful sovereign and prevent him from dominating."[14] Friedrich von Gentz observed that "an union between several regents ha[s] been always considered as a barrier against lawless power, and the passions of an individual oppressor."[15] Lord Palmerston declared that "'balance of power' means only this—that a number of weaker States may unite in order to prevent a stronger one from acquiring a power which should be dangerous to them."[16] In Germany, Leopold von Ranke, reviewing the history of modern Europe, concluded that "in great danger, one can always trust in the guiding Genius which ever protects Europe from a one-sided and forceful dominating tendency. Every pressure from one side is resisted by one from the others, and their connection into a whole [...] has happily preserved the freedom and particular development of all."[17]

The role of the *balancer*, as pointed out by various scholars and observers of the balance of power, consists purely in wisely deciding which side one should ally one's forces with, or in deciding to remain on neutral ground. In other words, it consists in adopting a careful alliance policy.[18]

More recent reflections emanating from the realist tradition tend to echo these historical views. In the words of Morgenthau, alliances are "the historically most important manifestation of the balance of power" (1948/1973, 188), and international politics as a whole could easily be seen from the point of view of alliances, according to two models. In the first, the balance of power consists in competition between a hegemonic power on the one hand and a coalition of all those states opposed to this power on the other; in the second model, there is the opposition between alliances, each of which tries to protect its members from the attacks of other alliances, and in general to further the interests of those members (ibidem, 194–200).

However, it was above all the neorealism of Kenneth N. Waltz (1979) that led to formulation of a general theoretical-conceptual interpretation of international relations, which was to have considerable influence thereafter. To put it briefly, Waltz believes that the characteristic results of interaction among states can be explained in terms of the structure of the international system; this is defined by an ordering principle, namely anarchy, and by the distribution of power among the various states, whereby an international system may be deemed either bipolar or multipolar. Within such an anarchical international setting, devoid of any central authority guaranteeing the defense of the system's member states in the event of aggression, and thus the protection of their vital interests, the same states have to rely on their own forces. In fact, Waltz refers to the international system as a *self-help system*: states are functionally undifferentiated within such a system, in that their primary objective, one that is shared by all, is security. According to Waltz, this sheds light on certain international outcomes that constantly emerge, regardless of the domestic make-up of the states in question, starting with the balance of power itself.

Although neorealism is occasionally ambiguous on this particular issue, we could say that the traditional term *balance of power* can be ascribed to this general trend when it is perceived as a systemic effect, whereas the term *balancing* would be more appropriate if the trend in question concerns the behavior of the states themselves. In addition, such a tendency takes on a number of more specific forms and means, depending on the type of international system in question. In a bipolar system the two dominant powers try to preserve the balance between themselves using mainly "internal" means, that is, rearmament; whereas in a multipolar system states adopt "external" means, namely alliances. Worried about its own security, when a state realizes its resources are insufficient for it to deal with an adversary on its own, it tends to seek the help of other states that are equally as concerned to contain the "common enemy."

That a common enemy is required first of all in order to form an alliance is a frequently raised issue. If an enemy is not specified, as Morgenthau points out (1959, 187), no alliance can ensue. In Liska's view, the move toward creation of an alliance is triggered by the threat represented by a third state (1962, 13); being a "latent war community," an alliance presupposes a common interest in opposing the threat from certain specific states (Osgood 1968, 17). A shared perception of danger and insecurity is the most frequent reason for creation of military alliances (Holsti 1977, 120); the principal prerequisite for forming an alliance is that its members feel subjected to a common threat (Bladen 1970, 121). The list of such observations could go on.[19] The question of the underlying threat triggering formation of an alliance has been thoroughly examined by Stephen M. Walt (1985 and 1987), who has made it the key issue in his well-known, much-debated theory of the origins of alliances. Walt critiques classical balance of power theory for its exclusive focus on power. In fact, in Walt's view the behavior of states is based on the need not to rebalance power but to deal with threats. In deciding whether a given state represents a threat to our security, we need to take account not only of its aggregate power (population, economic base, industrial and military resources) but also of its geographical proximity, offensive power, and aggressive intentions.[20] However, what Walt stresses as a "balance of threat" theory (not to be confused with traditional balance of power theory) is more of clarifying worth than of any real innovative value, since it expresses a concept which is already an integral part—albeit not always expressed explicitly—of traditional thinking regarding the balance of power.[21]

Whether alliances be seen as a reaction to an imbalance in the distribution of power, or to a threat, they are nevertheless dealt with as an aggregation of diverse powers against a common enemy.[22] It is worth repeating that this conception is broadly shared, and as such it explicitly or implicitly guides not only the majority of studies of the origins of alliances but also numerous analyses of the workings and effects of such alliances. The threat of aggression plays a key part in the creation of alliances, but it is also considered a fundamentally important factor in keeping the alliance going and in ensuring that it continues to perform those functions for which it was designed. In fact, one of the most common generalizations is that the cohesion of an alliance depends on the external threat; as the latter grows or diminishes, the alliance does likewise.[23] Consequently, the duration of an alliance will also depend on the persistence of the threat that led the various states to come together in the first place. Should the danger be dispelled altogether, then the allies will tend to go their own separate ways, especially in the case of war alliances.[24]

The effects of alliances, both from the member states' point of view and from that of the international system, also are examined in terms of the aggregation of power between states sharing the same interests. With regard to individual allies, scholars have studied the strategic-military repercussions and the economic (mostly commercial) implications of alliances. The former include above all consolidation of deterrence (Huth and Russett 1993; Sorokin 1994a; Smith 1995, 1998). In terms of their economic effects, if we assume that an increase in the wealth of one ally means economic reinforcement of the entire alliance, then it has been suggested that free trade is more likely among allies than between states belonging to different alliances (Gowa 1994; Gowa and Mansfield 1993, 2004; Mansfield and Bronson 1997; Long 2003). Finally, a number of analyses regarding the effects of alliances on the overall international system have been based on the very conception of the alliance as an aggregation of power; this is evident from those studies that focus on the role of alliances in creating an international order based above all on a balance of power[25] and also from those highlighting the destabilizing impact of alliances,[26] or those that draw differing conclusions, depending on the type of alliance in question (Mueller 1995).

BALANCING VS. BANDWAGONING, EXTERNAL VS. DOMESTIC CAUSES

However, states do not always unite *against* a state that threatens them (balancing); sometimes, on the contrary, they form alliances *with* the latter, thus adopting a policy known as *bandwagoning*. The dichotomy of balancing versus bandwagoning has been hotly debated. Walt (1987, 17–49), for example, discusses bandwagoning in some depth and argues that such a policy can have defensive grounds (appeasement), offensive grounds (the possibility of sharing the direct or indirect fruits of victory through alliance with an expanding power), or a combination of the two. According to Walt (1987 and 1988), however, the most commonly found form of behavior is balancing, and the reason for this is clear: given that nobody is sure what today's ally will do tomorrow, siding with the strongest party is always going to be risky business. Nevertheless, bandwagoning remains an option (1) for weaker states that cannot possibly hinder the progress of the probable victor, (2) when there are no potential allies with whom to join forces against the strongest state, or (3) during the final stages of a conflict, when those who can will be tempted to move across to the victor's side.[27] In the latter case, the resulting alliance may still be seen as an aggregation of power against a common enemy; in the first two cases the situation is very different, since the state with whom one eventually forms an alliance is, in fact, the enemy itself. It is clear that in this kind of situation, the term *alliance* takes on a completely different meaning. However, Walt goes no further than circumventing the problem by stating that bandwagoning is a much less common occurrence than balancing; this generalization, which is disputed by a number of other scholars, if nothing else deserves further specification.[28]

The power aggregation model, in its various formulations, perceives alliances as phenomena entirely projected outward; in other words, the common enemy plays a fundamentally important, catalyzing role. On the other hand, there are a limited number of studies that attempt to offer an alternative interpretation of the phenomenon. All of them focus on examination of cases of alliances involving states that are not only weak from the international point of view but are also internally fragile; in doing so, such studies look to this internal fragility as a possible explanation of alliance policies. The stance adopted by the weaker powers in central-eastern Europe, in relation to Germany during the second half of the 1930s (Larson 1991), and the politics of alliance adopted by many middle-eastern countries,[29] by third-world countries in general,[30] and also by certain former soviet republics (Miller and Toritsyn 2005), are in fact associated not so much with the presence of external enemies as with the presence of internal dangers. The uncertain legitimacy and doubtful efficacy of the political institutions in these countries, together with their chronic economic fragility, are such that their political elites constantly see themselves as under threat; hence their willingness to form any kind of alliance that can enable them to deal with such problems. Such studies criticize the power aggregation model for its purported neglect of the impact of internal forces, and its underestimation of the fact that an alliance may be both a guarantee of security and a source of economic and political resources to be used internally. At the same time, however, these studies do not really constitute a viable alternative to the traditional approach, in that they are concerned either with the analysis of a single state or with cases that are wholly unrepresentative; as such they reveal very little of any real use in constructing a general theoretical framework.[31]

A more effective criticism of traditional theory (but not of the power aggregation model) was submitted by Randall L. Schweller (1994, 1998), who argued that the term *bandwagoning* should be used to refer to the process of alignment not with the state posing the threat but simply with strong states. Walt admits, as we have already said, that the bandwagoning option may be seen as a choice guided by the desire to enjoy the fruits of the victory of the strongest party; however, this does not lie well with the general hypothesis whereby alliances are created as a response to a threat of some kind. In Schweller's view, the theories of both Waltz and Walt are implicitly suited to conservative powers, or to those powers satisfied with the status quo, which as such tend to form defensive alliances. However, this viewpoint fails to consider a number of other possibilities. To Schweller, the most important factor affecting alignment is the compatibility of various states' political objectives, rather than the power imbalance or the imbalance created by the emergence of a threat. If one state is satisfied with the status quo, it will join a conservative alliance, even if the latter is the stronger force; on the other hand, a revisionist state will be driven more by the desire for "profit" than by the desire for security and will thus align itself with the strongest revisionist power in ascendance at the time. Thus there are two types of bandwagoning: the "jackal," when the state in question allies itself to an expansionist power in order to share in the spoils of victory; and "piling on," whereby a state, at the end of a war, aligns itself with the victorious coalition that is likely to shape the new international order.

However, just as Walt himself is forced to admit certain exceptions that weaken the principal association between threat and alliance, Schweller has to acknowledge that the pursuit of profit is not everything. Even in his hypothetical cases of bandwagoning, in fact, he foresees the possibility that aligning oneself with the strongest power is done also out of fear. Thus on the one hand Walt emphasizes the existence of a threatening state, but as we have seen the ensuing alliance may be just as much against this threatening power as with it. On the other hand, Schweller insists on the importance of the idea of profit, which may induce a state into siding with the strongest power, while at the same time admitting that this decision may also be influenced by the fear factor. Both Walt and Schweller see alliance as an aggregation of power against a common enemy situated on the outside. In Walt's view, an alliance represents a reaction to a commonly perceived threat, whereas Schweller believes that it is a response to the opportunity of gaining something from the outcome of conflict. In a certain sense this distinction is a clear one: Walt implicitly examines the case of satisfied, conservative powers, while Schweller examines the case of unsatisfied, revisionist powers. The two theoretical approaches in question explain differing phenomena and forms of behavior. The problem is that, when put in such terms, the contrast between balancing and bandwagoning fails to stand up to closer examination; indeed, both Walt and Schweller perceive the need to qualify their fundamental generalizations. For both of them, there is a general rule accompanied by certain exceptions; these exceptions cannot be ignored, but they do tend to be marginalized, and consequently examination of the question in hand tends to go no further.

The distinction between profit and threat, which in theory appears to be clear, encounters serious problems in the transition from the conceptual level to the empirical. Whereas in the case of the smaller powers the meaning of the term *threat* is fairly clear, in the case of middle-sized and larger powers the distinction between profit and threat becomes blurred to the point where it is almost imperceptible. Even in those apparently clear cases of alliances based on a potential profit, there is still a noticeable threat; for example, the alliance between Germany and the Soviet Union in the summer of 1939 was undoubtedly based to a certain extent on the profit motive, in that it entailed territorial gains for both sides. Nevertheless, both countries feared being isolated in the event that Great Britain came to an agreement with one state or the other. By contrast, in those alliances that can be explained mainly in terms of the presence of a common enemy there is always some form of profit. For example, within the various coalitions opposing Napoleon's France, for many years both Great Britain and Russia took advantage of the difficulties of their allies, Austria and Prussia, in order to make unilateral territorial and political gains. In other words, threats and opportunities are often inextricably entwined; failure to grasp such an opportunity could lead to a nation finding itself in a tight situation, and in reacting to the threat in question a nation may also stand to gain something from the move.

In short, relationships between allies are often much more complex than current theory would have us believe. Opposition to a common enemy, where present, may be less firm and insistent than talk of balancing would suggest; similarly, the common expansionist policies of the allies in question are often implemented with a watchful eye on the gains made by the other member(s) of the alliance. Even jumping on the victor's bandwagon at the end of a war has the dual purpose of obtaining some form of recompense and of avoiding the punishment dealt out to the vanquished powers. In joining an alliance, states not only side with, or against, the strongest power, oppose a threat, or side with it; in practice, they also do a series of other things that in certain cases have nothing to do with any of the above. For example, in the case of the 1833 Russo-Turkish alliance, although it may be claimed that Turkey counterbalanced Egypt, Russia's behavior would not seem to be explicable solely in terms of the two alternative options. Similarly, in 1904 Germany, seeking to build an alliance against Great Britain, turned to Russia, which was busy fighting Japan. At the same time, German policy was also directed against France, an ally of Russia at that time; if France were excluded, its ties with Russia would become meaningless; whereas if it could be sucked into the German system, it would cease to be a worry for Germany. By describing these intricate maneuvers simply as cases of balancing or bandwagoning, or by simply referring to a generic threat or a profit, we would fail to recognize the complexity of the situations in question.

Balancing and bandwagoning, in their purest forms, thus prove to be rather problematic conceptual categories. Indeed, some believe the dichotomy to be unsatisfactory for a number of other reasons as well (Snyder 1991 and 1997, 156–58). To begin with, states may counterbalance one another by other means, such as rearmament.[32] Furthermore, there is a much wider range of alternatives than the rather drastic choice of being either with or against the strongest would lead us to believe. For example, a state may decide to remain strictly neutral, or it may create ties with other states; a state may still reach a compromise with the strongest state without necessarily forming an alliance with it. Indeed, this form of conciliation, despite its precariousness, may guarantee preservation of a certain degree of freedom of movement, which would be seriously compromised in any alliance. Moreover, the two terms encapsulate a further dichotomy, namely between offensive and defensive alliances, and between resistance to or accommodation of a potential enemy. For example, Walt is closer to the second of these two dualisms; however, as we have already said, there are a number of ways of rendering an adversary more amenable to one's position than forming an alliance with that adversary. In addition, classifying alliances as either offensive ("revisionist") or defensive ("conservative"), as Schweller suggests, raises more problems than it actually resolves. First, just as it is difficult to trace a clear demarcation line between a profit and a threat, likewise it is generally very difficult to distinguish between offensive and defensive alliances. Each state tries to consolidate its own position, be that conservative or revisionist, either directly by increasing the total resources at its disposal or indirectly by damaging or weakening the other states. As a rule, even what we generally consider to be a revisionist power will probably not be following any clearly defined expansionist plan; it will more likely be taking advantage of those opportunities that arise, often for the simple reason that it is in a position to do so. Then there are numerous cases where an expansionist policy derives from the need for security, and thus by trying to "conserve" the existing status quo the state in question ends up contributing to revision of that same status quo.[33] If this is the case for individual states, then it is easy to see just how difficult it can be to interpret any inter-state union in such terms.

THE COMPLEXITY OF ALLIANCES

All of this leads us to make one further observation: the so-called power aggregation model assumes that the allies' interests coincide regardless of whether the alliance is offensive or defensive. This is a cornerstone of the various realist approaches to the question: Liska (1962, 27) makes reference to "identical interests," Morgenthau (1959, 186) to a "community of interests," and Schweller (1994, 88) to a "compatibility of political goals." The meaning of such observations is clear: they deny that alliances may have foundations (ideological or otherwise) other than those constituted by the interests of the states in question.[34] However, by doing so they tend to ignore one very important, fundamental fact: as well as identical, common, or compatible interests, allies may also possess a number of other, very different interests that, when interwoven with the power relations within the alliance, give rise to a whole series of problematic issues that are often neglected.

This question is even more paradoxical if one considers that many classics, often invoked by contemporary realism, were perfectly aware of the fact that relations between allies go beyond pursuit of a common interest. For example, Thucydides often mentions that when faced with the hegemonizing efforts of the Athenians, the weaker, more vulnerable states tended to form alliances by clearly adopting balance of power policies. However, having said this, on more than one occasion Thucydides also reveals the multifaceted character of alliances; the Delian League was transformed by

Athens, the "dictator city," into a genuine empire (I, 89–117); the Peace of Nicias triggered the serious suspicions of Sparta's allies (V, 29); and Persia, although aligned with Sparta, refrained from giving the latter its full support and opted instead to watch over the simultaneous weakening of both Sparta and Athens (VIII, 46). On frequent occasions, city-states behaved in a completely opportunistic manner, looking to profit for themselves from the situation rather than focusing on the benefits to be gained by the alliance to which they belonged. According to Themistocles, the Athenians, when fortifying the city right after the Persian wars, were well capable of distinguishing between general interests and their own interests (I, 91, 4), and construction of the city walls meant that some form of balance must be preserved between allies—and that if there is no military parity between them, then alliances tend to become a means whereby the strongest member of the alliance dominates the others. Not to mention the sinister words of the Mytilenians, according to whom "in an alliance the only safe guarantee is an equality of mutual fear; for then the party that wants to break faith is deterred by the thought that the odds will not be on his side" (III, 11, 2).[35]

In modern times, there are innumerable cases of observations highlighting the less reassuring aspects of alliances. Jean Bodin, immediately after having acknowledged the utility of alliances ("for by this meanes they are not onely the more strengthened, but they also take from the enemie those succours which he might draw from them"[36]), quickly added—echoing the words of Machiavelli—that it is advisable to remain stronger than the allies ("for he alwayes commands the state that is the master of the force, and will make himselfe an absolute lord upon the least occasion if he have any desire").[37] Paolo Paruta focused on the inevitable dispersion of interests within an alliance, on the substantial difference between the parties' intentions at the moment of stipulation of a treaty and how said treaty is implemented, and concluded that "he who will confide too much upon such Unions [...] will soon find he is deceived" and "may become a prey as well to him who appears to be his friend, as to his formally declared enemies."[38] Also, Botero warned against placing too much trust in alliances, since "it is impossible that the interests of each of many rulers will be involved in an equal degree."[39] Such questions were very much at the center of debate up to the 18th century; on the one hand, opportunistic allies were criticized for burdening their fellow members with the costs of war,[40] but on the other hand one never lost sight of the risk that defeat of the enemy could be overly advantageous to one's ally.[41] The interest that such observers showed in the often ambiguous relations between allies can be misleading: remember that such figures explicitly theorized the balance of power, and as such were fully aware of the importance of the union of forces in preventing the unchecked domination of one excessively powerful state. However, at the same time they pointed out that this common objective fails to remove certain aspects of rivalry between the allies in question: furthermore, the approximately equal distribution of power between allies constitutes a guarantee not only in relation to the disturbing force, but also as far as the allies themselves are concerned.

In short, those usually deemed to be the precursors of contemporary realism, share this perception of the dualism of alliances—namely their orientation towards the common enemy and towards their own members. Contemporary realism, it should be said, is well aware of the difficulties and tensions inherent in relations between allies, as is shown by frequent warnings about the limited reliability of such alliances. However, this point has never been the subject of any systematic analysis until very recently.[42] It was Paul Schroeder—a diplomatic historian, not a political scientist, interestingly enough—who really broke new ground in the mid-1970s; yet with few exceptions his appeal fell on deaf ears.[43] Schroeder (1976) criticized the common belief that alliances were principally *weapons of power*, suggesting instead that they were really *tools of management*. His views, based on a rapid (albeit incisive) survey of the most important alliances witnessed in the period from 1815 to 1945, can be briefly summarized as follows. First, the wish to "aggregate power" against a threat is not always of vital importance for creation of an alliance. All alliances work, to a certain degree, as *pacta de contrahendo*, that is, restricting and controlling the actions of the allies themselves. Certain alliances may be employed in order that an adversary joins our side, thus avoiding open conflict. Finally, bandwagoning may be adopted with the precise aim of creating a pactum de contrahendo.

According to Schroeder, this conception of alliances lies halfway between two opposite views of international politics, one seeing such politics in terms of conflict, and the other placing the emphasis on its cooperative aspects. In fact, alliances encapsulate elements of both cooperation and conflict. However, Schroeder also underlines one crucial factor that has escaped the attention of the realist school, thanks to the latter's near obsession with the balance of power, namely that *the rivalry between states extends to within the alliances they themselves are members of.* One step further, and alliances can actually be transformed into the proverbial "kiss of death," whereby a given ally is neutralized in order to control it better. Fear and profit remain the key elements once again; however, the feared thing, or the thing that an ally thinks it can benefit from, no longer exists outside the alliance but within it. In this case, therefore, our position is the exact opposite of the one commonly adopted. Nevertheless, the remarkable thing is that such a perspective is perfectly in keeping with the realist stance. The fact that alliances, designed and created as "tools of management," sometimes succeed in preserving a certain international order can be misleading; Schroeder's reconstruction of a number of alliances clearly shows the almost systematic attempt by allies to influence one another, together with their shared awareness that merely being members of an alliance does not eliminate their rivalry. Ultimately the most important thing, and one that Schroeder calls our attention to perhaps unwillingly, concerns the dynamics of inter-ally power: alliances hardly ever consist solely in countering the advance of a common enemy, even if such an enemy actually exists.

This is clear even if one embraces the friend-enemy dualism implying exclusion of any third party. It was Julien Freund who treated the ally as a specific kind of third party, one that does not constitute an independent pole but represents a third party for one or the other of the two opposing factions (Freund 1983, 291–94; Portinaro 1986). So even though it may be true that there have been very few cases of armed conflict in which three forces confront one another in an independent, equally hostile manner, and we admit therefore that conflict is basically dyadic,[44] this does not mean that the third party gets canceled out within the alliance. In fact, one ally may commit itself more to the cause of the alliance than the other ally; the one may try to destroy the enemy, while the other opposes such destruction. Indeed, Freund himself acknowledges the existence of tension between allies resulting from one ally's fear that the other may become too strong or benefit from the alliance unilaterally, or resulting from disagreement over the role of each ally within the alliance. He adds that "politics and the relation of forces are never suppressed by an alliance, since [...] the agreement is never perfect, if only because all alliances are characterised by a hierarchy, more or less acknowledged by the members, and at times by a genuine hegemony" (Freund 1983, 293). In other words, Freund understands that the aim of an alliance is not to be confused with the other vested interests of the individual members of the alliance. Diplomatic history—or, if you like, diplomatic practice—clearly reveals constant attempts to try and bow the alliance in question to a party's own interests, by taking advantage of the ally's weaknesses, and maneuvering things so that the other ally is increasingly dependent on the alliance, or by trying to free itself from the excessively tight grip of that other ally.

INTER-ALLIED RELATIONS

The spread of the power aggregation model has meant that the problem of inter-ally relations has not received the attention it deserves. However, this does not mean it has been ignored completely. We are now going to briefly mention a number of directions taken by such analysis, and the limits of those studies in question. The first, which has been frequently applied to the case of NATO, is the "economic theory of alliances." This theory is the result of extending the traditional collective action dilemma, as done by Mancur Olson and Richard Zeckhauser (1966, 1967)[45]; their model applies to all voluntary international organizations (in particular NATO) in which the members share one or more interests. In the case of the NATO alliance, the common interest par excellence is deterrence, which constitutes a public (or collective) good in that it is characterized by its "non-excludability" (in other words, whoever fails to contribute to its production cannot be excluded from its consumption) and "nonrivalry" (in that if it is available to one member of a group then it can be made available to the other members at little or no marginal cost). The members of the group have no incentive to provide optimal amounts of such goods, given that the benefits of any action an individual member takes automatically extend to the other members of the same group. The larger members of the group will tend to place a higher absolute value on the public good and as such will bear a disproportionate share of the cost of production of that good. In an alliance between unequal states, if the stronger state hopes to protect the weaker one, while increasing its own resources by means of those of its ally, it will soon realize that the two aims are mutually exclusive; unless the weaker state is forced to do so by the stronger state, or finds itself in an emergency, it will not contribute to the alliance in a manner proportionate to its means, and the stronger state will have to choose between protecting the weaker ally and renouncing any increase in its own resources.

Olson and Zeckhauser's theory stimulated numerous subsequent empirical studies, but it was also widely criticized.[46] One critique rejected the claim that deterrence is a public good (Russett 1970); the principle of non-excludability, in fact, is not fully observed here, given that in cases of "extended deterrence" (one state wishes to protect another state from attack from a third state), there is always the problem of the credibility of the protection afforded, as this credibility is greater in the case of some states and lower in the case of others. The more exposed ally will thus have good reason to create a certain quantity of additional security, which in turn strengthens the alliance overall. If we now abandon the assumption that military expenditure serves solely the purpose of deterrence, then smaller allies may have other reasons for pledging more than was foreseen by Olson and Zeckhauser. In fact, military expenditure may also produce "private" goods, that is, goods associated with the requirements of an individual state (such as contingencies not provided for by the alliance), with domestic security requirements, or with the attempt to stimulate the overall economy. As far as regards the "substitutability" of the allies' military forces, it has been pointed out that in the past such forces were not generally considered interchangeable, partly owing to the competition between the great powers—each of which was jealous of its own prerogatives—and partly because of the technical difficulties involved, related to the limited development of means of transport (Thies 1987). This implies that defense was a very "impure" public good.[47] However, this impurity has persisted into the modern age; indeed, it is a characteristic of NATO itself. France and Great Britain (like China in the communist bloc), being aware of the risk they would run by behaving as free-riders in relation to their respective protectors, decided to bear the burden of developing their own national nuclear weapons (Goldstein 1995).

Another path that has been followed takes the type of international system as its point of departure. In the view of Waltz (1979, 161–93), there are a number of important differences distinguishing the relationship between allies in a bipolar system from that among allies in a multipolar system. In the latter case, given that friendships and enmity are somewhat more ambiguous and unclear, the greater complexity of such a system predisposes the states in question to two kinds of error: of getting too close to those allies whose support is vital ("chain ganging"), thus running the risk of getting dragged by such allies into a dangerous situation, or even a war; and relying too much on others to deal with any threats that arise ("buck passing"), meaning that chronic uncertainty about the reliability of alliances may lead to failure to offer a sufficiently strong challenge to an aggressive state, in the hope that others will do so (i.e., passing the buck on to others).[48] A bipolar system, on the contrary, does not have such problems, according to Waltz. In such a system, the poles are clearly defined—friends and enemies are known to all—and everyone knows who will step up and lead the alliance should this prove necessary. In fact, the two largest powers cannot rely on allies in the event of instability, and they know that it is up to them to govern the system themselves. Furthermore, given the disproportionate relationship between the leader's forces and those of its allies, the former does not really have any vital need of the latter—unlike diverse states of equal ranking in a multipolar system—and thus can withstand any pressure from an overly exuberant ally and control that ally more closely.[49] This point has been examined in greater depth by John J. Mearsheimer (2001, 267–333), who distinguishes between "unbalanced" and "balanced" forms of multipolar alliance, which depend respectively on whether the international system is characterized or not by a state aspiring to a position of hegemony. In the second case, there will be a more marked tendency to pass the buck, since in the absence of any serious immediate danger each member will try to burden the others with the costs of containing any aggressor. Finally, taking the polarity of the international system as a basis, Glenn H. Snyder (1984, 1990) formulated the idea that continues to be the best possible way of accounting for certain important aspects of the relationship between allies, namely, constant oscillation between their fear of abandonment and their fear of entrapment. Efforts to avoid the first outcome make the second more likely, and vice versa. Hence Snyder's concept of the "alliance security dilemma." Given the considerable importance of this point, we shall discuss it in more detail in the coming pages; for the moment we would like to stress that according to Snyder this dilemma takes a more acute form in multipolar systems than in bipolar ones. In fact, in multipolar systems the considerable interdependence of the allies is accompanied by the likelihood of realignment; hence the allies' need to avoid being abandoned leads to adoption of policies that produce the risk of entrapment, which is where the dilemma arises. Conversely, in bipolar systems abandonment is less likely, and thus the dilemma arises in a more latent, diluted form.

The contrast between bipolar and multipolar systems is of general use, especially if we wish to highlight certain basic differences in international relations before and after the Second World War. However, it clearly reveals little about the extreme variety of situations that may be encountered in a multipolar system. Second, categories such as buck passing, chain ganging, entrapment, and abandonment always presume, to a lesser or greater degree, the existence of a clear common enemy and the real likelihood of open hostilities; thus such categories are incapable of accounting for those situations in which the states in question run different, albeit still serious, risks, such as the risk of diplomatic defeat, of isolation or immobilization, or of impotence in the face of a negative international situation. In other words, little heed is paid to those cases in which there is no common enemy, or there is little likelihood of war (or such a likelihood is not the major worry), or where above all the allies' attention is focused more on their mutual relations than on any external threat or problem.

A number of conclusions may be drawn from this brief survey of the most commonly debated and most frequently studied aspects of alliances. Even though the existence of a threat or the prospect of a profit is often of vital importance to the foundation and survival of an alliance, alliances are not merely a means by which to deal with such threats or pursuing potential benefits, as they invariably go beyond dealings with the external world. Hence the need to carefully examine the internal affairs of such alliances, especially given that this is one area about which relatively little is known. The starting point for the present study is a simple one: although, as a rule, allies are brought together by some common interest or other, this does not mean that one ally does not have certain other interests not shared by another ally. In addition, both the cooperative aspects of alliances (the means and nature of cooperation) and, perhaps more important, the conflicting aspects thereof reflect the dynamics of power in various ways. Thus any overall picture of alliances must take into account these various aspects at one and the same time. Finally, we should point out a further limitation to the most highly acclaimed theories of alliances: even the most cursory look at the history of international relations, together with our observations to this point, show that the term *alliance* conceals a vast range of policies implemented by all kinds of states in a variety of contexts. Can we really deal with the question of alliances while ignoring or undervaluing their truly varied nature? It is no surprise that the generalizations one comes across in existing studies are so vague, fragile, and often contradictory. To clarify matters and introduce a little order into the debate, we need to formulate a clearer picture of the types of alliance we are dealing with; only after doing so can we then submit more accurate, specific hypotheses. However, before embarking on this task we would like to reformulate the indispensable theoretical-conceptual instruments we intend to employ, given the inadequacy of those available.

TWO

The Relational Nature of Alliances

ANARCHY AND SECURITY

The fact that alliances are a common, constantly present phenomenon, and that nearly all states at some time in their history have formed alliances, means any theory of alliances implies a general theory of international politics and shares the limitations and problems of such a general theory. For those mainly interested in the study of the repetitive phenomena of international politics, that is, the inherent regularities therein, the best approach to a theory of alliances is undoubtedly the systemic-structural variety. At the same time, however, the most influential structural theory, neorealism, fails to offer any genuinely satisfactory results; it sheds light on *only a limited number of alliances*—those formed exclusively in response to a power imbalance—or on *only one aspect of the majority of alliances*—their external orientation against an actual or potential enemy.

Neither of the neorealist independent variables—international anarchy and the distribution of power (bipolar or multipolar)—is of any great help when it comes to analyzing a specific phenomenon in depth, for a series of obvious reasons. The number of poles, as we have seen, offers a limited explanation of the major differences between the *functioning* of alliances in bipolar systems and in multipolar systems. The same could be said of the *formation* of alliances. In fact, a polar interpretation of their origins can provide only the most general of conclusions. According to Glenn H. Snyder (1990), in bipolar systems the structural pressures present seem to play some kind of role; the two superpowers have no reason to form an alliance with each other, because there is no third party threatening either power. In fact, what happens is that each superpower tends to protect the weaker states against the real or presumed threat posed by the other superpower. By contrast, in a multipolar system the logic of alignments cannot be explained merely in terms of the number of poles.

The question of anarchy is a more complex one. What conceptual use can be made of anarchy when studying alliances? Raymond Aron (1962/1967, 5–6) observed that the distinguishing characteristic of international politics is the fact that they are always conducted in the shadow of war. An anarchical context is one in which the law of the stronger holds. There is always the chance that violence will be resorted to; each individual state has to count on its own force, because there is no guarantee of it being protected or being helped. Hence the neorealist interpretation of the international system as a system of self-defense where states pursue their own security above anything else. This also explains, according to Kenneth N. Waltz once again, certain repetitive behavior and outcomes, such as the limited success of cooperative effort, the low degree of interdependence between the great powers, and the recurrent emergence of a balance of power. Thus anarchy lies at the basis of a general theory of international politics that aims to explain "a small number of big and important things" (Waltz 1986, 329) at a highly abstract level. It is no surprise, therefore, that alliances become mere expressions of the balance of power, with all the limitations that such a formulation implies. There can be no doubt that anarchy induces both *the need for others' support* (given the constant possibility of being attacked) and *concern for the ends that others come to* (an aggressor who gradually overpowers others becomes increasingly stronger) and thus encourages states to form alliances with others (Snyder 1997, 52). However, this does not explain why alliances are formed *even when* an act of aggression is highly unlikely, or why the functions of alliances extend beyond mere defense.

Waltz believes that the immediate effect of anarchy is to cause states concern about their own security. But what exactly is this security that all states desire and pursue? At first it would seem that security is the guarantee of a state's survival, and as such it is pursued through a process of deterrence, or through building a suitable defensive barrier against real or potential attacks from outside. However, can we plausibly assert that states actually live in constant fear of being attacked? Understandably, frequent attempts have been made to broaden the meaning of security to incorporate a more general form of protection of those objectives judged to be of real importance, including not only a state's boundaries but also its political independence and economic well-being.[1] If this is true, then nearly all forms of state behavior may be interpreted in terms of the need for national security, and of threats to that security. This may well be so, but what exactly does such a vague statement tell us? Claiming that alliances are always the result of the need for security deriving from a situation of anarchy is in truth either too vague or too specific. It is certainly true to say that states' behavior reflects their concern about national security. However, comparing such clearly different cases as Italy, whose membership of the Triple Alliance in 1882 ended its international isolation, and Turkey, which, facing defeat by an insurgent Egypt, in 1833 signed an alliance with its traditional enemy, Russia, would not seem to tell us much about the nature of alliances. Conversely, if we define *security* as protection from a threat in the sense indicated by Walt, then it is not difficult to observe this is less often the case than one might believe, within the framework of the wealth of alliances characterizing modern history.

Placing the emphasis on the question of security is not wrong, but it is certainly not enough, since it fails to account for the specificity of alliances. This point has been clearly expressed, once again, by Schroeder (1994a), who ably demonstrates how states, when faced with a threat, do not always resort to balancing or bandwagoning policies. They may, for example, "hide" in the hope that the storm blows over without excessively onerous consequences for them, while other states take it upon themselves to deal with the aggressor. Or they may "transcend" the threat, trying to resolve the dispute(s) by institutional procedures based on consensus or formal agreements. Furthermore, if the objection is now made that all such strategies nevertheless respond to the very same need for security, then we have to ask ourselves what explanatory power the "need for self-defense" actually has, given that it can be used to account for such different responses.

Despite being a structural theory, neorealism tends to remain indeterminate. Waltz (1986) claims that his is a theory of international politics and as such is capable of accounting for only the most important *outcomes* of interaction between states at the systemic level, and not for the *behavior* of individual states. However, the dividing line between a systemic result and a state's behavior is sometimes not that clear. Indeed, many criticisms, and attempted revisions, of neorealism tend to focus on this very point; some deplore the contradictory results of various balancing theories that derive from it (Vasquez 1997, 1998),[2] while others try to establish more specific conditions under which the structural mechanisms operate. Hence the tendency to develop not so much a theory of international politics as a theory of foreign policy based to a certain degree on Waltz's ideas (Elman 1996a, 1996b);[3] hence the contrast between what have been called "defensive realism" and "offensive realism," and the attempt to formulate causal frameworks containing both structural and domestic independent variables (the neoclassical realism).[4]

All of this notwithstanding, the anarchical assumption remains of importance in framing (albeit in general terms) not only the relationships between states and alliances but also the circumspect, prudent, calculating behavior of states *within their very alliances*. If the absence of a supreme authority helps explain states' decisions to come together and form alliances, it is undoubtedly a decisive factor in accounting for the skepticism often accompanying such alliances once they have been constituted (Snyder 1997, 17–18).

SYSTEM AND SYSTEMIC POSITION

Is it possible to remain within a systemic framework while going beyond the simple, albeit debatable, consequences of anarchy and the distribution of power? As Waltz himself observed, a system is composed of a structure and a series of interacting units. The question is, How are we to study the interactions of states without simply concluding that they are the result of a broad need for security? Talking about a threat does not really suggest how the threat is to be dealt with (Schroeder was right on this point) if we do not possess other items of information. For example, do any other potential allies exist? Is anyone in even greater danger? Are there any grounds for disagreement and conflict with those powers willing to join us in an alliance? Which circumstances work in our favor, and which work against us? In other words, which opportunities and constraints lead us to react in a certain manner? Holding anarchy constant, we need to focus on the *positions* that the states adopt at various times in relation to each other; such positions cannot be determined simply by anarchy, or by the bipolar or multipolar nature of the international system.

Diplomatic history often gives the impression that the geopolitical context, *from the point of view of each state's relations with others,* is constituted by "spaces" that open and close, leaving little choice to those who basically have to look after themselves. States move around in the available cracks and openings, at times finding themselves excluded from action and at other times brought back into play; at times they have their back to the wall, and at other times they are given the chance to take advantage of a favorable international configuration. At each given stage in history, what is a constraint for one state may well represent an opportunity for another; state A takes advantage of the fear that state B has of state C acting unscrupulously on its own, or of forcing B to make concessions that in other circumstances it would not make. For example, at the end of the 1930s, Anglo-French ambivalence and Soviet weakness enabled Germany to choose between turning against the USSR, with the approval of the Western powers, or against the West, in concert with Moscow. In turn, the British guarantee to Poland freed the Soviet Union from the potential nightmare of finding itself having to face up to Germany alone, and it predisposed Moscow to make a deal with Berlin.

When can one speak of open spaces? The immediate response might be: when there is no immediate danger. However, even in the presence of danger, a state may well have its hands free if another state is even more exposed to the same danger, and forced to do something about it. Spaces open up when one state becomes of importance to others, or when the state that could impede the actions of another is too busy with more pressing matters to do so. Spaces open up thanks to the multitude of relations that a state can entertain with other states; such varied interactions enable one to accumulate assets that may be employed at different negotiating tables. Furthermore, spaces open up to those who are fortunate enough to be able to set long-term goals; free of any immediate concerns, they can calmly evaluate the various options available, accept certain offers, refuse others, and wait for the right moment to make their move. Spaces close, on the other hand, when one faces enemies posing a serious, and at times immediate, threat that other states fail to take into account or when one state finds itself isolated because of its own weakness, or pursuant to agreements made by other states, or when it needs the support of someone else. Moreover, the greater the perception of urgency, and the more pressing the feeling that an immediate solution has to be found, the more spaces close; if you find yourself with your back to the wall you can, by definition, be blackmailed.

In sum, the foreign policy of nations reflects the spaces and the moments in time in which they find themselves. As they open and close, the spaces offer opportunities or impose limits; and though this does not strictly determine the decisions made by the states in question, it does nevertheless render them intelligible.

Similar dynamics are in fact clear, in a stylized form, in three-way relations.[5] An improvement in relations between two adversaries means that the third party loses a certain degree of bargaining power. By contrast, a worsening in relations between two states means that the third state's bargaining stance is strengthened; it is now freed from the potential nightmare situation of finding itself up against a union of the other two, and it is now in a cast-iron position in which neither of the other two will want it to side with, or fall into the hands of, the other (Jervis 1997, 177–91). George Simmel adopted a similar point of view in introducing the figure of the *Tertius Gaudens*, the third party that benefits from the conflict between two other states, either because the latter both see themselves in a checkmate situation and thus let the third party act undisturbed or because one of the two obtains results that also benefit the third party (Freund 1983, 287–301).[6] It is obvious that for a third party to be so important, it must be in a position to modify existing power relations. However, this does not necessarily imply that it has to be a major power; sometimes the Tertius Gaudens is a small state that takes advantage of the situation in order to offer itself as an ally, in the knowledge that its bargaining power depends more on its ability to tip the balance in favor of one state or the other than on a substantial amount of any resource it may possess, thus obtaining advantages out of all proportion with its economic-military capabilities.[7] Conversely, the third party can be a *Tertius Dolens*, that is, a state excluded from negotiations between the other two states, and perhaps even directly harmed by the joint hostile action of the other two states, or of one of them as the second looks on indifferently (Portinaro 1986, 225–31).

Glenn Snyder offered similar observations to those made here concerning spaces and position, within the context of his own alliance theory (1996 and 1997, 1–39). Snyder, like Waltz, starts from the structure of the international system and moves on to add a new conceptual category, the "relationships,"[8] defined as the "situational context of behavior" (Snyder 1997, 20). Relationships are situated between structure and action; they are the channel through which structural effects are reflected in actual behavior, called "interaction." There are four components constituting such relationships. First, there are "alignments"—the expectation of being supported, ignored, or hindered by the other states. Second, relationships are also defined by "conflicting or common interests," and these interests in turn may be "strategic" if they derive directly from the structure (anarchy, for example, encourages forestalling a potential adversary's expansion or growth) or "intrinsic" in the case of objectives that are of value in themselves (for example, saving an unredeemed national group). Interests may also be "general" if they refer to the international system as a whole, or "specific" if they refer to certain countries or objectives. The third aspect of relationships is "capabilities," the resources of power conceived not so much in the aggregate sense (overall power) but as specific assets available to one state relative to another state in any given situation. Finally, "dependence" is to allies what capabilities are to adversaries; it is also based on the degree to which the parties involved may harm each other, with the obvious implications this may have for their respective influence. Relationships and interactions (the behavior adopted) are very closely linked: the former shape the latter, while the latter modify the former. Negotiations for creation of an alliance (interaction) mix up the alignments (relationships); an arms race (interaction) affects capabilities (relationships); a crisis (interaction) changes the level of conflict between enemies and the degree of interdependence among allies (relationships); and a war (interaction) probably changes the entire system of relationships.

Thus anarchy generates latent fears, which in turn give rise to indeterminate forms of behavior; however, specific common or conflicting interests, power relations, and reciprocal dependence clarify such fears and limit the number of available options. Relationships, for example, make it possible to account for the rapidity or slowness with which a balance of power will emerge. That is, without prejudice to the system's trends as elucidated by Waltz, Snyder's categories help us understand the timescale of such trends and how they develop. Likewise, the diverse reactions to a threat can now be better understood with reference not so much to any generic need for security but rather to the specific position of the threatened state in relation to the other states. It should be pointed out that this argument remains a systemic one, in that none of the components of the relationships directly concerns the attributes or characteristics of individual states: alignments, capabilities, dependence, and common or conflicting interests are all *relational* categories. The preference given to the systemic viewpoint is closely linked to the type of problem we wish to address. Here we are interested in grasping the nature of constant features, trends, temptations, and fears; that is, we are interested in regularities. A systemic theory aims to explain why similarly placed states tend to behave in a similar manner (if and when they do, of course) despite their domestic differences (Waltz 1996, 54).

The social sciences generally explain behavior as the result of a combination of constraints, opportunities (those actions compatible with the constraints in place), and preferences (how the possible results of an action are ordered by the individual on the basis of their desirability). However, it is still unclear exactly how objective elements (opportunities) and subjective elements (wishes or preferences) interact to produce an action (Elster 1989, 13–22).[9] In fact, opportunities and wishes often influence each other; the former shape the latter (one wants what one can have), and wishes can alter opportunities (when a given strategy manages to change the context within which we operate). Furthermore, it is often true in international politics that constraints may be so strong that they leave little room for expression of any real preferences. It is easy to see that this is particularly true of small and medium-sized powers; however, even the major powers, rather than being "masters with free hands," resemble more a series of "Gullivers, more or less tightly tied" who "usually lead troubled lives"(Waltz 1979, 187). Thus it is that they move off, frequently without any specific aim, filling any spaces opening up before them, for the simple reason that nobody is capable of stopping them.

THE SEARCH FOR CONFORMITY

Snyder should be praised for having formulated an innovative theoretical-conceptual framework whereby a structural perspective is associated with the specific, systemic positions adopted by various states. Categories such as dependence, interests, and capabilities are going to be of considerable value in the rest of the present work. However, Snyder continues to perceive alliances from a basically traditional viewpoint: he sees them simply as the means by which to continue the battle against threatening third-party states, and this defensive understanding of an alliance as the union of one state's own forces with those of another state tends to limit the weight of his analysis. In this sense (and in this sense only), Snyder's views are not that much different from those most commonly held. So it is now time we take a step backward and deal with the problem from a broader perspective.

The fact that states interact in an anarchical setting, where resources are dispersed, means that each state requires some degree of cooperation of other states in order to pursue its most pressing objectives, including security. It will thus use all available resources in order to obtain the conformity of others. In other words, the anarchical international system is constantly characterized by bargaining and conflict, and by latent uncertainty and insecurity: uncertainty, since distribution of resources needs to be modified to only a slight degree, and a state will attempt to modify the terms of exchange in its own favor, thus breaking the previous agreement; and insecurity, because given the presence of destructive means, there is always the danger that such means will be put to use. Whatever the specific interests pursued, such interests can be made safe only if there is some guarantee of conformity.[10] If power is understood to comprise the overall resources an actor possesses compared with those resources held by others, then the pursuit of conformity among states is the pursuit of power, regardless of whether such power is immediately used in order to obtain final values.

As we all know, classical realism strongly emphasized the very pursuit of power as an essential trait of international politics.[11] In the words of Hans J. Morgenthau, "international politics, like all politics, is a struggle for power. Whatever the ultimate aims of international politics, power is always the immediate aim" (Morgenthau 1973, 29). Morgenthau perceived the behavior of states as an expression of the "lust for power" so deeply rooted in human nature; other realists took international anarchy as their starting point and concluded that "the pursuit of power [...] tends to become an end in itself rather than a means to other ends" (Schuman 1948, 374); that "there is [...] no possibility of drawing a sharp line between the will-to-live and the will-to-power" (Niebuhr 1932, 42); that when a state, in order to achieve its objectives, depends on the actions of other states, "the improvement of the relative power position becomes the primary objective of the internal and the external policy of states" (Spykman 1942, 13, 18); and that "the pursuit of 'security' by satisfied Powers has often been the motive of flagrant examples of power politics" (Carr 1946, 105). Even neorealist thought has something very important to add to this question. Although Waltz is clear that states' primary objective is not power but security, it has been pointed out (Zakaria 1992) that the pursuit of security leads to states behaving in such a way as to maximize their own power. Indeed, the so-called offensive form of realism insists on this point. John J. Mearsheimer, for example, claims that "survival mandates aggressive behaviour. Great powers behave aggressively [...] because they have to seek more power if they want to maximize their odds of survival" (Mearsheimer 2001, 21), and that "the best way to ensure [...]

survival is to be the most powerful state in the system" (ibidem, 33). From this comes the motivation to fight for hegemony, a characteristic trait of the foreign policy of the great powers.[12] Given this viewpoint, the contrast between balancing and bandwagoning is replaced by the contrast between balancing and buck passing; joining forces with a stronger potential enemy is counterproductive almost by definition, because the latter will gain a greater relative advantage from the alliance. The real alternative options available to the major powers consist in their uniting forces against a common enemy, or leaving (or even inducing) the other state to take on the burden of the cost of containment by itself. If the choice exists, any such state will choose the second option (ibidem 134–35, 138–67).[13]

More generally speaking, if a state can maintain a certain degree of power, this will enable it to regularly enjoy certain advantages over other states. For example, stockpiling arms is not necessarily geared to their eventual use, just as an alliance is not necessarily designed for the purpose of waging war against a common enemy. In both cases, preservation of (or increase in) one state's power—that is, its capacity to obtain the cooperation of other governments—is equally important as, and often more important than, the actual use of that power. Regardless of the material objective of a state's foreign policy (whether this is acquisition of raw materials, control of shipping, or changes in national boundaries), the actions of other states have to be controlled by trying to influence the will of those states.

Alliances need to be perceived from within this general framework. Alliances are first of all a means of circumscribing and mitigating the constant insecurity and uncertainty present in the context described here, a means by which states exploit those spaces that open up or try to force them open again after they have closed. An alliance attempts to render an ally's behavior predictable, that is, to eliminate the uncertainty resulting from the same ally's freedom of movement, by guaranteeing its cooperation. This vitally important function, which logically precedes all other functions, is clear if we look at the mutual exchange of pledges that generally underlies any alliance. In fact, by means of a mutual pledge one ally circumscribes the other's behavior while accepting limitations to its own actions. The pledge is, in this sense, a genuinely strategic move designed to induce an ally to act in a certain manner (in favor of the other ally), conditioning the former state's decisions since it influences its expectations. Promising another state that it will not be harmed, or that it will be helped, does not necessarily mean doing it a favor; such a pledge puts it in a position where it has to opt for a given strategy, and the other ally, knowing this, may take advantage of its predisposition.[14] In other words, the self-imposed limitation of one state's freedom entails constraints not only for that state but also for its ally, and alliance strategy consists in creation and exploitation of such constraints, whereby an ally is induced into moving in a certain foreseeable manner.[15]

It follows that combating a common enemy is *one of the many objectives* made possible by those constraints placed on the behavior of one's ally. In fact, the conformity of an ally enables a state to obtain the conformity of those other states against whom the alliance was formed. Any alliance consists in two principal spheres: the allies, and the other states. The conformity of the former is often instrumentally important to the conformity of the latter. Yet if the basic purpose is pursuing conformity, then it is also easy to see why, as we have already pointed out, certain alliances cannot be understood merely in terms of security. According to the traditional interpretation of alliances, A and B join forces against C because C is the common enemy. However, it may also be that from A's point of view C is above all a means by which B may be constrained, rather than an enemy to be dissuaded or fought.[16] This is why the debate over which is the most characteristic form of coalitional behavior—balancing or bandwagoning—is basically misleading. It is not a question of understanding whether states tend to ally against, or with, the strongest state, or against the state threatening them or with that same state. *All of these policies* reflect the pursuit of an ally's conformity, a pursuit consisting in those methods and timescales dictated by the available spaces, or, if you like, by the relationships in question. It goes without saying that the specific meaning such a pursuit takes on will vary according to the ranking of the states in question, and the nature of their power relations. In the case of a hegemonic power, the conformity of a weaker ally tends to consist in transformation of the latter into the stronger ally's own policy instrument. With a smaller state, by contrast, the cooperation of a major ally may mean guaranteed protection or a special agreement whereby in exchange for the smaller state's substantial subordination to the greater power it maintains a degree of formal autonomy. Between states of equal standing, finally, there will always be a constant tug of war between the two, with each trying to convince the other to support it with regard to those objectives deemed to be of greatest importance. As far as relations with the adversaries are concerned, the pursuit of conformity is achieved either through deterrence (the alliance makes A and B stronger in relation to C and thus prevents C from taking steps that could harm the allies) or through an act of war (the alliance puts A and B in a position to get C to behave as they wish through the actual use of force).

In an alliance, mutual pledges are codified, and this formalization makes the various commitments specific and reciprocal, implying certain obligations that render the undertaking in question more credible (Snyder 1997, 8–12). Given that alliances generally concern only some of the allies' interests, the expectations they create are in fact more specific; a sense of obligation, which is underlined by the solemn stipulation of the treaty, derives from the more or less generally accepted convention whereby pledges made must be kept, while the reciprocal, mutual aspect of the alliance means that one party's observance of the agreement depends on its observance by the other party. This is the point made by many observers. Despite the generally precarious nature of cooperation between states, or rather, as a result of this precariousness, alliances introduce a modicum of order and predictability into international relations (Rothstein 1968, 54); they constitute an element of stability in a world of uncertainty (Haas and Whiting 1956, 161), and they represent the most stringent obligation one state can have with another (Osgood 1968, 161). In other words, formalizing such an agreement strengthens the allies' commitment to it. Despite all of this, however, the political impact of alliances is the result not so much of their contractual nature as of the changes they produce, as pledges, in the international system; or rather, as a result of the changes they lead to in the relationships Snyder mentions. An alliance closes spaces to some and opens up spaces to others, and in doing so it forces (or allows) parties to act in a way that at first appeared problematical, or that was simply unthinkable. In other words, alliances represent a message of intent. They represent one's own intentions and those of others, and the credibility of such intentions is often strengthened by the costs borne; pledges are made *despite* the implied limitation to a state's freedom of movement (Morrow 1999, 103–106).

Of course, in a situation of international anarchy the simple fact that a formal agreement has been stipulated does not in itself guarantee the agreement will be observed.[17] The problem of the reliability of alliances is generally dealt with by underlining the central role played by both the strategic interest and the so-called reputational interest that the signatories have in keeping their part of the bargain. According to Snyder (1997, 52–55), defensive alliances perform two basic functions: identifying the enemy, and aggregating power. Thus once such alliances have been formed, defending one's ally becomes vitally important—and virtually automatic. Then there is the reputational interest resulting from the exchange of pledges. Anyone failing to honor pledges cannot expect the other party to honor its own pledges. Moreover, any state with the fame of being an unreliable ally will lose credibility and find it increasingly difficult to reach subsequent agreements with other states (Snyder and Diesing 1977, 432).[18] However, were things quite so simple, it would be hard to explain the frequent about-turns made in relations between allies, or the willful ambiguity that often characterizes the wording of treaties. War alone is the only real test of the solidity of an alliance.[19] Although the pledges codified in a treaty are, on the one hand, constraints binding upon all parties, on the other they reflect a contingent solution, the position of the signatories at a particular moment in time. Consequently, those pledges made are neither neutral (because they favor one to the detriment of the other) nor uncontested (given that attempts will invariably be made to modify the terms of exchange as the situation changes). Now, if new constraints and new opportunities alter the relational context of the alliance, then it is reasonable to doubt the importance of reputational interests. The famous warning to French diplomats to beware of Frederick the Great's intentions is a clear case in point. He will certainly have no fear of rendering himself "hateful" since "over the course of time, the hateful nature of the means by which the State has grown will be forgotten, while the power remains" (quoted in Sorel 1885–1904, 27).[20] On the other hand, even though one cannot be sure that pledges are going to be honored, neither can one be sure that the opposite is true, or that the pledges will be taken lightheartedly. The care with which negotiations are conducted, together with the caution with which words and terms are chosen, clearly shows that treaties are not simply pieces of paper to be signed one day and disregarded the next.[21] Despite the uncertainty (or, if you like, as a result of the uncertainty) that constantly permeates relations between political units in anarchy, alliances lead to changes in the relative positions of the states in question, and everyone concerned—be they allies, adversaries, or neutral states—are called on to take account of such changes.

EXCHANGE AND POWER BETWEEN ALLIES

The reciprocal undertakings of allies limit their freedom of movement to a greater or lesser degree, since an alliance calls for some coordination of its members' foreign policy and armed forces; but why do states accept this limitation? The answer is simple: because they get something in return, as we have already seen. An alliance is thus basically an *exchange*, whereby the parties give and receive something, and each tries to obtain the behavior of the other on which its own capacity to act depends. Now, exchange is not always equal; in a situation of unequal exchange, *power* comes to the fore. "Remuneration," based on bestowal of "emerging benefits" (Stoppino 2001, 163–73),[22] is the characteristic form of exchange witnessed in an alliance. The typical form of remuneration among allies is support, while the most common form of punishment is withdrawal of that support, and thus abandonment of the punished party. So relations between allies are imbued with forms of mutual dependence, by virtue of which each party controls or influences the other's conduct, granting or denying it the services it desires. The principal form of tension running through the majority of alliances is clear here. On the one hand, the exchange of pledges is designed to render the behavior of others foreseeable by constraining our own behavior. On the other, however, the more B manages to negotiate its performing the act A asks it to perform, that is, the more B manages to maintain its future conduct unforeseeable in the eyes of A, the more the terms of exchange are going to be in B's favor (Crozier and Friedberg 1977/1980). Power thus lies in the margin of freedom each state enjoys; that is, in the possibility each state has of refusing what the other state asks for. Each ally tries to impose itself on the other as the only possible partner, while trying to reserve some alternative solutions, constrain the other party in order to satisfy its own needs, and free itself from the other's attempted constraints by systematically defending its own margin of freedom. If the parties to the alliance stand to benefit from the resulting agreement, then they will have a common interest in ensuring it is carried out, although they will nevertheless disagree over the terms of exchange. Each party will thus exert pressure on the other to make the latter accept the heavier burden, while its own burden is limited as much as possible—right up to the point where the relationship between the two allies is in danger, but not beyond that point (Blau 1964, 315–16).

Therefore, in every interaction between the allies, each will try to influence the other,[23] using its own resources, to obtain the highest possible ratio of benefits to costs. This strategy underlies bargaining, a communicative process in which each party threatens (diminishing benefits or emerging costs) or promises (emerging benefits or diminishing costs) so as to obtain the best possible terms of exchange. The necessary precondition for bargaining is coexistence of common and conflicting interests. Also, the shared interest in reaching some form of agreement must be strong enough (or the conflicting interests must be weak enough) to create a "bargaining range," a series of possible agreements each would prefer to no agreement at all (Snyder and Diesing 1977, 476–77). To rephrase the concept again, the necessary condition for bargaining is both parties' conviction (or hope) that the common interest reflected in an agreement is enough to counterbalance any concessions having to be made to reach this agreement. It may be pointed out that the four types of relationship identified by Snyder describe the initial components of any bargaining. Alignments specify the type of bargaining we are talking about (resolving conflict between adversaries, achievement of common goals among allies). Interests establish the aims of bargaining and the degree to which these aims are compatible with one another. Capabilities and dependence indicate the relative power to pursue the objectives held by the states in question (Snyder 1997, 32–33).

If the relation between the parties to an alliance is well balanced, each party will continue to exercise substantial influence over the other, and both will be controlled by their very relationship (Emerson 1962). However, the exchange is not always balanced. Sometimes B gives greater value than A does to the advantage it gains from the exchange; or B has no alternative but to turn to A. The difference lies in the *strategic force* of the actors, where strategic force for each individual resource consists in a combination of the degree of control by the actor holding the resource, and the degree of importance given to the resource by the others (Stoppino 2001, 167). Specific military means, financial resources, the importance and prestige enjoyed in relation to the other states, and an advantageous geographical position are any ally's most coveted resources. The greater the inequality of resources, the more a remunerative relationship tends to become one based on coercion. In this case, A is in a dominant position, B is dependent on A, and the basis of their interaction is no longer the promise of emerging benefits but the unilateral threat of diminishing benefits, that is, of losses. Thus we can imagine a continuum stretching from a pure exchange of benefits to the most extreme form of dominion and dependence. Even in the latter case, however, a form of mutual exchange still exists (each remunerative action is, ipso facto, an exchange relationship), although the degree of reciprocity is very limited because of the dependent party complying basically to avoid punishment. In equal relationships, the behavior of both parties is conformity because each party is remunerated.

Power thus develops between allies through a mechanism of unequal exchange, where inequality stems from the differing degrees of dependence of the parties in terms of the exchanged resources and their respective options for action.[24] An ally's power over another ally is exercised either directly or indirectly (Stoppino 2001, 150–60). In the first case, as well as the remuneration used to manipulate behavioral choices, through the promise of support (or the threat of abandonment), persuasion is also employed. This involves intervening in relation to the other party's factual knowledge, and even in relation to its value beliefs. In the second case, the first party intervenes indirectly with regard to its ally's circumstances. Its actions in relation to third-party states, by means of which it modifies the distribution of resources, beliefs, and the freedom to act, as well as having an immediate impact on the relationships of the states in question, may also be seen as a means of achieving more or less systematic conditioning of its ally. If state A manages to influence state C, this influence may be profitably used by A to bind ally B to it even more closely. For example, in the event that the relationship between B and C is conflict, A may offer its services as mediator and guarantor. By definition, it is to A's advantage to be in a position to influence C's policies. However, in such a situation, the conformity of C is even more advantageous in that it increases the conformity of B. Those alliances that for long periods in the history of modern Europe characterized the most important phases of war and peace were in fact often founded on similar mechanisms governed by great powers capable of controlling the foreign policy of their allies to a substantial degree.

THE COSTS AND BENEFITS OF ALLIANCES

One generally observes that the alliances whose creation is most likely, as well as those whose conservation is appreciated to the greatest degree by the parties concerned, are the ones in which the members have substantial common interests. Given that each party is clearer about its own intentions (and thus the associated costs) than it is about those of its ally (and thus the potential benefits of the alliance), the costs tend to be lower in those situations where there are shared interests at stake, since neither party promises to do more than it would do in any case. If there are limited shared interests, the costs will be higher, since the parties pledge themselves for a cause that is not really theirs. Likewise, the benefits of such an alliance are going to be limited; an ally cannot place too much trust in the other (Snyder 1997, 10). Cases of alliances of this kind are in practice rather common. In fact, allies often do have shared interests, but their objectives differ, because each ally has its own vision of the purposes of the alliance and will thus tend to consider its own limited objective as the alliance's principal objective. In addition to such inevitable tensions, there will be others if the prize at stake is, above all, one ally's control of the other.

The question remains as to how the costs and benefits of an alliance are to be perceived in conceptual terms. Snyder is one of the few scholars who have posed this question seriously (Snyder 1997, 43–49). He believes that the costs of an alliance may be seen as reduction in the *autonomy* of its members, while the advantages can be evaluated in terms of an increase in *security*. This conceptual framework, though plausible for defensive alliances (the subject, in fact, of Snyder's analysis), fails to offer the basis for a wider-ranging reflection. First, Snyder is forced to excessively broaden the meaning of the two concepts employed. The advantages of security are claimed to include not only dissuasion of the enemy, or in the worst-case scenario a war conducted from a more advantageous position, but also control over the ally. By contrast, the price to be paid in terms of autonomy is said to include the need to move in conjunction with the ally and also the risk of finding oneself facing a counteralliance and involved in a war against one's own will. Second, the costs and benefits may be of a more complex nature.[25] As for costs, it is true, as we have seen, that an alliance is an exchange of pledges and obligations, by definition it limits the autonomy of its members. However, it is also true that some members may assume obligations that they would have taken anyway, or that do not curtail their freedom of movement to any significant degree. Furthermore, an alliance may be costly not only because it leads its members to behave in a way they would not normally behave in, given the choice, but also because it may endanger security itself. Given that the stipulation of an alliance treaty marks the boundaries between friendship and enmity, it officially sanctions, as it were, the existence of an enemy; to find oneself involved in an undesired war is a risk affecting security to a greater degree than autonomy. This means, among other things, we must constantly bear in mind the uncertainty that permeates the behavior of our ally toward the enemy. In addition, the benefits of an alliance are not always associated with security alone. By blocking our ally, we gain room for maneuver and thus autonomy. This means, among other things, that we must constantly bear in mind the uncertainty permeating our ally's behavior toward us.

Snyder's concept of relationships offers a detailed picture of the "situational context" of behavior. If this picture is, in turn, connected with the pursuit of power, as we have chosen to do here, then it is possible to broaden the discussion of costs and benefits by making explicit reference to the two relational levels at which costs and benefits are evaluated, namely, relations with the enemy and relations with the ally.

Despite being an extremely stylized picture, Table 2.1 does show those incentives and disincentives characterizing inter-ally relations. The 1–4 combination reproposes Snyder's insight: an ally gives up some of its freedom of movement and obtains the military support of the other(s). However, as we can see, there are certainly a number of other possible solutions. The 2–3 combination also implies simultaneous involvement of relations with the ally and relations with the adversary. In this situation, however, the costs and benefits are inverted. The alliance enables one ally to keep the other under strict control, in such a way that it is prevented from taking any independent action but may act only in conjunction with the other ally. This objective is deemed so important that it induces one to accept the risk of war. But in the case of some states finding themselves in a particularly advantageous position, it may well be that an alliance essentially produces benefits rather than costs (combination 2–4), in enabling us to block the ally, prevent it from aligning with any other powers, while ensuring a feasible form of cooperation. Conversely, there are states for which an alliance means not only reduction in freedom of movement but also excessively high risk of war. For such states, therefore, the alliance is a heavy burden to bear, and a dangerous one at that, which they would do well to free themselves from at the first opportunity (combination 1–3). Finally, we may imagine other situations in which the costs and benefits accrue at just one level: that

TABLE 2.1

Costs and benefits of alliances

	Costs	Benefits
Vis-à-vis the ally	1 My freedom of movement is constrained	2 Your freedom of movement is constrained
Vis-à-vis the adversary	3 "Official" enemy; counteralliance; war	4 Deterrence; in the case of war, additional resources

of the ally, or that of the enemy. For those who find themselves in the 1–2 combination, the alliance basically represents a mutual conditioning agreement, and the important thing is not to join forces against the common enemy but to keep a close eye on one's ally. In the second combination (3–4), the alliance is played out almost entirely at the level of relations with the enemy. In this case, the cost is the risk of war, while the benefit is to fight that war with greater forces than one would have if the alliance did not exist.

The combinations described here denote pure situations, or in any case rare ones: benefits only, costs only, or combinations of one type of cost and one type of benefit. It goes without saying that history is full of even simpler cases (one benefit only or one cost only), and also of much more complex cases (various combinations featuring more than two types of cost and benefit). The usefulness of this framework, nevertheless, is its emphasis on the fact that costs and benefits may be expressed in a less obvious manner than that represented by a simple trade-off between security and autonomy.

THREE

Types of Alliance

ALLIES AND DILEMMAS

So far we have seen that the dynamics of exchange and power examined here work through remuneration and constraint mechanisms that are based on the promise of emerging benefits and the threat of diminishing benefits. In the specific case of inter-ally relations, such mechanisms center on the promise of support or the threat of withdrawal of such support. Within this broader framework, we can now examine the famous "alliance security dilemma" formulated by Glenn H. Snyder (1997, 180–86).[1] In every alliance, as we have already said, states tend to oscillate between two opposite fears, abandonment and entrapment. The former fear is that an ally abandons us, either directly (by abrogating the treaty, for example) or in a more covert manner (by doubting that the *casus foederis* ever existed, or more generally by denying its diplomatic support during a crisis involving the adversary). The latter refers to the risk, as a result of the obligation assumed, of being drawn into a war provoked by an intransigent or reckless ally. Such fears give rise to different forms of conduct. The common response to the fear of abandonment is to "get closer" to the ally, that is, to increase those incentives that may induce the ally to keep its initial pledge; the usual response to the fear of entrapment, on the other hand, is to "get away," that is, to reduce one's obligations or threaten to withdraw one's support. We can speak of a genuine dilemma here for the simple reason that if a state chooses to get closer it reduces the risk of being abandoned but increases the risk of becoming entrapped; on the other hand, if the state chooses to get away, then the opposite will be true. Thus the policies adopted to prevent abandonment make entrapment more likely, and those policies designed to avoid entrapment may well lead to abandonment.

Once again, Snyder's framework is highly effective here. The alliance security dilemma often has a profound impact on inter-ally relations. However, as we have seen in the previous chapter, Snyder is forced to broaden the meaning of autonomy and security to an excessive degree; this entails that the perspective resulting from his alliance security dilemma be in a certain sense distorted, and suffer from the traditional, narrow understanding of alliance underlying it. In fact, abandonment and entrapment represent a significant dilemma in those cases where war is a real possibility and relations between allies are structured defensively, in view of the presence of an adversary. Each state fears being abandoned to face the enemy alone, or being forced to wage war despite not wanting to. Indeed, Snyder talks of a *security* dilemma because the risk is one of being left at the mercy of an *enemy*, or becoming caught up in a *war*. In this kind of situation, one can undoubtedly claim that the allies' major concerns are abandonment and entrapment; however, can the same be said of all alliances? Let us look at the opposite case: in a purely offensive alliance, it makes little sense to speak of abandonment or entrapment, unless we substantially dilute the meanings of the two terms, which would lead to their losing immediacy and analytical worth. In general, a state tends to withdraw its support not only when it finds itself in a situation where there is a risk of entrapment but also when the ally stands to gain what are deemed to be excessive advantages. There are numerous examples of alliances that failed to achieve the success they could have achieved, or that failed to take advantage of excellent victories gained in the field as a result of the allies' differences, differences that cannot be simply described as manifestations of the abandonment-entrapment dilemma. In short, one ally often distances itself from the other despite there being little chance of it becoming entrapped. Similarly, according to Snyder a state gets closer to its ally in order to avoid abandonment. Yet a state may get closer to its ally or allies even when the likelihood of abandonment is remote. Furthermore, as has already been pointed out, Snyder's dichotomy loses much of its significance in the absence of any clear threat; it depends very much on the existence of a hostile environment.

Now, if alliances are, first and foremost, means by which the behavior of others is rendered predictable regardless of the specific objectives pursued, then it could be said that Snyder's dilemma is in turn a specific case (played out in the name of security) of the latent power struggle between allies, whereby each ally attempts to control the other's movements. This means that the alliance security dilemma is logically circumscribed to within what could be described as the "alliance power dilemma," which may be defined as follows: even prior to fearing abandonment or entrapment, an ally will worry about the other party becoming too strong or too weak. Once again, the two fears are inversely correlated; those measures taken to produce one result help produce the opposite result. The abandonment Snyder talks about is the likelihood of one ally finding itself facing the enemy on its own, since the other ally has retreated. The weakening of an ally, though, is not a question of failed loyalty; the other ally does not withdraw but is simply incapable of doing its job and is thus a burden for the first ally. This is why Snyder's policy of getting closer appears a better idea when there is a risk of the weakening of one's ally, rather than it abandoning the field altogether. In fact, this abandonment may be due to one or more of a series of causes, and there can be no guarantee that provision of closer support to that ally will avert the latter's withdrawal. Moreover, fear of entrapment always implies the risk of an unwanted war; the fear of excessive strengthening of the ally implies the risk—perhaps less dramatic, but serious nevertheless—of becoming so dependent on this ally that all of one's foreign policy becomes conditioned by the ally as a result. Hence the characteristic tension accompanying evaluation of an ally's successes: if an alliance were a mere aggregation of power, then one ally should be pleased with the strengthening of the other ally, because this would put all concerned in a position to achieve their purpose more easily. However, given that an alliance is not simply a union of forces designed for a commonly shared purpose, it is always going to be better if an ally is never in a position to free itself from its partner, because its emancipation would amount to the end of the latter's influence over it. Furthermore, the alliance security dilemma concerns allies' *intentions*, given that it is characterized by the uncertainty surrounding their actions; the other dilemma results from the *means* actually available to allies, because these means establish their propensity, rather than their intention, to act in a certain way. If an ally is too weak, it will not be of any great use and will not be in a position to keep its pledge, regardless of what it would like to do. If it is too strong, it will invariably be in a position to subtract itself from the other ally's control, or even in a position to control this ally. Finally, from a behavioral point of view, fear of excessive weakening of one's ally will result not so much (or not only) in renewed commitment to the alliance and the offer of new incentives to one's ally but also in provision of direct support, that is, of the aid required to keep the ally on its feet. On the contrary, one ally's fear of the excessive strengthening of the other will result not so much in the former moving further away from the latter but also its in attempting to hinder the latter's plans.

All of this can then be related to the much-debated question of "relative gains," which the neorealist school considers one of the major structural obstacles to cooperation between states within an anarchical context. In the words of Kenneth N. Waltz, when states are given the chance of cooperating with one another "they are compelled to ask not 'Will both of us gain?', but 'Who will gain more?'" (Waltz 1979, 105). Consequently, one state may even be prepared to give up certain benefits offered by cooperation, if they can be obtained only by conceding even greater benefits to the other parties involved. Neorealism links this reaction to the need for security induced by anarchy; the uncertainty regarding implementation of agreements, together with the ever-present possibility that force might be employed, means states are basically "defensive positionalists" (Grieco 1988) and as such are more interested in relative gains than in absolute ones. In an attempt to grasp the problem clearly, it was also pointed out that the sensitivity of one state regarding the difference between its own gains and those of others is of a conditional nature and thus tends to be greater in certain circumstances and less in others. More specifically, it has been claimed that in the presence of a common enemy, allies' concern over relative gains tends to diminish (Grieco 1993).[2] This hypothesis is hardly surprising, given that it duly reflects the characteristic neorealist approach. However, according to the line of argument developed in the present study, such concerns over relative gains are bound to be felt even among allies. The problem is not only that today's ally could become tomorrow's enemy; any imbalance in distribution of gains will have immediate consequences, regardless of whether an alliance risks seeing the former ally become the current enemy and vice versa (a suggestive possibility, but a rare occurrence). If an alliance between A and B enables B to obtain greater gains than those obtained by A, this will put B in a stronger bargaining position than that of its ally—a position enabling it to subtract itself from A's power, or to exercise power over A.

ADVERSARIES, ALLIES, AND DILEMMAS

Up to now we have focused mainly on inter-ally relations; we now need to examine relations between allies and their adversaries. From a strategic point of view, analysis of the dynamics of inter-state conflict has traditionally been based on the contrast between the "deterrence model," which underlines the benefits of a strategy of firmness, and the "spiral model," which focuses on the reasons for adoption of a strategy of flexibility (Jervis 1976, 58–113). In the first model, a conciliatory approach could be interpreted as a sign of weakness, leading the adversary to submit further demands; for this very reason a firm stance needs to be taken. In the second model, an overly firm approach with regard to the adversary could force the latter to also adopt a stricter policy, thus creating a vicious circle of reciprocal fear, actions, and counteractions that could quite easily get out of control. For this reason, a more conciliatory approach is suggested. As we can see, we are faced once again with a dilemma: on the one hand, those steps taken to avoid the risk of being manipulated by the adversary actually increase the likelihood of a confrontation that neither party really desires, and on the other hand any measures taken to avoid escalation of the situation may lead not to a cooling of tensions but instead to demands for further concessions.

For our purposes, we need to understand, first and foremost, how the two relational levels—that is, relations with the ally and relations with the adversary—interact.[3] According to Snyder (1997, 192–99), adoption of a firm approach with the adversary reassures the ally and thus reduces the risk of abandonment. However, at the same time it also increases the risk of entrapment and reduces one's bargaining power over the ally. Conversely, a conciliatory approach to an adversary will have an inhibitory effect on an ally (the latter no longer being certain of our support if it forces our hand), thus reducing the risk of entrapment and increasing our bargaining power in relation to that ally (since we now have less need of our ally's support due to the improvement in relations with the adversary). Nevertheless, the risk of upsetting the ally remains, and it could even lead to the latter's withdrawal from the alliance. As for the impact that strategies concerning our allies have on our adversaries, it may be summarized this way: full support for an ally will have a dissuasive or coercive effect on the adversary (the deterrence model), but this tightening of the alliance may also frighten the adversary to the point where it reacts by radicalizing the confrontation (as foreseen by the spiral model). Similarly, if we distance ourselves from an ally, this will temper tensions with the adversary, thus reducing the likelihood of escalation; nevertheless, the dissuasive effect will also be diminished, and the adversary, having noted the counterparty's prudence, may be encouraged to increase its demands.

At the risk of repeating myself, the perspicacity of Snyder's theory should be underlined once again. It clearly reveals some of the characteristic difficulties and uncertainties encountered by states faced with the complex task of handling the combination of relations they have with both allies and adversaries. Nevertheless, this result is obtained at the price of a series of simplifications we are now going to examine. In fact, on closer inspection we find that a firm attitude with the adversary does not necessarily have the effect of reassuring an ally; nor does a strategy of flexibility necessarily lead to abandonment of the alliance by one's ally. To begin with, firmness with the adversary may even have the opposite effect from what is hypothesized by Snyder; rather than tranquilizing the ally, the latter may become even more worried to the point where it concludes that continuing with the alliance represents too great a risk. Containing an enemy does not necessarily mean going to war; even in cases of actual warfare, there are various levels of involvement and obligation. In other words, an intransigent approach to an adversary may put our ally in a position to either entrap or abandon us. Moreover, adoption of a firm approach in relation to an adversary may lead to entrapment not so much of ourselves but rather of the ally. If the latter has no way out, it will find itself faced with a fait accompli, bound to the alliance even more than before, and forced, against its will, to follow us. Likewise, adoption of a conciliatory approach with regard to an adversary will lead to abandonment of the alliance by our ally only if the latter can do without our support or, more realistically, has any genuine realignment options; but if its spaces are closed, it will again be forced to fall into line, regardless of how unhappy it is with the alliance.

The impact that the approach to our ally may have on relations with the adversary also merits further consideration. The effects of our support for the ally, as Snyder himself admits, may vary considerably. In fact, it may lead to opposite reactions, based on the terms of the deterrence model and the spiral model. However, failure to support the ally does not simply result in a relaxing of relations with our adversary; there is another possibility that Snyder, in his traditional understanding of alliances, neglects, namely that failure to support the ally implies an agreement with the adversary, to the detriment of the same ally, thus leaving the latter either to the mercy of the enemy or increasingly entangled in the alliance that has just caused it damage (the Tertius Dolens mentioned earlier).

In the final analysis, by asking ourselves what the effects are of a firm or flexible approach to an adversary, or of providing (or failing to provide) support to an ally, we are asking questions with no answers if we do not possess "relational" information, that is, information concerning the positions held by the various states with regard to both allies and enemies, at that specific moment in time. We therefore need to focus more clearly on the conditions under which the dynamics described in general terms so far are more or less likely to emerge, and on the specific forms that such dynamics may take. Although it is fair to say that power struggles and security concerns characterize the majority of alliances, we nevertheless have to admit that the degree to which one or the other influences such alliances, and as a result (partly or completely) affects relations between allies, may vary considerably. In other words, not all alliances are characterized by the same tensions and the same ambiguities; hence the need to distinguish between types of alliance.

TOWARD A TYPOLOGY OF ALLIANCES

The most common trait of the specialized literature is to focus, either implicitly or explicitly, on defensive alliances alone, that is, on those alliances created in order to counter a common threat. However, this approach not only precludes any meaningful examination of power struggles among allies but also prevents us from examining those alliances that cannot be defined in purely defensive terms. There is no shortage of classifications, of course. However, they are often rather limited contributions consisting in mere lists of alliance types.[4] Although on the one hand this approach represents an initial attempt to put some order into a mass of complex phenomena, on the other hand it has certain clear limitations. For example, there is very rarely any explanation of why certain criteria are employed rather than others, while the various types of alliance identified are never subjected to any real theoretical analysis. Be that as it may, it is common practice to distinguish between alliances in terms of their duration,[5] their effectiveness,[6] their objectives in relation to other states,[7] the nature of the casus foederis,[8] the required military effort and integration,[9] the interests at stake,[10] the geopolitical positions of their members and adversaries,[11] the obligations undertaken,[12] the power relations between the allies,[13] and the distribution of gains among alliance members.[14] As we can see, there is plenty of choice here. So, although it is clear that each empirical universe can be organized in many ways, it is also true to say that if we wish to avoid being submerged by a plethora of classifications with a purely descriptive purpose, we require the guidance of a theoretical framework capable of indicating the most important criteria on the basis of which to proceed.

Although contemporary theory fluctuates from complete disinterest in types (often going no further than an analysis of defensive alliances) to a hurried listing of the possible classifying criteria, the classics once again offer the most interesting ideas. Paolo Paruta, for example, emphasizes the conflict of interests among allies when he writes that in "Leagues of Princes, every one harth his own conveniencie, and particular benefit for his aimed at end, and then the like of others onely so far, as by accident may square with his. But it commonly falls out, that what makes for one makes against another."[15] Those alliances created for purely defensive purposes, or designed to help a state under attack from a stronger power, are the ones that offer the best form of guarantee. However, the former are the result of a "fear which makes a Prince take up Arms, which likewise makes others joyn with him, who otherwise do much differ from him in desires and interests"[16]; hence their fragility, and the tendency of each member to "change War for Peace" as soon as the occasion to do so arises. The latter, on the other hand, are susceptible to friction and tension as soon as the opportunity arises to "increase in State and power" by destroying the enemy, since "the purchase that is got, or which is hoped for, cannot be so equally divided and agreed upon, but that some of the Confederate Princes will happen to have a greater share than the rest; and every increase [...] doth easily cause jelousie, or at least envy in the rest."[17]

Finding oneself in a precarious situation, as a result of the disinterest, or diverse interests, of one's ally is not the only risk a state runs. An even greater risk is how an asymmetric power relationship between allies is transformed, ipso facto, into a relationship of subordination of the weaker state to the stronger one. Giovanni Botero, for example, distinguishes between "equal" and "unequal" alliances. The latter are those in which "one [partner] dominates the rest," or those in which "one partner in the joint enterprise contributes more, or derives more advantage from victory than the other"; little trust should be placed in such alliances.[18] Jean Bodin recommends that "the succours of the confederate must not be such as they may force or prescribe a law";[19] and in reference to treaties of protection, he advises against allowing the protector to take over fortresses and station troops in the cities of the protected parties, if the alliance is not to be transformed into "seigneurie."[20] According to Machiavelli, a state should not create an offensive alliance with a stronger state "because if you are the victors, you emerge as his prisoner."[21] A state that is on an equal footing with, or is even stronger than, each of those states already fighting will find itself in an extremely advantageous position as a result of the control it may exercise over its ally: "you help destroy one combatant with the help of the other, who would be helping him himself if he were wise. If you are the victors, *your ally is at your mercy*, and with your help it is impossible for him not to win."[22] Furthermore, Machiavelli considers an intelligent alliance policy to be the best possible instrument of expansion. Such a policy consists in "forming alliances in which you reserve to yourself the headship, the seat in which the central authority resides, and the right of initiative."[23] That is exactly what Machiavelli believed republican Rome did with the Latin and Italic peoples, who "without being aware of it, fell under her yoke and laboured and shed their blood on her behalf."[24] Although the words of Machiavelli refer to those cases in which there is a clear power imbalance among allies, the underlying logic is not that much different when the parties in question are of substantially the same importance. One excerpt from the writings of Francesco Guicciardini illustrates the dualism of alliances perfectly. In reference to the triple alliance between Milan, Florence, and Naples at the end of the 15th century, he writes that "this alliance easily curbed the cupidity of the Venetian Senate" and immediately adds, however, that at the same time the allies "full of emulation and jealousy among themselves [...] did not cease to assiduously observe what the others were doing, each of them reciprocally aborting all the plans whereby any of the others might become more powerful or renowned."[25]

The configuration of interests among allies, and the nature of their power relations once again emerge as key categories, relational categories concerning the position held by each ally in relation to both the other allies and to third-party states. As we have already mentioned, Snyder too defined his relationships in terms of "interests in common and in conflict" and "dependence" (among allies). At which point, some questions need to be answered. Have the allies taken similar stances with regard to their common enemy, or is one ally more concerned about the enemy than the other ally is? Are they prepared to pay the same price and run the same risks, or is only one of them prepared to push the confrontation with the enemy to its extreme consequences? Do the allies fear each other? Do they possess similar power, or is one noticeably stronger than the other? To what degree are they interdependent? It may be a good idea to formulate various types of alliances on the basis of such questions. To put it more precisely, given that allies act to try to obtain reciprocal conformity, two basic lines of thought emerge. The first is centered on the question, "Is the strategic force of the allies equal or unequal?" This enables us to distinguish between *symmetrical* and *asymmetrical* alliances. The second is centered around the question, "Is the bargaining range between allies broad or narrow?" This enables us to distinguish between *homogeneous* and *heterogeneous* alliances.

SYMMETRICAL AND ASYMMETRICAL ALLIANCES

In the previous chapter, the "strategic force" of an actor is defined as the combination of the degree of *control* over certain resources, and the *importance* that the other actors attribute to such resources. An alliance composed of two (or more) states of similar strategic force is deemed to be a symmetrical alliance. In this case, equality underlies a remunerative relationship based on an exchange of benefits between interdependent parties. When the strategic forces of the states differ, their union gives rise to an asymmetrical alliance, and in this case their inequality underlies a relationship that tends to be restrictive, that is, based on the dominance of one ally and the dependence of the other. When power relations are very heavily weighted to one side, the conformity pursued by the most powerful ally is at its greatest, influencing as it does the foreign policy of the weaker states (which are asked to have the same friends and enemies), their military organization (the most powerful ally monopolizes command of the armed forces), their economic and financial decisions (through demands for the granting of trade rights and contributions for their joint defense), and in some cases their domestic affairs (through ideological and cultural penetration, as well as the legitimization of institutional arrangements and forms of regime; Colombo 1994, 39–52).

To a first approximation, the distinction between small and large powers is important. Even though it may be said that in theory the pursuit of power (or of security in the pure neorealist version) permeates the behavior of all states, it is also true to say that this fundamental attitude may vary considerably, and that such differences can be explained in part by the ranking, size, and resources of the states in question. In other words, the needs and ambitions of a major power are different from those of a small state, and the foreign policies of the two will resemble each other only in very general terms. The same is true, of course, for their alliance policies. Minor powers cannot simply be thought of as major powers on a smaller scale.[26] The difference between the two classes of state is not only a quantitative one but above all a qualitative one. In fact, the distinguishing characteristics of a minor power go beyond its relative weakness, even though this still needs to be borne in mind; they also include a whole series of implications deriving from that weakness. First of all, unlike major powers, which possess much greater means and can thus choose from a wider range of options, minor powers are more often than not forced to seek external support and place their faith in the guarantees offered by other states, which are often of an ambiguous nature. As a rule, the stakes are also different. If a small state is threatened by a large state, the former's very survival may be at stake, whereas a war between major powers may not necessarily affect their vital interests. This does not mean a minor power is always concerned exclusively about its own survival; however, whereas a major power usually plays the field, a minor power's scope is much narrower. Furthermore, the latter's margin for error is much smaller; a modest territorial size, scarce resources, and unpredictable friends mean that a small state could pay a high price for adopting a rash policy. Finally, it may be true that every alliance by definition limits the freedom of movement of its members, both large and small, but this limitation is generally greater in the case of a smaller state. In other words, if an alliance creates a situation of asymmetrical interdependence—that is, a situation in which breaking off relations between the parties would damage one party more than another—as a general rule it is the small state that is going to find itself in the most vulnerable position.[27]

If we now look at things from the point of view of the major power, the latter may be encouraged to ally itself to a weaker state for a variety of reasons (Liska 1968, 23–43). The possibility of increasing its own capabilities, even to a moderate degree, is something that appeals to both great and small alike, or at least this was the case until the end of the 18th century, that is, up to the point when even a small military contingent could be of some value for the purposes of warfare. Moreover, an alliance with a minor power means subtracting a potential ally from other states, which could be more important than the limited direct contribution that such a state could offer. Finally, an alliance allows a major power to control its smaller ally, in ways that range from genuine vassalage to blander forms of surveillance and control. Despite the multiplicity of possible arrangements, all such relationships have one feature in common: when the client state makes foreign policy decisions, it has to take account of the more powerful state's interests.

Nevertheless, the power relationship between allies is based on both the entity of their resources and the perceived importance of such resources. Thus even if A possesses fewer resources than B, A may be less dependent than this inequality would have one believe; vice versa, even if A possesses similar resources to B, A may be more dependent than would appear to be the case at first glance.[28] The potential relations between each ally and other states outside the alliance play an important role here. A state that, despite its substantial resources, still looks for the support of another smaller or weaker state at a given moment in time could pay dearly for such a policy. On the other hand, a state will be in a strong bargaining position vis-à-vis an ally if it can turn to others for support without too much difficulty. In other words, a state with options is going to bargain hard, whereas a state with no alternatives is going to have to beseech the other. However, even in a desperate situation, the supplicant party may still exercise a limited degree of bargaining power. If satisfaction of the major ally's interests depends on the survival, or on a specific foreign policy, of the minor ally, then the major ally will have to take it upon itself to look after its weaker partner.[29]

According to Snyder (1997, 187–88), the type of dependence that binds allies is one of the most important factors that shed light on the alliance security dilemma; such a dilemma is more acute in symmetrical alliances as a result of each member's awareness of just how important the other's support is, although the risk of abandonment is tempered by the very reciprocal nature of this need. In asymmetrical alliances, it is the more dependent member who feels the entire weight of the dilemma. It fears being abandoned above all, and as a result it is also concerned about becoming entrapped. The less dependent ally, on the contrary, fears entrapment most of all. Yet it could be objected that in symmetrical alliances an equal distribution of power is not enough to avert the risk of abandonment-entrapment. This is only true if such alliances are also homogeneous, in the sense we shall be giving to this term shortly; that is, if the allies are actually prepared to exchange services. Things are different, however, in the case of heterogeneous alliances, in which, if power relations are evenly balanced, each member tends to hinder the other's movements in order to avert the danger of entrapment. However, going back to the effects of symmetry and asymmetry, we are now in a better position to specify the consequences that a firm, or a flexible, approach to one's enemy will have on inter-ally relations. As we have said, according to Snyder, a strategy of firmness implies the risk of becoming entrapped. Yet this is especially so for the more dependent ally. The risk is lower for the less dependent because it could feasibly threaten to exercise the abandonment option, or indeed do so. Similarly, a flexible approach to one's adversary will only lead to abandonment in the case of the ally that can afford to do so, that is, the less dependent state once again. The more dependent state has no choice but to accept the policy of its less dependent ally.

All of this would seem to suggest that prior to shedding some light on the alliance security dilemma, knowing whether an alliance is symmetrical or asymmetrical helps us understand, in more general terms, who exercises power over whom. In symmetrical alliances, this restraint is genuinely reciprocal and consists of thrusts and counterthrusts between the parties, each of which possesses the means with which to enforce its demands (those resources desired by the other party). In asymmetrical alliances, the restraint is unilateral, and the decisions taken inevitably reflect the imbalance in power relations; for this reason, such alliances are always characterized by a degree of unilateral constraint. The leader of the alliance generally has a lot of cards to play. The conformity of the weaker ally is obtained by offering the ally security if it feels threatened, or economic aid if it needs resources; and if the weaker ally cannot be either protected or aided, then it will be intimidated.

As we have said, the threat of withdrawal of support—in its various forms—is the most commonly used bargaining instrument among allies. Snyder (1997, 321) explicitly links this threat to the policy designed to avert the risk of entrapment, whereby restraint of the ally performs this very function. However, inducing an ally to follow a certain, foreseeable direction remains an advantage, regardless of whether the risk of entrapment exists or not. The less-dependent ally finds itself by definition in an advantageous position, which it cannot really be expected to renounce. The importance of this point cannot be emphasized enough, since providing benefits that the others cannot easily do without is the commonest way of obtaining power. According to Peter M. Blau (1964, 15–142), if B needs a service offered by A, it has four options: (1) it may supply A with a service the latter needs, in exchange; (2) it may find the service it needs elsewhere; (3) it may force A to furnish it with the service; or (4) it can resign itself to doing without the service in question. However, if it is not in a position to do any of these things, then it can be said to be within A's power. With the exception of the third option (direct recourse to physical coercion is uncommon among allies), the conditions established by Blau also describe certain forms of behavior adopted by a state trying to subtract itself from an ally's control. It will be prepared to offer further services (diplomatic support, additional military services, funding, military bases), thus balancing its own dependence with that of the other partner; it will look for alternative courses of action, first and foremost promotion of agreements with potential new allies; and finally, it may even review certain of its foreign policy objectives and accept, for example, a lower international profile in exchange for greater independence. Conversely, Blau's conditions also suggest the moves that a state wishing to strictly control its ally will make. First, it will try to remain indifferent to those services it is offered, perhaps by finding them elsewhere independently, or with the help of yet other states. Furthermore, it will try to maintain a monopoly over the benefits the other state needs ("only I can help you; only I share your interests"), by rendering the search for alternatives more difficult and costly. Apart from the diplomatic and military support characterizing all alliances, financial aid, trade concessions, and more recently the supply of arms usually render an ally increasingly dependent. In addition, in those alliances composed of three or more allies, attempts will be made to ensure that they cannot coordinate their movements in order to extract concessions or enjoy greater freedom of movement. Finally, the importance of the alliance's role in the given international context will be underlined, both by encouraging the ally to pursue certain foreign policy goals rather than others, and by using propaganda and ideological means. Just as the belief in the positive character of the church's approval tends to reinforce the power of the clergy, so political and strategic belief in the key role of an alliance tends to reinforce the power of that alliance's leader. From this point of view, the alliance power dilemma appears clear. Broadly speaking, every ally has good reason to fear the excessive power of every other ally. If they are on a par, then the strengthening of one ally will lead to unbalanced relations in the latter's favor; if, on the other hand, their relationship is an unequal one, then the strengthening of the weaker ally will mean diminished control by the stronger ally, whereas further strengthening of the latter will result in even greater dependence of the weaker member of the alliance.

The characteristics attributed here to asymmetrical alliances may be more or less accentuated, depending on the degree of inequality between members of the alliance. The measure of unilateral restraint and control that A exercises over B is increasingly evident as the degree of asymmetry rises, as A moves from a position of simple preponderance to one of complete domination. Given the range of arrangements characterized by unbalanced power relations, we can expect the class of asymmetrical alliances to be empirically far larger than the class of symmetrical alliances.

HOMOGENEOUS AND HETEROGENEOUS ALLIANCES

The power relations between allies thus offer important initial information. If the allies are of similar strategic force, then their relations will be of exchange; if, on the other hand, they are unequal, then their relationship will be one of dominion and dependence. We now need to examine the bargaining range between allies, that is, the space delimited by the possible agreements both parties would rather come to than have no agreement at all. In fact, even if one party possesses resources important for the other party, this is no guarantee that an exchange will take place. Moreover, relationships of dominance and dependence may oscillate between a symbiotic situation characterized by the mutual satisfaction of both allies and a situation characterized by latent or evident tension arising from exploitation of the weaker member by the stronger one. Redefinition of those pledges constituting the basis of the alliance, for example, is the structurally induced outcome of a change in the power relations between the allies; however, this outcome may be of a varying nature, ranging from break-up of the alliance to mere redistribution of roles and responsibilities. We are now going to take up where we left off earlier in pointing out that despite the positions implicitly or explicitly adopted by the majority of scholars, allies' interests cannot simply be boiled down to their opposition to a common enemy. In other words, we need to distinguish between the interests of the alliance as a whole, where such interests exist, and the national interests of its member states (Aron 1962/1967, 137–38) as well as to examine their systemic-relational aspects.

Homogeneous alliances are those in which the states comply with convergent constraints or respond to compatible opportunities. Such a context encourages the allies to cooperate in a way that is potentially beneficial to all. By contrast, those alliances in which the member states comply with divergent constraints or respond to contradictory opportunities shall be deemed to be heterogeneous. In such cases, any close cooperation is discouraged because it could prove counterproductive, or in any case disadvantageous, for at least one of the members.[30] In other words, in homogeneous alliances the states find themselves in a situation in which withdrawal of support by one or both parties would be detrimental to both. That is, A lends B its support because if it did not do so, it would lose out. In heterogeneous alliances the context in which the states find themselves is such that it is the very support offered to the ally that constitutes the source of potential harm. That is, A is not going to lend B its support, because if A did it would be harmed as a result. Yet another way of expressing this is shown in Table 2.1. In homogeneous alliances, each state deems the benefits—in relation to the ally ("your freedom of movement is constrained") and the enemy ("deterrence, and in the case of war, additional resources")—to be greater than the costs to be borne in terms of relations with the ally ("my freedom of movement is constrained") and the enemy ("official enemy, counteralliance, war"). The opposite is deemed true in heterogeneous alliances. The presence of a common enemy is the clearest sign of the homogeneity of an alliance (Colombo 2001, 151–55). However, even the presence of several enemies, provided they are associated with an interactive situation shared by the allies, renders the alliance a homogeneous one. This is true in the case where the defeat of A, who is fighting C, has serious consequences also for B, who is busy combating D. In other words, the "common enemy" may be perceived as a species of a larger genus. When the enemy is not the same for each member, or when the various enemies are in no way shared by the allies, then the latter are going to be reluctant to get too involved in any cause that may not be theirs. As far as opportunities are concerned, the opportunity to expand implies results that may be more or less compatible. The agreed sharing out of a territory enables the allies to act together, but if both are interested in the same portion of that territory then this will introduce a degree of rivalry into their union. Similarly, the difficulties of a third state may present an opportunity for both allies to gain certain advantages over that third state, but if one of the allies does not want the third state to be further weakened this may complicate the allies' relationship. In more general terms, homogeneous and heterogeneous alliances can also be conceived of independently of the presence or absence of a clearly identified enemy or target. Where an alliance basically constitutes an element of the international order, the nature and meaning of that order, together with the role assigned to each of the allies, often need to be defined, and there can be no guaranteeing that the allies in question are capable of giving the same answers to such questions. To sum up, in homogeneous alliances, there is a strong common cause that monopolizes the allies' attention. In heterogeneous alliances, the common cause is a less clearly defined one and coexists with a whole series of "particular causes," and it may even play an instrumental role in pursuing such particular causes. Balancing together with bandwagoning (conceived as the joining of forces with the strongest state for revisionist purposes) are associated with the class of homogeneous alliances. Bandwagoning seen as the joining of forces with the state posing the threat belongs to the class of heterogeneous alliances.

The decisive point in distinguishing between homogeneous and heterogeneous alliances should be clear by now; it concerns the link between the common cause and the particular causes. Notwithstanding that every alliance inevitably features both types of cause, homogeneity is given when pursuit of the common cause is not particularly affected by requirements deriving from the particular causes and does not, in turn, prejudice pursuit of such particular causes. State A is trying to achieve objectives X and Y; state B, in turn, is in pursuit of objectives X and Z. Their alliance, which centers around objective X, will be homogeneous if in order to achieve X, A does not have to forgo Y and B does have to forgo Z; similarly, the alliance is considered homogeneous if the policy implemented by A in order to achieve Y, and that implemented by B in order to attain Z, do not compromise the common objective X. Thus, for an alliance to be considered homogeneous it does not have to be devoid of interests other than the common, shared interest; nor does there necessarily have to be any ideal convergence of interests such that pursuit of Z by B, and pursuit of Y by A, also contribute to achievement of the common objective, or vice versa. Of course, the presence of such conditions would clearly strengthen homogeneity. However, the minimum requirement is that the allies be in a situation in which one ally does not represent a hindrance to the particular causes of the other, and that the common cause not be compromised by the various particular causes. When an alliance is heterogeneous, one has to forgo particular causes if one wishes to safeguard a minimum degree of cooperation. At this point, power relations come into play. As we shall see, in heterogeneous symmetrical alliances neither member is prepared to make concessions to the other, while in heterogeneous asymmetrical alliances the weaker party is forced to give up a series of substantial interests for the sake of the alliance.

The distinction between homogeneous and heterogeneous alliances casts further light on the alliance security dilemma. As Snyder himself observes (1997, 186–88), when allies have a clear common enemy or shared enemies there is less likelihood of abandonment; in fact, they have a considerable strategic interest in giving each other support, since neither is prepared to see the other ally's resources being taken over by the enemy; at the same time, the risk of entrapment is low since there is already a certain propensity to fight. In our terms, the allies in this case are both subject to similar constraints, and for this reason their alliance can be considered homogeneous. However, if the allies have different enemies, or if one ally's cause of friction with the same enemy differs from that of the other ally (that is, if they are not both subject to the same constraints), then the dilemma returns to the fore, because the likelihood of abandonment and the costs of entrapment are both greater. Given that the strategic interest in defending the other is now weaker, there is a palpable risk of abandonment; furthermore, the different conflicts with the common enemy, or the conflicts with different enemies, evoke the specter of entrapment. In homogeneous alliances, the allies tend to put aside their potential differences, as they are induced into helping one another. In heterogeneous alliances, dispersion of interests complicates things. Each ally would like to be supported by the other, but on its own questions and with regard to its own interests that the other ally does not share; hence the generalized uncertainty over reciprocal commitment (Colombo 1994, 107–38). Here too, something more specific may be said regarding the effects that behavior toward the enemy may have on one's ally. It is especially in heterogeneous alliances that a firm stance with regard to the enemy is more likely to lead to entrapment or abandonment. In homogeneous alliances, such risk will be lower.

Furthermore, the homogeneity or heterogeneity of an alliance affects the alliance power dilemma. In general, we have seen that the prevailing tendency is to fear the strengthening of an ally. Nevertheless, in homogeneous alliances this competitive logic is to an extent extenuated by similar positions held by the allies in relation to the outside world. The importance given by all to the common cause will mean that each ally is worried above all about the other ally becoming too weak, and as a result one will be prepared to tolerate the reinforcement of the other. At the specific moment of the conjuncture that renders the alliance homogeneous, it is better to have a solid ally. In heterogeneous alliances, the imperatives dictated by competition between the parties tend to prevail, and fear of excessive strengthening of an ally tends to be greater. In other words, the competitive forces that characterize this kind of alliance accentuate an ally's fear that if the other ally strengthens its own position, the former will be forced by the latter to comply with a series of policies it does not share.

Finally, focusing on the homogeneity or heterogeneity of an alliance enables us to understand the nature of any bargaining that is going to take place between the allies. In homogeneous alliances, the bargaining will be of an "accommodative" variety, whereas in heterogeneous alliances it will probably be of a "coercive" nature.[31] The former term refers to those situations in which the parties judge their shared interests to be more important than their conflicting interests. In such a situation, the allies are less concerned about the outcome of secondary questions and tend to adopt cooperative strategies, with occasional expression of firmness through which each party tries to obtain its share of benefits. The aim of such negotiations is to reach an agreement that both parties deem satisfactory, within the context of the common cause; the constraint conditioning their moves is the attempt each makes to grant as few concessions as possible during the course of negotiations. The extreme accommodative move, when power relations are asymmetrical, is capitulation. Such a move preserves the common interest, to the detriment of all other interests. Conversely, if power relations are symmetrical, then the allies will enter into negotiations consisting in offers and demands, refusals and concessions. As for coercive bargaining, such a term is used when the conflicting interests are deemed to be just as important as, or more important than, the shared interests. Each party tends to impose its will on the other, despite both parties preferring some form of agreement rather than breaking off. The party's aim in coercive bargaining is to get the alliance to conform to his own objectives, basically by turning it into an instrument for the pursuit of his particular causes; the constraint conditioning their moves is avoidance of breaking off the alliance.[32] The outcome of this type of interaction will thus be characterized by considerable constraining of the weaker party, in the presence of a power imbalance; in the event of equal bargaining power, either an agreement is reached as the parties concerned reluctantly concede some ground or reciprocal paralysis is the result.

Some of the differences between homogeneous and heterogeneous alliances can be illustrated with the aid of simple matrices taken from game theory. To illustrate this point, let us take the case of two allies, each of which has to choose between two strategies, "North" and "South" (Tables 3.1 through 3.4).

In a homogeneous alliance, the parties give priority to their joint action. As Table 3.1 shows, the two allies obtain the best results by coordinating their movements, whereas if they act separately they are both penalized by the poorest end result. In this game there are two equilibrium points, corresponding to adoption of the same strategy by the two players involved (4,3 and 3,4). This situation represents a "dilemma of common

TABLE 3.1
The homogeneous alliance

	North	South
North	4, 3	1, 1
South	1, 1	3, 4

TABLE 3.2
The homogeneous alliance with altered payoff

	North	South
North	4, 3	1, 1
South	1, 1	3, 2

TABLE 3.3
The heterogeneous alliance

	North	South
North	4, 1	2, 2
South	2, 2	1, 4

TABLE 3.4
The heterogeneous alliance with altered payoff

	North	South
North	4, 1	2, 0
South	2, 2	1, 4

aversions," whereby the two players' strategic problem is to avoid a certain result—here, two results—in the presence of more than one equilibrium point (Stein 1983). In heterogeneous alliances, if the allies choose the same strategy, one obtains the best possible result while the other obtains the worst possible outcome. In Table 3.3, these two results are located in boxes 4,1 and 1,4. In other words, the most satisfactory result from the point of view of the individual player is achieved by pushing or dragging the other player where it does not want to go, and the best result for one player is the worst for the other. Such a situation illustrates the gap in interests that characterizes this class of alliance. Preference for outcome 4,1 (and 1,4) forces both allies to adopt coercive tactics, given that this result may be obtained only by imposing it on the other party. In this game, there is just one equilibrium point, situated in square 2,2 (top right); compared with the first game, the interests in the second are spread out to a greater degree, and thus the margins for agreement are much narrower. Furthermore, this equilibrium, achieved while avoiding coordinated action, does not allow either of the two to obtain the best possible result. This is a further illustration of the difficulties inherent in this alliance, and of how each party hinders the other's movements.

Now, if together with the configuration of interests we also take into consideration the distribution of power, as we did when distinguishing between symmetrical and asymmetrical alliances, then further observations may be made. The first game does not feature a problem of coordination alone, but also a distributive one. Each party would rather have one equilibrium point than the other. In situations of this kind, it is often suggested that the winner will be the party that is more convincing in threatening an outcome neither party wishes to see, and that the credibility of such a threat lies in the cleverness of the player. However, Stephen D. Krasner (1991) rightly pointed out the importance of power in determining the outcome of such interactions. If one party manages, thanks to its greater resources, to duly modify the other party's structure of preferences, the latter will be forced to offer its conformity. For example, the stronger ally can create incentives or disincentives capable of altering the weaker party's system of preferences, thus inducing it to review and modify its strategy. A credible threat of withdrawal of support, or of other forms of retribution, may counterbalance or nullify the benefits that the ally hoped to receive as a result of an adoption of an independent policy. As Table 3.2 shows, if the row player is capable of reducing the payoff that the column player expects to receive in the event of convergence on "South-South," then the latter will be induced to shift toward "North," that is, to adopt the same strategy as the former; 4,3 is now the only equilibrium point. A similar action is conceivable in the event of asymmetrical power, also in a heterogeneous alliance, according to Table 3.4. Here the new equilibrium point is 4,1. The new positions that the weaker allies are forced to adopt in Tables 3.2 and 3.4 clearly illustrate one of the most significant differences between homogeneous and heterogeneous alliances when power relations are unbalanced, and which we examine in greater depth later on. Although in both cases the weaker ally ends up by following the stronger ally's lead, in a homogeneous alliance this at least enables it to obtain certain appreciable benefits, whereas in a heterogeneous alliance it is simply the lesser of two evils.

FOUR TYPES OF ALLIANCE

If we intersect these two basic classifications, we get four types of alliance, each of which is characterized by certain essential features:

The aggregation alliance, the result of the combination of homogeneity and symmetry

The guarantee alliance, characterized by homogeneity and asymmetry

The deadlocked alliance, made of heterogeneity and symmetry

The hegemonic alliance, defined in terms of heterogeneity and asymmetry (Table 3.5)

TABLE 3.5
Types of alliance

	Symmetrical Alliances	Asymmetrical Alliances
Homogeneous Alliances	Aggregation alliance *The allies exchange services under terms jointly agreed; cooperation is advantageous for all.*	Guarantee alliance *The allies cooperate under the terms preferred by the guarantor; cooperation is advantageous for all.*
Heterogeneous Alliances	Deadlocked alliance *The allies inhibit each other; the alliance does little or nothing for the security and power of its members.*	Hegemonic alliance *The hegemon imposes its policies on a reluctant partner; hegemonic policies harm the more dependent ally in various ways.*

The Aggregation Alliance

A symmetrical, homogeneous alliance is one characterized by the prevalence of a common cause between allies whose power relations are approximately balanced. This type of alliance is thus based on a transaction consisting of mutual "emerging benefits," a genuine exchange of services between the parties, all of which is generally centered on a common policy toward the adversary. The allies adopt a linear strategy of mutual support and joint action with regard to the enemy. The importance that each party gives to reciprocal conformity is clear; without B's support, A cannot take any action, and vice versa. As a result, each member of the alliance is of necessary importance to the other, because the conformity of the one enables the other to act. Furthermore, given that homogeneity facilitates coordinated movement, the result of the allies' interaction is of a cooperative, mutually beneficial nature. Decisions are taken by consent, and no one party can decisively influence the outcome of negotiations, while both parties gain satisfaction from their agreements.

On the one hand, symmetry renders each ally sensitive to the strengthening of the other; on the other hand, homogeneity tends to reduce this concern and may even engender the opposite fear, namely that the ally becomes excessively weak. Symmetry implies a bargaining process conducted from similar positions of power, thus each party conditioning the other to a similar degree; homogeneity lends this process an accommodative character. Finally, symmetry means that either party's abandonment of the alliance would give rise to serious consequences, while homogeneity strongly encourages the parties to remain united and thus lessens the likelihood of being abandoned, and as a consequence also the likelihood of becoming entrapped. Whether allies adopt a policy of firmness or flexibility in relation to the adversary does not affect their own relationship; the important thing is that they move as one. One could say, to put it succinctly, that this is the model implicitly adopted by those studies that, in neglecting the power relationship between allies, see their association as basically a union of forces for the clear purpose of defense or attack. Hence the term *aggregation*, which we have adopted here for the sake of simplicity.[33] However, even in this particular case, although the parties agree on the objective to be pursued and there are no serious conflicts of interest, the alliance still relies on a process of constant negotiation concerning, if nothing else, the costs to be borne by each party.

The aggregation alliance thus requires a double form of equilibrium: equal dependence and a series of external constraints going in the same direction, be it defensive or offensive. It is therefore easy to see that of the four types described here, this is the rarest and most fragile because it does not take much to alter one of the two conditions and transform the alliance, or, more simply, break it up completely. The aggregation alliance is often an impromptu system, which does not have (nor can it have) any hope of lasting very long, despite potentially offering considerable benefits to both parties. Rather than requiring an unlikely "harmony of interests," the aggregation alliance is based on the agreement of its members in relation to a given objective, the common cause; as far as concerns the other particular causes, the allies can safely ignore one another. Thus the true condition is of the negative type. The various interests in question, other than the shared common interest, only have to be separated from one another in order not to constitute an obstacle to cooperation in view of the common cause. In such circumstances, power relations need to be equal; if this balance is modified in any way, one party will inevitably be tempted to use the other's conformity to other ends, or to impose less beneficial conditions upon that other party, as happens in the case of guarantee alliances. Similarly, homogeneity is just as vital if a satisfactory agreement is to be reached in conditions of symmetry. If power relations are on a par but the allies tend to move in divergent directions, their interaction will result in only partial support being offered, or even in a situation of mutual immobility, as happens in the deadlocked alliance. Despite the common enemy being only one of the possible sources of homogeneity, traditional theory may be useful here. The exchange of "services" in an aggregation alliance is justified in terms of a specific external objective, and once this has been achieved (or has failed) the two allies will tend to withdraw their conformity, given that being of equal strategic force neither can seriously hope to convince the other to follow its lead.

The Guarantee Alliance

A homogeneous, asymmetrical alliance is characterized by the existence of an important common cause binding the allies together; however, one is more powerful than the other. This power imbalance is clearly a decisive means by which the stronger ally conditions its weaker partner. Homogeneity means that negotiations between the two parties are conducted in an accommodative manner, and the weaker party's substantial interests are preserved. This is the meaning of the guarantee offered by the stronger ally. However, the contents of agreements tend to reflect the preferences of this stronger ally. Thus in the guarantee alliance the allies cooperate on the basis of the conditions established by just one of them (the stronger power).

As with the aggregation alliance, the guarantee alliance, thanks to its homogeneity, entails a more or less clear contrast between the allies and the outside world. However, in this particular case the parties no longer perform the same functions. Smaller allies tend to focus their energies on countering the enemy, while the leader—or if you like, the guarantor—fighting for the same common cause secures the conformity of the other members, whose previous sovereign prerogatives diminish to a certain degree as a result. The most characteristic example of such alliances between unequal forces is perhaps an alliance of protection, whereby a major power guarantees the security of other smaller states that feel threatened, in exchange for their obedience.[34] As the major power's policy does not merely consist in the response to an external threat, the guarantee alliance is no sheer union of forces against a common enemy. The more the power relations between allies are uneven, the more the relationship of mutual exchange becomes one of dominion and dependence. Thus in the aggregation alliance the allies offer their conformity, since all obtain something in their exchange; in the guarantee alliance the remuneration factor persists, but the conformity of the weaker ally rests on a certain degree of constraint. Diminishing benefits may well replace the emerging benefits promised by the guarantor. In the abstract, the leader's threat of withdrawal of support is a credible one, since in the event of a breakdown in relations the latter would be harmed to a lesser extent than the smaller ally would. As a result, the leader will try to maintain those conditions that would render the end of the alliance a more costly experience for its allies than for itself, and will therefore perpetuate a situation in which these minor allies continue to follow its leadership if this is the price they have to pay to maintain their ties with it.[35] Moreover, if the smaller power were certain of the guarantor's support, it would be more difficult for the latter to put pressure on the former. Hence the inevitable tendency that transpires from the major power's movements in dealing with its weaker ally, namely satisfying the latter's needs, but not to the point where it feels it can fully rely on the major power's constant support. Such an approach is particularly evident not only (and not particularly) with regard to the common cause but above all with regard to the particular causes; the guarantor subjects the minor ally's attainment of interest Z to the latter's commitment to the pursuit of interest X, the common cause.

In asymmetrical alliances, as we have seen, the weaker ally tends to fear being abandoned; the usual response to this concern, namely strengthening their relationship, implies the increased likelihood of entrapment (for example, becoming involved in a war between major powers). Thus the alliance security dilemma is strongly felt by the smaller allies. By contrast, the major ally is more concerned about becoming entrapped, or more simply about being manipulated by its smaller ally. However, although the leader's firmness toward the enemy places its smaller allies in the position of becoming entrapped, the firmness of these minor allies does not involve the same risk for the leader, which can always resort to threatening withdrawal of its support. The leader may tolerate the minor allies' flexibility toward the enemy, provided this does not constitute an actual rebellion against the leader's directives. Rather than being tempted to abandon the alliance, the leader will resort in turn to various means with which to circumscribe the impact of such flexibility, including (first and foremost) the attempt to maintain a constant, albeit controlled, degree of tension with regard to the enemy, such that the smaller allies are constantly reminded of just how important the leader's protection and support actually is. If it is the alliance's leader who decides to adopt a more flexible approach to the enemy, then once again the allies' reaction will not necessarily be that hypothesized by Snyder; their dependence on the major power will force them to follow its lead even on policies that they do not really believe in.

Such dynamics, which are structurally induced by the power imbalance, are nevertheless tempered to an extent by the homogeneity of the allies' position, which in creating a substantial bargaining range weakens any tendency toward, or probability of, defection and coercion. The position in which the minor ally finds itself leads it to maintain ties with the guarantor, and not to make any real attempt to end its own dependence, provided the risk of entrapment is under control. As homogeneity creates the necessary preconditions for a mutually beneficial form of cooperation, albeit subject to the terms established by the guarantor, we can expect the minor ally to accept its subordinate role without too much trouble. After all, it is only asking to be "guaranteed" by its more powerful ally, and it does not really matter whether its independence is limited or not, provided its most important interests are satisfied to a certain degree. In other words, despite having to accept a certain limitation to freedom of movement, the smaller ally obtains from the guarantee greater benefits or gains than it would be likely to obtain were it to act alone.

This same homogeneity also ensures that the guarantor does not force things too much. Although it may well be true that it is in a much stronger bargaining position than its weaker ally and thus can control the latter's movements by making its support conditional on the smaller power's conformity, it is also true that homogeneity means there is normally no need to resort to coercion; in the majority of cases, persuasion is enough. Paradoxically, the weakness of the minor ally is not only an opportunity for the guarantor but also a constraint on the latter. If the minor ally does not receive the support of the guarantor, it will collapse, and often the major ally cannot allow this to happen. Thus minor allies may use this fact to their own advantage and behave as free riders, burdening the leader with the costs of the alliance. We should not forget here that in the accommodative form of bargaining so characteristic of homogeneous alliances, the principal dispute will be over the sharing of the burden of costs among those concerned. Furthermore, in an aggregation alliance symmetry tends to discourage free riding; in guarantee alliances the minor powers may be induced to take advantage of the protective cover offered by the major power. The latter will then encourage strengthening the minor ally to the point where this serves the common cause, and where it aids achievement of the major ally's other purposes, but no further than this. The golden rule is that the minor ally must never be put in a position to free itself from the need for the major ally's protection and support. From the minor allies' point of view, consolidation of the major power's domination means a greater degree of security, or improved gains, but also greater dependence in both cases. They will thus willingly accept the lead of the guarantor and will be concerned about any weakening of the latter's power if they themselves require greater protection, or if they hope to obtain substantial benefits from this guidance.

The Deadlocked Alliance

A symmetrical, heterogeneous alliance is one where the allies each possess a similar strategic force, and where the common cause coexists with a series of particular causes deemed to be just as important as the common cause, if not more so. In symmetrical alliances, each party offers services to the other, and each party gives equal importance to what the other has to offer. This creates a situation of mutual conditioning that, if the bargaining range is ample, predisposes the allies to coordinate their movements in view of a possible agreement, but that, if the range is limited, provides each party with a genuine veto power over the other based on the threat of diminishing benefits. The allies would be capable of exchanging services, but their unilateral preferences render such an exchange difficult.

In other words, symmetry means that no one party can act freely without the support or agreement of the other; however, by virtue of the heterogeneity that characterizes the alliance, such agreement is unlikely to be given except in rare cases, and as the result of some hard bargaining. The characteristic feature of this type of alliance, therefore, is the reciprocal impeding of the other's actions, which results from a coercive type of bargaining conducted from basically similar positions of power. In short, the allies are condemned, as it were, to coexist; they are often at loggerheads on important matters and thus attempt, frequently with little or no success, to forge ahead in different directions. Such alliances are thus paradoxical, in that they do very little for the signatories' security or power (as perceived by traditional alliance theory). Furthermore, the allies' forces are not really aggregated, and often there is no common enemy (or enemies) capable of catalyzing the alliance. Nevertheless, despite the scant support received, none of the allies would seriously consider dissolving the tie uniting them. Often involved in a process of coercive bargaining, they are nonetheless sensitive to the principal constraint characterizing this type of bargaining, the unwritten law not to break up the alliance. The deadlocked alliance enables us once again to grasp the importance of its members' pursuit of conformity, because it tends to consist in a form of reciprocal control. If supported, an ally will drag the other in a direction it does not wish to go in; if released, it may turn elsewhere, perhaps to the adversary, and harm the other ally even further. This is why the tie constituted by the alliance is so important. The most representative case here may be the union of major powers, each of which is incapable of obtaining the other's support with regard to certain questions. Given that neither is prepared to uphold the other's actions, each tends to keep the other in check.[36]

As with the aggregation alliance, in a deadlocked alliance symmetry gives rise to fears of both abandonment and entrapment. Whereas in the former type homogeneity tempers this twin fear, in the latter heterogeneity accentuates the same fear. In fact, each ally is aware of the importance of the other's support; at the same time, however, the enemies in question are either different or, if identical, do not pose the same problems to each ally or, more generally speaking, what could be beneficial to one ally would damage the other. For this reason, there is a real likelihood of abandonment. If, in order to avoid being abandoned, the allies were to get too close, the cure would be worse than the ill, for it might lead one ally to having to get the other out of trouble. Hence all the allies in this particular case feel the entire weight of the alliance security dilemma. The interweaving of inter-ally relations and relations between allies and the enemy is equally problematic. If the parties adopt different stances with regard to the enemy or enemies, then the firmness of A may easily evoke the specter of entrapment to B and encourage it to abandon the alliance.

Finally, heterogeneity and symmetry render all allies particularly sensitive to the potential excessive strengthening of one of them. The problem of relative gains is particularly evident in this kind of alliance. Given the basic rivalry between the allies, neither is prepared to see the other obtain gains that could alter the relation of forces between them, giving one the opportunity to overcome the other's resistance. To use Guicciardini's term, in this case each ally "aborts" those plans which, if implemented, would allow one of them to increase its power. Of the four types described here, the deadlocked alliance is the one most likely to yield unintentional results, given the contrasting forces and impulses running through it. This alliance, which is similar to Schroeder's pacta de contrahendo (1976), may be associated, among other things, with lengthy periods of peace, since it has the effect of preventing destabilizing actions being taken by its more disruptive members. In the words of Guicciardini, even though the allies tried to hinder each other's movements this "did not result in rendering the peace less stable; on the contrary, it aroused vigilance in all of them to carefully stamp out any sparks which might be the cause of a new conflagration."[37]

The Hegemonic Alliance

Like the deadlocked alliance, the hegemonic alliance is also composed of states that, at one and the same time, are united by a common cause but divided by a series of particular causes. Once again, heterogeneity implies the coercive character of negotiations between allies. However, unlike in the deadlocked alliance, the members of the hegemonic alliance possess unequal powers. Hence exchange is uneven, tending toward a relationship of dominion and dependence based more on the threat of diminishing benefits than on the promise of emerging benefits. So even if both allies adopt coercive tactics, the outcome of their interaction usually leaves no way out for the weaker state, which is generally taken advantage of by the stronger state, that is, by the hegemon.

Herein lies the main difference between the two types of asymmetrical alliance. In the guarantee alliance, the weaker ally, despite its subordinate position, nevertheless obtains certain substantial advantages from its ties with the major power; in the hegemonic alliance its emerging benefits are limited at the most to a mere lesser evil, which is the logical outcome of its precarious position. In fact, in this particular type of alliance the minor ally really has no genuine alternatives, since any other course of action is deemed worse than its relationship with the hegemon. In other words, whereas the guarantor and the minor ally may create an almost symbiotic, albeit troubled, relationship, the hegemon systematically exploits its own position. The heterogeneity of the alliance leads the hegemon to adopt policies detrimental to the lesser ally, while the asymmetrical nature of the alliance offers it the means by which to implement such policies. The pursuit of conformity thus takes different forms for the two allies; the hegemon uses the weaker ally as an instrument of its own policy, and the minor ally tries to contain the actions of the hegemon because it is the weaker party that pays the highest price for such actions.

The combination of heterogeneity and asymmetry underlies certain other characteristic features of this type of alliance. Asymmetry produces the familiar effects on the alliance security dilemma. The more dependent member of the alliance wavers between the fear of abandonment and the fear of entrapment, while the hegemon has to beware above all of becoming entrapped. However, even though in the case of the other asymmetrical alliance (the guarantee) such concerns are tempered by homogeneity, in this particular case they are much more real thanks to heterogeneity; and of course it is the more dependent member that finds itself in greater difficulty. Vulnerable as a result of its dependence, and on the way to clashing with its more powerful ally as a result of heterogeneity, the weaker partner finds itself in the most difficult position of all for an ally. Its firmness with the enemy may be thwarted by the clear refusal of the hegemon to give it necessary support or may be the cause of further embarrassment should the major ally force it forward, thus compromising it even more. In other words, the minor ally could even end up entrapping itself. In relations with the enemy, it is generally the hegemon that dictates the terms and conditions, adopting a more flexible or firmer approach depending on the circumstances, and counting on the constant presence of its minor partner. It is unlikely that, as a result of the minor ally's flexible approach to the enemy, the major ally abandons the alliance, given that it is in the major ally's interest to maintain such an advantageous relationship. Flexibility, if anything, may have the effect of upsetting the hegemon and inducing it to pursue an agreement with the adversary, thus side-stepping its weaker ally altogether, which in this case would not find itself abandoned in the true sense of the word, but in an even worse position still. Here, once again, we encounter a paradoxical situation characterizing all asymmetrical alliances, but particularly evident in the hegemonic type. On the one hand, the major power may use the threat of abandonment to force the hand of a weaker ally refusing to offer its conformity, and on the other hand such a threat is not wholly credible, given that the major ally has a vested interest in continuing to influence the minor ally's policies. Indeed, as we have seen, in a process of coercive bargaining both parties are subject to the same constraint, i.e. not to break their relationship. The real risk the minor ally runs, therefore, is not so much being abandoned to its own devices[38] (it is unlikely that any party exercising power is going to surrender such a prerogative) as being dragged unwillingly in a certain direction, or being immobilized; the hegemonic alliance compromises the weaker ally's position, denies it other options, and compresses any realistic room for maneuver.

Each ally thus tries to prevent the strengthening of the other. In the case of the weaker ally, this would mean subjection to an even greater degree of coercion exercised by the hegemon, while for the latter the strengthening of the weaker party would mean not being able to use it as before. In a guarantee alliance, the minor ally may be tempted to play the role of the free rider; in a hegemonic alliance such an option is not as attractive, for two reasons. First, it cannot be sure that the hegemon is going to shoulder the burden of the costs involved; and second, even if the hegemon were prepared to do so, this would further exacerbate the minor ally's dependence, rendering it even more visible than was previously the case. Furthermore, a minor ally in a guarantee alliance can tolerate losing a degree of autonomy in exchange for certain services offered by the leader; in a hegemonic alliance the minor ally will do everything within its power to avoid remaining totally controlled by its more powerful partner. This would seem to suggest a further difference between the two types of alliance. In a guarantee alliance, the weaker party will be tempted to adopt an opportunistic behavior, whereas in a hegemonic alliance the stronger party will be tempted to do so, and occasionally it will also harm its weaker ally more than the enemy, as it attempts to gain the maximum possible benefit from the favorable position.

The most characteristic form of hegemonic alliance is one in which a major power maintains a tight hold on a small or medium-sized power, or even another major rival power in difficulty, thus neutralizing it within its grip.[39] The ambiguous support offered by the hegemon may not be the only reason the lesser ally accepts the conditions imposed on it. In fact, the hegemonic alliance, seen from the point of view of its weaker members, resembles the situation known as *collective binding* (Grieco 1995, 1996), which is based on the celebrated concepts of *exit* and *voice*, coined by Albert O. Hirschman (1970).[40] When an exit (in our case, the act of freeing themselves from all alliances, or from this specific alliance) is not feasible, the weaker allies will bind themselves to the stronger ally in the attempt to have a voice, that is, to influence the latter's decisions in some way, as members of the same alliance. Bandwagoning, as perceived by Walt (formation of an alliance with the state posing a threat), is an extreme variant of the hegemonic alliance, that is, the attempt to placate a major power by negotiating with it before it is too late, since prompt negotiations may sometimes offer the chance to gain certain concessions that it would be difficult to obtain thereafter.[41] In other words, this represents the weaker states' attempt to get a more powerful state to listen to, and take into consideration, their needs and demands, and to convince it to undertake certain obligations; in short, this is their effort to circumscribe the major power's actions. In relations with adversaries, this often means working to mediate between them and the major ally. This attempt is a very real one, in that it reflects the precise aim of avoiding entrapment; nevertheless, it is often hindered by the hegemon, which is tempted to submit demands to the adversary that the latter is unlikely to accept, counting as it does on the support of the minor ally, who is then entrusted with the task of formulating an agreed compromise solution.

The dynamics of the hegemonic alliance thus consist in unequal conditioning of the reluctant minor allies. Although the latter need the major power's support, they nevertheless harbor a certain rancor against a partner that systematically tries to embarrass them and take advantage of the difficult position in which they find themselves.

To sum up, the distinguishing characteristics of the types of alliance described here may be grasped from various perspectives, in terms of class and type. Although *all* alliances are characterized by a certain degree of cooperation and conflict, homogeneous alliances differ from heterogeneous ones in that the former are characterized by a greater degree of cooperation between allies, whereas the latter are distinguished by a more markedly competitive spirit. The very names given to the types of alliance are designed to highlight, among other things, this basic diversity. On the one hand, there are aggregation alliances and guarantee alliances—terms that convey the idea of some form of joint action beneficial for both parties. On the other hand, there are deadlocked alliances and hegemonic alliances—terms denoting reciprocal denial of cooperation (in the first case), or imposition by one ally of onerous terms on the other (in the second case). As noted above, the alliance is either disadvantageous for both (in the first case) or beneficial to only one of the two (in the second case). If we now examine the other dimension of alliances, the difference is one of power relations. Thus the terms used try to convey the equal or unequal nature of the bargaining power of the allies. *Aggregation* and *deadlocked* imply a certain degree of reciprocity when it comes to giving and taking, in the first case, and the absence of any give or take in the second case. *Guarantee* and *hegemonic* imply the asymmetrical nature of bilateral relations. Where there is a guarantor there is also a guaranteed party; similarly, a hegemon is such because of its superiority compared with the other players.

As far as individual alliance types go, a comparison of each with its neighbors, be they on the same row or column of Table 3.5, may be useful here. The aggregation alliance and the deadlocked alliance are both composed of states with similar levels of bargaining power; however, whereas the former reflects a homogeneous situation, the latter is the result of a heterogeneous context. The heterogeneous alliances in turn feature both the deadlocked alliance and the hegemonic alliance, where the bargaining power of the allies is even, or uneven, respectively. Furthermore, the class of asymmetrical alliances contains both hegemonic and guarantee alliances (where homogeneity prevails over heterogeneity). Finally, within the class of homogeneous alliances, the differing distribution of bargaining power establishes whether an alliance is to be considered of the aggregation variety or a guarantee. The terminology used accounts for this "circular" nature of the typology in question. The same unequal power relations putting one ally in a position to offer a guarantee to the other, in a situation creating a propensity toward cooperation, lead to the hegemony of one over the other when the two allies find themselves in diverging positions. The solution adopted by the stronger inevitably harms the weak. The same differences between allies will give rise to a deadlock when their respective forces annul each other, and neither of the two is capable of convincing the other to offer its services. The equality of bargaining power between allies, in turn, may allow aggregation of their resources when an exchange of services promises to be mutually beneficial. Finally, when the forces are united in this manner of an unequal entity, the preponderant party will grant the weaker party a guarantee, reassuring it that certain of its interests will be satisfied in exchange for obedience. In short, a guarantee gone malevolent, as a result of the different systemic positions held by the two parties, constitutes a hegemony whereby the weaker party is taken advantage of by its stronger ally; between equals, any attempt to take advantage of the other will result in a deadlock; in the presence of conditions that encourage cooperation, the allies' powers, rather than holding each other in check, give rise to an aggregation; and an aggregation where one party plays a preponderant role represents a guarantee offered to the weaker party by the predominant party.

FROM THEORY TO HISTORY

The next step is to examine the characteristics of the four types of alliance in greater depth, and take a closer look at their "rules of functioning." To this end, four particularly important cases are cited from 18th century European politics. International relations scholars have only on rare occasion gone back as far as the 18th century, mainly within the context of statistical-quantitative studies. This omission is not only paradoxical—the period from the Peace of Westphalia to the French Revolution is considered by many to represent the classical period of the modern state system—but also particularly regrettable given the wealth of material available. The 18th century witnessed a number of alliances come and go, some short, others longer, involving practically every single European state at one time or another. From the Peace of Utrecht to the French Revolution, Europe went through a dozen or so wars of various sorts, and war can be considered the true test of any alliance. Then there were periods of peace, based once again on systems of alliances, some of which involved the traditional balance between opposing blocks, while others represented more complex forms of reciprocal conditioning of allied states, as highlighted in the present study. The 18th century was also one in which the principle of the balance of power was explicitly theorized as the cornerstone of international order and security; this should not be underestimated here, in light of the previously mentioned close relationship between alliances and the balance of power.[42] Finally, 18th century foreign policy was completely de-ideologized. Although inter-state relations took place formally in the name of some "international public law," such law was of a prevalently factual nature, whereby sovereignty was legitimized by the acknowledgment thereof by other states, with no concern for the origins of such power. Extremely different forms of government coexisted, but no politician would have ever thought of declaring one form superior to the others. *Raison d'état* was the rule in politics, just as enlargement of the state represented the objective of politics. The resulting foreign policy was of a calculating nature, with politicians waiting for the opportunity to take advantage of favorable circumstances. The general rule of conduct appeared to be to avoid being cheated, and to cheat others whenever possible.[43]

Many 18th century alliances may appear, at first sight, to have been mere aggregations of power for purely offensive or defensive purposes. Yet this aggregational aspect was not their only function. Likewise, it would be reductive in the extreme to perceive the intense diplomatic activity of the European powers of that time merely in the light of balance of power theory. Through alliances, each state pursued its own interests, and such interests would suggest containment of the strongest state, but only if threatened by it, and provision of support to the weakest state, but only if there is some chance of subjugating it. This is not to mention the many cases of stronger states coming to agreement without consulting the smaller states, and without taking the latter's interests into account. Neither may the complex interweaving of alliances and counteralliances be seen as a willing attempt to achieve a lasting general system capable of placating the major powers, for the simple reason that these powers often gave conflicting definitions of the balance of power.[44] Finally, although many alliances arose to a certain degree from the logic of the balance and aggregation of power, some implications went well beyond such logic. For decades, Great Britain, which at the time was the least vulnerable power within the international system, courted Russia—another relatively safe power—with the purpose of countering France. In doing so, it indirectly lent support to the expansionist policies of Catherine the Great. Russia used its alliances with Prussia and Austria to control, and then divide up, Poland; annex parts of the Ottoman Empire; rule the Baltic; and increase its influence in Germany, while keeping its allies paralyzed by their very own rivalries. And, as we shall shortly see in greater detail, the Franco-Austrian alliance following the Seven Years' War failed to increase the power of the two countries in question, as the two allies denied each other certain important foreign policy targets (Schroeder 1993, 50–51).

This picture clearly reveals why we have chosen this specific period in history. In fact, 18th century doctrines and practices enable us to immediately grasp the significance of those calculations of interest and power mentioned in the previous pages, and thus to present a meaningful historical basis for the most important variables, the most characteristic forms of conduct, and the foreseeable results of states' interaction as emerge from our typology of alliances. The four chosen cases—one for each type of alliance—are thus designed to show how certain basic tendencies, portrayed in an abstract manner, may take on a specific historical-empirical aspect. Thus, examination of a clear phase (1702–1756) in the long relationship between Great Britain and the United Provinces highlights the most characteristic aspects of a guarantee alliance; Anglo-French relations between 1716 and 1731 illustrate the hegemonic alliance; the Anglo-Prussian partnership during the Seven Years' War (1756–1762) offers an example of an aggregation alliance; and reconstruction of the difficult union of France and Austria during the second half of the 18th century (1756–1785) enables us to appreciate the contradictions of a deadlocked alliance.

It should be pointed out that the intention here is not to "prove" anything, but simply to clarify the interrelations of systemic forces and the behavior of states that constitute, according to the viewpoint adopted herein, the key to understanding alliances. The probatory value of the analyses is strictly limited to what may be termed a "plausibility probe" (Eckstein 1975, 108–113), in that should the present hypotheses fail to find any support even in such favorable circumstances, then they would be very unlikely to possess any universal or generalizing value. The cases examined here may also be seen as a touchstone with which to identify and assess all the other cases that diverge from the characteristics of the four types. In this sense, they constitute the starting point for more specific, in-depth evaluations.

PART TWO

Four Case Studies

FOUR

The Guarantee Alliance

Great Britain and the United Provinces, 1702–1756

A HOMOGENEOUS, ASYMMETRICAL ALLIANCE

In homogeneous alliances, the presence of a common enemy constitutes the strongest element, albeit not the only one, binding the allies together, because it encourages them to cooperate, especially when it becomes a real threat for both allies. Generally speaking, inter-ally relations are bound to be affected by the position the adversary adopts vis-à-vis the allies, starting from the degree of hostility, or willingness to come to a conciliation, displayed by the enemy toward each of the allies in its attempt to loosen their alliance. Furthermore, homogeneity means that negotiations between allies are often of an accommodative nature, whereby each ally generally tries to find a solution that the other party will accept as satisfactory, while attempting to minimize the costs ensuing from such an agreement. Finally, even if the common cause is more important to both allies than any particular causes may be, the latter still exist, and their weight is generally inversely correlated to the weight of the common cause; when the common enemy constitutes a serious, immediate danger, the allies focus all their attention and energies on this enemy, and cooperate closely to counter its moves, but when the danger posed by the enemy is deemed to be less serious, then the particular causes come to the fore once again, either for one ally or for both of them, thus rendering their cooperation that much more problematical.

Homogeneity is one of the two characteristic features of the guarantee alliance, the other being the asymmetrical nature of power relations between the allies. The mere existence of unequal power relations enables the stronger ally to condition the weaker ally more than the latter can influence the former. Regardless of the degree to which the weaker ally interiorizes the common cause, its policy is always going to be subjected, to a certain degree, to the coercion exercised by its stronger ally, as a result of its dependence on the latter. Regardless of how beneficial working with the stronger ally may be, such cooperation will nevertheless be conducted under the terms and conditions established by the latter, and it will often represent a certain limitation of the weaker ally's freedom of movement. These are the effects of the asymmetry in power relations most clearly distinguishing the guarantee alliance from the other homogeneous arrangement analyzed here, the aggregation alliance. For the junior partner the alliance is basically a protection against the common enemy; for the major ally—the guarantor—the alliance is beneficial not only in terms of the military support provided by the minor ally but also (and above all) because it enables the major ally to demand the conformity of the weaker partner with regard to other matters that go beyond the immediate question of the common enemy. Finally, unlike the other symmetrical alliance analyzed here—the hegemonic alliance—the guarantee alliance sees the minor ally prepared to remain bound to the major ally, without doing anything seriously designed to free it of the larger partner's grip other than what is strictly necessary to avoid the risk of entrapment. The minor ally is inclined to cooperate with the guarantor since it receives a payback from the latter, in the form of a series of benefits it would not be able to obtain merely by using its own means. Its autonomy is limited, owing to the asymmetrical nature of the alliance, as in the case of the hegemonic alliance. However, whereas in the latter the minor ally is generally harmed by the decisions taken by its more powerful partner, the hegemon, the homogeneity of the guarantee alliance means that the results the minor ally obtains by sacrificing a degree of autonomy are often substantial.

For a number of decades, the alliance between Britain and the United Provinces was characterized by its homogeneity and asymmetry. The original tie uniting the two countries goes back to 1678 and at least on paper lasted for more than a century, that is, until Britain's declaration of war in

1780. For a number of reasons, the scope of the present analysis is limited to the period between the War of the Spanish Succession and the Seven Years' War. The first such reason is that the real anti-French alliance began about ten years after the treaty signed in 1678, that is, on occasion of the War of the League of Augsburg, between 1689 and 1698. During that period, nevertheless, the two nations were both ruled by William III of Orange, who combined the role of stadtholder of the Netherlands and king of England, making it difficult to separate the English role from the Dutch role. Furthermore, during the early part of their union the two nations were fairly evenly balanced, whereas we are more interested in analyzing the asymmetry that was to clearly characterize the alliance from the War of the Spanish Succession onward. Finally, we have decided to adopt the declaration of Dutch neutrality in 1756 as an *ad quem* term, since this declaration rendered the previous treaties devoid of meaning, despite their continuing to remain in force for many years thereafter.

During the first half of the 18th century, the expression "maritime powers" was part and parcel of the language of European diplomacy and politics. Furthermore, these maritime powers, together with Austria, formed what the English called the "Old System," that is, the anti-French diplomatic device originating from the times of the struggle against Louis XIV, and constituting a reference point for European politics up to the diplomatic revolution of 1756 (Scott 1989). The maritime powers were united not only because the power and wealth of both derived from the sea but also because it was commonly assumed that they shared similar interests and were thus "natural allies"; this is also the way the two nations saw each other.[1] For those members of the post-1688 generation, concern about French expansionism was enough to eclipse any colonial or trade rivalries between the two states (which nevertheless continued unabated during the years thereafter). Both nations wanted to restrict the naval, colonial, and trade expansion of France, and in particular they wanted to defend the Low Countries;[2] the United Provinces wanted to protect the Low Countries because they were fully aware of the extreme vulnerability of their southern border, while Britain was keen to do likewise, thanks to its deeply rooted, traditional concern about being invaded across the "narrow seas." In other words, Britain saw its alliance with the United Provinces as an indispensable link to mainland Europe, and a point of reference and support should the need arise. The British appreciated the ally's strategic position, its naval force, and above all its army (the Dutch had a standing army at that time, which had handled itself very well in the wars against France and which could be reinforced by British contingents if need be) as well as its wealth, in an age in which British allies often asked for large subsidies. From the Dutch point of view, the nation's alliance with Britain was, quite simply, the key to their security, and those who remembered the wars against France knew this only too well.

This joint need for security was satisfied by the 1715 Barrier Treaty, the most tangible product of the wars previously fought against Louis XIV, and a genuine symbol of the Old System. However, Anglo-Dutch interest in the Low Countries went beyond their joint commitment to preventing France from dominating them. This interest also extended to preventing Austria, when it took possession of them, from regaining their commercial prosperity, thus making them an ipso facto rival. During the 1720s, the joint efforts of the maritime powers to get the Ostend Company closed down perhaps represent the best example of this further convergence of interests. Generally speaking, the emperor's attempts to encourage the independent development of the Low Countries helped keep the two allies together even as France's change in policy tended to divide them (Horn 1967, 96). A close religious tie accompanied this fundamental strategic and economic interest in the Low Countries and France. The United Provinces were also the guarantors of protestant succession to the English throne. A Stuart king would have meant the return of the Dutch Republic's nightmare of being surrounded by Catholic powers, and no politician could ignore the emotional impact on his country of a regular Jacobite threat, even if such a threat was increasingly unlikely (Carter 1975, 40).

The homogeneity of the alliance, however, should not be allowed to conceal its asymmetrical nature, which was already evident at the beginning of the century and became increasingly so during the period in question. This imbalance in the Anglo-Dutch alliance can be clearly seen in the English monopoly of military control. During the War of the Spanish Succession, despite the Dutch army being much larger than the English army, the Duke of Marlborough was always in command of the allied forces. Likewise, at sea, as early as the time of William III an English admiral commanded the allied fleet and had the final vote on the war councils (Eyck 1990, 4–5). Furthermore, it should not be forgotten that from 1689 on, each generation of Dutch naval officers was called on to serve for a certain period in the English fleet, thus creating personal and institutional ties between the two navies that were to survive the vicissitudes of the alliance (Rodger 1990, 27). Generally speaking, Britain was the predominant party, so much so that

Frederick the Great was led to observe: "A la suite de l'Angleterre se range la Hollande, comme une chaloupe qui suit l'impression d'un vaisseau de guerre auquel elle est attachée,"[3] while Simon van Slingelandt[4] had these bitter words to say: "Notre situation et notre dépendance [...] nous forceront toujours de suivre le torrent"[5] (quoted in Rodger 1990, 24). Compared to Britain, the United Provinces were much smaller, poorer in raw materials, more vulnerable, and less populous. In particular, the wars fought against France (which were an almost constant feature of the period from 1672 to 1713) underlay a financial crisis the country was never to recover from, one that led it increasingly to withdraw from the international scene and give up the idea of any further independent, significant role in international politics (Aalbers 1977). In other words, the Dutch Republic now had limited room for maneuver, greatly reduced means, and a more circumscribed range of action than its English ally. If the Dutch managed to influence British foreign policy to any significant extent after 1713, it was only because nobody realized the extent of the Dutch Republic's economic and naval decline. In fact, it was still considered a great power until the mid-18th century.

Although failure to play any part in the European wars waged after 1713 was, on the one hand, the almost inevitable consequence of the nation's gradual decline, on the other hand it could only exacerbate this decline. In fact, the commercial oligarchs in charge of the country constantly refused to implement those reforms so urgently required if the Dutch Republic's naval power was to be resurrected. The longer this situation continued without the onset of catastrophe, the more difficult it became to change things. Midway through the 18th century, the United Provinces' fleet had been reduced to a mere 30 warships. The result was the nation's increasing dependence on its English ally, which was asked to supply necessary protection so that the Dutch could continue trading. However, Britain was not prepared to offer such protection for free, since the United Provinces constituted its greatest trade rival. Hence one of the most common features of a guarantee alliance emerged. Once the weaker ally obtained the security it sought, it tended to behave as a free rider, systematically trying to avoid further commitments and pursuing its own freedom of movement. To this end the weaker ally was even taking advantage of any difficulties in which its stronger partner found itself, so long as such actions did not compromise their joint security. For its part, the major ally, as guarantor of their joint security, tended to use the other's dependence to ensure involvement in areas not strictly provided for under their alliance.

WEALTH AND SECURITY: THE 1674 TRADE TREATY AND THE 1678 NAVAL TREATY

The French attack on the Dutch Republic in 1672 (marking the start of the Dutch War, 1672–1678) is generally considered to have been a genuinely traumatic event for the United Provinces (Carter 1975, 12). Thereafter, and for the best part of the following century, France was seen as the main enemy and the greatest threat to national security. A tenacious resistance to this French threat characterized the foreign policy of William III of Orange, who was in fact acclaimed stadtholder after the French invasion. His incessant diplomatic activity saw him make numerous attempts at creating alliances and coalitions against Louis XIV's hegemonic policies. Britain and the United Provinces, it should be pointed out, had only just fought three wars to gain control over the shipping lanes (1652–1654, 1665–1667, and 1672–1674) and were anything but natural allies. It was not until the crowning of William as king of England in 1689, following the "Glorious Revolution," that a close anti-French cooperation emerged between the two countries. It is nevertheless significant that a sovereign such as Charles II, who had often been criticized by the opposition within his own country for his pro-French policies, was the one to sign two treaties with the United Provinces—a trade agreement and an alliance—that together constituted the basis for Anglo-Dutch relations during the century that followed.

At the end of the third Anglo-Dutch war, a trade agreement was signed (1674) that was to prove extremely beneficial to the United Provinces. If one of the signatories was at war while the other was neutral (as was Britain's case in 1674), the "free ships, free goods" principle stood. In other words, the neutral power could trade with the ally's enemy, in everything but armaments.[6] Britain was the major beneficiary of this agreement at the time it was stipulated, but the roles were inverted following the Peace of Utrecht. The United Provinces' efforts not to get involved in further wars enabled the country to take full advantage of the 1674 treaty, and of the wars that Britain found itself fighting, in order to make substantial gains to the detriment of British trade, not refraining from supplying Britain's very enemies.

This extreme freedom of movement afforded to both parties was, however, restricted some years later. In 1678, the English Parliament, concerned about the risk of the Flanders coast remaining in French hands, forced Charles to agree to a defensive alliance with the United Provinces (Haley 1958). The alliance treaty specified, among other things, the exact type and entity of aid that one party would offer the other should the latter be attacked. Britain was to supply 10,000 men, while the Dutch Republic was to supply 6,000 men and 20 ships. The casus foederis was limited to Europe, and this condition was to be very important for the Dutch during the following century, as a colonial war between France and Britain became increasingly likely.[7] However, from our point of view, an even more interesting aspect of this situation is that the combined effect of the trade agreement and the alliance treaty quickly become rather paradoxical, and the full weight of this effect was felt during the course of the 18th century. Britain was not happy about the trade agreement, for both economic and strategic reasons, and given the likelihood the Dutch would take advantage of England's wars by remaining neutral, the 1678 alliance became increasingly important. The United Provinces were less of a concern as an ally, which could be pressured into contributing to the war effort, than as a neutral power enjoying considerable trading rights. As a result, the English made systematic efforts to get the Dutch involved in Britain's wars after 1715. As long as the United Provinces were prepared to fulfill those obligations afforded under the 1678 treaty, and to fight alongside Britain, their trading rights, albeit restricted to the requirements of war, were preserved. As the Dutch increasingly adopted a neutral stance, there was serious debate in Britain on whether it was better to have the United Provinces as a declared enemy or as a neutral power helping England's foes more than it would do if it fought alongside them. This dilemma was even more complicated for the Dutch. Without the naval alliance, the Dutch would have been exposed to French aggression, but at the same time the naval alliance could have represented the means by which Britain then restricted Dutch trade (Eyck 1990). Paradoxically, the trade agreement was perhaps more likely to force the Dutch Republic into war than even the naval alliance with Britain was.

Finally, the strategic and religious questions of the time were closely interwoven. The wife of William III was the elder, protestant daughter of James II, who had succeeded Charles to the English throne in 1685. James's second wife, a catholic, gave him a son in June 1688, who was also baptized catholic, and this event brought into question the protestant succession to the throne. This, together with the fear of an imminent, close alliance between Britain and France, led William III to invade England, causing the immediate fall of James II. The following year, the two countries, Britain and the Dutch Republic, constituted the principal axis of the League of Augsburg, which for 10 years fought an isolated France. The protection agreed by Louis XIV to the deposed James II meant that a French victory would probably have led to restoration of an absolute, catholic monarchy subjugated to French power—an outcome that the Dutch and British leaders were keen to avoid. The landing of James II in Ireland, in 1690, was the first act in the Jacobite rising that would last for more than half a century.

This was the basis on which the two allies cooperated throughout the 1690s, under the same political leadership and substantially on par, in the attempt to contain France's naval and commercial power, and to defend the Low Countries. Both countries contributed in roughly equal terms to military operations. As for the navy, the 1689 agreement established that five English ships were to be provided for every three Dutch ships, while the commander of the combined fleet was to be an English admiral;[8] however, as far as operations on land were concerned, the United Provinces were to furnish more troops than their ally, and William III was exclusively seconded by Dutch and Huguenot generals and advisors. Even though the war against France was cleverly presented as a grand struggle for the liberty and prosperity of the whole of Europe, William III's real aim was to defend the United Provinces and his own position in Britain.[9] During the course of the war, the Dutch Republic gradually abandoned the traditional idea of the Low Countries as a buffer zone and replaced it with the new strategic concept of the fortified line, initially centered around certain particularly important points, but subsequently taking in the entire border between France and the Low Countries. Given that Spain had proven incapable itself of defending those territories, the direct involement of the Dutch was deemed desirable (Carter 1975, 25–26). This was what gave rise to the "Barrier Treaties," signed during the War of the Spanish Succession and in its aftermath.

During this phase of the Anglo-Dutch alliance, the States-General of the United Provinces were even more prompt than the English in providing William III, the stadtholder-king, with the financial aid he requested; overall the Dutch Republic cannot be accused of having failed to fulfill its duties as ally at this time, as in fact was the case increasingly during the following decades. However, Britain used the war to create a fleet of ships that gave it naval supremacy, organize a fair-sized army, and reform its financial system. Thus the initial evenly balanced alliance soon gave way to a much more asymmetrical arrangement, in which pursuit of the common cause was dictated by the stronger party. The events during the latter part of the War of the Spanish Succession were the first signs of this transition.

THE FUNCTIONING OF THE ALLIANCE

In all asymmetrical alliances, the stronger ally's pursuit of the other's conformity takes the form of a series of policies that become increasingly evident as the relation of bargaining power between the allies grows more and more unbalanced. The favored means of obtaining this conformity is to threaten withdrawal of support (diminishing benefits) and the promise of even greater gains (emerging benefits). In the case at hand, Britain often exploited the Dutch Republic's constant wish to expand its trade in order to obtain the latter's political cooperation. Within this general context, we are now going to examine the most important theoretical propositions regarding the policy adopted by the guarantor with regard to its weaker ally.

First, the major power tends to control its smaller ally's foreign policy and point out who the ally's friends and enemies are. The smaller ally's involvement in the diplomatic-strategic maneuvers conceived by the guarantor is always convenient: it confers multilateral legitimacy on the actions taken; it serves to lend practical support (for example, a limited degree of military aid), which is always appreciated; and above all it prevents the minor ally from undertaking activities that could harm the major power. In fact, in this case Britain tended to absorb the United Provinces within the various diplomatic arrangements put in place from the Peace of Utrecht onward, namely, the Triple Alliance (1717), the Alliance of Hanover (1725), the Treaty of Seville (1729), and the second Treaty of Vienna (1731). The Dutch Republic was rarely left out of such arrangements (one occasion being the Quadruple Alliance of 1718), and when this happened it was because the Dutch asked too high a price for their involvement, which in the end proved unnecessary. Likewise, Britain tended to involve the United Provinces in wars that did not directly concern Dutch security: in the Baltic, up to the end of the Great Northern War (1721), against Spain during that same period, and against Austria during the latter half of the 1720s. However, the only time that the English achieved any real results with such a policy was, significantly enough, when the United Provinces were still involved in combating French aggression during the War of the Austrian Succession (1740–1748).

For the leader, the ally must be strong enough to contribute to the joint security of the alliance, but not strong enough to elude the grip of its own dependence. Although the weakness of the minor ally is, within certain limits, beneficial to the guarantor, because it enables the latter to exercise power, beyond those limits the same weakness becomes a constraint because there is now a real danger that the leader has to take on board the entire security of this minor ally, which, being aware of this, is strongly tempted to act opportunistically. Hence the insistence with which the minor ally is asked to invest a sufficient quantity of resources in its own security, and thus in the security of the alliance as a whole. In fact, if the imbalance is considerable, the guarantor knows that it has nothing to fear—indeed can only gain—from the strengthening of its ally. The minor ally, though, sees the effort required as a mere waste of resources that would not in any case affect the power relationship between the two. In other words, the weaker ally may well decide to take full advantage of its own weakness by burdening the leader with the costs of joint security. The result of such a situation is constant recriminations accompanying interally relations, and in particular the accusation that the weaker ally is not doing its part. The breaking point comes when the weakness of the minor ally is such that the stronger partner concludes that the alliance merely constitutes a burden it would do well to rid itself of as soon as possible, especially if other options are available.

All of these dynamics are clearly illustrated in this case. From the final phase of the War of the Spanish Succession to the outbreak of the Seven Years' War, the English constantly complained about the limited contribution made by the Dutch and systemically called for "augmentation" of their armed forces. At that time, the United Provinces were still considered to be the wealthiest nation in the world, and this only served to increase English resentment; if they had only wanted to, the Dutch could have done so much more (Rodger 1990, 14). It proved discouraging and frustrating for the British to witness their ally's relentless decline, which had become of little or no use but nevertheless often interfered in Britain's decisions. At the same time Britain wanted to involve the Dutch in every single one of its offensive alliances for fear that unless it did so, this profiteering ally would become even richer (Hatton 1950, 10); at the end of the War of the Austrian Succession, the exasperated British likened their alliance with the United Provinces to being "tied to a corpse"[10] and began to take into consideration a possible alliance with Prussia.

The final feature that as a rule characterizes the policy of the guarantor with regard to its weaker ally is interference in the latter's domestic policy. Here, English interest in the domestic affairs of the United Provinces took the form, above all, of support for the stadtholder's party, that is, for those who would have looked favorably on restoration of the office of stadtholder, which had remained vacant since the death of William III in 1702—in the hope that a stadtholder would render the United Provinces a more reliable ally than it actually was at that time. So, from 1718 onward the English government began to work on a plan for the marriage of the oldest grandchild of George I (the daughter of the future George II) and William III's heir. Another fifteen years went by before the marriage finally took place (in 1734), since the Dutch were very touchy about this matter and fully understood the implications of the possible future stadtholder being the son-in-law of the king of England. In fact, when William IV was made stadtholder during the turbulent events of 1747, the English ships positioned along the Scheldt River played an important part in resolving the Dutch constitutional crisis.

If these are the main features of the behavior of the guarantor, what can be said about the minor ally's behavior? To start with, it always follows the lead of the major power on all questions regarding the common cause, that is, defense of the Low Countries (we shall see the importance given to this in the 1715 Barrier Treaty) and the protestant succession to the throne (the United Provinces sent the 6,000 troops envisaged in the alliance treaty each time there was a danger of a Jacobite rising, in 1715, 1719, and 1745, and refusal to furnish troops in 1756 was to be one of the causes of the breakdown of the alliance). In more general terms, the common cause was also represented by a European arrangement guaranteeing the peace and stability that Dutch trade required, here meaning the alliances negotiated by Britain, which the Republic was also party to. It should be pointed out that these were the elements rendering the Anglo-Dutch alliance homogeneous and making for a wide bargaining range between the two allies. Negotiations on those issues tended to be accommodative, and the terms of the agreements often included a certain remuneration for the weaker party. As a rule, a settlement was reached, and the discussion centered mainly on distribution of the burden of costs and of the ensuing benefits. However, given that negotiations were conducted from diverse positions of power, the outcome thereof tended to reflect the leader's preferences in the first place. Moreover, Britain had various possible means of damaging Dutch trade, starting with privateering, and this became increasingly clear during the final years of their alliance.

The minor ally is thus encouraged to increase its demands, if for no other reason than it knows it will always obtain less than what it asks. The United

Provinces were able and insistent bargainers, partly due to the institutional framework in place in the Republic.[11] Every decision was debated at various levels, and every amendment made at one level required a new round of discussions. However, this style of bargaining proved extremely effective if time needed to be gained, so that larger concessions could be obtained from a major ally in a hurry to conclude matters, and so that the minor ally could free itself from pressing demands that, as time passed, became superfluous or somewhat less of a burden. Even if the country always found good reason to complain about the outcome of those negotiations that Britain had induced it to take part in, it has to be said that as a rule the United Provinces gained more than they would have done without Britain's support. The minor ally thus followed the guarantor, but only after having attempted to obtain the highest possible remuneration for its involvement, that is, to be allowed to enjoy conditions enabling it to gain the greatest possible benefits from the agreements it stipulated, at the lowest possible cost. The Dutch "want [...] everything for nothing," the English observed in desperation (quoted in Hatton 1950, 229). Besides, the United Provinces were not entirely defenseless against pressure from their more powerful ally. Once again, we would do well to remember those strategies, mentioned by Peter Blau (1964, 118–25), adopted within the context of the struggle between the party that wishes to exercise power and the party that wishes to free itself of this power. It is true that the United Provinces needed the "services" offered by Britain; however, it is also true that they were in a position to offer something in exchange, in accordance with the provisions of the 1678 treaty. Britain needed certain Dutch services, and the States-General, who were well aware of this, were determined to grant those services at a high price. Whether this was actually an act of cold political calculation, or simply the result of a weakness too great to offer any alternative strategies, the effect was that this opportunism irritated the guarantor. It is consequently no surprise to find that from time to time the major ally chose to do without the minor ally's support, provided of course that this did not result in the Dutch being thrown into the arms of the French, or in any case being put in a position to take advantage, as a neutral power, of English belligerence. Finally, this negotiating style was pushed to the very limits of obstructionism when the risk of becoming entrapped in hostilities became increasingly tangible. Britain had good reason to want the United Provinces to always fight by its side, but the United Provinces had equally good reason to keep a low profile anytime their own security was not at risk. A war would have harmed trade, the country did not possess the financial wherewithal to adopt an interventionist foreign policy, and as far as France was concerned everything depended on the benevolence or hostility displayed by this nation. Which brings us to the final point to be examined here, the relationship between the allies and the common enemy.

In homogeneous alliances, the two parties see adoption of a joint policy with regard to the enemy as a positive thing. In fact, the United Provinces followed Britain both when it formed an alliance with France (between 1716 and 1731) and, albeit more reluctantly, when the two major powers found themselves fighting each other during the War of the Austrian Succession. In 1733, the Dutch Republic caught its English ally on the hop by declaring its neutrality as the War of the Polish Succession broke out; this time it was the English who toed the line, remaining neutral themselves on that occasion. To put it briefly, the important thing is to act in unison. However, as we know, in any asymmetrical alliance the minor ally is structurally induced to fear abandonment; this means that the minor ally actually runs the risk of entrapment. The fact that Britain was capable of abandoning the United Provinces was evident at the time of the separate peace agreement stipulated by the English in the last phase of the War of the Spanish Succession; furthermore, during the final stages of the War of the Austrian Succession, Britain clearly lost interest in defending the Low Countries. To avoid both abandonment and entrapment, the minor ally is therefore prepared to come to some form of agreement with the common enemy, provided the latter acts less aggressively. Thus if the guarantor tries to get closer to the common enemy, the minor ally will follow its lead, even though this may not prevent the two major powers from reaching an agreement to the detriment of the minor power, as indeed happened in the case of the Treaty of Utrecht. However, if the minor ally agrees to a compromise solution with the common enemy, then the guarantor is not going to be happy. The latter knows that its relationship with the minor ally is based, first and foremost, on the minor ally's relationship with the common enemy, and it fears that if the latter gets closer to the common enemy, this will render the alliance devoid of all meaning. Following the death of Louis XIV, the French adopted a more conciliatory approach to the United Provinces, and the Dutch took advantage of this opportunity to move closer to France, thus often managing to circumscribe the abandonment-entrapment dilemma. Britain, for its part, was not prepared to lose control over its Dutch ally and often stood in the way of those measures designed to facilitate this thawing of relations between the French and the

Dutch (such as the French proposals designed to guarantee the Barrier Treaty, or the neutrality of the Low Countries, submitted between 1715 and 1716). The English blackmailed the Dutch with regard to trade, or as was the case in 1756 by trying to force their hand by calling for application of the naval treaty when the premises for such application did not exist. George I and James Stanhope were well aware of the dangers posed by an excessively close relationship between France and the United Provinces; the British influence was to be "so much stronger in Holland as they are under the fewer Tyes to France" (quoted in Hatton 1950, 130).

The obedience of the minor ally is a function of the protection afforded to it by its more powerful partner. It follows that if this protection is not forthcoming then the obedience will also cease. The United Provinces' declaration of neutrality in 1756 was the logical consequence of a process that had been ongoing for just under 10 years, whereby France had increasingly become less of a threat to the United Provinces, and Britain had increasingly become disinterested in defending the Low Countries. The diplomatic revolution of that time completed this process, giving it the decisive push.

THE WAR OF THE SPANISH SUCCESSION AND BRITAIN'S SEPARATE PEACE

Even though William III was immediately against the idea of a Bourbon—Philip of Anjou, the grandson of Louis XIV—inheriting the Spanish throne following the death of Charles II (in November 1700), large swaths of public opinion and the political leadership in both Great Britain and the United Provinces were not inclined to launch another war against France, which this time around was allied with Spain. Nevertheless, a series of decisions and steps taken by Louis XIV and Philip V within the space of just a few months seemed to confirm William's darkest predictions regarding the dangers inherent in that succession. Philip reached Madrid escorted by French troops, and it was French troops that took control of the Low Countries, in Philip's name, forcing the Dutch to evacuate their fortresses. The new king also granted certain substantial trade concessions to France, while Louis XIV, for his part, kept open the possibility of his grandson succeeding him on the French throne as well. Finally, on the death of James II, the Sun King recognized James's son, James III (the Old Pretender), as the legitimate heir to the English throne. Within the space of a year, there was the risk of Bourbon hegemony, which could not be ignored by either the emperor (who claimed rights to the Spanish succession and to Italian lands) or the two maritime powers (concerned with the plight of the Low Countries, the protestant cause, and their trade with both Spain and the Spanish colonies in Latin America).

The Great Coalition of the Hague, officially stipulated in September 1701, was on first appearance the coalition of three countries against one common enemy that threatened their most important interests. The maritime powers' aims were clear: prevent the dynastic union of France and Spain; give Archduke Charles, son of the emperor, the Low Countries, which served as a protective barrier for the Dutch Republic's southern border, together with Spain's Italian territories; divide up all those Spanish colonies they could conquer; obtain trade concessions from Spain; and guarantee the protestant succession to the English throne (McKay and Scott 1983, 57–59). During this phase, the homogeneity of the Anglo-Dutch axis could not have been any clearer. The two countries reacted to the same threats and tried to take advantage, in a mutually compatible way, of the various opportunities that came along.[12] The death of William III, in April 1702, did not prevent the maritime powers from preserving their close alliance. Anthonie Heinsius, grand pensionary from 1689 to 1720, on the one hand, and Sidney Godolphin and (above all) the Duke of Marlborough on the other guaranteed the required continuity. The Great Coalition also included Hanover, Prussia, and other German principalities, and from 1703 onward the Savoy and Portugal as well. However, it was led by the two maritime powers, which provided the naval forces, the majority of land forces, and above all funding to the other allies, starting with Austria.

Whereas in the previous war against France Great Britain had been somewhat ill at ease moving around mainland Europe, it now often took the initiative, especially after the Duke of Marlborough's sensational victory at Blenheim (in August 1704). It was an English idea, which the United Provinces then agreed with, to extend the aims of war to include the removal of Philip V from the throne of Spain. Even though expulsion of the Bourbons from Spain was a Portuguese request, the English willingly took up the challenge. They not only obtained, in exchange, access to Portugal's ports, which were of vital importance for the war in the Mediterranean, but saw the replacement of Philip V by Archduke Charles as an opportunity to obtain substantial trade concessions. Furthermore, they stipulated a series of highly advantageous trade agreements with Portugal itself. The year 1703 also witnessed an important amendment to the 1678 Anglo-Dutch Treaty. The

United Provinces, which at that time were threatened by another French invasion, insisted that the casus foederis be broadened to include "warlike preparations." This meant that one party could ask for the other's help even before being attacked. Although tied to guarantees of protestant succession, this clause implied that from then on, Great Britain could demand Dutch help even if word got out that the French were preparing a fleet in their Channel ports to lend support to a Jacobite invasion (Carter 1975, 28). In other words, the Dutch Republic was forced, by necessity, to get even closer to an ally that at that point in time was clearly outdistancing it.

This new British assertiveness was met by a certain passiveness, or reluctance, on the part of the Dutch. In fact, differences were quick to emerge between the allies, in terms of the distribution of the costs of their joint operations. For example, in 1704–05 the Dutch Republic's vessels did not take part, as promised, in the siege of Dunkerque but chose to escort trade vessels in the Baltic; then, immediately after the conquest of Gibraltar (1704), they retreated at the first sight of the French fleet. Generally speaking, the United Provinces were increasingly reluctant to get involved in oceanic expeditions, especially in the West Indies (Rodger 1990, 16). This behavior was, at least at first, the result of certain understandable technical and strategic considerations. For example, the Dutch warships were better equipped to protect convoys than to be involved in naval sieges. Nevertheless, it also reveals a growing weakness relative to the ally. In fact, while Britain moved very comfortably across the various fields of play, both on land and at sea, the United Provinces' interest seemed to be focused ever more on the Low Countries, where the battle against the French was particularly hard and demanding. The enormous effort required on that particular front soon began to take its toll. Even though Amsterdam remained the financial center of the coalition, the Dutch Republic found it increasingly difficult to find the necessary resources for the 100,000 troops (120,000 by the end of the war) spread out across the Low Countries, to the point where it had to ask the English to take on the burden of two-thirds (rather than the previously agreed half) of the subsidy agreements that they had stipulated together. Likewise, the United Provinces were no longer able to supply two-thirds of the ships, as they had agreed to do (Geyl 1964, 311–12). Furthermore, in the case of the war in Spain, after the Dutch Republic's initial involvement things were left entirely in the hands of Britain, which believed itself to be free to use those strategic positions won (such as Gibraltar and Minorca) as it saw fit, and to exercise exclusive control over the Mediterranean.

With the expulsion of the French from Flanders and Brabant in 1706, the United Provinces' involvement in the war became even more restricted to the European mainland. The aim of the Dutch at this point was to obtain Britain's promise of support in the negotiations to be held at the end of the war with the new Austrian sovereign, in order to reach a satisfactory agreement with regard to the barrier fortresses. Britain accepted the Dutch idea that the security of both countries was strictly interdependent and could only be guaranteed by massive Dutch involvement in the defense of the Low Countries. However, the Low Countries had by then acquired a certain economic importance for both powers, and this was quickly to prove a source of contention between the two. During the course of the war, the Dutch used those cities they had previously occupied in order to promote their own trade interests, to the detriment of Britain's trade interests. For this reason, Britain did not wish to allow the United Provinces to include Ostend, the only port in which English goods could evade Dutch control, in their future defensive border. Relations between the two allies worsened even further when the problem arose, once again, of the legality or otherwise of trading with the enemy. At the beginning of the war, the Dutch had accepted the English ban on trading with France, but by 1704 they had gone back to their traditional ways, having noted that their refusal to trade with the French did not damage the enemy but merely afforded unforeseen advantages to the Hamburgers, the Swedish, and other neutral powers. Although at the beginning the English turned a blind eye to the renewed Dutch trading with the French, aware as they were of their ally's financial plight (Pares 1938, 238), the question became particularly delicate as the United Provinces' contribution to the war effort waned, and Britain inevitably began to complain about its ally's behavior. Predictably enough, Britain resorted to threats and promises, all centered on the future trade gains to be negotiated with the French at the end of the war.

By 1706, Louis XIV had stated he was prepared to discuss a peace agreement, which many Dutch were interested in, but English and Austrian demands were deemed excessive and the war continued, even after the objectives the Great Coalition had set itself in 1701–02 were in fact achieved. The importance that Britain gave to the conquest of Spain prevented the establishment of peace, and the United Provinces, despite the further financial burden this involved, continued to follow their ally's policies (Coombs 1957), even though they were to have the chance to come to a direct agreement with France, since the Dutch hoped to obtain a favorable deal regarding the Low Countries in exchange for such an agreement. The 1709 Barrier Treaty gave the Dutch Republic all the guarantees it had asked for: a triple defensive line of fortresses, a free hand in the region's financial and trade matters, English promises to share the trade concessions that were to be negotiated with the new king of Spain, and support for Dutch designs on the Upper Quarter of Guelders.[13] It is clear that Britain was far from keen to make such concessions, but as the English negotiator, the Viscount Townshend, knew only too well, they represented a means of tying down the Dutch Republic and avoiding the risk of a separate peace agreement between the Dutch and the French. If France had managed to wrest the United Provinces away from Britain, it would probably have made even greater concessions to the Dutch in the Low Countries (Geyl 1964, 318–19). However, a separate agreement with the French was no longer attractive for the Dutch. Even if they had managed to obtain a satisfactory arrangement with regard to their southern border, they would have found themselves defenseless at sea and in their colonies, and faced with a former ally, Britain, intent on making them pay for their betrayal. Indeed, Dutch trade in the Mediterranean and in South America could only be preserved with the help of the English, and the weakness of the Dutch Republic's naval forces was clear for all to see at the end of the war, when French privateers got away with pillaging Dutch holdings in the West Indies.

The English promise, however, was quickly broken. In 1710 the Tories took power and decided to put an end to a war that had lasted too long and cost far too much, even if this had to be done to the detriment of the allies. On top of the constant problems in Spain, one year later Joseph I died, which meant the imperial crown now passed to his brother, Charles—that is, to the person who according to the allies' plans was to take the place of Philip V in Spain. The prospect of replacing a Bourbon hegemony with a Habsburg one was thus more reason to end the war. The English government quickly arranged secret negotiations with France, declaring that it was prepared to leave the Spanish throne to Philip V in exchange for Gibraltar and Minorca, a privileged position with regard to trade with the Spanish colonies in South America, certain acquisitions in North America, and the demolition of fortifications in Dunkerque. The allies were asked to take part in the international peace congress to be held in Utrecht, without being offered any specific guarantees. Indeed, the United Provinces were asked to renounce the 1709 treaty; otherwise France would not fulfill its pledges. When the Dutch objected to this proposal, the Tories were not afraid to push matters to the breaking point. The treaty was declared null and void, being deemed contrary to British interests, while the famous press campaign was launched against Britain's greedy, ungrateful allies in which Jonathan Swift's pamphlet "The Conduct of the Allies" was the most influential voice: "No nation was ever [...] treated with so much Insolence, Injustice and Ingratitude by its foreign friends."[14] Despite the attempt to continue the war alone, the Dutch Republic had no choice in the end but to *submit* (this is the term used by Viscount Bolingbroke, the English secretary of state) to that which Britain deemed opportune to grant it and to obtain for it from France. Britain's terms were far from generous, it should be added, with their exclusion of the United Provinces from trading rights in South America, together with the Republic's giving up of both the Upper Quarter of Guelders and the previous financial and trade agreements regarding the Low Countries. Thus diplomatic humiliation was exacerbated by this substantial reduction in Dutch financial power, at the hands of their own ally, Great Britain. It was not France, as was feared, but Britain that closed the Mediterranean and South American trading ports. Concerning the barrier fortresses, this defensive line was reduced in size because Britain could no longer demand further concessions from France, and the United Provinces failed to obtain those internal lines of communication that would have enabled them to exploit the region economically. Nevertheless, the defensive arrangement was still an improvement over the one that had been established at Ryswick in 1698, while the river Scheldt was closed to navigation, and the English government pledged to support its ally in future negotiations with Austria (Geikie and Montgomery 1930, 284–320).

It is no surprise, therefore, that the Utrecht Peace proved particularly advantageous for Britain, but rather unsatisfactory for the United Provinces, given the promises made in 1709. However, we should not forget that William III's original aim of preventing the French takeover of the Low Countries was in fact achieved, and from this point of view the Dutch Republic came out on the winning side after four decades of war with France. To conclude, without harming their common strategic interests, namely the defense of the Low Countries, Britain had no qualms about adopting a coercive policy—to the point where the United Provinces was faced with a fait accompli and abandonment—for its own purposes. Overall, this outcome clearly reflects the change in the relation of forces between the two states, in a process that had been ongoing for many years and was now complete. The lengthy wars fought against the French had caused far less damage to

British trade than to Dutch trade. From the end of the 17th century onward, Great Britain boasted clear naval superiority, in both technical and quantitative terms. Above all, the English had managed to finance their war effort with greater ease than their Dutch allies. In fact, from 1707 onward the British bore the larger part of the costs of war and managed to be active on all fronts nevertheless. The British success, in turn, reflects the weakness of the Dutch. At this point, it was clear that the Dutch had neglected their interests at sea, which was the inevitable price to pay for an interminable war on the mainland. Just as it had been impossible for them to disengage from the mainland during the war, now it was equally difficult for them to do so during peacetime, whereas their British ally would now enjoy an ever greater degree of freedom.

THE ALLIANCE AND BRITAIN'S "PREPONDERANCE"

The period from the Peace of Utrecht (1713) to the second Treaty of Vienna (1731) was one of relative stability in Europe. Although it is true that fighting continued in the north until 1721, on the rest of the mainland there were no wars as such, with the one exception of the brief conflict with Spain (1718–1720). However, tension and crises continued to be a frequent feature of European international politics, the true reflection of a peace that undoubtedly was not to everyone's satisfaction. The linchpin of the diplomatic system during that period was the Anglo-French alliance, whereby the two great enemies temporarily put aside their historical rivalry; this inevitably affected the relationship between Britain and the United Provinces, if for no other reason than their latter alliance was, from the outset, an anti-French agreement.

The 1715 Barrier Treaty saw the two allies involved in lengthy negotiations, during which Britain often acted as mediator between the Dutch proposals and the Austrian counterproposals. Given that George I was pursuing an agreement with the emperor, which was indispensable for his Hanoverian policy, constant pressure was brought to bear upon the United Provinces for them to moderate their requests. The Jacobite uprising in Scotland (during the summer of 1715) strengthened the Dutch Republic's bargaining power, which then enabled it to obtain better results in the end than had seemed likely only a few months earlier (Geikie and Montgomery 1930, 334–58). The bilateral agreement, which three years later was followed by an agreement to which Austria was also party, involved a series of complex reciprocal undertakings by the three Old System allies, concerning the occupation of fortresses, garrisons, loans, artillery, and supplies. The maritime powers thus managed to create a common defensive barrier in the Low Countries, which were not to be attacked again until 1745. However, in a certain sense the new system was already out of date when it was created. Conceived when the Spanish held the Low Countries, and designed not only for defensive purposes but also with a view to the maritime powers economically exploiting the region, the Anglo-Dutch arrangement meant that Austria immediately lost interest in its new possession, seeing it more as a burden than an acquisition to be defended and valorized. This was to be one of the reasons the French managed to conquer the fortresses so easily some thirty years later.

Anglo-Dutch relations during this period can be subdivided into two phases: a tense initial phase, ending with the death of Stanhope in 1721, during which George I and his minister were highly critical of Britain's ally; and a warmer phase, during which Charles Townshend and Robert Walpole proved to be much abler at ensuring Dutch involvement in English foreign policy.[15] However, certain important constant features may be identified during both phases. The British, for their part, systematically tried to get the United Provinces involved in all diplomatic projects, and above all in those that implied the risk of war. From a political point of view, Dutch involvement gave greater weight to Britain's initiatives. From a military point of view, the Dutch contribution, despite its being an increasingly limited entity, was nevertheless still appreciable. Above all, as we have said, Britain did not want to allow the United Provinces any real freedom of movement, especially when preparations for war were being made, for fear that it might enjoy excessive trade gains, at Britain's expense, from its neutrality. Britain's leaders, both in Parliament and in government, were in complete agreement on this matter, to the point where Dutch involvement was often sought by English ministers so as to ensure the support of Parliament on major foreign policy decisions regarding both international agreements and, more important, war. Perhaps the clearest example of this was witnessed between 1715 and 1717, when George I tried on numerous occasions (and using deceit if necessary) to drag the Dutch Republic into a naval conflict with Sweden. The United Provinces were asked to contribute to the security of the convoys in the Baltic, but while the Dutch ships were sent with instructions to remain strictly neutral, the British ships had the task of attacking the Swedish if occasion to do so arose. It was only Dutch reluctance that prevented George I from pursuing his Hanoverian aims to the end. Then in 1719, when Britain was at war with Spain, the problem arose once again, this time in an even more evident form, and the English decided to intercept those Dutch vessels trading with Britain's enemies.[16] The stick was accompanied, as it were, by the carrot: the promise not only to grant trade gains, but also to pay off previous debts. Settling these debts, constantly requested by the Dutch, was always being put off, clearly in order to render the Republic more malleable.[17]

The United Provinces, for their part, cautiously followed Britain's lead. The decline of France, and the death of Louis XIV in 1715, put the Dutch in a favorable position, almost one of Tertius Gaudens; by using the threat of close cooperation with the other maritime power and with Austria, the United Provinces managed to limit France's economic penetration in the Low Countries, and through the threat of their getting closer to France hoped to induce Britain to tolerate not only Dutch trade in the Low Countries but also expansion of Dutch trade (in collusion with France) in the event of a new Anglo-French war (Horn 1967, 97). However, the 1716 Anglo-French alliance dramatically reduced room for maneuver, which reappeared only when the two big powers went back to fighting each other in the War of the Austrian Succession and the Seven Years' War. For the moment, the regents were fully aware there were no alternatives to a close relationship with the English, and the English in turn also realized it; Dutch involvement was almost taken for granted, and this calculation often proved to hold true.

Dutch policy could thus be summarized as adaptation to Britain's actions, while trying to get the highest possible returns at the lowest possible cost, and in any case never at the risk of war. From the point of view of the United Provinces, the alliance possessed above all conservative value, and the country was prepared to support the alliance on condition that it did not get dragged into any ventures that could complicate its relationship with Austria, or that could lead France to take the road toward Brussels, or that could lead to the closure of its last remaining channels of trade to Spain and its colonies. The lessening of the tension with France led the regents to pursue interests of a prevalently economic interest, while renouncing any specific proactive foreign policy and a costly security policy, which would have meant in particular restoration of an ancient naval power. Hence the constant fear of becoming entrapped in a war, together with the constant temptation to take full advantage of the successes of British diplomacy in order to transform them into concrete trade gains. Thus it was that interally negotiations quickly took on this character of the Dutch being generally prepared to follow Britain's lead, but only after long, drawn-out negotiations had tested the English government's patience to the full.

On occasion the bough broke, as happened when the Dutch Republic failed to join the Quadruple Alliance. That event was particularly significant because it revealed both Britain's behavior towards its ally and the limited bargaining power of the Dutch. The Quadruple Alliance, which despite its name was negotiated in 1718 by three states (France, Great Britain, and Austria; the United Provinces never actually became a member) was designed to force Spain to comply with the signatories' plans, in particular in Italy. Britain, after having obtained Dutch membership of the Triple Alliance with France, almost took it for granted that the ally would follow its lead in this latest venture; in any case, it concealed from the Dutch certain secret clauses providing use of force against Spain, in order to get the Dutch to believe there was no danger of war. The Dutch Republic, which had been reluctant to fight Sweden, likewise had no intention of risking involvement in a war against Spain. At the same time, however, it was attracted by the possibility of having, in exchange for such involvement, part of the trade gains the English procured in the Baltic in the meantime, and frightened by Britain's threats to damage Dutch trade with Spain and no longer mediate with Austria regarding conclusion of the Barrier Treaty. In this situation, negotiations dragged on for such a long time that when the United Provinces finally came to a decision, news arrived of the fall of Cardinal Alberoni, which made Dutch membership of the alliance that less important, and which led the British to renege on the promised concessions, thus putting an end to negotiations (Hatton 1950, 166–205; Carter 1975, 47–49). Under other circumstances, it was the Dutch who decided not to be part of British diplomatic arrangements; this was the case with the 1721 Triple Alliance among France, Spain, and Britain. Once again, the Dutch were held back by their fear of being involved in a European war—in the south, between the Bourbon forces and the emperor, or in the north, following Russian attacks in the Baltic. In addition, the English did not even notify them of the specific terms of the alliance, which further contributed to Dutch wariness. Similarly, British plans to involve the Dutch in the Anglo-Prussian Treaty of Charlottenburg (1723) also failed to achieve their purpose (Dunthorne 1986, 31–39).

More often than not, however, the two nations managed to come to an agreement that, although nearly always proposed by the British, proved mutually satisfactory. When the United Provinces joined France and Britain to form the Triple Alliance in 1717, the role of the Dutch, although somewhat peripheral, was nevertheless important as it disguised the dynastic interests of the previous year's Anglo-French agreement. The United Provinces obtained a guarantee for the Barrier Treaty concluded with the emperor, together with trade gains from France. Finally, the Dutch guarantee afforded to the other two signatories was limited to their European possessions (Muret 1949, 78). Dutch membership of the 1725 Hanover Alliance was to prove of even greater significance. Once again, the United Provinces behaved in a very cautious manner—joining the Alliance in 1726, only after protracted negotiations—which was due to their desire to avoid war but also obtain the best possible terms for involvement therein. From the early 1720s on, the Dutch Republic protested the creation of the Ostend Company, which was seen as a rival of its own trading companies (Hertz 1906). Dutch concerns did not initially find much sympathy from the British; however, it was not long before the British government backed suspension, and then permanent closure, of the Ostend Company, to encourage the United Provinces to join the Hanover Alliance, which was a coalition created by the British to counter the Austro-Spanish axis that had emerged during this period (Dunthorne 1986, 57–74). The risk of war, which had been substantial in 1725, diminished during the course of 1726. In addition, there was a strong enough likelihood of British support in future negotiations over the Ostend Company to convince the United Provinces to take part in the most important diplomatic actions witnessed in the years thereafter, the results of which were encouraging. One problem of the relationship between the two allies during the early 1720s derived from Britain pursuing political and diplomatic objectives on a European scale, whereas the United Provinces were mainly concerned with their own trade activities. The political and economic dangers posed by the Austro-Spanish alliance now led to the two allies coming closer together.

After the crisis involving the two blocs had been momentarily resolved by the preliminary peace agreements signed in Paris in 1727, the two allies began planning a series of joint land and sea operations. Britain seemed more inclined than the United Provinces to use force, and the latter, together with France, often had to hold their more bellicose ally back. However, generally speaking they both pursued the same objective: implementation of the Paris agreements. The United Provinces, despite being excluded from France and Britain's negotiations with Spain, promptly acceded to their Treaty of Seville (November 1729) and in doing so obtained substantial trade gains in the Mediterranean, as well as more favorable commercial terms from Spain's subjects and allies. Moreover, France and Britain undertook to close the Ostend Company and support the Dutch in their dispute with Prussia over East Frisia, in exchange for a Dutch pledge to send a military contingency to Italy that was only half the size of those sent by the other allies, in the event of war between the emperor and Spain (Carter 1975, 58). Finally, the United Provinces were, from the very outset, involved in the negotiations between Austria and Britain that led to the second Treaty of Vienna (March 1731). Once again, the Dutch evaluated things with their traditional circumspection and became party to the treaty the following year, having stuck to certain points in their usual tenacious manner. Once again, the parties did not dispute the crux of the transaction. It involved resolution of the Italian problem, that is, the emperor's acceptance of the immediate entry of Spanish garrisons into Italy's dukedoms and winding up the Ostend Company in exchange for Anglo-Dutch recognition of the Pragmatic Sanction. However, the United Provinces bargained very hard on a whole series of issues pertaining to the costs and benefits of their involvement, notably reduced military involvement; prohibition of all "fraudulent, indirect trade with the West Indies"; and a pledge to maintain the existing advantageous tariffs in the Low Countries. With regard to the latter two points, two separate articles were needed to convince the Dutch Republic to adhere to the treaty.[18] Once again, the "Dutch sloop," a combination of free rider and subordinated ally, followed in the wake of the British, being careful not to run any unnecessary risks, while taking advantage of any interesting opportunities that arose. This difference in the two allies' approaches to risk is the almost inevitable result of the imbalance in power within an asymmetrical alliance. There is little the guarantor can do to affect its ally's risk propensity. Far more influential, in this regard, is the attitude taken by the common enemy.

THE COMMON ENEMY: FRANCE AND THE WARS OF POLISH AND AUSTRIAN SUCCESSION

Despite the fact that the second Treaty of Vienna had formally reinstated the Old System, the ties between the three allies were never to be as strong as they had been at the time of the struggle against Louis XIV. Indeed, the maritime powers beat a retreat at the very first opportunity, leaving Austria to deal with France on its own. The pretext for this new European war (1733–1735) was the Polish succession, about which France and Austria had very different ideas; the latter took this opportunity to settle its score with

France in Italy as well, with the aid of Spain and the Kingdom of Sardinia. August II died in February 1733; already by April of that same year the United Provinces expected France to attack Austria in Germany or Italy and also expected the emperor to request help from the maritime powers. This time round, the Dutch Republic took the initiative, forcing its more powerful ally, which had been caught unawares, to follow its lead. In fact, during the course of the summer it negotiated an agreement with France that basically saw Dutch neutrality being offered in exchange for a French pledge not to invade the Low Countries. The chronic state of its finances, the likelihood of compromising trade with France, and above all the increasing lack of faith in the defensive system of the barriers had placed the United Provinces in a very difficult position: if France were to attack the Low Countries, the Dutch had no real chance of defending themselves. This precarious situation was also the result of the two allies, Britain and Austria, who had increasingly lost interest in the state of the fortresses, thus substantially compromising their defensive capabilities (Dunthorne 1986, 265–68). The agreement with France enabled the United Provinces to get out of a difficult situation by placing themselves on the same level as their British ally; the Dutch Republic no longer needed to fear for its safety, just as Britain was not directly affected by the events of the Polish succession. This could be seen as a negative form of homogeneity, if you like, but nevertheless an important factor in accounting for the subsequent joint actions of the two allies.

Naturally enough, the British were not at all happy about the Republic's actions; however, the very fact that events on the mainland did not directly damage its interests led Britain to make the best of a bad bargain. Dutch neutrality led the British to remain neutral as well—as the French expected—for the familiar reasons Robert Walpole summed up this way:

> Great Britain can neither with safety nor prudence enter into this war but in conjunction with the States. . . . I will not enter into the consideration of the advantages [sic] and prejudices that must attend our being engaged in a war against France and Spain, and the Dutch continuing in a state of neutrality; they are too evident, and we must conclude it is what this nation cannot, will not bear [quoted in Wilson 1936, 246].

Thus it was that Dutch neutrality, despite being officially condemned, became a useful justification for avoiding a war that very few, apart from the king, were prepared to wage. When the emperor actually asked for help, the United Provinces took their time before responding, claiming they wished to consult with the British before offering a joint reply in conjunction with the latter, while Britain played along, offering a somewhat ambiguous, evasive answer itself, and the same scenario was played out again in 1734 and in 1735 (Dunthorne 1986, 283–84). Together, the two maritime powers strived to mediate; once again the Dutch took the initiative, while Britain followed suit. The two allies were driven by divergent considerations here: the British joined negotiations in order to prevent the Dutch Republic itself getting too close to France (Black 1991, 189), while the Dutch were highly suspicious of Britain's aims. They feared that their ally, in taking up a pro-Austrian stance, could take advantage of negotiations in order to drag the Dutch into a war, and the same fear clearly emerged when, during this very period, the marriage of the heir of William III to the daughter of George II was announced. If the king's son-in-law were to become stadtholder with the help of the British, the latter could use this to push the United Provinces into an unwanted, unnecessary war. Together, the maritime powers failed in their attempt at mediation;[19] however, they both reaped considerable trade gains from their neutrality (Carter 1975, 59). Finally, both witnessed a decline in their importance and esteem during the course of that decade, as France increasingly became the key player in the European diplomatic game.

The behavior of the common enemy, France, is thus an important factor in establishing the tone and nature of the relationship between the two allies. From the Dutch point of view, given the extreme weakness of the country and the vulnerability of its southern border, its security basically depended on what France intended to do. The Dutch Republic was not completely without bargaining power; indeed, it was fully aware of exactly how much importance the French placed on the neutral Dutch fleet and knew that the government in Paris was aware that any further French attacks in the Low Countries would not only strengthen Anglo-Dutch relations but could also have unforeseeable repercussions, as indeed was to happen in 1747 with the restoration of the stadtholder. By contrast, in adopting a policy of conciliation France managed to ensure the neutrality of the Dutch and that of its British ally. The fact that Louis XV waited until the completion of negotiations with the Dutch Republic before declaring war on the emperor is of some significance. As long as France did not represent an immediate threat, Britain's grip on the United Provinces was anything but firm.[20] The Dutch government adopted a low profile once again, in 1739, when Britain found itself at war with Spain which continued to capture English ships involved in illegal trade in the West Indies.

The agreements between the two allies did not cover the colonies, and the Dutch were clearly not prepared to fight Spain in order to protect British trade. All Horace Walpole managed to obtain from his visit to the Hague in the summer of 1739 was a modest promise of an "augmentation" in military spending, which among other things was seen by the Dutch more as an increase in their own national security than as support for the English cause. Walpole returned from the Hague totally convinced that the United Provinces had become a dead weight that could no longer be relied on to lend support under any circumstances, especially in the event of war with France, and he suggested that Prussia would be the best ally on mainland Europe (Dunthorne 1986, 321–22). However, his views were not shared by the majority of the British, who were still not really aware of the extent of the United Provinces' decline; and of course, the trade rivalry between the two allies persisted. At the outbreak of the war with Spain, Britain threatened to capture all neutral vessels found trading with the enemy. Despite the Dutch being informed, in accordance with the 1674 treaty, that this measure did not concern their ships, in practice this threat was carried out on more than one occasion with regard to Dutch vessels.[21]

The events related to the War of the Austrian Succession (1740–1748) clearly show both the results of the excessive weakness of the minor ally and the important role played by the enemy in the relationship between the allies. To start with, it was the behavior of France that strictly conditioned that of the United Provinces. Britain, for its part, subjected its ally to systematic pressure in an attempt to get it to make a greater contribution to their joint war effort. It was only when the guarantor had finally achieved this aim that it realized the truly sorry plight of an ally it was now forced to carry completely. Hence the decision to put a quick end to the war. Despite being obliged by the provisions of the various treaties—the Barrier Treaty forced it to defend the Low Countries, while the second Treaty of Vienna made it one of the guarantors of the Austrian succession—in 1740 the Dutch Republic decided to take the middle path, which was the logical consequence of the extremely difficult position it found itself in with the war at its door. The United Provinces paid the due subsidies to Austria and sent 20,000 troops to the Low Countries. In doing so, the Dutch were in fact taking part in military operations against France; yet not only did they arrange things so that their troops never actually joined the allied forces (other than by chance in 1745), but they also abstained from declaring war against France. Indeed, they maintained healthy relations with the latter since the French, for their part, did not want the Dutch Republic to intervene directly in the war, and the French ambassador in the Hague had the specific task of preserving the fear among the Dutch that they risked immediate attack should they give in to British pressures (Coquelle 1902, 13). Thus the Dutch Republic's concern over France's declaration of war against the British (in March 1744) was understandable: the Republic's neutrality was now even more difficult to preserve. Nevertheless, it still tried to remain neutral; on the one hand, it promised its allies an additional 20,000 men, to be sent to the Low Countries, but on the other hand it informed France of its desire for peace (ibidem, 21–22).

For its part, Britain, which was already at war with Spain, repeatedly demanded its ally's fuller involvement. Together with the usual commercial reasons for this,[22] there were now also strategic-military considerations. In 1744, France prepared an invasion, which came of nothing, and the United Provinces declared that they were prepared to provide the support envisaged in the treaties; the following year, at the time of the new Jacobite uprising in Scotland, 6,000 men were sent to fight at the side of the ally's forces. Despite British complaints about the increasingly impalpable nature of Dutch naval support,[23] the Dutch nevertheless observed the letter, if not the spirit, of their treaties and in doing so exposed themselves to serious dangers. The Jacobite threat in 1745 led to the British recalling its entire military contingent from the Low Countries, which together with the sending of the Dutch contingent to Scotland left the defensive line of the barriers extremely vulnerable. In February 1746, the French reached Brussels, and a few weeks later they were at the gates of Antwerp. Even though Britain failed to convince the United Provinces to declare war against the French, it did manage to force it to prolong its state of belligerence, by impeding the peace proposals made by France in 1746, which the Dutch Republic would have been happy to accept. The desire to hold on to the important conquered territory of Cape Breton in North America encouraged the British to try everything to get the French out of the Low Countries, in order to avoid having to hand the island back in peace negotiations (Geyl 1925–26).

Then in April 1747 France put an end to all the obstacles in its way and finally declared war on the United Provinces. The aim of this was to impose peace on Britain from Amsterdam and the Hague. The rapid invasion by France, as in 1672, led to a violent popular groundswell against the government of the Dutch Republic, which in turn led to restoration of the stadtholder. Initially, this may seem to have been a great victory for the British and a defeat for the neutralist, pro-French positions of the business oligarchy, especially in the province of Holland; this outcome was in large part thanks to Britain's money and the British ships moored along the Scheldt. In fact, the British government had great hopes for the return of the stadtholder.[24] However, it quickly became apparent that William IV possessed neither the force nor the means with which to impose an abrupt change in policy. The promises of subsidies and troops were never kept; indeed, the United Provinces even tried to get the British to shoulder the cost of, and responsibility for, the defense of Dutch lands. In other words, when Britain finally witnessed its ally at war with the French, it realized that this was not a help but a burden, from a military point of view. To the very end of 1747, the Duke of Newcastle continued to place great faith in Britain's alliance with the United Provinces and Austria[25] (and this was to become an important element in his policy even after the war ended). However, the repeated defeats suffered by the Dutch between 1747 and 1748, together with William IV's request for a loan to continue the war, convinced the British to seek a peace agreement. Parliament was not at all prepared to subsidize the war any further, and without the Dutch presence the British could not continue to fight as they needed to on the European mainland. In conclusion, the financial and military weakness of the minor ally induces the leader to renounce its more ambitious plans.

THE FINAL DEMISE OF THE OLD SYSTEM

The Peace of Aix-la-Chapelle (1748) restored the status quo in the Low Countries, including the presence of Dutch garrisons in the barrier fortresses. However, many Dutch were aware that the peace treaty had been made possible by the very fact of the nation's decline, and that if the country had made more of an effort in both military and financial terms and continued to fight the French then all it would have succeeded in doing was to allow Britain to keep possession of Cape Breton. After 1748, France was increasingly the only power still in a position to push the United Provinces into British hands; given that France had already paid the price for its declaration of war—with the return to power of the House of Orange—from that point onward it adopted an even more cautious approach. Indeed, Dutch security was not threatened again until 1793, and this time by a very different France.

What had been revealed to be a rather threadbare diplomatic arrangement—the anti-French alliance involving the two maritime powers and Austria—was nevertheless tenaciously promoted by the Duke of Newcastle, the leading figure behind Britain's foreign policy during the period, and William Bentinck, the most influential leader of the Orange Party. The sudden death of William IV in 1751 led to the crowning of his wife, since their son was only three years old at the time. Britain was now the natural protector of the Orange succession; Joseph Yorke, the English ambassador to the Hague, was explicitly given the power to intervene, albeit discreetly, in the Dutch Republic's domestic affairs (Scott 1989, 73). The imbalance in the Anglo-Dutch relationship was becoming increasingly evident. British policy toward Austria was, however, clumsy; Newcastle's plans to crown Joseph, Maria Theresa's son, king of the Romans and thus appoint him emperor, rather than consolidating Anglo-Austrian relations, was coldly met by the Austrians (Browning 1975, 159–80). One fundamentally important instrument for the relaunching of the Old System was represented by the negotiations over a new barrier system; yet they were afflicted by insurmountable problems from the very outset. As we have seen, even prior to the French victories in the War of the Austrian Succession, the vulnerability of the barrier was clear for all to see. Anglo-Dutch attempts to restore a credible defensive line in the Low Countries, and in particular to convince Austria to take upon itself the greater part of the financial and military costs involved, clashed with the realism of the Austrian chancellor, the prince of Kaunitz, who believed that the region constituted a burden that should be off-loaded as soon as possible; in any case, Austria now perceived its major enemy to be Prussia, rather than France, with whom it hoped to eventually come to an agreement.

In 1755, with a new Anglo-French war ongoing in North America, Austria's disengagement from the Low Countries was evident. There was lengthy, unproductive debate in the United Provinces as to whether it was a better idea to increase land forces, as the Orange Party and the British had hoped, or naval forces, as proposed by the Republican Party (which was more concerned about protecting overseas trade) and also suggested by France. English diplomacy's aim of obtaining an "augmentation" of the Dutch army now went beyond purely military considerations; if adopted, this measure would have created suspicion and resentment among the French. The latter saw their most realistic ambition as being Dutch neutrality and consolidation of the Dutch fleet. French insistence on this second point ran contrary to the British aim of augmentation and as such was designed to create tension between the two maritime powers. However, the ensuing discussions once again revealed the enormous financial problems the country had at that time (Carter 1971, 36–43). In such a situation of great uncertainty, Britain refused to take responsibility for the cost of reinforcing the fortress at Namur: "As the House of Austria will not, and the Republic cannot, take the share which they have hitherto done in the affairs of Europe, it is impossible to imagine that His Majesty will [...] launch out into a still more extensive scheme, the burthen of which would be insupportable to this Nation."[26] This marked the end of the barrier system, and the very fact that the Low Countries were now defenseless contributed to Dutch neutrality at the outbreak of the Seven Years' War; it would have made little sense for France to push into the Low Countries once the Austrians and British had withdrawn from the region (Carter 1971, 33–34).

Thus, while the Anglo-French naval conflict was about to have repercussions on mainland Europe, the United Provinces found themselves once again having to deal with the dilemma of their neutrality, caught as they were between their British ally, which sought to drag the Dutch with it into war, and the French enemy with whom the Dutch had been negotiating since the spring of 1755 in pursuit of guaranteed security. Things were further complicated by the traditional competition between the two trading powers, which as always increased as the prospect of war appeared on the horizon. The Dutch, for their part, were tempted to remain neutral in order to exploit the commercial advantages that only neutrality could offer, while the British were intent on granting no concessions this time round. In fact, it was Britain's wish to force its ally's hand that led it to sound out the United Provinces in October 1755. Newcastle feared a French invasion and so appointed Yorke to ask the Dutch what their response would be if they were requested to send 6,000 troops to support the British army, as was provided for under the 1678 treaty. This was a cleverly conceived move, with two aims. Had a positive answer been offered, it would have had the effect of compromising the ally in relation to France; on the other hand, had the answer been a negative one, then the Dutch government would have been deemed in the wrong, thus justifying a British trade reprisal, which would have forced the Dutch government to earn the right to enjoy, once again, part of its traditional privileges.[27] In his interviews, Yorke explicitly insisted on the relationship between the 1674 trade agreement and the 1678 defensive alliance; if the United Provinces had sent their contingent, then Britain would not have interfered with Dutch trade activities (Carter 1971, 55). The Dutch Republic was tempted; on first sight it appeared that the Dutch were offered the chance to continue trading with France in exchange for the reasonable price of 6,000 men. However, had it accepted this offer, one may realistically presume that British demands would not have stopped there. Both Newcastle and Yorke saw application of the 1678 treaty as implying not just simple provision of aid but war against France (Pares 1938, 245). In any case, the problem did not actually arise, since the French informed the Dutch that the only thing France would accept was complete neutrality (Coquelle 1902, 62–66). Furthermore, Britain made another attempt to resolve this impasse by embarrassing its ally even further; this it did by sending those ships needed to transport troops before the United Provinces had reached any official decision, which put the Dutch back up even more. The resulting position, especially in Holland, was that the Dutch would be prepared to aid their British ally in the event of a Jacobite invasion but were not at all prepared to take any action that would provoke the French if such an invasion were merely feared or hypothesized (Carter 1975, 83–84).

The diplomatic revolution simply completed the picture, reinforcing the Dutch decision to remain neutral. Under the Franco-Austrian alliance, following the first Treaty of Versailles (May 1, 1756), the Low Countries were now in the hands of an ally (rather than an enemy) of France, which meant there was no longer any need to worry about the region's defense. Furthermore, the treaty explicitly guaranteed the Low Countries against French military occupation. The United Provinces' declaration of neutrality on May 25, 1756, was the logical consequence of a profoundly altered relational framework, and it is, not surprisingly, considered by many to have been the death knell of the Anglo-Dutch alliance.[28] Subsequent attempts to obtain the 6,000 men provided for by the 1678 treaty, now that war had been declared against France, led to an official negative response from the United Provinces, justifying their failure to provide the due support on the basis of the non-European nature of the Anglo-French war (Schweizer 1989, 87). The process that was brought to fruition in May 1756 may be seen, according to our framework, as a radical change in the allies' relational system, that is, a transition from homogeneity to heterogeneity; the common cause was gradually diluted while the particular causes of each party emerged as preponderant. The Republic's commercial opportunism, now further reinforced by the French pledge not to attack, was the counterpart of the growing reluctance of the British to pay for the defense of such an unreliable, quarrelsome, ineffective ally, and their search for a new partner, now that a European war seemed imminent. The continued trade rivalry between the two allies merely completed the picture; immediately after the United

Provinces' declaration of neutrality, Britain took a series of steps to impede Dutch trade with France.[29]

Dutch neutrality, as agreed with France, was no novelty; as we have seen, they had already adopted such a position in 1733. However, on the first occasion this decision was in keeping with the British position, whereas the later declaration was quite clearly not, given that Britain was now at war with France, and thus France no longer represented the common enemy for the two allies in question. The heterogeneity of Anglo-Dutch relations, which had been latent for some years beforehand, was clearly evident in the changed positions of the two allies with regard to the enemy; one ally had now come to an agreement with France, while the other was at war with it. Where there was no longer any need for protection, there was also no longer any obedience. Once this tie was removed, the guarantee alliance no longer existed, thus producing standard coercive politics and similarly tenacious resistance thereto; but both were now devoid of the meaning they had been given by the alliance itself. Whereas beforehand British leadership tended to take the form of actions and solutions that offered undeniable, albeit limited, advantages to the minor ally, they now promised nothing but disadvantages. Given that the United Provinces could (using the terms employed here) "resign itself to doing without" the services offered by its ally, it now eluded British power. This does not mean the Dutch Republic shifted from an alliance with Great Britain to a privileged relationship with France; just as siding with the British would have meant having to face a French attack on land, against which Britain no longer seemed capable of offering due protection, likewise siding completely with the French would have meant challenging Britain's naval power, with the risk of incalculable losses to trade and no chance of being properly defended by France. Therefore, a precise limit remained—neutrality—beyond which the United Provinces could not go; when they eventually did try to breach that threshold, a quarter of a century later, they immediately found themselves at war with their old ally.

FIVE

The Hegemonic Alliance

Great Britain and France, 1716–1731

A HETEROGENEOUS, ASYMMETRICAL ALLIANCE

In the hegemonic alliance, the asymmetry in power relations between the allies is accompanied by the heterogeneity of their respective relational context. Thus even though there is a common cause, this cause is coupled with a series of other particular causes, the pursuit of which prejudices the shared interest, or is prejudiced by the same shared interest; and the sacrificing of those particular causes comes at a very high price. As is the case in the other type of heterogeneous alliance, the deadlocked alliance, the allies are faced with constraints or opportunities that tend to lead them in separate directions. However, whereas in the case of a deadlocked alliance such contrasting tendencies are inclined to block each other as a result of the symmetry in power relations, in the hegemonic alliance one party manages to force the other into following its lead. We have already seen the kind of impact that asymmetry may have in inter-ally relations; unlike in the other asymmetrical alliance presented here, the guarantee alliance, the hegemonic alliance is characterized by heterogeneity, which tends to give negotiations between the parties a definite coercive character. The only binding constraint is that of avoiding the breakup of the alliance, as this would prejudice the common cause. The end result of inter-ally interaction is thus unilateral conditioning, whereby the weaker member of the alliance is forced to follow the stronger member, comply with its decisions, and pay the price that all this entails. Whereas the major ally in a guarantee alliance is predisposed, by homogeneity, toward safeguarding some of the minor ally's interests, the heterogeneity of a hegemonic alliance gives it reason to take advantage of the minor ally's dependence. This heterogeneity in turn leads the minor ally to try to influence the behavior of its stronger partner. The outcome of this pursuit of the conformity of the other is decisively affected by the power imbalance, which leads the weaker party to give in to the stronger party's demands.

Historians have convincingly showed that following the Peace of Utrecht, France and Britain were subjected to diverse constraints and contrasting opportunities.[1] For a start, they were the two most important great powers at the time, and given that Britain had attained this position thanks largely to its role in the defeat of Louis XIV, the two countries were positional rivals, as it were. The simple fact that they were geographical neighbors generated a traditional hostility among the British toward nearby France, from the Middle Ages onward, and this hostility was now exacerbated by rival national interests, together with defensive concerns that came increasingly to the fore during the better part of the 18th century. Furthermore, there were also a number of religious and economic grounds for tension between the two powers. Although the religious factor remained more or less of secondary importance, there were times when Britain explicitly appealed to the protestant cause in an attempt to obtain the cooperation of other European states; religion sometimes emerged as one of the grounds used to justify the government's foreign policy; and France, the only nation seriously capable of shouldering the Jacobite cause, was often portrayed as the long hand of the pope (Horn 1967, 31–34). Even more important, Britain was, first and foremost, a "trading island" (Sorel 1885–1904, 261), and its policies were based on this fact. It produced more than it consumed and could expand only through the colonies. Hence its refusal to entertain the idea of sharing command of the seas and oceans with France, and its constant opposition to any moves that would increase France's oceanic channels of trade. Britain also wanted to reserve German supplies for itself and so would not allow the French to establish bases in Antwerp and the Low Countries. Britain's policy of containment, which was to survive up to the end of the century, was based on one simple principle: extension of its own maritime empire, and restriction or destruction of that of France. Trade rivalry with France became increasingly acute as the two countries' economies grew; it was generally accepted that, according to the mercantilistic principles of the time, France was the one benefiting the most from bilateral trade with Britain. This helps explain a whole series of British measures, adopted between stipulation of the Utrecht Treaties and the onset of the French Revolution, specifically designed to hinder trade with France. This aspect of Anglo-French rivalry was also the basis of both British policy in the Baltic[2]—given the declined trading power of the United Provinces, it became necessary not only to take that country's place but also to prevent France from doing so first—and of Britain's colonial policy from the middle of the century onward, which was justified in anti-French terms: the growth of British trade, it was argued, would put the country in a stronger position than that of France (Horn 1967, 34–39). To conclude, it is hardly surprising that at the time the two nations were perceived as natural enemies.[3]

A simple calculation of the resources possessed by each rival at the time reveals a more or less balanced relationship. France and its possessions had been somewhat reduced in size, but not downgraded, as a result of the War of the Spanish Succession; its now more restricted borders were easier to defend. Furthermore, France's population, which was about three times that of Britain, together with the nation's thriving agriculture and considerable industrial capacity meant it could avail itself of more men, materials, and money than any other nation on the European mainland. However, it is also true that in 1714 France was in a rather delicate position: its warships had been destroyed, its army had failed to match those of the maritime powers and their German allies, its foreign trade had been reduced to the bare minimum, and its public debt stood at a worrying level (McKay and Scott 1983, 97–98). Historians almost unanimously conclude that the country needed a long period of peace in order to gather itself together and reorganize its domestic affairs. A certain passive predisposition was accentuated by another two factors, which are very much focused on as a rule. The first was the problems associated with the succession, and the regent's intentions regarding the matter. The second was France's diplomatic isolation. If we put all this information together, the picture that emerges is one of a country that, although potentially stronger than its ally (in terms of available resources), was nevertheless dependent on the latter, and this dependence meant that for many years it remained subject to the wishes of its partner. Yet Britain's position on various important issues could not be easily reconciled with France's. As a result, British policies could not be particularly beneficial to France, just as France's conformity could not be but reluctant and resentful.

OPPORTUNITIES, CONSTRAINTS, AND DEPENDENCE: THE ORIGINS OF THE ALLIANCE

It is widely recognized that during this historical period both France and Great Britain's movements were influenced by a series of national forces and dynastic requirements that were not always mutually compatible. The harmonization of such forces, which was a necessary prerequisite of any coherent foreign policy, proved more successful in the British case than in the French one. Some believe that France was diplomatically dependent on Britain, as a result above all of the personal and family interests of the regent, who was prepared to sacrifice the independence of French policy in exchange for British support.[4] Although this view is widely shared, it should be pointed out that French subordination extended beyond the deaths of the regent and his advisor (and later minister), the abbé Dubois (both died in 1723). Furthermore, though it is true that the policy of the regent and Dubois was undoubtedly inspired by dynastic considerations, it nevertheless took some account of the country's traditional security imperatives—basically to counter the threat posed by Austria—while the need for peace was acknowledged by everyone. However, the price that had to be paid for British support was Britain's acquisition of the status of world power, in both economic and military terms, together with a reduction in the importance of France itself (Shennan 1979, 74–75).[5]

In brief, following the Peace of Utrecht both France and Britain were afflicted by serious domestic instability, associated with the succession to their thrones. In the summer of 1714, George I of Hanover was crowned king of England, and from the very beginning of his reign he had to deal with the threat posed by the Stuart pretender to the throne, James III, who enjoyed French sympathies. The crowning of George I also meant the redesign of British foreign policy in Northern Europe, in particular constant focus on the plight of the Hanover electorate, and on the complex affairs of the various important regional powers.[6] As far as France is concerned, the death of Louis XIV in 1715 led to Philip II, the Duke of Orleans (the future Louis XV was born in 1710), being made regent of the kingdom, a precarious position owing to the hostility of Philip V of Spain (nephew of Louis XIV);

the latter, in turn, could count on considerable support in France, both at court and among the populace. Hence Philip II's need, first, to continue as regent and second to ensure the Orleanist succession to the throne in the event Louis XV died heirless. From this arose also Philip's preference for a policy of peace, designed to prevent any possible political upheaval.

Following the crushing of the 1715 Jacobite uprising, two basic strategies emerged in Great Britain. The first strategy, adopted by the king, his Hanoverian ministers, and a section of the Whig Party, consisted in creation of a network of agreements and alliances that would discourage any further sudden attacks by James Stuart, the Old Pretender, and consolidate Britain's international position; the keystone of such a system was an alliance with France. The regent would accept those conditions set by Britain, and Britain would then be free to get closer to other powers. The second strategy, favored by the majority of Whigs, was characterized by a proud, anti-French patriotism, and as such it aimed to rebuild the former Grand Alliance among Britain, the United Provinces, and Austria that had worked so well against Louis XIV (the Old System), and even to recoup Spain in some way. Townshend and Stanhope were the politically able ministers who managed to combine the two strategies, and in doing so they succeeded in projecting Great Britain to the center of the European diplomatic stage.

The situation that emerged may be summarized as follows. France, exhausted by war and governed by a vulnerable regent, would lend its support to George I against the Jacobites, in exchange for British support against Philip V. It may have appeared inevitable that the two weak rulers would join forces; in fact, negotiations proved difficult,[7] among other things because Stanhope really did believe that he could rebuild the Grand Alliance, and to this end he went in person to the Hague and to Vienna at the end of 1714 to discuss matters. However, Austro-Dutch differences over the Low Countries, and demands from Vienna for British naval support in the Mediterranean against the Spanish, effectively prevented restoration of the Old System. All that Britain's energetic diplomacy managed to achieve was a series of bilateral agreements with Spain, the United Provinces, and Austria (concluded between the end of 1715 and the summer of 1716). Certain doubts may be expressed regarding the actual importance of those treaties,[8] but at the very least they did succeed in isolating France at a time when the regent was forced to come to terms with the powerful domestic groups willing a return to Louis XIV's "*anciennes maximes,*" that is, to a strictly anti-Austrian and anti-British policy.

It is therefore understandable why one observer commented that "circumstance largely dictated the coming together of two powers whose basic interests were scarcely compatible" (Langford 1976, 78). In our conceptual scheme, circumstance refers to the relational context within which French and British foreign policies were situated, in that the negotiations conducted between the two countries largely reflected their relations with other powers and cannot be interpreted simply from a bilateral perspective. Even though Britain's agreements with Spain, Austria, and the United Provinces were not entirely satisfactory from the British point of view, they nevertheless close off the space available to French diplomacy, and the regent had to seriously consider the idea of reaching an agreement with Britain at a time when the recent crushing of the Jacobite uprising mitigated doubts about the Hanoverian succession, thus strengthening the bargaining power of George I.

It was within this diplomatic context that the regent, urged on by Dubois, decided to negotiate with the British. The ensuing agreement, which gradually emerged during the summer of 1716, included recognition of the Protestant succession in Great Britain and expulsion of the Pretender from French territory, in exchange for a new, solemn formulation of the Utrecht Treaties, which implied confirmation of the renunciation of the thrones—including Philip V's renunciation of the French throne, which was of essential importance for the Duke of Orleans and his house. However, apart from the family interests in question, George I also defended a specific national interest, namely the closure of the port of Mardick to warships (the port of Dunkerque had already been dismantled following the Utrecht Treaties). This implied further reduction in France's naval power in the Atlantic. Great Britain, which found itself in the enviable position of being beseeched by its ally, consequently raised the stakes further during the course of negotiations, after Austria's victories against the Turks made London more reluctant to abandon Vienna for Paris: the port of Mardick now had to be completely dismantled.[9]

From the French point of view, the interests at stake may be traced back to the Orleanist succession to the throne and the preservation of peace; from the British point of view the question was more complex and centered around issues arising from the war still being fought in Northern Europe. In this war, Sweden, expelled from Germany, was contemplating redirecting its policy toward the North Sea, which would have set it on a collision course with Britain, and was also keen on reconciliation with Russia, which would have been the preamble to an alliance involving Prussia and Poland as well, to the detriment of Denmark and Hanover. Britain, which was concerned about the likelihood of such a scenario, was contemplating getting closer to Austria; but to do so it had to concede more than was done a few months earlier. In December 1716, therefore, a second Austro-British treaty was concluded, whereby Britain found itself implicated in Austria's Italian affairs, while Austria for its part promised to lend Britain support in Northern Europe.

As one can see, this policy led to Britain's substantial involvement in European affairs, which was a risky venture indeed. However, these risks could be limited thanks to the conformity of France; it was France, and its system of traditional friendships and old alliances, that Britain was counting on for support. In negotiating the alliance, Stanhope undoubtedly had a mental reservation about seeing France being used, for policies conceived without her interests in mind, by Britain, Austria, and the House of Hanover in Northern Europe—to discourage Swedish and Russian maneuvers by separating Prussia from Russia—and in Southern Europe, where the regent was expected to comply with Austrian desires, thereby leaving Spain and the Kingdom of Sicily to their fates. This arrangement was particularly appealing, since it promised Britain substantial benefits at very little cost; the planned measures centered around British interests, they could be implemented without the dangers and costs of a war, and the odious nature of such measures in the eyes of those who were inevitably to come off worse could be ascribed to France, forced as it was to abandon its old friends. The official explanation, of course, was the need to "safeguard peace" against "disruptive forces," and this was to become the underlying theme of British diplomacy at that time. The official explanation, however, attempted to conceal certain other important results of British policy.

The agreement, stipulated at the end of August and then ratified in October, clearly reflects the imbalance in the allies' respective bargaining power. In fact, the contents of the treaty were very much weighted in Britain's favor. By getting closer to Britain, the French managed to ward off the specter of a new Grand Alliance, to strengthen the peace that was so important for domestic recovery, while their regent guaranteed himself the Orleanist succession to the throne.[10] Although these results were of much importance, they were obtained at considerable cost. As well as conceding the dismantling of the port of Mardick and expulsion of the Pretender, France also undertook to cooperate with Britain in maintaining the Utrecht system, and to convince, or force, those powers still at war—in particular, the emperor and Spain—to accept the peace terms proposed by the two allies. France guaranteed George I all those dominions and territories in his possession, in the event of an act of aggression. This meant, among other things, giving up Bremen and Verden (territories possessed by its old ally Sweden) and in the battle conducted on the ruins of Sweden, between Hanover (supported by Britain) and the tsar (supported by Prussia), siding with Britain. As a result, the coalition that the elderly Louis XIV wished to create, during the final months of his life, among France and Austria, Prussia, Spain, Sweden, and the Jacobites, against Britain was now inconceivable. Austria was more hostile than ever, Spain was unhappy with French policy, and Sweden and the Jacobites had been abandoned to their fates. Britain no longer ran the risk of encountering a formidable coalition of European powers; on the contrary, it was now the arbiter of European affairs and could consolidate and improve through peace on what it had previously acquired through war.

The Anglo-French alliance, a genuine diplomatic revolution, was always going to be rather precarious, never very popular in either country, and constantly burdened by the pressures put on the two allies as well as by their reciprocal suspicions (Black 1986, 12); notwithstanding this, however, it was to last all of 15 years, until 1731 (and it was not until 1744 that it was officially abrogated). Even though it was transformed into a triple alliance as a result of the addition of the United Provinces in January 1717, it essentially remained a two-party coalition led by Britain, with France often diplomatically dependent on the latter, conditioned by the regent's desire for peace, and always concerned about the possible reaction of the British government. The common cause uniting the two countries was preservation of the European order that emerged from the Utrecht Treaties. In fact, the alliance worked better when both parties perceived a threat to this order; Spanish revisionism in 1717 and 1718 could have had repercussions that both allies feared, and similarly the sudden alignment of the two dissatisfied powers, Austria and Spain (the first Treaty of Vienna 1725)—strengthened shortly afterward by the involvement of Russia and Prussia—represented a substantial challenge to France and Britain, who were thus forced to reiterate their relationship, first with the Treaty of Hanover (September 1725) and then with the search for new allies.

None of this could conceal the heterogeneous character of the alliance, however. First, the two nations feared one another, if for no other reason than that in theory one could have decided to form and lead an alliance against the other. Second, both allies had particular causes that had to be sacrificed in the name of the common cause; it was France that in the end had to forgo the most, given that any alternative to its alliance with Britain, and thus to conformity with British wishes, was judged to be worse than a close relationship with Britain. This was to become clear in the two fields of play, the Baltic and the Mediterranean, in which Britain now expected French support for its ventures. France had previous interests and a consolidated presence in both regions, which made it particularly difficult and costly to accept British leadership. Hence the French attempt to influence in turn their ally's policies and also their constant dissatisfaction with that ally every time such efforts failed.

THE FUNCTIONING OF THE ALLIANCE

In a hegemonic alliance, the more powerful ally adopts a broad-ranging policy, while the smaller ally is merely a means by which such policy may be implemented. The favored means of obtaining the conformity of the minor ally is the threat of withdrawal of support (diminishing benefits), since the heterogeneous nature of the alliance leaves little room for positive inducements (emerging benefits). Briefly, a number of theoretical propositions regarding the behavior of the hegemon may be extrapolated from our model. Within the context of the asymmetrical dimension, given that the exercise of power is advantageous, and given that those who do exercise power will want to continue to do so, we would expect the major ally to act to prevent the minor ally from becoming independent. The only constraint on the hegemon is that it should avoid carrying things too far, since there is always the danger that the alliance might collapse as a result. On the rare occasions when Britain slowed down its ventures, subsequent to pressure from the French, or indeed settled for a less favorable outcome than expected, this came about owing to the serious risk of exasperating the ally. In our terms, Britain repeatedly used those strategies that Peter Blau (1964, 118–25) suggests are adopted by those who possess power and wish to maintain it. First, Britain often obtained the cooperation of other states, thereby avoiding having to rely solely on France. The diplomatic-military schemes designed by Britain during that period involved not only France but also the United Provinces, Austria, and Prussia, and furthermore the opening up to Austria and Spain (between 1728 and 1729), at the very moment France was also carefully cultivating relations with the same powers, to a certain extent falls within this logic. Second, Britain systematically hindered France's search for alternative support, thus rendering itself indispensable to the French. British policy led to the French government abandoning its old allies (first and foremost, Sweden), while preventing it from acquiring new ones (starting with Russia), or more simply from acting as an effective independent mediator (between Sweden and Russia during the early years of the alliance, and between Austria and Spain during the entire period in question). Finally, Britain encouraged France to pursue certain foreign policy objectives by using "ideological" or propagandistic means, in particular the safeguarding of peace.

The weaker ally, for its part, plays a basically passive role. It debates matters, but in the end it follows the lead of the hegemon and has no real foreign policy of its own, since it is not in a position to overturn what it complies with. Once again, it may help to briefly recall Blau's analysis (Blau 1964, 118–25). If the minor ally needs those services offered by the major ally, it can either offer the latter something in return, look elsewhere for the services, or resign itself to going without. However, if none of the three solutions is feasible, then the minor ally will find itself dependent on the hegemon. France often tried to render itself indispensable to Britain (for example, its Northern European policy in 1719 was totally designed to satisfy British interests), but often to no avail. The search for alternative solutions was also problematic, thanks to both the behavior of the other powers toward France and the ability of British diplomacy to prevent any realignments centered around Paris. Reconciliation with Spain in 1721, and the central role played by French diplomacy in European affairs between 1727 and 1729, once again in cooperation with Spain, come within this logical framework; however, such measures were never taken to their logical conclusion—breaking off ties with Great Britain—as a result of the very dependence the French wished to circumscribe. Finally, given that France could not "resign itself to doing without" those services offered by Britain, it found itself ipso facto subject to British power, and often forced to comply with that nation's wishes.

Not surprisingly, the support France needed came at a very high price in terms of freedom of movement and decisional autonomy, since as a result of the heterogeneous nature of their alliance the solutions imposed by the hegemon required a sacrifice in terms of material interests, together with reduction in the prestige of France. In other words, given that the two allies were both sensitive to the constraints and opportunities separating them, the power imbalance characterizing their relationship meant that the conformity of the minor ally led to results that satisfied above all the interests of the hegemon. To limit the damage, France tried to modify British behavior, expressing its views and proposing compromises between the various adoptable policies (in other words, the French did exert the voice option). However, given that France's bargaining power was limited, it often succeeded in obtaining only marginal results. Bargaining between the two allies was, as a rule, of a coercive nature, shadowed by the threat of diminishing benefits. Withdrawal of British support could have led not only to a dynastical crisis but also to the country's diplomatic isolation, or even to a reworking of the Old System. Thus the Anglo-French alliance was the principal instrument of British "preponderance" right up to the beginning of the 1730s, while this same preponderance was accompanied by a reduction in the influence exercised by France. The common cause, in other words, was little more than a pretext designed to serve Britain's particular causes, at the cost of prejudicing France's particular causes. Hence the reluctance of the French to follow its ally's lead, and the recriminations that accompanied this subjection.

These dynamics were particularly evident in relations with the enemy. One would expect the stronger ally, the hegemon, given its power over the weaker partner, to display a certain determination in relation to the enemy, dictate the terms of any agreements, and threaten the use of force should the enemy resist. In fact, on more than one occasion Great Britain prepared for war on the basis of France's expected support. France, for its part, could only try to mediate between Britain and the third power, while being subjected to Britain's increasingly tough and specific demands, and often under the threat of being abandoned or dragged unwillingly into a war by the latter. This is exactly what happened not only with Sweden in 1716 and with Spain in 1717–1718, during the early 1720s, and between 1726 and 1729, but also with Russia (early 1720s) and Austria (between 1726 and 1729). Some of the problems in question did not directly affect French interests; others—primarily those regarding trade concessions within the Spanish empire—were of considerable importance, and such problems were resolved to the detriment of France (Black 1986, 14). Until the signing of the Treaty of Seville (1729), France was forced to grant concessions that were hard for the country to swallow. Consequently, as far as relations with the enemy were concerned, the heterogeneous, asymmetrical nature of the alliance meant that to avoid abandonment the minor ally would often risk entrapment; in other words, France frequently found itself in a position of taking part in a war that was unnecessary and that it did not want to be involved in, a war that would merely contribute to strengthening the position of the hegemon. In fact, this occurred in the case of the war against Spain (1718–1720), a war that France unwillingly got involved in and toward which it tried to contribute as little as possible.

The fear of entrapment was justified by the fact that the enemies of the two allies were often different. From the French point of view, the real enemy in mainland Europe remained its old foe, Austria (Black 1988b); but from the British point view, Austria was an important potential partner, since it hoped to be offered this nation's support in Germany and Northern Europe, and because it was useful in inducing fear into the French. From the British point of view, Russia represented the principal concern at the beginning of the 1720s, while Prussia was to become the main source of worry toward the end of the same decade. In this case, the minor ally's vocation as mediator was displayed in its attempts to curb Britain's actions—whereas the latter forged ahead and forced France to follow in its footsteps—and to mediate between Britain and the British enemy. However, since the hegemon has every interest in adopting intransigent positions, the minor ally's mediation proves to be a difficult task. The alternatives, on the other hand, are even worse. A policy of firmness with the enemy, in keeping with the position adopted by the hegemon, could lead to the minor ally becoming entrapped as a result of its very own actions (as happened to France in the previously mentioned case of the war with Spain), or at the very least could mean compromising itself even further (as happened to France in the complex affairs of Northern Europe during the early years of the alliance). Yet a more flexible stance could have upset Britain to the point of inducing it to seek other options elsewhere. Furthermore, in both cases the hegemon might have been encouraged to try to come to an agreement directly with the enemy; thus there was also the danger that France became a Tertius Dolens, which is in fact what happened when Britain reached an agreement with Austria in 1731.

In light of all this, it is clear that both the hegemon and the minor ally are loath to see the other strengthen its position. A stronger, more confident France would have meant a France no longer subject to the will of its ally; a Britain further strengthened by military victories and diplomatic success, likewise, would have meant the never-ending subjection of France, with all the ensuing costs that such an outcome implied. In a hegemonic alliance, therefore, it is clear that the alliance security dilemma is connected to the broader alliance power dilemma; the game being played out here is one of two allies each finding the other's services useful and fully aware that such services are subject to the relation of forces between the two.

In heterogeneous alliances—and thus in the case of the hegemonic alliance—bargaining between the parties is constrained by the need to avoid the break-up of the alliance itself. However, should this constraint be removed, as in one party having other options that are considered better than continuing with the alliance, or because it is subjected to even stronger constraints than avoiding the break-up of the alliance, then the party may well be tempted to simply present its ally with a fait accompli. At this point, one would need to see how the domination-dependence relationship has been modified. The minor ally is unlikely to be able to carve out any room for maneuver, unless of course its spaces suddenly open up. As a rule, it is the major ally that, as a result of its more advantageous position, is likely to take the risk of ending the alliance. However, if the party presented with the fait accompli proves capable of "resigning itself to doing without" those benefits the alliance offers, then it will withdraw; should this not be the case, it will simply be forced once again to accept the other's decisions. When France found itself playing the part of the Tertius Dolens in 1731, its domestic and international position was stronger than it had been in previous years; this meant it was less dependent on Great Britain and could thus dissociate itself from British policy, and in practice terminate the alliance.

THE ALLIANCE AND BRITAIN'S "PREPONDERANCE"

Within the space of two years (between 1716 and 1718), the Anglo-French alliance took up a key position in the broad diplomatic arrangement that allowed Britain to arbitrate European conflicts from the Baltic to the Mediterranean. During the period between the summers of 1716 and 1717, both Sweden and Russia asked France to mediate between them. This was clearly dangerous for Britain, and Stanhope averted the chance of France returning as an independent player by creating such tension between Britain and the two Northern European powers that it was impossible for France to reconcile its alliance with Britain with an independent policy in the Baltic (Muret 1949, 93–94). In other words, by taking a firm stance toward its enemies, Britain tied its ally's hands. The fear of upsetting the English was exacerbated by Britain's intransigence with regard to Russia and Prussia; Britain was prepared to negotiate only if Russia gave up Mecklenburg, and if Prussia joined Hanover to fight the Russians.[11]

France was also obliged to tailor its actions to British policy further south. Here, Britain allied itself with Austria, as the latter provided Britain with vital support in Germany and Northern Europe; consequently, Britain was induced to support Austria in its disputes with Spain and the Kingdom of Sicily. Once again, France played a very important role, serving to share responsibility for those decisions taken against Spanish and Sicilian interests. Here again, the compromising of the ally was functional, in a twofold sense. When Spain rebelled against the Austro-British plan and occupied Sardinia in August 1717, the use of force became a genuine possibility. Indeed, the British rejoiced: "La conduite de l'Espagne déterminera le Régent à conclure avec l'Empereur, à l'exclusion de l'Espagne, et à pousser l'affaire du plan avec fermeté."[12] Though Britain was ready to support Austria, even if this meant war with Spain, French support was more essential than ever if such a war were to be circumscribed and rendered less costly for the British. On that occasion, Dubois acted as if he were playing the part of mediator (though he would have needed his hands free to actually mediate between the parties in question). In practice, the only concession he managed to obtain from the British, in exchange for France's acceptance of the plan, was further recognition of the regent's rights; with this, France found itself in an even more subordinate position in relation to its ally.

The problem for France was that George I was elector (that is, prince of the empire) and king of England, and as such he had to take into account the needs of both empire and country. After having been led to make certain sacrifices for Britain, France was now forced to make further sacrifices for the emperor, thereby continuing to give the regent hope of being guaranteed succession to the French throne. Such a subordinate policy in turn provoked strong anti-Austrian, anti-imperial feelings among those who looked favorably upon Spain, including members of the regent's Council itself, Marshals d'Huxelles and Tallard, and many other officials (Bourgeois 1909, 225–27). France badly needed peace, especially in Southern Europe; Britain needed it in particular in the north, where the resumption of fighting could have compromised Hanoverian interests and led to the king's ministers being accused of concerning themselves more with Hanover than with the country as a whole. This further difference between the two allies illustrated once again the diverse constraints the two were subjected to. Negotiations eventually led to a three-way agreement, starting with an accord between the two allies (signed in February 1718) and followed by one with the emperor (in April 1718). However, in the summer of that same 1718, when Austria, following its victory over the Turkish forces (Peace of Passarowitz), also became intransigent over Italian affairs, Britain found itself faced not only with the problem of avoiding supporting Austria to the point where this would have led to a definitive break in relations with Spain (at a time when Britain shared important trade interests with Spain) but also with preventing France from acting as independent mediator between Spain and Austria. In such uncertain circumstances, France had to curb Austria's actions, which although apparently in Spain's favor would in fact have safeguarded British interests.

The outcome of British diplomacy was a series of trade and political treaties, designed to counter Russia in Northern Europe, together with the Quadruple Alliance (August 1718) binding Britain and France to the United Provinces and Austria in the south, and featuring a precise plan for the territorial and dynastic arrangement of all those matters not concluded at Utrecht.[13] Furthermore, given that Spain refused to yield at all, not even after its Mediterranean fleet was destroyed by the English (at Cape Passero, Sicily, in August 1718), France was given the task of putting it in line by declaring war. This was perhaps the most critical moment for Dubois's diplomacy. From the French perspective, the Quadruple Alliance served to avoid a general war that would have been extremely unpopular, and the regent and Dubois calculated that it would be easier to maintain peace by convincing Austria to join the Anglo-French alliance than by welcoming the overtures from Madrid and allying itself with Spain. This is why France had tried to get Britain and Austria to make certain concessions to Spain, albeit to little avail. Despite considerable domestic resistance, the regent and Dubois eventually managed to get France to go to war alongside Britain. Objectively speaking, this war cannot be judged to have been beneficial to France, given its dynastic ties with Spain, their common aversion to the Habsburgs, and the recent damage to the French navy and trade inflicted by the very same Britain.[14] Indeed, attempts were made to lay responsibility at the door not of the king of Spain but of his minister, Cardinal Alberoni (Bourgeois 1910, 20–41).[15] Once military operations began, Dubois tried to conciliate requirements that were basically incompatible: the recouping of domestic consensus without losing the international standing obtained thanks to Great Britain, while fighting Spain without exasperating Philip V. Hence the decision to conduct limited military operations and not get too involved in matters, while insisting that peace talks continue. Spain, which was quickly defeated, was subsequently forced to temporarily join the Anglo-French alliance and renounce exercise of the Spanish Bourbons' rights to the French throne.

To limit the war against Spain, France also promised involvement in Northern Europe, thus preventing Philip V from finding other allies among those nations, and committed itself to reconciliation of Sweden and Russia; at the same time, fear of upsetting the British led France to reject the offers made by the two northern powers. At the beginning of 1719, this hesitation allowed Britain to set up a league that was to prolong the Great Northern War for a further two years, following the collapse of Sweden. France was as a result relegated to a secondary role and threatened with another futile war. Isolated and discredited, it decided to try to obtain recognition from George I; in 1719, France persuaded Sweden to cede Bremen and Verden to Hanover, in exchange for subsidies to the Swedish fleet and the guarantee of a defensive alliance between Sweden and Britain, while granting Britain the money it required to convince Russia's last remaining ally, Denmark, to leave Pomerania to Sweden. In other words, France acted to defend Britain's basic interests in the region: containment of Russia's naval power and protection of trade in the Baltic. The chairman of the foreign affairs council, d'Huxelles, exclaimed bitterly, "Nous étions enchâinés à l'Angleterre avec la dernière servitude" (quoted in Bourgeois 1909, 207).[16] France was left with the honor of a sterile mediation, and the right to see its guarantee recognized in subsequent treaties, which Britain was nevertheless still reluctant to concede.

The price France paid for its alliance with Britain, during the first five years thereof, was high. The country was forced to suffer destruction of its naval power in the English Channel, and of its trade with the Baltic region. It had to go to war against Spain and contribute to the destruction of the Spanish fleet. At the same time, it abandoned Sweden, the traditional ally in the north, without replacing it with Russia. It also lost a considerable degree of influence in Italy and the United Provinces, leaving the field free for Austria and Great Britain, respectively. On the other hand, during these early years of the alliance Britain managed to obtain significant results, thanks to French support: it organized a directory of European powers, which in the name of peace enabled it to dictate conditions in both the Baltic and the Mediterranean; it put the Spanish navy out of action; it neutralized Sweden and curbed Russia's movements; and it managed to maintain traditional ties with Austria and the United Provinces.

These results were, however, rather precarious, and it was this very precariousness that for the second time revealed Britain's strategy to deny France any real freedom of movement. In fact, several great powers quickly became restless. Sweden and Russia gave signs of a desire to get closer, while Austria did not seem intent on observing agreements regarding Italy, thus placing Britain in an embarrassing position with regard to Spain, with which it was already in conflict over the question of Gibraltar. Furthermore, Austria, which had been forging and leading the Catholic movement in Germany, was now directing the attention of the international community toward the Pragmatic Sanction,[17] which was not simply a dynastic problem but one that implied the unity and indivisibility of the Habsburgs' dominions. Britain was not interested in meeting demands from Charles VI; on the contrary, it intended to leave this matter unresolved until his death, to get Austria to pay the highest possible price. Charles, who fully understood the policy aims of the British, had no intention of giving in to Britain and the United Provinces, which meant among other things not finding oneself in the situation of receiving subsidies from either maritime power. The question was how to guarantee other forms of revenue. From about 1720 onward, Charles had begun to take an interest in the Asian business dealings of the Austrian Low Countries' merchants and shipowners, and in 1722 he chartered a private trading concern called the Ostend Company, which was deeply resented both in the United Provinces and (albeit mainly as a conditioned reflex) in Britain.

The greatest danger for Britain now was that other countries in question would turn to France, which is in fact exactly what Russia, Spain, and Austria promptly did. Dubois realized the nature of this opportunity and would seem to have taken advantage of it. Spain, after having been forced to accept peace, asked France for its help—in exchange for recognition of the regent's rights—with getting Gibraltar back and with concluding a number of other open questions, including (above all) its request for immediate imperial investiture of Don Carlos, the son of Queen Isabella Farnese, in Parma, Piacenza, and Tuscany. Given the Anglo-Austrian refusal, this time the regent stood his ground, and in March 1721 the treaty of conciliation between France and Spain was signed. In September of that same year, the Peace of Nystad, the best part of which had been negotiated under the auspices of French diplomacy, put an end to the long-standing Great Northern War. However, in this complex diplomatic game Dubois failed to exploit the opportunity France had to get free of Britain's grip. In fact, its ties with Britain remained of vital importance for France because, apart from the dynastic interests at stake, they prevented creation of a new Grand Alliance. But above all, Dubois was deeply convinced that a whole series of interwoven guarantees would render the polarization of the system, and thus any war, less likely. In other words, the aim was to get Spain on one's side without losing Britain, or if you like, to adopt once again the Bourbons' anti-Habsburg policy and conciliate it with the alliance with Britain. As a result, Dubois ended up by bringing the two maritime powers back into the picture. Having convinced Philip V that it was a good idea to have Britain on his side in the event of war with Austria, Dubois invited the British to accede to the 1721 Franco-Spanish treaty, restoring British influence in Spain to a certain degree and accepting payment of a substantial price for British involvement in terms of French and Spanish sea trade (Shennan 1979, 71).[18] All that France and Spain managed to obtain was a call for a congress of Cambrai, which was to deal with this and certain other unresolved questions, but which failed to produce any significant results as such.

THE ALLIANCE OF HANOVER

The chickens came home to roost, as it were, in 1725 when the two dissatisfied powers, Spain and Austria, stipulated a peace treaty that represented a revision of the arrangement put in place in Utrecht, to the detriment of Britain. At the same time, in the north a coalition among Sweden, Russia, and Austria was impending. All of the previous years' successes of British diplomacy were now being questioned: trade with Spain and with America, the balance of power in Italy, the warding off of Russia from the northern straits. Worse still, however, was the gradual emergence of a continental European system that offered little reassurance to Denmark and Hanover in the north, and for Gibraltar in the south, and that, beginning with Sicily, tied the Mediterranean to the Low Countries. The challenge that was launched appeared to concern the economic and trade sectors, in the main.

So Britain, whose preponderance and selected specific interests were now under threat, began readying for war against Spain and Austria as of June 1725; its military preparations were accompanied by untiring diplomatic efforts. Once again, France was of vital importance. From the British point of view, France had two options: either it adopted a strictly defensive stance, which would have made Britain lose the initiative, or it exchanged its support for British support of French policy in Germany, which would have prevented Britain from making peace once again with Austria. As was the case in 1718 and 1721, it was once again important for the British to suppress any French dreams of independence. The alliance of Hanover (Britain, France, Prussia, and Hanover, together with subsequent addition of a number of other member states), signed in September 1725, was structurally more advantageous for Britain than it was for France, in light of all this.[19] More specifically, the membership of Prussia, which the British were really keen on seeing, gave the alliance a clearly anti-Russian, anti-Saxon (and thus pro-Hanoverian) flavor; however, by opposing the Russians, France could no longer play any significant role in the affairs of the north.

The alliance of Hanover encouraged Austria and Spain to come even closer together, by means of both marriage and a military agreement (the first Treaty of Vienna, signed in November 1725); during the subsequent months, Austria also pursued an agreement with Russia and got closer to Saxony, while France and Britain for their part looked for new allies. At the end of 1725, the European system seemed to be strongly polarized around two large alliances. In such circumstances, France's position was a particularly delicate one; it did not possess the financial resources to have a large-scale army of its own, and so it needed the support of others. Furthermore, the two alliances would have been quite prepared to make a settlement, if they had been given the chance to do so, to the detriment of one isolated power. A choice had to be taken, once again: Spain was not sufficiently trustworthy, and Austria was excluded given that France did not intend to guarantee the Pragmatic Sanction. Indeed, there was no real option but to get closer once again to Britain, and to count on Britain's need for French support in turn. However, once again the reciprocal dependence was not of a symmetrical nature, and the constraints on the two allies differed substantially. Suffice it to say that the Vienna alliance jeopardized Britain's wealth, whereas it potentially jeopardized France's territorial integrity. Therefore France had to resign itself to measures that were more advantageous to its stronger ally, the British, especially in the trade sphere (Wilson 1936, 117–28).

In 1726, when Cardinal Fleury came to power, France's dependence on its ally was such that it not only obliged France to accept terms that were more beneficial to Britain but also conditioned relations between Paris and all the other European capitals. Relations with Prussia were dictated, first and foremost, by France's attempt to convince Friedrich Wilhelm to remain loyal to the Hanover alliance. With regard to Russia, although Dubois in his later years was inclined to stipulate an alliance with Peter the Great, these plans failed because of Britain, since Dubois wanted to include London in his scheme of things whereas the tsar would hear nothing of it. Then after the death of Peter the Great in December 1725, Catherine I carried on Russia's anti-British policy, which in turn made the country hostile to France as well. In Sweden, the new French ambassador received instructions to work closely with his English counterpart. Denmark, which was useful in defending Hanover, agreed to sign an agreement with the allies in 1727, thanks largely to French money. Turkey was pushed by the British into the war against Austria and Russia, thus ensuring a reduced Russian presence in the Baltic. The Kingdom of Sicily was evaluated in light of its potential contribution to the anti-Austrian cause, at a time when Britain, to a larger degree than France, was on a collision course with Austria.

Until May 1727, France basically pursued four objectives, in the attempt to govern the crisis rocking Europe at the time. These objectives clearly reveal the difficulties and ambiguities faced by the weaker party in a hegemonic alliance in relation to the stronger ally and to the alliance's enemies. First, France cooperated with Britain in the search for new allies; at the same time, it restrained the British from committing themselves completely to the war. In addition, it constantly communicated and kept a dialogue open with Spain. Finally, it exercised pressure on Austria to accept the conditions imposed on it. Given Britain's intransigence, the only nation that could help Fleury was Austria. By getting closer to Austria, France could also get Spain on its side, which could have counterbalanced British power within the larger scheme of things. In other words, France had to convince Austria and Spain to yield, while at the same time holding Britain back. Although French policy remained subordinate to British policy, Fleury nevertheless managed to recoup a little diplomatic independence. Despite British pressure to do so, France refused to recognize the existence of a casus foederis in the siege of Gibraltar, begun in the meantime by the Spanish; it treated Spain more tactfully than its British ally would have liked to see, and though Britain wanted to deal first with Spanish resistance and then with the Austrians, France proposed to do things in the opposite order (Wilson 1936, 151–67).

Britain began naval operations in the Baltic, in the Indies, and in Spanish waters. These military measures, which increased the risk of a generalized war, were accompanied, however, by diplomatic measures designed to prevent the outbreak of hostilities. To Austria, war would entail a considerable risk; had the promised Spanish subsidies materialized, this would have rendered Austria even more dependent on the Spanish. There was also a serious risk of a French invasion of the Low Countries, and a French and Protestant attack in Germany. Finally, it was also practically impossible to defend the Ostend Company at sea. Indeed, it was no surprise that Austria pursued French involvement, in the hope that the French would be the artifices of an honorable compromise for all concerned. In the other camp, the United Provinces refused to take part in military operations, while Prussia beat a retreat. From the very beginning, Frederick Wilhelm had strong reservations about a war fought on behalf of "Messieurs les Hollandais," in order that the latter could sell "le thé, café et fromage, porcelaines etc. plus cher" (quoted in Gibbs 1958, 417). With regard to France, faced with the real possibility of declaring war on Spain once again (for the second time in the space of a few years), it looked for a way out. Discontent abounded, and nobody really wanted to get involved in a long, uncertain war over the Ostend Company, Gibraltar, and Britain's trading interests in Spain and the Americas, while complaints from various quarters were heard (as happened during the regent's time) about Britain's domination of France (Rain 1945, 164). The scenario was a well-known one: the major ally acted in a bellicose, determined manner, counting on the support of the minor ally, which in turn was called on to double its efforts at mediation, if it wished to avoid entrapment. It is true, on the one hand, that France, together with the United Provinces, tried on more than one occasion to curb Britain's actions between 1726 and 1729[20]; on the other hand, it is also true that Britain was not really unhappy at being held back, provided that its interests were safe.[21]

In practice, Fleury acted as spokesperson for Britain's considerable demands, which were temporarily accepted by Austria (at the Paris Preliminaries in May 1727). Spain, however, did not intend to give in, and its own demands were designed to divide the allies. It seemed to have succeeded in doing so, and French mediation saw Fleury at the center of the diplomatic stage for several months. This marked the beginning of a phase in Anglo-French relations during which it was clear not only that France was trying to escape the grip of the British, by exploiting those spaces that were opening slightly and appealing to Spain's reaction, but also that Britain was responding by closing the French spaces once again, coming to terms with Spain and trying to reach an agreement with Austria.

Between 1727 and 1729, French diplomacy's support for Spanish demands was constant, albeit of a moderate nature. France continued to serve British interests, but this support could no longer be taken completely for granted, and a series of events pointed to the country maneuvering to free itself from the yoke of British dominance. For example, the French ambassador in Madrid received secret orders contrasting with the joint line agreed with the British, while the appointment of Chauvelin, one of the most tenacious critics of British preponderance, to the position of foreign minister (in August 1727) had a clearly anti-British flavor about it (Wilson 1936, 175–76). During those months, France bought time, negotiated, and never tried to speed up discussions. Its reluctance to declare war against Spain encouraged the resistance of the Spanish; and while Britain's ministers were in a hurry to finalize negotiations to show to the English Parliament that the money had not been spent in vain, the French were in no hurry to do so and often acted to check their impatient ally.[22]

It is true that the British were increasingly frustrated by French policy. However, it is also true that in the end British interests were invariably catered to. Moreover, Britain handled such obstacles to its plans well, primarily by cautiously opening up to Austria; some form of agreement with the government in Vienna was needed not only for the purposes of the German policy adopted by George II (who had succeeded to the English throne in 1727) but also in order to prepare the Congress of Soissons, where French diplomacy could have played an important role if only France were to arrive at an agreement with Spain and Austria in advance, thus isolating Great Britain. Moreover, by getting closer to Austria, Britain could frighten France enough to get it to meekly follow British policy (Black 1987, 42–43). As far as Spain was concerned, even though everyone could see that France had no wish to declare war against it, at the same time the French position was not such as to encourage Spain to resist to the very last. Proof of this came in March 1728, when Spain seemed to give in (at the Convention of El Pardo) and agree to the terms dictated by the British.[23] However, not even this was enough to lay British suspicions to rest; Fleury's work as negotiator and mediator had placed him at the center of European diplomacy, and the British were far from happy with this situation (Muret 1949, 179). Hence the British proposal that the members of the Hanover alliance resolve their differences prior to the upcoming congress and present a united front at the negotiating table. This proposal was promptly rejected by the French.

As soon as the Congress of Soissons got under way (June 1728), it was clear that the Spanish and British positions were not going to be easily conciliated. Spain demanded the return of Gibraltar and an end to the illegal activities of British ships in the West Indies, whereas Britain was not prepared to give up Gibraltar and demanded payment of damages for the

Spanish attacks on British ships. Britain hoped that, as had been the case in previous months, France would take its side; however, Fleury often negotiated secretly, playing the part of arbitrator in European affairs and increasingly upsetting the British. Britain was also in a difficult position as a result of French policy vis-à-vis Germany, where French support was needed more than ever to protect the German princes—a role that France traditionally played and that was very dear to George II too. The defense of Hanover also appeared much more precarious without French support.

THE CRISIS AND THE END OF THE ALLIANCE

Thus the minor ally hindered the plans of the hegemon, in particular with regard to the latter's policy vis-à-vis its adversaries. France did not intend to become entrapped in another war with Spain, and so while taking care not to break the alliance it tried to hold Britain back. On two further occasions, between the end of 1728 and the early months of 1729, France, together with the United Provinces, refused to bow to the pressing British demand to declare war on Spain. For its part, Britain was unhappy with the position adopted by France and consequently began to look around for an alternative approach. It was during this period that Britain moved to create an alliance with Austria. Even though this plan failed as a result of Austrian disinterest, it was nevertheless significant for showing that the alliance with France no longer had the full support of the English cabinet. Upon rejection of the plan by Austria, Britain momentarily found itself in the position of having no alternative but to go back to the French and follow them in their negotiations with Spain. However, once again the heterogeneous nature of the alliance was clearly evident from the diverging constraints to which the two nations were subjected. One of the conditions set by Spain—immediate entry of a Spanish garrison in the Duchies and in Tuscany—was too much of a burden for France; this would have meant allowing Spain to alter the balance of power in Italy, and in theory to put it in a position to attempt further coups de main. What was at stake, in short, was the French position in Italy. From the British point of view, it was merely a question of garrisons, which is why it was more inclined to accept Spain's demands.

A similar divergence was increasingly witnessed in Germany, where in order to contain Austria and render it more malleable an agreement with numerous German princes was required, including the Wittelsbachs, who controlled four electorates at the time. France was busy pursuing this line and would have appreciated the involvement of Britain as well, if for no other reason than the subsidies this would have brought. However, as was the case with relations with Spain, relations with Austria also clearly displayed the heterogeneity of the Anglo-French alliance. From the British point of view, tying oneself to the Wittelsbachs would have meant, first and foremost, supporting their territorial claims against Prussia, thereby forcing Austria and Prussia to tighten their own relationship. Second, it would have meant abandoning the idea of a close union between Hanover and Prussia, in favor of a nonconfessional league protecting Wittelsbach interests and potentially capable of challenging Austria's position in central Europe. Here lies the heterogeneity: Great Britain was simply interested in seeing Austria weakened just enough to get it to bend to British demands, but France's aims were much more ambitious. Austria was France's traditional enemy, with whom there were a number of important territorial disputes pending (Württemberg, Alsace, and in particular the Lorraine), and it played a key role in discussions regarding French foreign policy right through the 1720s. The slow reconciliation with Spain, the support provided to certain important German princes, and the alliance with Britain itself were all justified in anti-Austrian terms in the eyes of the French. It was this constant need to bear in mind the potential threat from the Habsburgs, together with the reluctance of their German allies to comply with French plans, that largely accounted for the caution, if not the passivity, often displayed by Fleury during that period (Black 1988b).

In fact, negotiations involving the Wittelsbachs, France, and Great Britain, for formation of an alliance, came to nothing in the summer of 1729. There was much debate in particular about the clause that forbade each party to the proposed alliance from providing guarantees to third parties without the agreement of the other contractual parties, which was a clear (albeit implicit) reference to the Pragmatic Sanction. The comment made by the English plenipotentiary Poyntz at Soissons says a lot about what the British thought of their alliance with France: "I have observed hitherto admirable effects from France's apprehension of our making up with the Emperor which would in some measure cease when we should have tied ourselves up from giving the guaranty or somewhat equivalent to it without her consent" (quoted in Black 1987, 122). Furthermore, the Lords of the Council (George II's inner cabinet) expressed themselves in such a way as to leave no doubt about their views: accepting the clause would have meant "tying up His Majesty's hands from doing a thing, which perhaps thereafter upon a change of circumstances, His Majesty may think advisable"; the suggestion was made to do nothing that "should make the friendship of that Crown [i.e., France] absolutely necessary, or a reconciliation with the Emperor impracticable" (quoted in Black 1986, 18–19). In other words, the alliance with France was perceived as a temporary measure that might have helped obtain better relations with Austria and Spain.

At the end of the Congress of Soissons (July 1729), Spain turned to France in the search for support for its plans in Italy. At this point, all of the limitations of Fleury's prudent diplomacy were revealed. Compared with previous years, France seemed less inclined to follow Britain; notwithstanding this fact, its constraints remained strong enough not to allow it any resolute change in foreign policy. In particular, the French were worried about exposing themselves too much to the risk of war with Austria, so they hesitated to the point where the exasperated Spanish turned to the English. The Treaty of Seville (November 1729) was rightly judged to have been a genuine triumph of British diplomacy. Although jointly signed by the French as well, the document was of British inspiration and in clear contrast to Fluery's diplomatic principles. It contained substantial trading concessions to Britain, in exchange for which the Farnese family were immediately allowed to deploy Spanish garrisons in the Duchies of Parma and Piacenza and in Tuscany. In the event of a reaction from the emperor, British obligations were characterized by a whole series of distinctions, formulated in relation to a specific series of cases,[24] whereas French obligations were such that there could be no doubt France was to bear the burden of the war from the very start. The only thing France obtained was the guaranteed protection of its territory, which, at the time, was in fact under no threat from any other power. Once again, therefore, the outcome from the French point of view was disadvantageous; once again, it was conditioned by the need to avoid breaking up the alliance, as this would have granted the British an exclusive relationship with Spain, among other things. Chauvelin presented the treaty as "un de ces engagements forcés que la necessité, bien plus que les intérêts naturels, fait contracter"[25] (quoted in Muret 1949, 184). Chauvelin's notes, dictated prior to the conclusion of the treaty, reveal his perplexity and disenchantment: war had to be avoided not only because it would have damaged France but also because it would have favored Great Britain too much. A war against Spain would have enabled Britain to extend its commerce and consolidate its naval supremacy, and "while exhausting us can produce utility only for a nation whom she [France] has always rightly regarded as her rival in relation to trade" (quoted in Wilson 1936, 212).

British preponderance at the beginning of the 1720s was based on a diplomatic system involving all of Europe's great powers. Similarly, now that the British position had only just been restored, it was desirable to recoup Austria (this was achieved by the second Treaty of Vienna in March 1731) and reconcile it with Spain (achieved by the third Treaty of Vienna in July 1731). Austria continued to reject allied demands, and consequently Britain had to continue paying subsidies to the German princes in order to guarantee the safety of Hanover. There was a way of coming to an agreement with Vienna—by recognizing the Pragmatic Sanction—but Britain knew that France would not agree to such a move; nor did it wish to overly strengthen the authority of Charles VI over the empire's territories. At the same time, neither Britain nor France was seriously contemplating waging a war against Austria. The result was a deadlock, for which the two allies accused each other. France complained that the British were not prepared to pay the subsidies demanded by the German princes, while the British increasingly believed the French were not at all prepared to fight, or if they were to do so this would happen in the Low Countries (as Chauvelin had in fact suggested), where Britain could not tolerate their reinforcement. Even when the United Provinces realized the need to resort to arms, France once again hindered things by claiming that according to the treaty war had to be preceded by a clear agreement about its aims. In fact, Fleury had in mind readjustment of things in Italy in order to counterbalance Austrian influence.

The principal constraint for both allies, as we know, is to avoid breaking off the alliance. However, this is of course not an absolute constraint. Should an alliance be characterized by a high degree of heterogeneity, and should dependence become increasingly less asymmetrical, then the ally with genuine alternatives will inevitably be tempted to risk breaking off the alliance, especially if such alternatives are made more appealing by the emergence of new constraints. In the case of the Anglo-French alliance, Britain's irritation at the conduct of France and its suspicion of Spanish aims were followed by fear that Fleury's policy would once again push Spain into the arms of Austria, with disastrous consequences: cancellation of the Treaty of Seville, strengthening of Austria, Prussian reluctance to accept Britain's positions, further caution on the part of the German princes, and greater dependence on France. In this situation, Britain's decision to circumvent France and come to an agreement directly with Austria was almost a desperate gamble; even if Britain succeeded, the breaking off of the alliance with France would mean, first and foremost, that Britain would no longer be in a position to condition the decisions of that nation, as it had done for fifteen years, and second it would be the basis for a new Franco-Spanish alliance. If British plans failed, this would mean a reworking of the Anglo-French alliance, but now subject to the conditions established by France.

Two important new circumstances that appeared during the early 1730s were to force Britain into a decision. In Northern Europe, the worsening of British relations with Prussia and Russia led to reemergence of the old fear of a joint Prusso-Russian attack on Hanover. If this happened, could Britain rely on France's support? Doubts now began to surface about the utility of the alliance with France. The second circumstance concerned the outcome of the Anglo-French talks on the policy to adopt in relation to Austria. Vienna was prepared to accept the entry of Spanish garrisons into the Italian duchies and Tuscany, in exchange for recognition of the Pragmatic Sanction, but this proposal was rejected by France. While France continued to oppose the Pragmatic Sanction, it increasingly represented a way out for Britain. In British eyes, the alliance with France was no longer a defensive system for protecting Hanover, Gibraltar, and Britain's trading privileges, but an arrangement that demanded payment of subsidies to the Wittelsbachs and to the Kingdom of Sardinia, a war to get the Austrians out of Italy, and a possible guarantee of the Saxon succession in Poland. There was no real intention of breaking off the alliance with France; indeed, Britain's commitment to France had never been so complete, even in the past, to prevent it from cultivating relations with Austria.

The second Treaty of Vienna saw British and Dutch recognition of the Pragmatic Sanction in exchange for closure of the Ostend Company and Austrian acceptance of the part of the Treaty of Seville dealing with the Italian duchies. There were also two secret clauses, not actually part of the treaty, obliging the United Provinces and Great Britain to compel Spain and France, by force if necessary, to observe the Pragmatic Sanction and requiring Britain to pay Austria those subsidies it would have been due from Spain. The contents of the treaty, and more important how negotiations were conducted (the Treaty of Hanover banned secret, separate negotiations), in practice put an end to the Anglo-French alliance.[26] Fleury was never to forget or forgive that things were done over his head. In the years beforehand, on numerous occasions he could have come to an agreement with Austria himself; but he had been held back by the desire to keep open the possibility of a partition of Austria's dominions. Now Britain granted Austria a guarantee of their very indivisibility. Furthermore, France now found itself in a situation in which neither Austria nor Spain owed it anything, in that the negotiations were conducted by Britain alone. Finally, the worse-case scenario now on the horizon threatened the return of the specter of the Grand Alliance and its rather disconcerting implications.

The divergence between the respective constraints and opportunities that had characterized the relationship between the two allies from the very start culminated at this point in Great Britain coming to an agreement with France's principal foe. However, the asymmetrical nature of the relation of forces between the two nations was somewhat mitigated, as France was now less dependent on Britain than before. Peace, so tenaciously pursued first by Dubois and then by Fleury, in practice reinvigorated France's economic resources and gave the country a certain degree of self-belief once again. Furthermore, the birth in 1729 of Louis, dauphin of France and heir to the French throne, removed long-standing uncertainty over the future of the royal family, which as we know had a decisive effect during the initial phase of the alliance. The problems associated with the succession to the French throne were a factor leading to France's moving away from Spain; but now that such problems no longer existed, the way was clear for close cooperation between the two Bourbon powers. This meant France now had another card to play, as was clearly demonstrated by the Family Compacts agreed over the course of the years that followed. All of these observations point to the one main reason, this time around, France chose not to follow Britain's lead in pursuing yet another agreement that would have penalized French interests. Unlike in the past, France was now in a position to resign itself to doing without those services offered by its ally. Britain was therefore no longer capable of influencing France's decisions. Indeed, some observers believe that if Britain had not broken away from France when it did, France would probably have broken away from Britain shortly thereafter (Horn 1967, 53; Langford 1976, 102).

SIX

The Aggregation Alliance

Great Britain and Prussia, 1756–1762

A HOMOGENEOUS, SYMMETRICAL ALLIANCE

The aggregation alliance, which is the result of a combination of homogeneity and symmetry, consists in the union of two states that react to convergent systemic pressures, and whose bargaining power is approximately balanced. The existence of a common enemy, as we have seen, is one of the most important sources of homogeneity as a rule. However, we have also seen that a common enemy is not a necessary condition, since homogeneity refers to any situation in which close cooperation promises to be mutually beneficial; different, albeit shared, enemies create the premise for a strong relationship between allies. In more general terms, a situation that threatens both parties encourages them to coordinate their policies and strategies to a substantial degree, even if they do not have the same enemies. The most immediate consequence of homogeneity can be seen in the importance each ally gives to the common cause compared to any particular causes. Granted, the latter persist, since not even in the case of homogeneous alliances can one genuinely speak of a harmony of interests; however, any particular causes are either subordinated to or at least conciliated with the common cause. It is this interactive context that predisposes the allies to pursue accommodative bargaining designed to produce a compromise solution beneficial to both parties, with the sole constraint of minimizing the costs of the agreement.

Unlike the other homogeneous alliance examined here, the guarantee alliance, the symmetrical nature of power relations within the aggregation alliance means that both parties are actually capable of exchanging benefits judged by each party to be of similar value. One ally pursues the conformity of the other and is prepared to give the other the services it needs in order to obtain that conformity. This alliance too is first of all and once again an instrument by which each party tries to constrain the behavior of the other party, since the behavior of one ally conditions the other's capacity to act. Nevertheless, in this particular case the conditioning process is a genuinely mutual one; neither party is in the grip of the other, but both influence one another in different ways. As in the case of the other symmetrical alliance examined here, the deadlocked alliance, neither of the two allies is capable of forcing the other to substantially change its behavior. However, unlike in a deadlocked alliance, where the best one can hope for is reluctant and limited cooperation, in an aggregation alliance mutual support prevails thanks to homogeneity; as a result, the allies are prone to coordinate their movements and often work and act together on important diplomatic and strategic issues.

Historians have traditionally been skeptical about the relationship between Great Britain and Prussia during the Seven Years' War, and many seem to doubt the homogeneous nature of their alliance. For example, it has been said that "at no point in their relationship did the aspirations of the two powers converge, apart from the period between the Convention of Westminster and the invasion of Saxony"—that is, from January to August 1756 (Doran 1986, 383). The alliance suffered from a "fundamental weakness" due to the "divergent strategic priorities" of the two members. In Britain's case, the real battle was played out on the high seas and in the colonies, against France, whereas in the case of Prussia it was fought on the mainland, in particular against Austria and Russia. Thus "Prussia and England never actually had a common enemy" (Schweizer 1989, 40), and the Seven Years' War in fact consisted, from the very start, of two parallel conflicts, each characterized by aims that had very little in common with those of the other conflict.[1] Furthermore, it has been claimed that the alliance's aims were "obscure and indefinite," and that it was inevitable that Great Britain should pull out of mainland Europe in the end (Lodge 1923, 108). However, these same scholars also admit that "on the whole, the alliance [...] worked well" (ibidem, 107); they speak of the "harmonious years" between 1758 and 1761 (Doran 1986, 212–50) and they highlight the "common fear of isolation" of the allies and their "need for cooperation in the face of growing external threats and pressures" (Schweizer 1989, 39). On closer examination, therefore, the main criticisms that could be made of the Anglo-Prussian alliance are its brevity, its being played out in a constant state of emergency that invariably concealed some "true nature" of relations between the two countries, and the fact that the allies were involved in completely different fields of play.

However, all of this does not mean that the homogeneity of the alliance, as defined here, is in question. Whether a convergence of pressures is short-term or long-term does not affect the *type* of ensuing relations, just as fighting in different and distant parts of the world does not necessarily hinder a mutually beneficial form of cooperation. Although it may well be true that the outbreak of war led the two countries to get much closer than they would normally have done just a few months earlier, this simply illustrates how interests are profoundly affected by the situational context in which one acts. War is, as a rule, the hardest test of any alliance; it forces those concerned to choose between supporting each other or withdrawing. In the case of the Anglo-Prussian alliance, war drew the two countries closer together. Besides, given the circumstances of the summer of 1756, this is hardly surprising, because each was the only ally available to the other, in a very real sense, and each performed certain extremely important (albeit very different) functions in the eyes of the other. The very same circumstances—that is, the potential isolation that both feared, for their own reasons—were what helped mitigate the effects of the considerable difference in resources between the two allies, and what bestowed a degree of symmetry to a relationship of dependence that, on paper, appeared heavily weighted in Britain's favor.

Even though Prussia emerged from the War of the Austrian Succession as a great power, it was still some way from achieving the territorial cohesion it desired. Indeed, it was only during the course of the war that the name "Prussia" began to be used collectively for all the territories possessed by the House of Brandenburg (Ritter 1954/1968, 94). Nevertheless, during the decade of peace that followed, Frederick II managed to partially counterbalance this structural weakness by means of a careful economic policy, an efficient form of administration, development and attentive use of human and material resources, and above all further consolidating of Prussia's army, which as well as receiving four-fifths of the state's taxable resources (Kennedy 1987, 91) was fully integrated into the nation's economic system. The Prussian army was considered to be "the best army in the world" (Ritter 1954/1969, 18) and "sans conteste la plus belle et la plus solide de l'Europe" (Waddington 1899–1914, vol. I, 2). Thanks to its regional organization, it had the twin advantage of rapid mobilization and guaranteed recruitment, and its training methods meant that under the direct command of the king (judged, in turn, to be the best strategist of his time) it performed better in battle than the other European states' armies (Showalter 1996, 105–116). Frederick thus hoped he could deal with the numerically superior joint Austro-Russian forces. In 1756, he could count on sufficient funding to cover about three military campaigns (Ritter 1954/1968, 96–100).

Insular Great Britain clearly did not have the same security needs as Prussia. Britain's military fleet was so strong that only France could have tried to take it on alone (Middleton 1985, 24), while the training of its crews was second to none. Furthermore, its remarkable financial resources, based on a solid system of public credit, put it in the enviable position of being able to spend more money on the war effort than was provided by tax revenue alone. The success of the "financial revolution" in turn was based on the government's ability to levy new taxes, together with constant expansion of trade thanks to the protection of the fleet, which proved very capable of hindering other nations' merchant vessels (Kennedy 1987, 80–81). From 1740 onward, these questions were at the center of a heated debate between the supporters of a purely naval strategy and those who believed in combating the enemy on land; this debate was to continue in this vein throughout the course of the Seven Years' War. Which approach was better for dealing with France? Should a predominantly naval strategy be adopted? This option promised reduced fiscal pressure, further growth of trade, and colonial conquests to be used in peace negotiations as a trade-off against France's conquests in Europe—starting with Hanover. Or should support be sought from one or more allies in mainland Europe, from among those who at a given time seemed most willing to fight France? Such a policy would deny France confidence in achieving its continental goals, but it would entail certain financial and human costs often deemed excessively high (Pares 1936).

Many English politicians supported the naval strategy when they were sitting on the opposition benches, but as soon as they got into power they ended up planning continental alliances. William Pitt was the best example of such a politician, and one who managed to combine the two strategies to great effect. Pursuit of an alliance with Russia toward the end of the 1730s and the attempt to preserve the Old System (the traditional alliance with Austria and the United Provinces) as long as possible during the first half of the 1750s are further proof of a constant feature of British foreign policy from the War of the Spanish Succession to the Seven Years' War. Pitt was subsequently to tenaciously defend the nation's recent alliance with Prussia. Commitment to a continental war was designed not only to prevent France from transferring resources from the army to the navy, as the Duke of Newcastle suggested,[2] but as well to pursue various other objectives: defending the Low Countries, allaying the danger of an invasion, keeping the Jacobites at bay, protecting Hanover, and last but not least making up for services that the allies would request but that the fleet was not capable of providing (Rodger 1992). In fact, Britain's naval power at the time was formidable, but it was neither unlimited nor fungible. This often created problems for Britain with regard to its alliance politics (Black 1988c) and was to be evident in its relations with Prussia as well.[3] In short, the country could rely on a naval policy only if it were completely indifferent to European affairs, which it never wanted, or was able, to be.

THE CONVENTION OF WESTMINSTER AND THE OUTBREAK OF THE SEVEN YEARS' WAR

To account for the Convention of Westminster, which although not a real alliance from the technical point of view nevertheless bound Britain and Prussia to an agreement, we could say that in 1756 both had good reason to fear a war in Europe, neither was under any illusion about the existing diplomatic arrangements, and each hoped to obtain (through direct agreement with the other) the conformity not only of the other party but also of that party's allies. Although Britain and Prussia were subject to very different constraints, these constraints led both countries in the same direction.

Since 1742, Frederick had feared that one day Austria would try to ally itself with France in order to win back Silesia, which Prussia had just conquered. In view of this possible event, in 1748 he proposed formation of an Anglo-Prussian alliance.[4] This idea, and the ensuing measures, were noticeable not only because of their long-sightedness but also because at that time there were various points of tension between the two powers. British diplomacy was busy trying to find a way to consolidate the country's ties with

Austria, Berlin was considered the focal point of Jacobite intrigue, and there were pending issues that made bilateral relations difficult. Indeed, between 1751 and 1756 there were no British diplomatic representatives in Berlin, while Prussia had only one agent in London (a certain Louis Michell, who was not even a secretary of legation). In other words, diplomatic relations at that time were almost completely suspended (Lodge 1923, 78–80).

The extension of hostilities between France and Britain in North America and at sea during the course of 1755 caused the British government concern regarding the fate of the Low Countries, and above all of Hanover, both of which would have been extremely vulnerable to a Franco-Prussian attack. Britain's response, consisting in three measures, was predictable enough. First, it decided to reinvigorate the Old System. Second, it was to offer subsidies to those German princes who were prepared to supply troops. Third, it wanted to come to an agreement with Russia, once again on the basis of financial aid, since Russia was the sole power that Frederick really feared (Pares 1936, 445–46). Newcastle's calculation was extremely clear: "The King of Prussia sees [...] that by taking part with France and introducing war in the Empire, he may draw upon himself seventy thousand Russians" (quoted in Browning 1975, 228). Austria, however, which had thrown itself headlong into the pursuit of an alliance with France, let all British proposals fall; the United Provinces moved increasingly toward neutrality, and as far as the smaller German states were concerned, in autumn 1755 an agreement was reached with Hesse only. As for Russia, a convention was signed at the end of September according to which Elizabeth undertook, against payment of subsidies, to keep more than 50,000 men in Livonia for four years, together with a naval force along the coast of the province (Kaplan 1968, 3–28). The secret clauses in the convention mentioned a "common enemy," without revealing its identity, and this was to create enormous problems over the following months. Moreover, the treaty had yet to be ratified, which would require some considerable time; yet more time was needed to gather the promised troops in Livonia. Then there was the fact that Livonia was situated a long way from the sites of those military operations that interested Britain most. In other words, the situation was far from reassuring; Hanover was inevitably going to be lost during the course of the first military campaign.

Prussia was not exactly in an enviable position either, threatened as it was by both Austria and Russia. The two empresses, allies since 1746, were waiting for the chance to settle their score with a problematic neighbor. In 1753, Frederick got knowledge of the secret clause in the Austro-Russian agreement concerning the reconquest of Silesia and stepped up Prussia's military preparations. However, he noticed that while British diplomacy was extremely busy on the mainland in an attempt to gather together the greatest possible number of forces to use in countering the Franco-Prussian alliance, France had adopted a hesitant, inconclusive stance. During the course of 1755, Frederick suggested to the French that they attack Hanover, only to be told that this was *his* duty; similarly, his attempt to convince Louis XV to invade the Low Countries proved to be in vain (Ritter 1954/1968, 101). The alliance with France was due for renewal in 1756, and both sides took it for granted that this would be done. However, Frederick also reached the conclusion that his ally would not be much help against an Austro-Saxon army on the Elbe, or a Russian army on the Niemen. Such uncertain circumstances formed the backdrop to an unexpected proposal in August of that year: Britain suggested an agreement designed to keep the peace in Germany. At first, Frederick's response was rather vague, but when he got word of the Anglo-Russian treaty he suddenly gave orders to Michell to immediately sign the proposed agreement—the Convention of Westminster (January 16, 1756). Under the terms of this document, Prussia and Britain undertook not only to refrain from attacking each other's territories but also to prevent foreign troops from entering and passing through Germany.[5] The aim of the operation was clear to all concerned: Frederick, by means of Great Britain, had "chained the Russian bear" (Ritter 1954/1968, 101), and Newcastle, for his part, obtained a dual guarantee concerning Hanover, according to which Prussia would not invade and France would find it much more difficult to do so thereafter (Pares 1936, 447). In other words, the two countries had the same aim, that is, to maintain peace in central-northern Europe, through the influence each had on its respective allies, even though both allies had different enemies in mind, and despite both of them believing they could reconcile their new agreement with their respective existing alliances.

At first sight, the two powers thus had good reason to be happy. Previous tensions were removed or resolved, and an official representative of the British government, Andrew Mitchell, was now in Berlin. However, their calculations proved groundless within the span of just a few months. At St. Petersburg, problems began to surface as of February concerning the identity of the common enemy, who had remained unnamed in the treaty signed the previous September. At the time of ratification of the convention, Russia submitted a clause according to which its armed forces were to attack Prussia only, should the latter attack either Britain or one of its allies (Kaplan

1968, 41). Even though Elizabeth's government continued to be considered corruptible and manipulable, the tsarina was motivated by strong anti-Prussian feelings, which became increasingly evident as time went by, and which the British proved incapable of mitigating. It took another year (until January 1757) before Russia officially sided with the Austro-French alliance; however, despite British diplomatic efforts and offers of financial support, the Russian position was already clear: in Elizabeth's view, the Convention of Westminster had removed any meaning from the subsidies agreement (Schweizer 1989, 18–19).

The second important consequence of the Anglo-Prussian alliance was the breaking off of relations between France and Prussia. Frederick counted on convincing Louis XV that neutralization of Hanover was compatible with French interests—the right time to attack it was before the conclusion of the Anglo-Russian treaty, whereas afterward would be too late—and until the end of March he tried to get France to renew their alliance. Furthermore, the King of Prussia saw the differences between France and Austria as incurable: "jamais la France ne méconnaitra ses intérêts au point de vouloir travailler à l'agrandissement de la nouvelle maison d'Autriche,"[6] he wrote in February (quoted in Doran 1986, 41). However, he seriously underestimated the pride of what was still considered the most important monarchy in Europe, which would not tolerate the idea that a client-state (as Prussia was considered at Versailles) would arrogate the right to tell it what it could and could not do. Moreover, the French were in a state of undeclared war with Britain, and it was not admissible that one of their allies would come to an agreement with their enemy. The French government's decision to cut its ties with Prussia, however, had the logical effect of pushing it toward Austria, thus completing the "reversal of alliances" (first Treaty of Versailles, May 1, 1756). This, and the declaration of Dutch neutrality, represented the end to Britain's dream of preserving the Old System; then in June, Russia repeated that the treaty with Great Britain would only be applied in the event of war against Prussia. In other words, the effects of the Convention of Westminster proved disastrous for its signatories.

Despite Britain's perseverance in trying to change the direction of Russian policy, Frederick was extremely skeptical about the outcome of such efforts. From May 1756 onward, when he learned of the Austro-French alliance, he constantly asked Mitchell: "Are you sure of the Russians?" (Doran 1986, 54). Then at the beginning of July, when Mitchell officially informed him of Elizabeth's position, Frederick came to the conclusion that the Anglo-Russian treaty was worthless, and that London was no longer capable of influencing Russian decisions. Movements of Russian troops in Livonia and Bohemia during the month of June had already led Frederick to begin mobilization of his own forces, and his suspicions about Saxony, Poland, and Sweden's intentions evoked the specter of encirclement of Prussia by powerful forces intent on dismembering the country. Frederick's difficult position, together with the international isolation of Britain, led Britain and Prussia to get closer; indeed, in June of that year the Earl of Holdernesse[7] went so far as to suggest that the two countries form a defensive alliance. However, such a move would have pushed Russia into the arms of Austria and tied Frederick's hands even further. Although this proposal came to nothing, it is nevertheless significant because it reveals the mounting pressures on the two countries (Lodge 1923, 89–90). During the same period (June 1756), Frederick made a long series of suggestions: Britain should reinforce the Hanoverian army, double the subsidies to Hesse and stipulate similar agreements with other German principalities, pull Denmark to its side, and rebuild relations with the United Provinces. The only request he made for Prussia was the dispatch of a British naval squadron in the Baltic (Doran 1986, 72–74, 82–84).

In July Frederick learned that Austria and Russia had put off any offensive to the following year; nevertheless, he decided to continue with mobilization of the army. At the same time, following Mitchell's advice, on three occasions he asked Maria Theresa for reassurances, only to receive a series of vague, somewhat disconcerting responses. The desire not to appear the aggressor (this was the sense of his requests to Austria) forced him to delay the start of hostilities. However, this delay proved useful, and not only from the diplomatic point of view, since as a result thereof France, and in particular Russia, could not enter the war until the following year. Having lost all remaining faith in Britain's ability to curb Russia's actions, Frederick prepared the country for preventive war: in other words, he preferred to take all the risks associated with such a move rather than passively wait until Prussia's enemies had the time to properly organize their own offensive, which would have given them an unbeatable advantage (Ritter 1954/1968, 103–107). At the end of August, Frederick's army thus invaded Saxony, which was about to join the anti-Prussian alliance, and in doing so began what was to be the Seven Years' War.

During the course of the previous two months, the British government had been debating whether the country should run the risk of definitively alienating Russia, or of losing the chance of finally separating France and

Prussia. In July, it decided in any case to support Frederick should Prussia come under attack, while at the same time trying to convince him not to attack first. British pressure was never applied with any great force, however, as Britain now realized just how vulnerable Prussia was on two separate fronts, given that Russia no longer paid any heed to British entreaties (Rose 1914, 82–83). Newcastle, in the face of Russian hostility toward Prussia and the virtual inevitability of war, saw Prussia as "the best if not the only card we have left" (quoted in Doran 1986, 84), just as Prussia saw Britain as the only power whose diplomacy could try to break up the coalition of nations encircling Prussia, whose wealth could be used to procure new allies, and whose navy could prove useful in the Baltic. The homogeneity of the Anglo-Prussian alliance was thus purely the precipitate of the situational context in which the two powers found themselves, despite their efforts, at the moment. This alliance, originally formed for peacekeeping purposes, now found itself conducting a war that went well beyond the signatories' original designs; given that each of the allies valued to a similar degree the services the other could offer, the second characteristic of their union was its symmetrical nature.

THE FUNCTIONING OF THE ALLIANCE

The most characteristic trait of an aggregation alliance, as we have said, is the reciprocal support the allies provide to one another, from positions of substantial parity. However, this support does not reflect a generic uniformity of views so much as a constant attempt to constrain the other's movements, that is, pursuit of the conformity of the other ally. The favored means of obtaining such conformity is the reciprocal promise of gains (emerging benefits). The underlying grounds for stipulation of the Convention of Westminster have already been examined (protection of Hanover, together with dissuasion of France and blocking of Russian actions), and we have seen how such requirements, despite their divergent nature, all point in the same direction: toward the prevention of war in central-northern Europe. Once war broke out, the pursuit of the other's conformity took a most typical form in banning any separate peace agreement, as decreed by the 1758 treaty and reiterated by each renewal thereof up to the crisis of 1762. It is also important to understand that neither party could ever dictate the terms of the agreement. According to Peter Blau (1964, 118–25), supplying those benefits that others cannot easily do without is the easiest and commonest way of obtaining power. However, if A needs a service offered by B but does not wish to find itself dependent on B, A may in turn offer B a service that the latter requires. The net outcome of this form of interaction is thus an exchange of services whereby A and B promise one another emerging benefits of comparable value. This is, to put it briefly, the situation that, in 1756, Great Britain and Prussia found themselves in.

What are the most important theoretical propositions that characterize this type of alliance? First and foremost, the interaction of symmetry and homogeneity produces an accommodative type of negotiating, resulting in a compromise solution that clearly reflects bargaining power parity. Homogeneity facilitates exchange of services, since the two allies take steps they would have taken in any case in such circumstances. Prussia was fighting for its own survival, and Britain had already come to the conclusion that it would support financially all those who were willing to contain a French offensive in Germany. In this way, Prussia and Great Britain gave rise to a kind of division of labor, whereby each saw to its own tasks and in doing so produced results that both parties judged satisfactory. That the agreement was the result of a compromise can be clearly seen from the negotiations leading up to the 1758 convention; both powers were forced to give up some of their initial demands—Prussia had to abandon its request for a British fleet in the Baltic, while Britain had to renounce any demands for a substantial Prussian contribution to the Hanoverian "army of observation."[8] Another of Frederick's demands was never going to be completely satisfied: the request for a veritable English army in Germany. Nevertheless, apart from carrying the burden of maintaining the entire army of observation, Britain also gradually increased its contingent, which by 1762 had reached a size unthinkable only six years earlier. The symmetrical nature of the relationship was evident even at the end of the alliance, during the early months of 1762, when the English government tried in vain to force Prussia to provide specific guarantees of peace in exchange for renewal of Britain's financial aid. Frederick's desperate military situation contrasted significantly with Britain's successes, and this gave Britain occasion to think it could dictate the terms of their alliance. However, the sudden defection of Russia reestablished the symmetry of the Anglo-Prussian alliance and allowed Frederick to get free of Britain's grip; he renounced the subsidies, thereby maintaining Prussia's freedom of movement.

Second, in an aggregation alliance both parties seriously fear abandonment, since the symmetry of the alliance makes one party dependent on the other and the defection of one ally could have extremely serious consequences for the other. The ban on separate peace agreements was specifically designed to avoid this. At the same time, the risk of being abandoned is mitigated by the homogeneity of the alliance. Neither of the two parties, both of whom are induced into remaining united by fear of isolation and by their own weaknesses, would ever entertain the idea of abandoning the other as long as the latter provides its support, and as long as such support is necessary.[9] In the case at hand, there was only one brief moment during the summer of 1757 when British policy still seemed unclear, and when Frederick actually thought of making a separate peace agreement with France. Pitt was well aware that Prussia had to be offered various inducements (prevention of the neutralization of Hanover, an offer of financial aid) to keep it from defecting. Finally, even after Britain achieved all of its war aims, it did not really think about abandoning Prussia but instead about making British support conditional: preservation of the tie was still considered important in that it could be used to induce the ally to adhere to British policy. As regards entrapment, such a risk is of limited importance in this kind of alliance; both parties are faced with hostile powers that have also formed coalitions, and their involvement in warfare is the logical outcome of such a situation. This is why neither is concerned about being dragged into a war that is not its concern. As we have seen, even though Britain would have preferred peace to war, in the summer of 1756 it did not really do very much to hold Prussia back, and it certainly did not threaten withdrawal from the alliance—the ultimate method of avoiding entrapment—in the event of Prussia declaring war.

A common policy with regard to adversaries is also in keeping with the characteristics of the aggregation alliance. Regardless of whether they adopt a strategy of flexibility or firmness, the two allies tend to act in concert. On two separate occasions during the course of the war (in 1760 and 1761), Great Britain and France negotiated in order to put an end to their colonial conflict; on both occasions, the British government had come to a previous understanding with the Prussian government, kept the latter constantly notified of the latest developments, and protected its interests vis-à-vis French demands. The 1760 negotiations led nowhere because, among other things, Britain and France failed to find a way of conciliating any eventual agreement with the claims of their respective allies. This does not mean, however, that the British government gave up on a beneficial agreement in the name of the Anglo-Prussian alliance; it means, more simply (and more importantly) that the failure of negotiations at that moment played into both

British and Prussian hands. Similarly, the allies informed each other of the overtures from their adversaries in 1757 and 1758, and Frederick notified Pitt of his contacts with France during the course of 1760. Up to the autumn of 1761, both parties basically agreed to continue with the war. Once again, it should be pointed out that their respective objectives differed: in the last phase of the war, Great Britain was essentially pursuing a crushing victory in the colonies and at sea, while Prussia was fighting for its very survival. However, this did not prevent the two allies from cooperating and working together not only on formulation of the policy to be followed with regard to both war and peace but also on how their military operations were to be conducted. The most famous example of this was the British raids along the French coast, suggested by Frederick and subsequently approved and put into practice by Pitt. Regarding relations with the other powers, there can be no hiding the fact that Britain coldly ignored Frederick's attempts to get the Ottoman Empire on their side, or to involve Spain in exchange for granting concessions in Italy. However, the two allies made considerable diplomatic efforts to find fresh allies and weaken (or prevent the strengthening of) the enemy alliance.

Finally, the symmetrical dependence that characterizes this type of alliance should lead each ally to worry about the excessive strengthening of the other, since this would fundamentally alter the relation of forces between the two. However, the homogeneity of their alliance substantially mitigates this fear. Consequently, the alliance power dilemma is far less dramatic, or may not even exist at all. During the course of the war, one ally was never tempted to withdraw its support for the other because it believed that the latter was growing too strong. In fact, British concern was focused in the opposite direction; there was a real risk that an exhausted Prussia would give in, and for this reason it had to be provided with all the support Britain could muster. It was only during the initial stages of the war that Holdernesse expressed doubts about the outcome of the first campaign; if Prussia were defeated, Hanover would also be lost; but if Prussia won, it would not be easy for Britain to convince the Prussians to use arms against the French.[10] The Prussians, by contrast, were not at all concerned about Britain's victories. The geographical divide separating the two allies, and their involvement in theaters of war so distant the one from the other, helped remove any potential sources of rivalry and friction that might exist between states bordering one another, or gravitating toward the same geographical area, and thus inevitably sensitive to any increase in a neighbor's power.

THE ADJUSTMENT PHASE

At the news of the invasion of Saxony, the British government reacted immediately.[11] Prussia had to be supported, and Hanover needed defending; hence the immediate deployment of an army composed of various German contingents, financed partly by Great Britain and partly by the king in his role as elector of Hanover. Nevertheless, Newcastle's resignation at the beginning of October marked the beginning of a phase of ministerial instability and delays destined to continue almost until the summer of the following year. Such slowness was partly due to George II being tempted to negotiate the neutrality of his electorate, and for several months in fact talks were held between Hanover and Austria that proved seriously embarrassing for Britain's ministers and came up against those obstacles put in place by French diplomacy (Lodge 1923, 98). It took a year to resolve the clash of Hanoverian and British policies.

Newcastle's place was taken by the Pitt-Devonshire ministry, until March. This short-lived, precarious arrangement lacked support from Parliament or the crown. As has been said, in the past Pitt had expressed the view that Britain should not have been involved in military operations on the European continent; however, recent changes, such as the Austro-French alliance and Dutch neutrality, led him to rethink his position on several issues. Furthermore, now that he was in power he had to make decisions that took account of both the interests of the crown—Hanover could not be left to its fate—and the views of Parliament and public opinion—defense of Hanover, a crown possession rather than part of British territory, was both costly and unpopular. During his first few weeks in power, Pitt received a total of four political-military documents from Frederick, containing a series of recommendations and suggestions: incursions along the French coast; diversionary attacks in Africa, India, and America; employment of the Ottoman Empire against the Russians, and of the Kingdom of Sardinia against the French; conquest of Corsica; funding of a German army; and sending English warships into the Baltic (Tunstall 1938, 173–74). The two leaders agreed on many of those matters. Even though the felicitous blend of naval and European operations that characterized Pitt's strategy was to emerge only gradually over the course of the following months, the underlying approach was immediately evident: the naval and land operations were both part of the same struggle against France. In mainland Europe, coordination between the two components was guaranteed by "containment operations" designed to hinder France's movements, thanks to a combination of British naval forces and Prussian and Hanoverian army forces (and in the end, British troops as well), and at sea by a blockade of French ports, under the cover of which offensive operations could be launched in North America, the West Indies, Africa, and India (Schweizer 1989, 44–45).

In February 1757, Pitt made his first important move when he created an army of observation, presented to Parliament and the king in a highly able manner. The task of this army, composed of contingents from Hanover, Hesse, and Prussia (the latter two funded by Great Britain), was to defend Hanover and protect Frederick's right flank. Given that Prussia could have been caught out along its flanks from Hanover, the army of observation was needed to ensure the success of the containment strategy. However, military operations proved unsuccessful;[12] after his initial victory in Saxony, Frederick now had to face the might of all those powers that had circled him in the meantime. In his second campaign, he found himself up against Austria, an imperial army, Russia, and Sweden, together with the worrying prospect of the imminent arrival of French forces as well. The bitter defeat at Kolin (June 16, 1757) effectively prevented him from providing support to the army of observation, and within the space of just a few months it was to cost him the loss of Silesia as well. In the meantime, the French army, having occupied Prussia's western provinces, now moved into Hesse and defeated the army of observation commanded by the Duke of Cumberland (the son of George II) at Hastenbeck (July 26, 1757), thus conquering the majority of Hanover and Brunswick. In September, Cumberland was forced to sign the humiliating Convention of Klosterzeven, obliging him to disband the army (Charteris 1925, 302–17). Prussia's central provinces were thus now exposed to French invasion, while the Russians seemed intent on occupying the whole of eastern Prussia.

Pitt, who together with Newcastle had returned to power in June, now had to remedy an extremely difficult situation. One of his major concerns was to reassure Prussia, which in the circumstances could be tempted to sign a separate peace treaty with France (Black 1992, 168). After the defeat at Kolin, Frederick asked Britain for three things: an immediate diversionary attack on French ports; reinforcements for the army of observation; and sending British warships into the Baltic, where the Russian fleet was blockading Memel (Schweizer 1989, 49). Even though the defeat at Hastenbeck had, in the meantime, reduced the military significance of the planned raid on Rochefort, it was carried out all the same (in September) to give an indication of a reaction to both France and Prussia (Middleton 1985, 29–30). Nevertheless, Pitt immediately rejected the idea of running to the ally's aid with men and ships, and this was met with a bitter reaction from Prussia.[13]

During the same period (in June to be exact), the King of Prussia also sounded out Mitchell with regard to the chances of receiving financial aid in the event of extreme need, and this time Prussia's request was met positively by Britain, which was prepared to offer its ally the highest sum ever paid in the form of subsidies, in exchange for Prussia's undertaking not to stipulate a separate peace (Eldon 1938, 96). These are the topics around which negotiations between the two powers centered until the agreement of April 1758, as we shall see shortly. However, the turning point that was to remove all doubts concerning the British position came in autumn 1757, when George II, who was extremely embarrassed about the humiliation previously suffered at Klosterzeven, turned to his ministers to get him out of this tight corner; the ministers, who pointed out to George that what he had done as elector was incompatible with his role as British monarch, convinced him to repudiate the convention entered into by his son. The British government was to pay the entire cost of the newly reconstituted army, which was to be commanded (another gesture toward Frederick) by Ferdinand of Brunswick, one of the King of Prussia's best-known officers. From that moment on, George II's hands were tied; operations in Westphalia became an integral part of British policy and were no longer influenced by Hanoverian considerations. The defense of Hanover was now the British government's task, and as such it was associated with the alliance with Prussia. The unexpected news of Frederick's brilliant victories against the French at Rossbach (November 5, 1757) and a month later against the Austrians at Leuthen (December 5, 1757), followed by the liberation of Prussia and Silesia, led to a level of popular support for the King of Prussia hitherto unheard of in Britain; the king was greeted as a "protestant hero," and it was now much easier for Pitt to stabilize relations with Prussia.[14]

From the summer onward, the two allies were busy negotiating the terms of their cooperation. The subsidy that Britain offered Prussia was substantial, but apparently not enough. As we have already mentioned, Frederick wanted British naval support in the Baltic; this demand, which dated from the previous summer, was reiterated on several occasions, albeit to no avail (Black 1988c, 100–102). From the British point of view, such a move would have been extremely risky, since entry to the Baltic was controlled by Denmark and Sweden at the time, and these two nations possessed considerable naval forces and were both inclined to support the French should that be needed. If the British could not be sure about the Danish position at least, an entire new fleet would have had to be commissioned, and this was something Britain could not afford to do (Middleton 1985, 22–23). A second Prussian request concerned the sending of English troops, as proof of London's commitment to the war on the continent. However, for some time now the British army had been undersized in relation to the armies of the other great European powers;[15] furthermore, half of it was busy on the other side of the ocean, while the other half was nonoperative (ibidem, 25). It was difficult to recruit more troops, for financial reasons officially (workers were needed in the industrial and trade sectors) although the real reasons were political: the deep-rooted belief that broad conscription was incompatible with the constitutional forms of the country meant that every British government was afraid to challenge Parliament on this matter (Eldon 1938, 108). Frederick did not try to hide his disbelief; calculations based on commerce and industry could not be more important than national security.[16] Despite his pointing out, ahead of Pitt, that the way to save America was to not tolerate the French becoming the leaders of Europe,[17] all the British government had to reply was that "money has always been looked upon as the proper and most effectual contingent of England"[18]—further proof of the ministerial doctrine whereby "we must be merchants while we are soldiers."[19]

Great Britain, in turn, asked Prussia to make a substantial contribution (12,000 troops) to operations in Westphalia. The King of Prussia, however, did not agree, not only because the military situation in which the country found itself meant he could not afford to do so but above all because he did not intend to play the role of a mercenary forced to accept terms dictated by another party. Thus it was that in February 1758 relations between Prussia and Britain reached a deadlock that was resolved only when both parties simultaneously submitted much more moderate demands. Prussia simply asked for the strengthening, by 10,000 men, of the army of observation (which would have brought it to a total of 50,000), a purely symbolic naval presence in the Baltic, and a token force to be used to occupy Emden, which had just been liberated. The British, for their part, dropped their request for Prussian troops and simply asked that Frederick pledge to leave Ferdinand the cavalry divisions that had been recently seconded to him (Waddington 1899–1914, vol. II, 195–208).

This then led up to the signing of the subsidies convention, on April 11, 1758. The document was accompanied by a statement made by George II, in which the king accepted Prussia's demands, with the usual exception of the request for British ships in the Baltic. The convention itself, stipulated for the term of one year, consisted of four articles, of which only two (the second and the third) were of any substantial importance. The second article was a British pledge to pay Prussia £670,000 (the equivalent of four million crowns) to enable Frederick to maintain and increase his military forces, which "shall act in the manner most advantageous to the common cause"; in fact, the convention acknowledged that the King of Prussia, having to deal with both Austria and Russia, could not take on any commitments to the army of observation and was free to act as he thought best. The third article bound both parties not to sign any kind of treaty—including any peace treaty, of course—with enemy nations, unless by joint agreement with the other party. This ban on separate peace constituted each ally's guarantee to the other (Schweizer 1989, 61).

THE PERIOD OF CONCORD

The exchange underlying the Anglo-Prussian alliance was thus clear. Britain's granting of a subsidy to Prussia guaranteed maintenance of the best European army of that age, while the army of observation, in defending Hanover, also protected Prussia's western flank. Ferdinand could now successfully counter French actions in Westphalia, Hanover, and Hesse, facilitating Prussia's bitter struggle against Austria and Russia. Even though Frederick continued to complain about Britain's failure to provide Prussia with naval support in the Baltic, he could not deny that the army paid for by Britain had succeeded in covering Prussia's western flank against attack from what could have been its most formidable enemy. This strategic arrangement also meant that a substantial part of France's resources were pledged to operations in mainland Europe that were both draining and of dubious utility. Naval incursions on the French coast completed the picture of containment. Thus it was that Britain could now commit all its energies to conquering the oceans and the colonies, while at the same time avoiding the danger of invasion and preventing the French from sending reinforcements overseas (Robson 1957, 472–73).

It has been pointed out that of all the alliance treaties signed during the Seven Years' War, the two Anglo-Prussian conventions were the least two significant, since both bore negative connotations; the first was designed to avert a war in Germany, while the second aimed to avoid any separate peace (Doran 1986, 175–76). This view, however, underestimates the great importance of simple, essential pledges. The division of tasks between the two allies allowed one to survive and the other to expand its colonial empire. The 1758 convention meant that Prussia was now tied to Britain, as Pitt finally succeeded in putting his continental European system in order; Prussia, for its part, managed to constrain British action and could now look forward to a diplomatic partnership that promised to put an end to isolation and influence British policy in Prussia's favor (Schweizer 1989, 62).

This, then, was the general framework within which the two allies operated for more than three years, and they both benefited from such cooperation. At the end of 1759, the tables were turned; Prussia's victories in 1756 and 1757 had come at a time when Britain had only defeats to show for its efforts, and as such they contributed to bridging the gap between the resources of the two powers, strengthening the symmetry of their alliance. The year 1759 proved to be Britain's *annus mirabilis*, with important victories and conquests in the West Indies, Africa, India, and North America (Middleton 1985, 130–46; and Waddington 1899–1914, vol. III, 252–344). Furthermore, France's invasion plan was thwarted, and with two decisive blows to Louis XV's fleet Britain finally gained naval supremacy (Corbett 1907, vol. II, 33–44 and 53–70). Prussia had just come out of two military campaigns in which it lost its eastern province together with parts of Saxony and Silesia, and as a result its position was increasingly in the balance (Robson 1957, 474–75). On top of this, there were also a number of misunderstandings and disagreements between the two allies; but notwithstanding everything, until 1761 the common cause represented a really strong tie for both allies. The crown's discourses during this period often contained words of praise for Frederick (Doran 1986, 213), and the original subsidies treaty was subsequently renewed through 1760.

The joint effort against the enemies was organized on two traditional levels, military and diplomatic. Despite the failure of the first naval attack on Rochefort, Pitt continued with his incursion strategy, launching raids on Cherbourg and St. Malo in 1758 and on Belle Île in 1761. Despite being of a limited nature, these military operations had the effect of alarming the French, causing them to call back troops employed in the war against Germany. The indirect consequence of raids was thus a reduction in pressure on Frederick and Ferdinand; indeed, it was Frederick who suggested to Pitt to adopt such measures, and although he would have preferred direct help in Germany or in the Baltic he nevertheless considered such diversionary tactics useful (Rose 1914, 92–93). Ferdinand, for his part, made a good start as head of the army of observation (now renamed "His Britannic Majesty's Army"), occupying the French to the full (Savory 1966, 47–66). From 1758, Pitt began to send an increasing number of troops to Germany, including English soldiers (Eldon 1938, 113–14); following Ferdinand's victory at Minden (August 1759), Pitt proposed that the army in Germany be strengthened by a further 10,000 men, and the year after he took similar measures. In 1760, the British contingent (cavalry and infantry) totaled some 20,000 men, thus accounting for a quarter of the entire army (Savory 1966, 202). Although this was a fairly modest entity, it still represented an incredible step forward given Britain's reluctance to provide troops only two years earlier. Within this context of naval wars of conquest and defensive wars on the European mainland, it was vitally important to consolidate European victories to avoid having to give up some of the colonial conquests to pay for territories lost in Europe. Hence the importance of Prussia's survival, which among other things explains the tone with which Pitt greeted Frederick's victories.[20]

Britain's behavior in relation to Prussia did not reflect any loyalty as such, of course, but rather the homogeneity of their alliance, as defined herein. This homogeneity was equally clear within the context of the diplomatic relations the two allies had with their enemies (during peace talks) and with other nations. Although some of the other ally's initiatives were occasionally met with a degree of coldness, there was nevertheless basic agreement between the British and Prussian governments. As early as the spring of 1758, in fulfilling its undertakings with Berlin, London tried once again to resolve the question of the neutrality of the United Provinces and Denmark in the alliance's favor, and to get Sweden to leave the enemy coalition. These maneuvers failed, however. Sweden even refused a British diplomatic representative entry into the country; Denmark signed a subsidy agreement with France (in May); and the usual trade issues with the Dutch persisted, given that Britain was not prepared to make any concessions to the United Provinces (Eldon 1938, 111–12). The most important thing at stake was the relationship with Russia. Britain continued to believe that a separate peace agreement between Prussia and Russia could be reached, which would relieve the pressure on Frederick and put an end to his insistent demands for naval support in the Baltic. British diplomats, having been informed about the disagreements between the Russians and their Austrian allies, offered a considerable sum in an attempt to bribe the Russian cabinet secretary and promised subsidies to Russia. But once again, Britain's policies did not succeed; at the end of 1758 Austria paid Russia a substantial sum, and it was Frederick himself who suggested to Pitt to break off negotiations with Russia in order not to give the latter the impression that Britain was pursuing peace regardless of the cost involved (Middleton 1985, 95–96).

Having lost the initiative in military terms, Frederick too was very active at the diplomatic level. During the early part of 1759, he contrived to destabilize the Swedish government, interfered in Polish affairs, drew up plans to force Spain against Austria in Italy, and above all tried to convince the Ottoman Empire to declare war on Russia. In fact, the Prussian and English representatives at Constantinople were in close contact with the Grand Vizier. Before taking any steps, the latter wanted a specific guarantee from the British, but Britain hesitated; there was the danger of alienating Spain (which Pitt was trying to keep neutral) and losing what was left of British credibility among Russian leaders. Thus it was that the operation failed, and Frederick, who it appeared never ceased to cultivate this plan in subsequent years, was now completely absorbed by the new campaign and its rather unfortunate results, so giving little weight to the matter (Waddington 1899–1914, vol. III, 110–14). The prudent behavior of the British did not give rise to any strain in the allies' relationship; similarly, the Prussian decision to decline Britain's invitation to adopt a position of détente with Saxony and Poland did not cause any great stir in the British camp (Rose 1914, 257–58).

The two allies' joint diplomatic moves in relation to their enemies were even more significant. In 1758, France tried to get closer to each separately, and in both cases the ally in question informed the other of proceedings (so as to avoid finding itself compromised in the eyes of the other) and refused to take up the French offer (Doran 1986, 222–23). The following year, the two allies acted jointly again, submitting a peace offer first in the autumn of 1759 and then during the course of a series of negotiations held in the Hague that winter. In particular, by the spring of 1759 the British government was split on the question of the country's financial standing in view of a further year of war. Frederick, worried about the possibility of Pitt finding himself in a minority, suggested to Britain that the two allies make a joint declaration in favor of a peace congress. Although Frederick did not believe that such an initiative would actually work, at least it would give Pitt the chance to silence opposition on the home front (Waddington 1899–1914, vol. III,

114). At the end of the summer of 1759, following two further defeats, Frederick asked George II to negotiate a separate peace with France; if the latter could be removed from the field of play, then it was likely that Austria would also be forced to give in. France itself was interested in a peace agreement with Britain that would resolve their colonial differences. This led both to an official request for a peace congress, at the end of November 1759, and to a series of informal meetings between representatives of the French and British governments, held in December 1759 and the spring of the following year. Now that they were aware of Prussia's desperate plight, neither Russia nor Austria displayed any real interest in peace; indeed, Austria exercised such strong pressure on the French ally that it harmed France's bilateral negotiations with Great Britain. Pitt had firmly decided to involve Prussia in peace talks, were such talks to proceed, but Louis XV would not allow it, the official reason being that France and Prussia were not formally at war; in reality it was because he found it difficult to ignore the veto applied by Austria.[21]

Pitt thus firmly defended Frederick's interests, and he perceived the French position as an attempt to divide Britain from Prussia. France could have made offers that, had they been accepted, would have immediately been made public as proof of Britain's greed and betrayal of its ally. Had this happened, then the alliance with Prussia would have been a dead letter even before Britain's war at sea was completed. When Frederick asked for an Anglo-French guarantee covering all Prussian possessions in 1756, prior to beginning work on a peace congress (a request France deemed totally unacceptable), not only did Pitt approve such a demand, but he even insisted that it be included in any preliminary discussions between Britain and France (Doran 1986, 240). Once again, the determined manner in which Pitt sided with Prussia should not be misunderstood. The English minister was negotiating with France in order to quell public opinion at home, and to publicly demonstrate his commitment to peace; his real intention was, on the contrary, to continue with the war for at least another year in order to take full advantage of the important victories gained during the course of 1759. From this point of view, preservation of the Prussian alliance was not so much a pretext for hindering negotiations as a reflection of Britain's strategic interest in keeping war going in Europe as well (Corbett 1907, vol. II, 86). From Frederick's point of view, on the one hand there was, of course, appreciation for how Pitt refused to abandon Prussia to its fate,[22] while on the other hand there was a certain degree of resurgent optimism regarding the possible outcome of the war (it seemed the Turks were finally ready to put an end to all previous obstacles, and Pitt himself now seemed better disposed toward them than before). The very terms Frederick set for a separate Anglo-French peace, in April 1760,[23] showed that he, just like Pitt, was now more inclined to continue the war than to end it quickly (Waddington 1899–1914, vol. III, 539–40).

Finally, in 1761 the enemy coalition submitted a request for a peace congress; at the same time, France offered to negotiate separately with Britain, in order to resolve their specific differences, on the basis of the principle of *uti possidetis*.[24] The French proposal was quite ambiguous and probably designed to test Britain's loyalty to Prussia after the crowning of George III. The British response was equally vague, with the exception of one thing: support for Prussia. Frederick, who had been immediately informed of proceedings, expressed his satisfaction and gave Pitt carte blanche with regard to negotiations, provided that the integrity of Prussian territory be guaranteed. Anglo-French negotiations centered mainly on the question of the colonies, and this is precisely where they got stuck. However, for their entire duration, Britain insisted that French forces leave those Prussian territories they had occupied and claimed its right to continue to support Prussia even in the event of a separate Anglo-French peace (Schweizer 1991, 129–30).[25] The only moment of tension, witnessed in June 1761, was when Pitt made mention to Frederick that Prussia would perhaps have to surrender some of its territory (Waddington 1899–1914, vol. IV, 585–86). The English minister had to take account of the growing demand for peace within government itself and in Parliament and among the populace, and he was thus worried about the rigidity of the Prussian position, which exposed him to the accusation of having condemned Britain to involvement in a never-ending war. However, there was also fear that Frederick's insistence on holding on to all of Silesia would ultimately be his downfall; the King of Prussia himself expressed serious doubts about his country's military situation, and England's ministers were informed of this since Prussia's secret code had just been broken (Doran 1986, 269–70). Frederick's firm opposition to any form of territorial loss nevertheless led the British government to immediately review the meaning of those "sacrifices" to which Pitt had previously alluded, and this diplomatic incident was over within the span of just a few weeks. Despite this, the King of Prussia followed negotiations apprehensively and was constantly afraid that Prussia would be abandoned by its ally, thus paying the price of an Anglo-French agreement. Hence his relief when negotiations finally fell through (Waddington 1899–1914, vol. IV, 599–600).

REALIGNMENT AND BREAK-UP

The causes of the break-up of the Anglo-Prussian alliance have been the subject of lengthy, intense debate by historians, centered on the responsibilities of both parties, and in particular of Frederick on the one hand and Lord Bute, Holdernesse's successor in the Northern Department in 1761, on the other. In particular, the bitter recriminations of the King of Prussia have been the focus of the attempt to establish whether the British really did betray their Prussian allies in a premeditated, cold manner, or whether the complicated affairs of the final months of the alliance's existence were the result of a more complex series of factors.[26] Within the context of the theoretical perspective adopted here, interpretation of the break-up of the Anglo-Prussian alliance goes beyond the personages involved and centers on the altered relationship between the two countries. Furthermore, from this point of view, talk of whether it amounted to an act of betrayal or not is largely meaningless. The events of the period between the autumn of 1761 and the spring of 1762 are a clear sign of the transformation of the alliance, from homogeneous to heterogeneous; bargaining, in turn, became increasingly tense, or to use our terms, it went from accommodative to coercive. The relation of forces would appear to have shifted decidedly toward Great Britain, and as a result Britain tended to impose its own terms on the ally. Despite this, Prussia was never forced to comply with British demands; on the contrary, it tried to get Britain to provide support for the forging of a new path forward. Since neither party proved capable of forcing the other's hand and molding the alliance to its own requirements, the almost immediate outcome was the end of the alliance itself.

Toward the end of 1761, it was clear that the two allies found themselves in positions that made it very difficult to reconcile the common cause with each party's particular causes. In Great Britain, the "party of peace"—or at least of peace in Germany—had grown in size, and its voice was increasingly insistent. A leaflet entitled "Considerations on the Present German War" appeared in autumn 1760; this publication was highly critical of British involvement in the war in Germany and of the Anglo-Prussian alliance, and its views were widely shared, causing the government considerable embarrassment and leading to a series of rebuttals in which the advocates of the naval strategy once again wrangled with the supporters of the continental strategy.[27] Many observers concurred that the cost of the war in Germany was increasingly difficult to justify once the major colonial objectives were reached; Pitt was well aware of this and had to take account of the fact (Spencer 1956, 104). At the news that Spain and France had formed an alliance in the summer of 1761, Pitt immediately wanted to declare war on Spain, but the reservations of the other British ministers led him to resign in October. However, the war against Spain was postponed for only a few months; in January 1762, Great Britain found itself faced with another enemy, and with another ally to support: Portugal. Prussia, for its part, had for some time been prepared to allow its ally to come to a separate peace agreement with France, as we have seen. But some of the conditions established by Prussia in December 1760 were deemed unacceptable by Britain; in particular, the request for a subsidy of nine million crowns (more than double the existing sum paid by Britain each year) was rejected outright by the British government in March 1761 (Schweizer 1989, 89–90).

The question of this subsidy came round again in the autumn of that year, when Britain began to secretly negotiate with France and review its position with regard to Prussia. Lord Bute offered Frederick six million crowns, including both the annual subsidy that had come up for renewal and a further sum designed to compensate for Britain's right to agree to a separate peace with France. Frederick, although not completely happy with this offer, had no choice but to accept. Prussia was in desperate military straits; for the first time ever, the Austrian and Russian armies had set up their winter quarters on Prussian soil, and the only hope for Prussia was the much-yearned-for intervention of the Turks (Ritter 1954/1968, 123–24). This time the fear of abandonment was palpable, and the King of Prussia chose to comply with the British position, above all "pour empêcher que la cour d'Angleterre ne prenne quelque parti prejudiciable à sês interêts au cas que sa négotiation avec la France vint à se renouer."[28] Consequently, Frederick looked for further guarantees. The draft agreement now proposed by Prussia, although complying with Bute's conditions, provided not only for the return of Prussian territories prior to the conclusion of any separate Anglo-French peace agreement—a condition that would have constrained Britain's diplomatic actions—but also for payment of a subsidy to Prussia until the latter made peace with its enemies, thus for an indefinite period of time. To free himself of these conditions, and to impose his own, Bute decided (in January 1762) to guarantee Britain's ally four million crowns only, and to offer this as a sum granted by the British Parliament rather than as part of a treaty. Moreover, in considering Prussia a defeated nation at this point (Colburg had also fallen at the time), Bute promptly advised Frederick to reach an agreement with Prussia's enemies as soon as possible, and to limit his demands to his means of enforcing them.[29] Even though the King of Prussia accused the British minister of negotiating "baton levé avec nous" (quoted in Doran 1986, 299), he was forced to agree. At this point, Bute went even further in his demands and made the granting of the subsidy conditional upon Prussia's notification of its plans for the following military campaign (Schweizer 1991, 142–96).

As we can see, Britain was involved in a coercive form of bargaining with Prussia, whereby it tried to gain the greatest possible advantage from the position of dependence that it believed Frederick found himself in at the time. British diplomats calculated that the pursuit of a peace agreement with France would be facilitated by some degree of Austrian involvement, which in turn would be subject to Austria receiving certain benefits concerning Silesia. Prussia, however, could not agree to any such concessions; asking it to constrain freedom of action without it receiving something suitable in exchange, and asking it indeed to give up part of its lands, was like asking Prussia to be something other than Prussia. This was the situation in which Newcastle attempted to circumscribe Bute, and to test Austrian opinion with a view to an agreement (Dorn 1929, 335–38). Kaunitz, the Austrian chancellor, thought this was a trap designed to separate Austria from France, and he ignored the British action; but Frederick was later informed of this move and thus realized that Prussia's ally had dealt with the enemy, unbeknown to him.

Within the context of this coercive strategy, British attempts to get Russia to continue exercising military pressure on Prussia were even more significant. The death of Elizabeth at the beginning of January 1762 changed the situation once again; the new Tsar of Russia, Peter III, was a keen admirer of Frederick, and just a few weeks after taking the throne he decided to withdraw Russia from the war. Sweden followed suit shortly afterward, which then meant that Frederick had only Austria to deal with. Furthermore, it was widely recognized that the new Tsar had hostile designs on Denmark. All of this was bad news for Britain. Frederick would now be even less malleable than before, and it was going to be even more difficult to attain the hoped-for peace in mainland Europe. It was at this point that the Russian envoy to London, Prince Galitzin, had an interview with Bute, and he referred the nature of these talks to the tsar, who in turn informed Frederick thereof. Briefly, Bute, who was still unaware of Russia's withdrawal from the war, complained of Frederick's obstinacy, claiming that Britain could not pander to Prussia's wishes to continue with the war, and that Prussia would have to make territorial concessions; moreover, he perceived Russia as the only nation capable of reestablishing peace in Europe, provided the tsar did not withdraw Russia from the war at that specific moment.[30] In other words, Great Britain was concerned that Peter III could ruin British peace plans; with Russian help, Frederick could now continue the war against Austria to the bitter end, and if he supported the tsar in his plans to attack Denmark then he could force Denmark into war at France's side. British suspicions were further fueled by the fact that Frederick failed to notify its ally of the instructions given to his envoy in St. Petersburg. Such suspicions were partly founded, since Prussia had offered its neutrality to the tsar in the event of a Russo-Danish war, and the Prussian envoy had been explicitly forbidden from informing his British colleague, despite the fact that the latter was initially responsible for maintaining contacts between the tsar and the King of Prussia (Dorn 1929, 543–44).

It was the death of Elizabeth, and the subsequent crowning of Peter III, that saved Frederick from his enemies, while at the same time enabling him to free himself of the grip of the British government: "at the moment that Russia detached herself from Austria, the bond between Prussia and England also broke" (Ritter 1954/1968, 125). The immediate suspension of Russian army operations, and the tsar's conciliatory attitude with Prussia, had the effect of reestablishing symmetry in the relations between the two allies. Bute's insistent questions about how Prussia intended to employ the money remained unanswered, and in the end, on March 17, Frederick ordered his representatives in London to stop asking for the subsidy. It was only the following week that Frederick was informed of Galitzin's report, and a further two weeks after that when he was finally notified of the Anglo-Austrian talks (Doran 1986, 319–20). Thus the decision to renounce the subsidy, if necessary, was taken regardless of any further British government maneuvers and was a reaction not so much to the betrayal by the ally as to its efforts to restrict Prussia's freedom of movement. It was natural for Frederick to turn to Russia, since this was the only power whose friendship could have guaranteed preservation of Prussia's territories, given that Great Britain was no longer prepared to do so. News of the Anglo-Austrian talks and of the contents of Galitzin's dispatch resulted in Prussia getting closer to Russia, that is, in giving further impetus to an existing shift in direction.

Frederick was now prepared to commit Prussia to another military campaign even without Britain's financial support; this showed both its newfound independence (the result of the nascent relationship with Russia) and Britain's clear miscalculation of the importance of British funds to the Prussian cause. British subsidies had always been willingly accepted, of course, but never played a decisive role. Even in the grave situation in which Prussia found itself during the winter of 1762, Frederick managed to keep the country afloat by squeezing Mecklenburg and Saxony dry, and by implementing certain drastic economic and administrative measures (Ritter 1954/1968, 125–26). Given Frederick's reticence toward Britain concerning his own relationship with Peter III, at the end of April the British government decided it had had enough and withdrew its offer of subsidies. Just as Prussia was not in the least interested in being forced into giving up land in order to ensure a peace agreement, Britain had no intention of paying for a possible war conducted by Prussia and Russia against Denmark.[31] In other words, both Prussia and Britain withdrew their conformity.

Bute was to justify his decision by placing emphasis on the changes in the respective positions of the two allies. From the beginning of the year, Great Britain had both an extra enemy to fight as well as another ally to support, whereas Prussia had two fewer enemies (Lodge 1923, 120–21). Despite Bute's words being judged by Mitchell himself as "tiré par les cheveux" (quoted in Doran 1986, 332)—Britain having promised on several occasions to renew the subsidy—they nevertheless hit the nail on the head: the situation of the two countries had changed dramatically compared to a few years earlier, to the point where it was no longer right to speak of any common cause. The last year of the war transformed the alliance from homogeneous to heterogeneous, but recent events even witnessed the disappearance of the one defining constraint of any heterogeneous alliance, the requirement not to break up. From the British point of view, Prussia's tenacity, which in the past had been much appreciated, was now one of the main obstacles to peace. From the Prussian point of view, now that military pressure had eased somewhat and there was no longer any risk of diplomatic isolation, British support was less important, and indeed counterproductive if subject to terms detrimental to Prussia's interests. Neither country was any longer in a position to offer its ally any essential services, and their bargaining range was reduced to the point of disappearing altogether; there was no point of agreement the two parties now preferred to no agreement at all.

In truth, the Convention of Westminster remained in force. This entitled Prussia to British support in getting the French to leave the western provinces, and in keeping hold of Silesia. The final months of the irredeemably damaged Anglo-Prussian alliance were characterized by reciprocal recriminations and accusations, including a violent press campaign led by Frederick against Bute in Great Britain, clearly designed to discredit him and get him replaced. During its negotiations with France, from April 1762 onward, the British government adopted positions that were increasingly distant from the Prussian position, but without informing the Prussian government. During preliminary peace talks held in Paris (November 1762), the two powers agreed on the withdrawal of French troops from the occupied territories, which in itself was something of a victory for the Prussians, but which opened the way to potential occupation of the same provinces by the Austrian army (Lodge 1923, 130–38). Accordingly, Prussia submitted an official complaint when the preliminaries were signed. It was only the fear that Frederick would in turn occupy the Low Countries that led France to return the Rhineland provinces directly to Prussia, and Austria had no choice but to follow France's example. Frederick, however, refused to have any indirect dealings with Austria, insisting that negotiations be conducted *cour à cour*, which subsequently resulted in restoration of the previous status quo (Peace of Hubertusburg, February 1763), thus guaranteeing the integrity of Prussia's territories.

SEVEN

The Deadlocked Alliance

Austria and France, 1756–1785

A HETEROGENEOUS, SYMMETRICAL ALLIANCE

A deadlocked alliance is characterized by a combination of the symmetry in interdependence between the two allies and the heterogeneity of the constraints they are subjected to as well as the opportunities they are led to take within a given relational system. In a heterogeneous alliance, the situational contexts of the allies do not sit together easily. A given set of constraints limit one ally's freedom of movement, while some opportunities predispose it to move in a certain direction. However, neither the former nor the latter is necessarily shared by the other ally. Examples of this are the presence of diverse enemies, or a differing degree of vulnerability in relation to the same enemy; their targeting exactly the same part of a given territory; their divergent positions with regard to a third state; and the dissimilar meaning that the international order (to which the alliance contributes) has for each of the allies. In other words, in a heterogeneous alliance the common cause coexists with a series of particular causes, some of which are incompatible with, or are judged to be as important as (or even more important than), the common cause. This is what underlies the characteristic coercive bargaining between the allies, each of which constantly tries to obtain the conformity of the other and drag the other along with it, in a permanent wrestling match where the only constraint is that the alliance must not be broken up. In addition, symmetry in power relations implies a substantial equality of those various resources employed in negotiations, or how such resources are evaluated in the circumstances. This parity underlies a remunerative relationship based on an exchange of potentially equal benefits. This means the two allies condition each other in a well-balanced manner, with each exerting pressure on its partner, which in turn counters such pressure, since both possess the means with which to enforce their demands. Even though a balanced relationship implies a mutual exchange of benefits, this does not mean such an exchange will necessarily take place. In fact, such a result is the logical outcome in conditions of homogeneity only, as we have seen in the case of the other symmetrical arrangement, the aggregation alliance. If, on the contrary, heterogeneity rules, things are quite different. The more the common cause is hindered by the particular causes, the more the symmetry in power relations between the two allies results in their mutual conditioning leading to an almost paradoxical outcome: rather than helping and supporting one another, the allies end up hampering each other, thus preventing anyone from achieving desired aims. Furthermore, the symmetrical nature of their relationship distinguishes this alliance from the other heterogeneous type; in the hegemonic alliance one ally is able to impose its will, and thus its policies, on the other, while in the deadlocked alliance the parties paralyze each other.

The alliance between Austria and France, stipulated in 1756 and preserved, at least on paper, until 1792, clearly illustrates these and other characteristics of the deadlocked alliance. The two nations joined forces at the beginning of the Seven Years' War (1756), for the usual reasons of power and security, and both were extremely disappointed by the outcome of the war. Nevertheless, they decided to preserve their union, since their alliance gave each a means with which to control the other, and also because without such an alliance they would probably have ended up fighting each other, as had happened so frequently in the past and was to happen again following the French Revolution. In fact, it has been pointed out that the Austro-French case represents a type of alliance that was to be more commonly found during the subsequent century, "a pact for management and mutual restraint of one's partner, not for capability aggregation and aggrandizement" (Schroeder 1994b, 42). Without achieving anything in terms of the power or security of its two members, the alliance nevertheless discouraged them from taking any actions that could have had destabilizing effects, thus contributing indirectly to maintaining peace in Europe and (paradoxically) enabling their adversaries to strengthen further (as in the case of Prussia) or even develop into hegemonic threats (in the case of Great Britain and Russia).

By the middle of the 18th century, the European state system formed a pentagonal arrangement devoid of any prevailing player.[1] The decline of Spain and the United Provinces was accompanied by the rise to power of Prussia and Russia, while Great Britain continued to rule the waves. France and Austria, on the other hand, had just come out of a war—the War of the Austrian Succession (1740–1748)—which, for a variety of reasons, had proved to be a failure for both, highlighting their financial limitations and in Austria's case its administrative and military weakness as well. However, despite being shaken by the Prussian attack of 1740 and the consequent loss of Silesia (together with other territories in Italy), Austria preserved its preeminent role in the Germanic world—although it now had to keep a close eye on its neighbor, Prussia—and the Habsburg succession had been guaranteed in the end. Moreover, a series of reforms of the nation's army and its administrative system immediately after the war were designed to make it a stronger, more centralized state (Bérenger 1997, 56–66).[2] France, despite the damage it had suffered in terms of trade and naval power, and despite being afflicted by a financial crisis that had already begun to have serious domestic repercussions (Muret 1949, 479–84), remained the strongest military power in mainland Europe, and the only such power that could hope to compete with Great Britain at sea. Within this international system composed of states of roughly equal strength, France and Austria were probably the most powerful on the European mainland, in terms of population, military capabilities (Kennedy 1987, 99–100), diplomatic traditions, and international prestige.

This rather evenly balanced relationship was also apparent subsequent to the Seven Years' War, as these two countries were the ones that came off the worst from that war. France was particularly badly hit in the colonies, and as the very result of its alliance with Austria (and its cooperation with Russia) it was shaken in its traditional role in Eastern Europe; Austria, which was incapable of winning back Silesia, now had to accept the fact that it was to coexist with an equally powerful Prussia and a much strengthened Russia. Furthermore, Austria's position within the Empire had become a lot more precarious as a result of its alliance with France. However, just as France had little choice but to remain tied to Austria if it wished to preserve the peace in Europe that its finances and overseas struggle with Britain required, likewise Austria had no real alternative to an alliance with France, especially after Prussia and Russia formed their own alliance in 1764. The alliance between France and Austria survived, therefore, but was never to be very popular in either country, despite the marriage of the future King of France, Louis XVI, and Austria's Marie Antoinette in 1770.

It was already clear that both countries were subject to diverse pressures during the lengthy, rather laborious negotiations that preceded stipulation of the original alliance treaty. Such divergences were also apparent during the Seven Years' War, which, from the Austrian point of view, was principally designed to regain possession of Silesia and destroy Prussia, whereas for France the war against Great Britain at sea and in North America was undoubtedly more important. Furthermore, their enemies remained different even after 1763. Indeed, it is hard to identify a solid common cause in this particular case. Following 1763, there were two main issues that dominated international politics: the maritime and colonial rivalry between Britain and France, and the Austro-Prussian competition for supremacy in Germany. Although these two international contexts were connected to a certain extent, in practice they constituted two separate scenarios; one concerned central-eastern Europe, and the other took in Western Europe and overseas territories (Anderson 1965). Until the end of the 1780s, no state within any one subsystem was really capable of influencing the other subsystem. In light of the contrasting geopolitical imperatives both countries had to cope with, it was no surprise that the alliance contributed to their security to such a limited degree, and that neither of the two allies was prepared to support the other against its respective enemies.

Furthermore, Austria's designs on Italy, Germany, the Ottoman Empire, and the Low Countries meant Vienna was structurally on a crash course with Versailles. The two foreign policy traditions—those of the Habsburgs and the Bourbons—were at odds in many ways. Regarding the empire, the obstacle was Prussia; if Austria wished to expand to the detriment of the Turks, Prussia was ready to threaten it from behind, and if it wished to forge into Poland, Prussia would want part of the spoils. The destruction of Prussia thus was the *conditio sine qua non* of Austrian policy. Such plans in turn moved Austria away from France's position. Busy as it was with its overseas ventures, France intended to keep peace established in Europe, and so Austria's plans could be implemented only by first obtaining France's conformity through forming an alliance with it. France, however, opposed any such Austrian designs, judging them to be dangerous for peace in Europe or for French interests in general, or for both of these things. This is why, from a French point of view, Austria's conformity was just as important. France's policy of systematic obstructionism was to lead to bitter recriminations in Vienna. Maria Theresa was patient and tolerant, but her son Joseph II (emperor and joint ruler of the Habsburg dominions from 1765 onward), despite preserving the alliance with France, hated it. He and his brother Leopold often talked of their deep resentment of Austria's ally, "de sa fausseté, son envie de nuire"[3]; of its "affreuse, contradictoire, outrageante"[4] behavior, and often accused the French of using "du titre de l'alliance, de la parenté et de l'amitié, que pour tromper sous main et pour insulter impunément"[5] Austria (quoted in Sorel 1885–1904, 352).

For France, the alliance with Austria just prior to the onset of the Seven Years' War seemed an effective way of neutralizing the only hostile great power (one that had traditionally been Britain's ally) capable of creating serious problems in mainland Europe. The sudden outbreak of war then transformed this effective expedient into a disastrous diplomatic-military device that was to lead to the very scenario it had been designed to prevent: war on two fronts. Furthermore, France was traditionally the focal point of all those nations that feared the power of the Habsburgs; forced to give up this role after the humiliating experience of having supported Austria against Prussia, France was then to witness the two formerly irreconcilable German states come to an agreement and, together with Russia, share the spoils of Poland, one of the oldest clients of the French monarchy. The fact that Great Britain remained France's implacable foe for the entire 18th century led several observers at the time to compare their rivalry with that between Rome and Carthage. However, the Habsburgs were the hereditary enemies of France, and the need to reduce their role as well as those alliances designed for this purpose were perceived by many as an established principle of state (Sorel 1885–1904, 227). The alliance with Austria, in other words, was seen as a humiliation. Moreover, Maria Theresa was highly religious, a friend of the Jesuits and an enemy of the *philosophes*; hence an even greater resentment. The alliance was unpopular among diplomats, the army, and even at court. From 1756 onward, the most influential royal advisors and ministers, including those connected to the "Queen's party," were lukewarm at best about the alliance. More in general, anti-Austrian feeling was so widespread that at the time of the French Revolution it was shared by both republicans and émigrés alike.

THE DIPLOMATIC REVOLUTION

The antagonism between France and the House of Habsburg was a virtual axiom of European politics from the very onset of the modern age. The reconciliation of these two great powers is thus considered the greatest of all diplomatic revolutions.[6] Midway through the 18th century, the two powers were still aligned in their traditional manner: France with Prussia, and Austria with the maritime powers. Until 1756, France's diplomacy in Europe was substantially conditioned by the nation's rivalry with Austria. In Germany, this meant providing support to the German princes (even if they were protestant), starting with Prussia, in the face of Austrian expansionism. The same concern with combating Austria led France to establish a solid friendship with those states forming the "eastern barrier" of Sweden, Poland, and the Ottoman Empire. This policy was accompanied by a poorly concealed mistrust of Russia, which had already tried to expand to the detriment of France's allies.

Despite not being appointed chancellor before 1753, for some years beforehand the Prince of Kaunitz had already been an important voice in Vienna. The War of the Austrian Succession taught him just how little Austria could place its trust in Great Britain, and already during the course of the war, and then at the time of the peace talks held in Aix-la-Chapelle (1748), he was making certain overtures toward France.[7] The very territorial arrangement of the Habsburg states—from the Low Countries to Italy and the Balkans—meant that, in Kaunitz's view, Austria was condemned to waste its energies and neglect defense of its central Germanic-Bohemian nucleus. The Prussian aggression of 1740 highlighted this weakness, and from then on Austrian diplomacy had to deal with the twin problem of reducing Prussia to the status of a secondary power while blocking Russia's military advancement. Given that the Low Countries could be defended from a French attack only by placing Austria in the hands of the maritime powers, Kaunitz was even prepared to hand them over to France if this was the price to be paid to get Louis XV to contribute to creation of a three-way continental European system involving France, Austria, and Russia, which could nullify or limit the advance of the medium-sized powers (Prussia and Sardinia) and prevent Austria from being involved in colonial wars, and which would thus enable the Habsburgs to conduct their own foreign policy (Schilling 1994, 226). In 1749, Kaunitz drafted an important brief, discussed by the *Staatskonferenz*, in which he claimed that, with Prussia being Austria's real enemy, it would be advisable to separate Prussia from France and come to an agreement with the latter. In 1750, Kaunitz was sent to Versailles as Austrian ambassador, with this very purpose in mind; however, it was a little early for such plans, and French opposition forced him to abandon them for the time being.

The border clashes between the French colony in Canada and the British territories in North America, which began in July 1754, led the two European powers to prepare for a new, large-scale war within the space of just a few months. Despite this war not being officially declared until 1756, the intervening two years were nevertheless characterized by a series of attacks, at sea and in North America, which had clear implications for Europe as well, starting with (from the British point of view) protection of Hanover. The British, disappointed by the conduct of the Austrians and the Dutch, now turned to the Russians, whose support was seen as a useful means of dissuading Prussia from attacking Hanover. At the same time, British diplomacy also got closer to Prussia itself, with Frederick seeing an agreement with Britain as a guarantee in relation to Austria and Russia and at this point distrusting any serious French support. The Anglo-Russian agreement (September 1755) finally convinced Frederick to act and was to lead to the Convention of Westminster (January 1756), whereby Prussia and Great Britain agreed to keep the peace in Germany, oppose the entry to or transition across the empire's lands on the part of any foreign army, and mutually guarantee each party's territories.

In the meantime, in the summer of 1755 Kaunitz went back to courting France's favor, increasingly convinced that French support was essential if Prussia were to be contained and Silesia won back. However, given that France would certainly have refused to be a member of any offensive alliance, it had to be convinced to take part in an exclusively defensive arrangement, according to which guarantees were to be provided to the Low Countries and France was to pledge not to attack Hanover. Although Louis XV did not disdain the offer from Vienna, and indeed appointed the Abbé de Bernis to conduct secret talks with the Austrian ambassador (the Count of Starhemberg), his advisors were opposed to the idea and suggested that he avoid making any pledges regarding Hanover, and that he include Prussia in the guarantees.[8] Initially, the respective bargaining positions of the two powers diverged considerably. The Convention of Westminster hit France where it hurt most: France's ally, Prussia, had secretly negotiated with France's principal enemy, and the country now found itself on the point of being abandoned, right at the beginning of the war, by its only ally, which, on top of it all, threatened to deprive France of its rights (as sanctioned by the treaties of Westphalia) to intervene in the empire on the side of the German princes. Even in such circumstances, there were still substantial differences between Austria and France when it came to negotiating an agreement, and the French government firmly rejected the explicit offer of an offensive alliance against Prussia (Broglie 1897, 249–343).

In the end, the prospect of Great Britain managing to reconcile new and old alliances—which evoked the specter of an isolated France faced with the joint forces of Russia, Austria, the maritime powers, and perhaps even Prussia—led to the first Treaty of Versailles (May 1, 1756). This treaty consisted of two conventions, one designed to guarantee neutrality, the other constituting a defensive alliance, together with five secret clauses (Horn 1957, 453–54). Under the first convention, Austria undertook to remain strictly neutral in the ongoing war between France and Britain, while France undertook not to attack the Low Countries or any other Austrian possession. Under the second convention, a defensive alliance was established according to which if either of the allies were attacked within its European territories, the other ally would give either military or financial support (with each undertaking to contribute the same quantity of such support as the other). Although the Anglo-French war was excluded from the convention, the first secret article stated that a Prussian attack on Austria would require France to intervene, just as Austria would intervene if Prussia helped Britain repel a French attack on Hanover (Horn 1957, 454). The other secret clauses provided for extension of an invitation to join the alliance to the Bourbons of Spain and Italy, and to the Grand Duke of Tuscany (Maria Theresa's husband); completion of the work undertaken by the congress of Aix-la-Chapelle; and their joint pledge not to stipulate or renew any treaty with any other power without having previously notified the other party, or without the involvement of the latter, which was clearly designed to exclude a return to the old system of alliances.

These were therefore the cornerstones of the diplomatic system that was to survive right up to the French Revolution. Its underlying principles showed that the signatories probably wanted to create a lasting arrangement. From the French point of view, these were the principles Louis XIV himself had indicated in his final instructions to his ambassador in Vienna; the treaties of 1648 were guaranteed, in keeping with the tradition of Richelieu and Mazzarino, the position of the Bourbons was further strengthened, and an end was put to a rivalry that no longer had any *raison d'être*. However, at the same time these principles were reiterated within a context characterized by the divergent positions of the two parties. For France, the alliance served to guarantee peace in Europe and isolate Great Britain, whereas from the Austrian point of view the alliance would avoid Austria's involvement in the Anglo-French conflict so that it could better prepare itself for war against Prussia with the help of France. The wording of the conventions and of the secret clauses gave no indication that France considered itself as having pledged to participate in an Austrian attack on Prussia. If anything, the truth is that the agreements implied that France risked a European war triggered by a Prussian attack, whereas Austria offered no guarantee to France should the latter be attacked by Britain. This quite unbalanced relationship was based on a misunderstanding that the treaty in question was a defensive one. Austria obviously counted on the fact that Prussia would be the first to attack, as it had already done in 1740, to entrap France at its side—and a highly skillful diplomat such as Kaunitz was right in believing that Austria would never find itself fighting an offensive war—whereas from the French point of view, a Prussian attack was seen as unlikely, because Frederick would not have the nerve to attack Austria again, as this time around such a move would risk triggering the joint intervention of Russia and France (Broglie 1897, 344–73).

In any case, the defensive treaty represented the failure of Kaunitz's original plan, which aimed to obtain France's active involvement in an anti-Prussian alliance. Indeed, the two countries continued to conduct feverish negotiations during the following months, and on several occasions Austria attempted, albeit to no avail, to convince France to lend the new alliance a more offensive character (Waddington 1896, 462–99). Austria had already played its best card; constrained as it was by the treaty, it could no longer threaten to ally itself with Great Britain, and all of France's ministers were rather perplexed, for a variety of different reasons, about the "diplomatic revolution" and were not prepared to strengthen France's relations with Austria. On the contrary; the fact that Austria was pushing for destruction of Prussia clearly revealed its fear of that country. France therefore had every interest in maintaining this dualism in Germany.[9] Underlying France's behavior toward its ally for decades to come, this was quite clear from the start (Muret 1949, 511). Despite Austria's very best efforts, alone it could not manage to overpower French resistance; it was only Prussia's brusque decision to break through the encircling cordon, by forcing its way over the Saxon border at the end of August, that eventually triggered events.

THE FUNCTIONING OF THE ALLIANCE

We are thus dealing with two states of equal standing whose respective situational contexts give them both occasion to pursue each other, without either ever really being in a position to meet the other. Each needs the other's conformity, yet neither is in a position to promise substantial gains (emerging benefits); as such, the only means to affect the other's behavior is the threat of withdrawal of support (diminishing benefits). What theoretical propositions emerge from the interaction of heterogeneity and symmetry once an agreement has been reached, and as such are to be found in the case at hand? Let us first examine the relationship between the two allies, and then move on to analyze their interaction with the adversaries in question.

First, given that the conflicting interests are deemed to be of equal importance to, or even of more importance than, their shared interests, each ally will tend to impose its will on the other within the framework of a coercive form of bargaining designed to shape the alliance to one's own specific aims. At the same time, there is a clear limit beyond which neither party dares attempt to go, and this limit is given by the likelihood that the alliance will fall apart. However, in a heterogeneous alliance a symmetrical relation of forces implies that neither party can easily get the upper hand. Their negotiations consist of a series of offers and rejections, requests and denials; hence the reciprocal recriminations and mutual suspicions and resentment. An agreement can be reached only if the allies allow each other some breathing space. This, however, rarely happens, and even when it does it leads only to a rather precarious and unsatisfactory arrangement, since the divergence of interests makes the two parties quite reluctant to grant their conformity, and neither has sufficient power to force the other to follow its lead. The most likely result is thus one of deadlock, or in any case an outcome that is of no benefit to either party. The events leading up to the Treaty of Versailles already pointed to something of this kind; the agreement was far from ideal from the Austrian point of view, despite the Austrians having made concerted efforts to achieve it, while France reluctantly accepted it as well. Indeed, France agreed to the treaty not so much because it was forced into doing so by the greater bargaining power of the other party but rather because it was convinced Prussia would not be the first to attack. When Frederick invaded Saxony then, though it was true that Louis XV went to Austria's aid, this decision reflected yet another autonomous (albeit mistaken) calculation by the French: that the war would be a short one.

Subsequently, once France realized the excessive cost of the war in Europe, it found the necessary force to free itself of Austria's grip and reduced the entity of its own undertaking.

During the entire series of events connected to the Seven Years' War, even though both nations were unhappy about the outcome of their alliance, neither seriously considered withdrawing from it. This basic line of conduct was to permeate their relationship over the following years. France was concerned with containing Austria and Joseph's ambitions without threatening the survival of the alliance. In other words, it could say no, but it would have to do so tactfully. For example, during the course of the crisis leading up to the War of the Bavarian Succession (1778–79), France, despite having notified Austria of French neutrality, avoided both making any public statements that would have further irritated Austria and undertaking to act as guarantor of the treaties of Westphalia, as Frederick would have wished; more generally speaking, Louis XVI abstained from taking any steps that could have been perceived as a condemnation of France's ally (Murphy 1982, 300). This does not mean, however, that France abdicated its European role; the two Bavarian crises were extremely delicate precisely because France had to demonstrate its determination to maintain a traditional role of protector of the German states, without alienating Austria in the process (Hardman and Price 1998, 112).

"Not breaking the alliance" of course implies continuing to strive for the conformity of the other ally, condition it, and deny it freedom of movement. From the French viewpoint, provided that Austria could be prevented from attempting any adventurous exploits, the alliance was beneficial since it maintained peace in Europe; this was the original reason, and one that was to remain valid even after the Seven Years' War, and it allowed France to concentrate efforts on settling a score with Great Britain. France did not enjoy the same continuity of leadership Austria did when it came to formulating foreign policy (Kaunitz continued to be chancellor until 1792). Nevertheless, its two most important ministers at the time, the Duke of Choiseul and the Count of Vergennes, shared very similar viewpoints on this and other questions;[10] both also believed that an Austria freed from its ties with France could be tempted to return to the Old System with its very enemy, Great Britain.[11] In short, this neutralized rival had to be held onto; proof of this was given by France acting to close off all spaces to Austria, at times by hindering all attempts the latter made to rid itself of the Low Countries, and at others by trying to prevent it from creating an alliance with Russia (Bernard 1965, 139). Austria was also subject to the same constraint, that is, of not breaking up the alliance. To do so, it had to swallow some bitter pills—in the Balkans, Bavaria, and the Low Countries—without getting to the point of dissolving the tie with France. In Kaunitz's view, the alliance with France at least had the merit of maintaining peace in Italy and the Low Countries, two regions in which Austria felt itself to be particularly vulnerable; and even if it was often exasperated by France's obstructionism, Austria was nevertheless well aware that if it ended the alliance, this would create the preconditions for a new Franco-Prussian alliance, just as France feared recreation of the Old System.

In a deadlocked alliance, the parties are particularly sensitive to the problem of relative gains. Heterogeneity and symmetry make it more likely that opportunities for cooperation, offering potential gains to both parties, are going to be rejected by the party standing to benefit less than the other; given that the parties are on an equal standing, the opposition of one party is enough to hinder the other. Although it is not clear whether Austria would really have been prepared to offer France compensations in exchange for the latter's support over annexation of Bavaria, it is very clear that Vergennes thought such an exchange would have benefited Austria much more than France. Similar considerations were made regarding Austria's offer of Egypt; although this might have been tempting, it would have led to dismemberment of the Ottoman Empire, which would certainly have benefited Austria more than France. In fact, the proposal was twice rejected by Vergennes. Similarly, the Austrians were glad to learn of France's domestic problems, starting with its financial difficulties, especially after France's involvement in the American War of Independence; a weaker France meant a more dependent, more malleable France, and at the end of the day greater room for maneuver for Austria.

As far as relations with the enemies are concerned, given that a deadlocked alliance has no one common enemy there is a considerable risk of entrapment as the result of fighting the wrong wars, as there is in all heterogeneous alliances. On the other hand, the equal bargaining power of the two allies means that neither is prepared to give in easily to the other's requests or pressures. Having learnt its lesson from the Seven Years' War, France was ever more careful not to get involved in another war that would have been advantageous for Austria alone, both in the case of the two Bavarian crises and in the Low Countries dispute with the United Provinces, regardless of the fact that Austria was indeed maneuvering to create a situation in which it could invoke the casus foederis. If heterogeneity is given by the situational contexts in which the allies find themselves, then in the present case it may be expressed quite simply in these terms: Austria was faced with a series of war scenarios, while France was not. Vergennes perceived the danger for France and informed the king: "Votre Majesté [...] peut être entrainée dans une et plusieurs guerres pour la défense de son allié sans que celui-ci soit peut-être jamais dans le cas de la payer de réciprocité."[12]

France would never raise its voice with Prussia, as Austria wanted it to do. On the contrary, it saw Prussia not as an enemy but as a partner that could help preserve the integrity of the Germanic and Ottoman empires. In other words, Prussia was a vital player in the German dualism that France was interested in maintaining, and it was the most effective instrument French diplomacy possessed with regard to relations with Austria. Austria feared Prussia, and France—well aware of this—duly used the situation to its own advantage. Everyone knew and talked about this, from Choiseul to Vergennes; in 1759 the former stated that "nous connaissons parfaitement que le roi de Prusse est assez abaissé et qu'il n'est pas de notre intérêt qu'il le soit totalement";[13] Vergennes echoed this sentiment in 1777, when he observed that "placé sur le flanc des états autrichiens, c'est la frayeur qu'en [of Frederick] a la cour de Vienne qui la rapproche de la France; cette même frayeur la retient encore dans nos liens et la retiendra aussi longtemps que son motif subsistera."[14] Hence the policy of maintaining an equal distance from both German states: "détruisons la puissance du roi de Prusse, alors plus de digue contre l'ambition autrichienne, l'Allemagne obligée à plier sous ses lois lui ouvrira assez facilement vers nos frontiers."[15] For its part, Austria did not hide the fact that in the event of a new Anglo-French war its role would be simply to contain Prussia by diplomatic means (Sorel 1902, 33), and in 1770 it rejected the French proposal of joint action in support of the Ottoman Empire (Rain 1945, 281). Just as France had no intention of opposing Prussia for the exclusive benefit of Austria, so Austria did not want to fight either Britain or Russia for the sole benefit of France; indeed, it was even to form an alliance with Russia, in 1781. In other words, the enemies of one ally represented a point of reference for the other, subject to one important constraint: the alliance had to be preserved anyway, not only for the reasons discussed here but also because this was the only way of avoiding conferring excessive power on third parties. Consequently, Vergennes believed that Austria should not have been allowed to become either too powerful or indeed too weak, because in the latter case Prussia could have moved in to take its place (Bourgeois 1911, 529); Austria remained wary of relations with Russia, to the point where it often tried to cover itself by using precisely the French alliance.

In the light of all this, therefore, one can see why a deadlocked alliance fails to contribute to its members' power or security, as usually conceived of, and why it tends to result in the two parties blocking each other's maneuvers. As with any alliance, the deadlocked alliance witnesses a struggle for power in which each, in pursuing the conformity of the other, is constantly trying to drag it along in the same direction; but given that neither really has the power to convince the other, this becomes a struggle for the power of interdiction, that is, for a negative power that can be used only to hold the other back, rather than encourage it to move forward. The members of a deadlocked alliance are too weak to do things on their own, but too strong to be pushed unwillingly in a given direction, so they end up neutralizing one another. According to Peter M. Blau (1964, 115–42), if B needs a service offered by A, it has three options: (1) it may give A, in exchange, a service that A needs; (2) it may obtain that service elsewhere; or (3) it may decide to do without. However, if B cannot do any of these things, then it will find itself within A's power. In the case in question, Austria tried repeatedly to employ the first of these strategies, offering France various forms of payment for its direct or indirect aid, but France always rejected Austria's advances. Austria even looked for help elsewhere, in particular from Russia, albeit rather reluctantly and without any great success. It cannot be said, either, that Austria accepted the situation and deliberately chose to do without France's services; the repeated attempts, and the insistence with which Austria looked for forms of compensation and expansion in the Balkans and in the Empire, clearly show how difficult Austria found it to renounce its own objectives.

Austria did not impede French moves in the same way France hindered Austrian maneuvers, if for no other reason than that the attention of the government in Versailles was focused in another direction, and France had no great plans for European expansion. Notwithstanding that in a deadlocked alliance the struggle waged is above all centered on the power of interdiction, it seems that in the case of the Austro-French alliance it was France that often got the upper hand, especially after 1774. This should come as no surprise, really; it is easier to hold the other party back than to push or drag it in a given direction, when power is evenly balanced and the parties in question tend to take diverging paths. This said, given that an independent Austria could always have gone back to allying itself with Great Britain, or could have taken measures harming French interests, or could even have threatened to trigger an undesired war; France needed Austria's services, it could not find such services elsewhere, and it was not in a position to offer other services in exchange that might have placated Austria. This is why French foreign policy was in any case conditioned by this tie; systematic rejection of Austrian offers of advancement, although effective in controlling the ally's actions, inevitably had negative repercussions for France in terms of power and prestige, and the various crises were resolved without either ally gaining any significant advantage.

THE SECOND AND THIRD TREATIES OF VERSAILLES AND THE SEVEN YEARS' WAR

Surprised, just like Britain, by Frederick's decision to attack, France at this point gave in to Kaunitz's arguments and accepted the idea of a partition of Prussia in favor of Austria, Saxony, Sweden, and the Palatine electorate; in its role as guarantor of the treaties of Westphalia, and as Austria's ally, it was to take part in a European war of conquest as the "principal power," paying subsidies to all concerned. In exchange, Louis XV was to get the Low Countries (to be shared thereafter with his son-in-law, the Duke of Parma), but only if Austria won back Silesia. This was all contained in the second Treaty of Versailles (May 1757), an unprecedented collection of military and financial undertakings that marked a real break with the past, albeit of a temporary nature.[16] French determination speeded up the decision-making processes in Russia, Sweden, and Germany as well; by the spring of 1757, in fact, Prussia was completely encircled, thus achieving Kaunitz's aim. This radical change in policy—which was to substantially affect the country's military and diplomatic future, and not surprisingly was met with a certain degree of disapproval domestically—came at a high price, which Louis XV must have been aware of. If, in the end, the king was convinced by Austria's reasoning, this was not because of any imbalance in mutual dependence but because of a specific calculation based on the belief (shared by many at the time) that such a coalition was capable of settling the score decisively within the space of just a few months; the war in Europe was to be short and was to end with the destruction of Prussia, the conquest of Hanover, and Austro-French joint control of mainland Europe, which, among other things, would transform the Low Countries into an annex of France. Thus

France was soon to be in a position to concentrate its energies and forces in the war against Great Britain, possessing as it did a formidable item to be offered during the course of peace negotiations: Hanover (Muret 1949, 513–14; Robson 1957, 466). By the end of the year, however, any hope of a quick victory had all but vanished; Frederick's two brilliant victories—the first at Rossbach (in November) against the French army, the second at Leuthen (in December) against the Austrians—clearly showed that it was not going to be easy to defeat Prussia.

This is not really the place for a detailed reconstruction of events during the Seven Years' War.[17] Suffice it to say that until 1760 it was a war of attrition on mainland Europe, and a (British) war of conquest in the colonies. Subsequently, exhaustion of Prussian resources, revision of French policy, and the offer of mediation from Spain were the premonitory signs of a change that Pitt tried to delay but that in the end resulted in the pursuit of peace coming to the fore. The anti-Prussian coalition, although appearing formidable on paper, very quickly revealed an intrinsic weakness, the result of the allies' divergent war aims; Russia concentrated on the eastern Balkans and Austria on Silesia, while France knew full well that the real battle was going to be fought at sea. Furthermore, the initial defeats led to a reemergence of historical differences, such as that between France and Russia in eastern Europe (Oliva 1964), while the allies had no real experience of coalition wars. All of this rendered any coordination of actions and decisions, which would have transformed their military potential into an unstoppable means, difficult. Having failed to gain a quick victory, France in particular soon realized that the enormous cost of the second Treaty of Versailles reduced the resources at its disposal for what was the most important struggle of all. However, it seemed quite difficult for France to free itself from Austria's grip, since any attempt to repudiate those obligations undertaken until then might have led to the end of the alliance with Austria, which would have given Britain considerable freedom of movement on the European mainland. In such circumstances, the constraint consisting in not breaking up the alliance was more important than ever. However, the disadvantages of the offensive alliance in Europe were so evident, and Austrian reluctance to reviewing the terms of French involvement so strong, that Bernis himself believed the only way France could have gotten out of this situation was by stipulating an immediate peace with Britain; only this direct form of agreement with the enemy could have removed the ally from the equation (Bourgeois 1911, 513).

Peace was also the objective pursued by Choiseul, who took over from Bernis in December 1758, although he chose to do so in a different spirit than that of his predecessor. Great Britain had to be induced into demanding that peace negotiations be started, if acceptable terms were to be obtained (hence his invasion plan, which quickly failed). Furthermore, Choiseul was determined not to give up the Austrian alliance, but he did wish to lighten France's involvement in European operations, by formulating the principle of the separation of two wars: France was to renounce the Low Countries, become an "auxiliary power," and undertake not to negotiate without Austria (since this would have been equivalent to terminating the alliance in Kaunitz's view). At the same time, Austria, which was not involved in the war against Great Britain, was not to be entitled to oppose talks between Britain and France designed to terminate their specific conflict. All of this was set out in the third Treaty of Versailles (March 1759). The plan for bilateral Anglo-French negotiations, however, was met by substantial resistance (as one would have expected) from both Prussia and Austria, who, fearing they might have been abandoned, stuck to the letter of their treaties. In any case, in March 1760 Austria signed an agreement with Russia under which the two powers guaranteed each other Silesia and Eastern Prussia respectively, which represented a mutual insurance policy against the concession that France perhaps wanted to demand of them. Austria then called for a general congress, which Choiseul was not at all happy with because he intended to reaffirm the principle of the separation of the two wars; yet it was precisely to preserve the alliance with Austria that at the beginning of 1761 Choiseul pushed his concessions to the very limit. A general congress was to be held, but France was nevertheless to have the opportunity to negotiate directly with Great Britain. The rather obvious intention here was to see that the congress went no further than reformulating the decisions taken by the two rivals, within the framework of a general peace agreement.

The Franco-Spanish alliance (August 1761), together with Russia's withdrawal from the war following the death of Elizabeth (January 1762), saw things change once again, leading to a further slowing of the peace process. Given the pending withdrawal of Russia, it was Austria that now called for a quick peace settlement, whereas France, bolstered by its new alliance, had no desire to reach an agreement that it saw as premature. So once again the two allies' roles were reversed, and once again they hindered each other's movements rather than coordinating their actions. The air of uncertainty was to last only a few months, however. The British fleet's conquest of Havana (August 1762), together with a new series of Prussian victories against Austria (now deprived of Russian support) in October and November of that same year, led all the parties concerned to rapidly conclude peace negotiations in February 1763. The Peace of Hubertusburg between Prussia and Austria, simply reconstituted the *status quo ante bellum*. Prussia pledged to support Archduke Joseph's election as emperor, thus guaranteeing the Habsburg succession, but Maria Theresa was forced to renounce Silesia once again, and to give up Glatz. France came out of peace negotiations even worse than Austria; the Peace of Paris established exclusion of the country from North America and India, to Britain's sole benefit.[18] Rather than gaining the upper hand over their respective enemies, the two allies were forced to recognize the failure of their policies.[19] Furthermore, Prussia's tenacious resistance had substantial implications for both parties; for the first time since the Saxon emperors an independent power capable of looking after itself was now emerging in northern Germany. Finally, from the French point of view the feeling of having fought a mistaken war, of having agreed a peace that was "neither good nor glorious" (as Louis XV himself defined it), and of having been led to taking such false steps by an untrustworthy ally was so deeply rooted that it was to shape French policy for decades to come.

THE EASTERN QUESTION

One effect of the diplomatic revolution was to move France further away from its old east European allies, as we have already said. The traditional ties with the states forming the eastern barrier had gradually been loosened by France's alliance with Austria, and by France's relationship, albeit never easy, with Russia. Indeed, it was the latter state that was to expand significantly, and France could do nothing to stop it from doing so. The Austrian case was very different, however.

Even though the period between 1763 and 1774 is generally considered the quietest time of the alliance, those years witnessed an event that was to seriously compromise France's position in eastern Europe: the first partition of Poland (1772). The fact that France was incapable of influencing Polish affairs to any great extent was already clear in 1763–64, when Catherine's candidate, Stanislaw Poniatowski, was elected to the Polish throne with the blessing of Prussia. Poniatowski's election, the alliance stipulated by Prussian and Russia that same year (1764), and Russia's expansion toward the Balkans were an early warning to Kaunitz of the fluid nature of the situation in eastern Europe. It was in this period that he formulated his concept of *convenance* politics and the idea of "relative power," according to which each territorial gain by one state must be balanced by the territorial gains of the other states. Hence his plans for controlled expansion, with a certain preference for Germany; if expansion was not possible in this direction, then the government in Vienna would look in the direction of Poland and the Balkans (Schilling 1994, 296–354).

Ottoman concern about Russia's policy in Poland led the Sultan—egged on by France—to declare war on Catherine in 1768. Between 1769 and 1770, Austria and Prussia got closer in order that both powers could mediate in the ongoing war. Choiseul was against this, because he would have preferred the war to go on in order to keep Russia busy and eventually weaken it. However, mediation offered Austria the opportunity to make gains, representing as it did a pretext for any kind of conquest (Sorel 1902, 79–80). Uncertainty over Austria's reaction to Russia's military victories was the underlying reason for Frederick's partition plan, which was designed to avoid both a dangerous new Austro-Russian alignment and the difficult task of taking sides, which Prussia would have faced in the event of a war between Austria and Russia. There was room for everyone in Poland.

Whether it was a largely obligatory choice reflecting the greater importance given to the naval and trade war against Britain (Scott 1979, 18)—which rejected the French proposal (made in 1769) for joint action against the Russian fleet—or simply the result of mediocre official diplomacy hindered by inconclusive secret diplomacy (Rain 1945, 269–87), France's policy forced it to stand by, powerless, as Poland was carved up.[20] During the most delicate phase of the crisis, Choiseul was dismissed as a result of a conflict within the French court, and for six months France was without a foreign minister. In the end, Kaunitz pointed the finger at French weakness and disinterest, claiming he would have preferred the preservation of Poland, and would have opposed Russo-Prussian plans if France had supported him. However, given that such support was not forthcoming, Austria decided to get involved in the partition of Poland, rather than stand by and watch Russia and Prussia expand excessively, or worse still rather than find itself having to fight a war alone against these two powers (Rain 1945, 285–86). Although it may sound rather specious, there is an element of truth in this argument. From Austria's viewpoint, the partition of Poland was the lesser of two evils, but it was still a bad result, since both Russia and, worse still, Prussia had taken advantage of this state of affairs. In fact, one has to bear in mind that Austria was mainly interested in unilateral benefits in compensation for its loss of Silesia. From this point of view, therefore, the partition of Poland was a failure for Austrian policy (McKay and Scott 1983, 226–27). As far as France was concerned, the Duke of Choiseul-Praslin himself[21] had already written (in 1763) that the states of the eastern barrier represented but a vague, indirect interest from the French point of view (Anderson 1965, 259). Indeed, there was no noticeable reaction at Versailles when the terms of partition were officially notified to the French government. However, many attributed responsibility for what had happened to the very alliance with Austria; on top of anger at being exploited during the course of the Seven Years' War, the French were now angry about being dispossessed by the same avid ally (Sorel 1885–1904, 228).

In 1774, Louis XVI was crowned king of France, and he subsequently appointed Vergennes as his foreign minister. In that same year, the Russo-Turkish war, which had begun in 1768, was brought to an end. The Treaty of Kücük-Kaynarca established a number of territories to be ceded by the Ottoman Empire and also granted Crimea independence, bestowing on Russia the right to protect the Christian subjects of the Ottoman Porte. Russia's plans greatly concerned France, because the fall of Constantinople would have deprived France of an ally, of important trading rights with the Turks, and of trade in the East in general. Austria, which until then had been the traditional enemy of the Ottoman Empire, was also worried; however, its rivalry with Prussia—the only power really capable of helping Austria—prevented it from coming to an agreement with Frederick. If, though, Austria had come to an agreement with Russia to divide up Turkish spoils, Prussia would certainly have asked for its part, thus strengthening its position even further. Maria Theresa was caught between an expansionist Russia to the east and Austria's principal enemy to the north; hence her resentment against its ally, which not only refused to mediate in relations between Austria and Russia but at the same time cleverly cultivated its own relations with Prussia. When Austria annexed Bucovina in 1775, Vergennes made it known that he was no longer prepared to stand by and watch the dismemberment of the Ottoman Empire, and that he would not agree to any further Austrian territorial acquisition to the detriment of the Turks (Murphy 1982, 292). In fact, Vienna made no such further moves until the end of the decade.[22] Despite this, France could do little to help the Ottoman Empire against the Russians. In the majority of the crises that followed, Vergennes tried to play for time, maneuvering and above all hoping that the state of constant tension between the Russians and the Turks did not develop into a full-fledged war leading to the destruction of the Ottoman Empire. It should also be pointed out that from 1778 to 1783 France was busy fighting Britain in the American War of Independence.

The year after the death of Maria Theresa, Joseph formed an alliance with Russia (in May 1781), which provided for limitless reciprocal aid in the event of a Turkish attack (Madariaga 1959). The pretext that Catherine was looking for came in the form of the Crimean revolt against the Khan, who was supported by the Russians, in June 1782. Joseph could also take advantage of this crisis in order to expand into the Balkans. However, Austria had to be sure of France's reaction, especially with Russia moving away from Prussia—as a result of the Austro-Russian alliance itself—which could have led Frederick to pursue an agreement with Louis XVI. France remained important for another reason as well; in Joseph's own words, by breaking off the 1756 alliance Catherine "verrait bien que je devrais être absolument à ses ordres, ce qui pourrait être très commode pour elle, mai trés-peu convenable pour moi."[23]

It was at this rather uncertain moment in time that Austria attempted to obtain France's agreement by offering it Egypt (August 1782). Despite Egypt having represented an appealing objective for France since the time of Louis XIV, and even though just a few years earlier the French ambassador to Constantinople had suggested its acquisition to his government given that the collapse of the Ottoman Empire appeared inevitable (Murphy 1982, 319), Vergennes convinced the king to reject Austria's offer. The French foreign minister withered the Austrian ambassador with the words: "L'Egypte! Nous ne voudrions pas de ces marabouts, quand même on nous les offrirait" (quoted in Salomon 1935, 164).[24] Once more, Vergennes wanted to preserve the Ottoman Empire and was therefore against any partition plan that, regardless of the portion assigned to France, would have been more advantageous for its rivals than for France itself. Even those ministers who were enthusiastic about French control of Egypt, such as the Marquis de Castries and the Baron de Breteuil, were not keen on the idea of a partition that among other things would have granted Austria control of the Adriatic, thus transforming it into a maritime power (Hardman and Price 1998, 141–42). There can be no doubt about the benefits France would have gained from such an operation, as is shown by Castries hypothesizing a scenario in which the Ottoman Empire itself handed Egypt over to France in exchange for the latter's protection. However, had the takeover of Egypt implied destruction of the Ottoman Empire, then it would have been better to reject the offer. Vergennes, aware of the limited means at his disposal with which to protect the Porte, and still engaged in the war against Britain, chose to adopt a simple line: he would keep the Turks quiet by advising them to accept Russia's demands but reject those of Austria. Such an approach had several objectives: to prevent a war that could have resulted in the destruction of the Ottoman Empire, to limit Russian acquisitions, and to prevent any further Austrian expansion, thus inducing it into abandoning its alliance with Russia.

In September, Catherine revealed her famous "Greek plan" to Joseph. This ambitious project provided for partition of the Ottoman Empire's European territories between Russia and Austria.[25] It was a grandiose and appealing (albeit rather vague) scheme that the Emperor was at one and the same time attracted to and worried about; he accepted the plan in theory—after substantial modifications were made—although he tried to avoid its practical implementation. As a result, on the one hand Austria supported Russia's November ultimatum and mobilized troops along Turkey's borders; on the other it helped France convince the sultan to accept Catherine's demands, thereby not giving her a pretext for declaring war. Encouraged by this success, in the spring of 1783 the Tsarina continued to look for a *casus belli*. The differences over the Russo-Turkish trade agreement that was negotiated during those months, together with the assassination of a Tartar official in Taman (on the Black Sea), constituted such a pretext for war, and in May Russia occupied the Crimea. Vergennes advised the Turks, who were increasingly worried about events, to ally themselves with Prussia and be more cautious than ever. However, the Porte was by now tired of always having to give in to other's demands, and Joseph, for his part, was convinced that the fate of the Ottoman Empire was sealed. Once again he attempted to get France's agreement, offering Egypt in exchange as before, and once again France rejected his offer. During this period, Vergennes was concluding a peace agreement with Great Britain, and from that moment on France could enjoy greater freedom of movement (Hardman and Price 1998, 131–32).

In June, Joseph went so far as to reveal Catherine's plans to Vergennes, claiming that Austrian involvement was necessary if Russia were not to be given a free hand. What he was particularly concerned about at the time was that France would come to Austria's aid if the latter were attacked by Prussia during the war against the Turks, pursuant to the 1756 treaty. In a series of talks held with the Austrian ambassador, the Comte de Mercy-Argenteau, Vergennes firmly spoke against any partition; he doubted the rationale of the plan (if Austria wanted to take part in the name of the balance of power with Russia, Prussia would want compensations in return in the name of the balance of power with Austria, and so on and so forth ad infinitum), and he insisted that it would have been against Austria's interests to strengthen two such aggressive neighboring states (Salomon 1935, 179–89). Mercy came away empty-handed. Vergennes, for his part, was determined to save what he could of the situation, and to stop Austria from acting, so he offered his good offices in the Russo-Turkish conflict. He was under no illusions; such mediation would inevitably be to the detriment of the Ottoman Porte. However, at least Russian power would be contained to a certain degree, and Austria would get nothing out of it. Furthermore, he spoke of involving Prussia in negotiations. Mercy and Joseph were well aware that it was impossible to come to a satisfactory agreement (from their points of view) with Prussia, but they also knew there was the risk that Prussia and France would come to an agreement between themselves, circumventing Austria. In fact, Vergennes's proposal concealed the threat of a Franco-Prussian rapprochement in the event that Austria forged on with its plans, and France's overtures were greeted warmly in Berlin, where Frederick was more than happy to cooperate with France (Anderson 1958, 35–36). Furthermore, when Joseph asked Vergennes to mediate between Austria and the Ottoman Empire as well, in the hope of obtaining some sort of result using pacific means, his request was again refused. France accepted Russian aggression only because it was not really in a position to do anything about it; however, it had much more powerful means of preventing such aggression in Austria's case. Joseph found himself blocked; without French agreement he could do nothing in the Balkans, and even if he decided to act of his own accord regardless, thus complicating matters and threatening the very existence of the alliance with France, he would have risked facing the combined forces of France and Prussia. In the autumn of 1783, therefore, he had no choice but to renounce any hope of expansion to the detriment of the sultan. The Russo-Turkish war then ended in January 1784, with Catherine making new acquisitions, but with the Ottoman Empire saved from partition.

The result was that during the course of 1783 the Austro-French alliance reached one of its lowest points ever. Both sides were on the verge of breaking off relations, but in the end both decided not to. The heterogeneous nature of the alliance was once again apparent from the diverse constraints and opportunities making up the context within which the two allies operated. Austrian policy cannot be explained purely by countering Joseph's ambition with Maria Theresa's moderation; Austria was clearly sensitive to what was happening around itself, starting from the unstoppable decline of the Ottoman Empire and the designs on that empire of its powerful Russian neighbor. France, for its part, despite being somewhat distracted by the war against Great Britain, could not support destruction of the Ottoman Empire, for both strategic and economic reasons, but it simply did not possess the means to directly prevent this from happening. France's stake consisted not only in its trade interests but also in the future of the remaining eastern barrier, in the threat that Russian annexations posed for observance of the treaties, and in relations with both Prussia and Austria itself. Despite the apparently hypocritical nature of the respective arguments (in Austria's case, this was a new "least of two evils" scenario, while in France's view its ally had failed to resist Russian designs to a sufficient degree), they nevertheless reflect the very real needs of the two countries, both of which were faced with a crisis neither could really control; each was induced into dealing with it in a different manner, while constantly trying to convince the other of the validity of its own reasoning (Anderson 1958, 30–33). The not-breaking constraint was thoroughly tested in such circumstances; when Austrian pressure was at its height (in August), Vergennes stated that should Austria have continued with its line the alliance would have been seriously questioned. Then in September, Mercy replied that the alliance was, in fact, over. However, just a few months later, Vergennes rejected an alliance proposal from Prussia, arguing that it "ne pourra que donner un juste sujet d'ombrage à l'empereur"[26] (Salomon 1935, 239); it was the fear of a Franco-Prussian realignment that also prevented Austria from acting on the harsh words of its ambassador.

So even though the balance sheet was undoubtedly negative from an Austrian point of view, France certainly did not seem to come off too well either. It was true that the dismantling of the Ottoman Empire was prevented in the end, but Russian expansion toward the Black Sea was not stopped; it was true that Austria was contained, but control over Egypt was sacrificed in the process. Finally, though it is true that French diplomacy continued to influence the Ottoman Empire's foreign policy, at the end of the day the role of protector of the Porte was passed on to Prussia and Great Britain, while France's position in eastern Europe was reduced even further. Renouncing acquisition of Egypt in particular deserves closer analysis, since this question was hotly debated among France's ministers, who, though sharing Vergennes's anti-

Austrian stance, saw Egypt as a valuable means of strengthening trade with India and of damaging Great Britain (Hardman and Price 1998, 135–44). In other words, in blocking Austria and slowing down Russia France gave up an acquisition that would probably have been of considerable value—as 19th century developments in the British Empire were to show—and that would have increased the monarchy's prestige after the unfortunate experience of the Seven Years' War. Nevertheless, the price to be paid was simply too high. The result, in any case, was that the Crimean crisis ended with Russia making net gains, whereas neither Austria nor France, trapped within their own deadlocked alliance, managed to achieve any such gains. France did not fare any better on the naval front, for which it sacrificed active involvement in eastern and Bavarian affairs (as we shall see shortly). Despite the damage to Britain's prestige caused by the loss of 13 colonies, the Peace of Versailles (September 1783) nevertheless confirmed Britain's dominance in both colonial and trading terms; indeed, its position in India was even stronger than before. Not only did France fail to recoup those losses it suffered in 1763, but Vergennes's strategy, designed to undermine the bases of British power by depriving it of American economic resources, proved to be a failure, since Britain continued to trade with its former colonies under semimonopoly conditions (McKay and Scott 1983, 264–65).

THE WAR OF THE BAVARIAN SUCCESSION

Austria had been contemplating the idea of annexing the Bavarian electorate, and possibly exchanging it for the Low Countries, since the end of the 17th century (Bernard 1965, 6–10). This would have meant not only the territorial expansion of Austria but also concentration of a more compact block of territories around the Danube—which would invariably have had an influence throughout the whole of central Europe—and control of the access routes to Italy and France. From 1774 onward, Austria began to gather the material it needed to reclaim its rights of succession, in anticipation of the death of the Bavarian elector, Maximilian Joseph. Neither Kaunitz nor Joseph was under any illusions with regard to Frederick's opposition to such plans; however, they thought that the King of Prussia could be persuaded to accept, in exchange, the succession to two principalities, Ansbach and Bayreuth, governed by a dying minor branch of the Hohenzollern family. In any case, French support was indispensable. Vergennes was probed about the matter in 1776. He then waited until the following spring before reflecting seriously on the proposal; for a time he contemplated asking for the Low Countries in exchange should Austria really expand into Bavaria, but then he refrained from notifying Vienna of this idea (Bernard 1965, 27). During this period, Vergennes was totally absorbed by developments in North America, which offered France the opportunity to seriously damage Britain. If France had played its cards right, it could have attacked the British at the very moment they were busy in America. One corollary of this plan, of course, was that France should have avoided a European war, or in any case involvement in such a war.

During the same period, prior to Joseph's imminent visit to Paris, Vergennes prepared a memorandum for Louis XVI concerning two principal points.[27] First, Vergennes suggested that should the emperor ask for a closer relationship with France, Louis XVI was to reject such a request, since it would inevitably be directed against Prussian interests: "il est si facile de faire venir la guerre sans être matériellement l'aggresseur que Votre Majesté se trouverait entraînée contre ses intérêts toutes les fois qu'il conviendrait à la politique autrichienne de la faire."[28] It is important to bear in mind here France's renowned policy of equidistance with the two German powers, and the useful role Prussia played in counterbalancing Austria. Second, should Joseph offer the king compensations (*equivalents*) in exchange for French agreement to Austrian expansion to the detriment of the Turks, even if such recompense were to consist in the Low Countries themselves, "il n'est point d'équivalents qui pourraient compenser le préjudice que causerait a Votre Majesté tout accroissement de puissance de cette maison [the House of Austria]."[29] The harm envisaged by Vergennes concerned both the *opinion* and the diplomatic-strategic consequences; if France accepted the Low Countries as a compensation, the Dutch would immediately turn to the British, and Prussia itself would move further away from France. In practice, it was in France's interest for the Low Countries to remain in Austrian hands, since as such they constituted "une sûreté de la conduite de cette maison envers Votre Majesté et un moyen de la contenir ou de la réprimer suivant le besoin."[30] Vergennes was referring to the possibility of Austrian expansion in the East, since everyone at that time thought that in the event of a new Russo-Turkish war Austria would take advantage of the situation as it had done in the case of Bucovina. However, he was probably also thinking of Bavaria. In fact, these were the arguments he was to use the following year, and then again in 1784, to oppose Austria's Bavarian plans; not even acquisition of the Low Countries would have counterbalanced such a formidable increase in Austrian power, and even if France benefited from such a project Austria itself would gain much more than its ally. In any case, during the course of the summer Vergennes appealed directly to Frederick, who ensured him that Prussia would impede any Austrian expansion, including into Bavaria (Bernard 1965, 27).

On the death of Maximilian Joseph (December 1777), Austrian diplomats immediately came to an understanding with his successor, Charles Theodore, who agreed to recognize Habsburg claims on approximately one-third of Bavaria, which was promptly occupied by Austrian forces. The plan also envisaged a further two possible developments, the more ambitious of which consisted in a scheme whereby Austria was to obtain all of Bavaria in exchange for granting Charles Theodore the Low Countries. Austria miscalculated things, however; not only would it never overcome Prussia's inevitable opposition to its plans, but it would not even convince Charles Theodore's nephew, and eventual successor, Charles Augustus (who was elector palatine, and thus traditionally sensitive to French pressure and wealth), and certainly not France itself, to agree to such an exchange. Vergennes, who at this point was about to declare war on Great Britain,[31] found himself in a very embarrassing situation: Prussia wanted France to react, and declare as much as guarantor of the treaties of Westphalia, which had just been violated by Austria; however, if France followed Frederick's lead this obviously would jeopardize the Austro-French alliance. Vergennes managed to get around this dilemma by guaranteeing "all existing treaties"—an answer that disappointed both Prussia and Austria, with the latter looking for France's support and not its neutrality, in order to both block and fight Prussia if dissuasion were to fail (Murphy 1982, 297).

Without reaching the point of breaking off the alliance, the French next adopted a more determined stance. In February, a document was approved warning of the risk that if it were seconded, Austrian policy could encourage creation of a protestant coalition headed, of course, by Great Britain; in addition, the document stated that France was to avoid, at all costs, getting involved in a European war by preserving the balance between Prussia and Austria. Just as France was putting the final touches to its plans for neutrality, Austria put the word out that its ally knew of, and thus approved of, Austrian designs on Bavaria. Faced with such a blatant attempt at compromise (and entrapment), the French government immediately reacted by sending a clear response—in the form of a document taken to the German courts by French government representatives—in which it expressly denied having supported Austrian policy in any way (Fagniez 1922, 163–64). Besides, in March 1778 France made an official statement regarding its ally's requests for support: in the event of war with Prussia, the 1756 defensive treaty could not be invoked because it applied only to Austrian possessions, and not to expansion thereof. In the end, all that Austria managed to obtain was the pledge that the statement of French neutrality not be made public. Vergennes continued to encourage negotiations between Prussia and Austria, but the latter was now bargaining with the clear intention of creating the due conditions for invocation of a casus foederis (Fagniez 1922, 170–73). Accordingly, Vergennes adopted an even more cautious approach; if he now suggested that Austria make one too many concessions, he could be accused of being the cause of Austria's failure, whereas if he suggested too little, Austria would have a pretext for demanding French military support (Murphy 1982, 301–02).

Once again it was Frederick who took action, when in July 1778 he started the War of the Bavarian Succession. This war of little military interest did not stop ongoing negotiations between the powers in question; nor did it put an end to Austria's demands for French help. However, Vergennes now had another reason to refuse such help. France was fighting a naval war against British aggression and could not therefore divert valuable resources. Furthermore, he informed Mercy that France could ask Austria for help in turn; each time Kaunitz raised the matter—even alluding to Austrian cooperation in the event that France wished to attack Hanover—Vergennes reminded him of the ongoing naval war, with the clear understanding that France was already doing its best for Austria by not calling for application of the 1756 treaty.[32] As far as Prussia was concerned, on the one hand Vergennes would never have given it an explicit guarantee of French neutrality, but on the other hand it would never have used the harsh tone that Austria wanted France to adopt. Vergennes was clearly interested in befriending Prussia, although at the same time he did not wish to alienate Austria to the point where the latter might put an end to the Austro-French alliance. When informed of the ongoing Austro-Prussian negotiations (August 1778), Vergennes unofficially offered France's mediation in the talks and stressed that he would be concerned if one of the two parties decided to continue the war—which according to Maria Theresa was an allusion to a possible abandonment of French neutrality, in favor of Prussia, if Austria continued with its obstinacy (Bernard 1965, 125). As soon as Austria decided to show a degree of interest in France's good offices, resigned as it was by now to accepting its ally's neutrality, Vergennes, who was always careful not to hurt Austrian feelings, immediately wrote a conciliatory message to Frederick.

However, termination of the war was not so much a result of French diplomacy as of Russian intervention. In fact, Catherine duly took the opportunity to increase her influence over German affairs, and in the autumn of 1778 she certainly was freer to act than Vergennes was. The Tsarina made no secret of her sympathy for the Prussian cause, and of her hostility toward Joseph; she made it known that if the two parties failed to find a peaceful solution she would feel obliged to protect the interests of her empire and of her friends and allies (Fagniez 1922, 174). France was rather unhappy about Russia's involvement in matters. Catherine's move may have been decisive in convincing Austria to adopt a more moderate stance, but what could be done if this were not the case and Austria were attacked by Russo-Prussian forces? Kaunitz did everything within his power to get France to side with Austria, but once again France drew back, and to avoid all misunderstandings (as in the spring of that same year) it decided not to offer its advice, but proposed joint Franco-Russian mediation instead. Faced with the choice between giving in and risking having to fight alone, in the end Austria yielded. The Peace of Teschen (May 1779) saw Austria accept that it was to get only a small part of Bavaria, and renounce any further claims on the electorate.[33] Of course, it is no surprise that in Vienna the French were openly accused of having abandoned Austria, or that the Habsburg court ostentatiously expressed its intention to get closer to Great Britain (Fagniez 1922, 203).

Austria's failure was clear for all to see, but France did not fare much better either, despite having avoided the risk of entrapment. Prussia now took up the role of defender of the empire's liberties, a role that was previously a French prerogative, while recent events saw Russia gain a certain importance in German affairs, for the first time, as Russia was another guarantor of the Treaty of Teschen, which in turn was connected with the treaties of Westphalia; from then onward (until the Napoleonic era), the "active influence" of Russia in Germany was one of the most important subjects of debate in St. Petersburg (Tratchevsky 1880, 278).

LOW COUNTRIES, UNITED PROVINCES, AND BAVARIA (ONCE AGAIN): EPILOGUE

Disappointed with the outcome of the War of the Bavarian Succession, and encouraged by his new alliance with Russia, from 1781 onward Joseph began to contemplate consolidation of his position in the Low Countries and raised two questions that saw Austria on a collision course with the United

Provinces. Since 1648 (the Treaty of Münster), the Scheldt River had been closed to ships not flying the Dutch flag, which significantly contributed to the decline of Ostend (with Amsterdam being the sole beneficiary thereof) and which continued to damage the Low Countries' trade. From 1697 (the Peace of Ryswick) onward, the Dutch had enjoyed the right to occupy a series of barrier fortresses designed to protect the Low Countries against French attacks. Having decided to remove the Dutch garrisons from his land and reopen the river to shipping, between 1782 and 1784 Joseph submitted requests to this effect to the United Provinces; the first demand was partially accepted, but the second was rejected. Stiffening of negotiating positions led to an Austrian ultimatum in the summer of 1784, which was duly rejected by the Dutch, and subsequently to the capture of a ship flying the imperial flag that was trying to force its way up the river. Shortly afterward, the government in Vienna recalled its ambassador, and the crisis threatened to turn into a war.

In the spring of 1784 the Dutch, concerned about the ongoing situation, turned to France (with whom they were negotiating an alliance) and asked Louis XVI to pledge to defend the Low Countries in the event of attack, to which the King replied that he would use his good offices to such effect. Vienna, of course, also looked to see what was being done in Versailles. France thus found itself once again in a rather embarrassing situation, caught as it was in the middle of a dispute between an old ally and a future one. One of the few positive results of the war against Britain was to separate the maritime powers, and so there was no desire to risk seeing this successful outcome ruined. Furthermore, the war left France weak and burdened with debt, which meant, among other things, that it had to avoid any further war at all cost. Finally, news got out that Frederick was inciting the Dutch to resist Austrian pressures, which made Vergennes even warier (Murphy 1982, 406–407). Although Joseph displayed great faith in French help, during the summer Vergennes advised him to moderate his demands, adding that France would not support him in submitting any ultimatums (Bernard 1965, 177).

At this point, the affairs of the Low Countries became interwoven with events in Bavaria. At the end of 1782, the question of the Bavarian succession resurfaced following Charles Theodore's illness, and this time around Austria sought exchange of Bavaria for the Low Countries from the very beginning. For the entire year thereafter, Austrian diplomats tried to get France's support, but the modest results of their efforts led Kaunitz, in December, to reach the sad conclusion (which was entirely true) that France continued to consider Austria a rival and as such would oppose any actions that were capable of increasing Austrian power (Bernard 1965, 149–50). Austria, however, did not give up. After all, unlike in 1778–79, this time round Russia was its ally. It was true that if things went wrong there would still be the risk of France allying with Prussia, but this was unlikely; it was more likely that France would remain neutral (due to Russian pressure to do so), at which point Prussia would be isolated. Catherine seemed to be on the side of Austria, at least on paper, and so Austria seconded the stipulation of the treaty on the basis of which Russia officially annexed the Crimea (January 1784), and then shortly afterward began to push through its Bavarian plan.

In the spring of 1784, Kaunitz's instructions to the Austrian ambassador in St. Petersburg contained, among other things, the recommendation to point out to Catherine that the exchange in question would enable Austria to free itself of France's hold, which showed that the Austrians fully understood the true reason for Vergennes's hostility toward their plan (Bernard 1965, 159–60). Indeed, they understood it so well, one could add, that when it came to officially informing France of the ongoing negotiations with Charles Theodore and Charles Augustus, Mercy was under no illusions; according to him, France would not allow the exchange to take place, because it was convinced that if Austria were freed of the Low Countries, it would become more dangerous (Bernard 1965, 178). In October, having realized the obstinacy of the two electors in rejecting Austrian demands, Kaunitz finally decided to appeal to France. However, at that very moment the crisis with the United Provinces reached its peak, and Joseph had the idea of connecting the two questions, believing that by making concessions on the Scheldt he could convince the French government to support him in his Bavarian plans.

During the previous months, France had behaved prudently with regard to the Austro-Dutch crisis, not because it shared Joseph's aspirations but because it was feared that Austrian intransigence would prevent emergence of a Franco-Dutch alliance (Grosjean 1925, 103–106). However, although on the one hand France could not stand by and watch impassively as Austria threatened the United Provinces, on the other hand France did not wish to extend sympathy for such a potential ally to the point where it might be induced to stiffen its position (Murphy 1982, 408). Now that Austria was threatening to declare war on the United Provinces, the French Council of State decided to adopt a clearer stand. On November 20, a statement was drafted containing not only an offer of mediation but also a clear refusal to take on the cause of the opening of the Scheldt; the document went on to state that the king "ne pourra même se dispenser d'assembler des troupes sur ses frontières," since "dans aucune hypothèse ne pouvait être indifférent au sort des Provinces-Unies."[34] The views expressed in Berlin were obviously not very different; Catherine went no further than sending a note to the United Provinces in which, although supporting the Emperor's requests, she expressed her wishes for a solution that satisfied both parties. Joseph was once again isolated; as a result, he had to make do with what French diplomacy could obtain for him.

During those very same weeks, the Bavarian question came to a head. Mercy officially notified Vergennes of the exchange plan, adding that the emperor would renounce his claims against the United Provinces if the Bavarian plan were successful. Vergennes gave an interlocutory reply;[35] however, immediately afterward, the French government alerted the Prussian and British governments, and around a month later (January 1785), when the king's council met to discuss the matter, there was almost universal hostility to the proposal, with some ministers even suggesting that France declare war on Austria.[36] Louis XVI thus wrote to Joseph, claiming that the exchange would have compromised the European balance of power and the Germanic constitution, and that such a transaction could not be made in any case without the approval of the king of Prussia. Austria's reaction to this was not difficult to imagine. As early as December, Joseph, who already felt himself completely in French hands, had written: "Si seulement nous pouvions avoir troqué les Pays-Bas, alors nous serions hors de leurs griffes, et l'on pourrait un jour peut-être les en faire repentir, s'ils avaient une nouvelle guerre avec les Anglais."[37] Louis XVI's letter led Leopold to observe that the king of France was "un homme sans charactère ni tête" (quoted in Tratchevsky 1881, 31), and Kaunitz then had Vergennes informed that if he thought it was so easy to get Austria to take one thing for something completely different, he was sadly mistaken (Bernard 1965, 206). The whole affair then finally collapsed shortly afterward, when Charles Augustus turned to Frederick for help in ridding himself of Austrian pressure and Charles Theodore, frightened by the way things were going, even denied he had negotiated the exchange. Now that the Austrian plan was made public, Prussia cleverly took advantage of the situation and in July set up a coalition of German princes worried by Austrian maneuvers. Austria's position in the empire became so precarious that Joseph was obliged to make a proclamation in which he pledged to comply with the terms of the Peace of Teschen.

The importance of the *Fürstenbund* should not be overestimated; only half of the electors, together with a dozen minor princes, joined. Nevertheless, Frederick's move further weakened France's remaining role in the empire; indeed, an irritated Vergennes advised the German sovereigns to remain independent from both Vienna and Berlin, and to form a "third party" (Tratchevsky 1881, 37) that France would have been happy to support. Not only did Vergennes's advice go unheeded but through Hanover (a member of the league) even Great Britain became involved in German affairs once again. Negotiations with the United Provinces dragged on until November of that year and were complicated by (among other things) Joseph's insistence in demanding the fortress in Maastricht, especially after the failure of the Bavarian plan. The Treaty of Fontainebleau (1785) gave the emperor a number of small territorial gains in the Brabant and Limburg regions, together with dismantling of certain Dutch fortresses and sovereignty over a section of the Scheldt; however, the river was to remain closed to navigation. Joseph also received an indemnity of approximately 10 million florins for having renounced possession of Maastricht, and half of this sum was paid by France despite the country's rather dire financial straits at the time. Although this was an unusual way of being recompensed for its role as mediator, a war would have been a worse outcome for France.

For our purposes, we can stop here. A deadlocked alliance no longer exists when one of its founding elements changes. For example, heterogeneity may become so acute that it renders any interaction between the allies one of pure conflict, or it may become sufficiently weak as to allow cooperation between those same allies. Alternatively, the relations of power and dependence cease being symmetrical, and one ally is capable of dragging the other along in its chosen direction; or it frees itself from the other's grip because it gets support from a new ally; or the original ally is no longer capable of fulfilling its role as such. This is what happened in the second half of the decade, during the final phase of a monarchy that had already been on the wane for some time, when France stood by, helpless, as Prussia moved into the United Provinces (1787). France was even incapable of finding the necessary resources for basic administrative purposes, having prevented the king from levying any new taxes without prior consultation with the States-General. In 1788, Austria and Russia once again turned against the Ottoman Empire and in doing so tried anew to involve France, and once more Louis XVI and the Count of Montmorin (who replaced Vergennes in 1787) refused to agree to French involvement. However, at this point France was completely absorbed by its domestic crisis and stopped playing any active role in international politics. Therefore it was not Austria that marginalized France, but France that abandoned the scene and turned in on itself. Joseph was already rejoicing at France's problems in 1782, because this gave Austria the chance to "do what it wanted";[38] this opportunity arose in 1788, although Austria once again failed to take it, notwithstanding France's evident decline.

It is true that the events of 1783 and 1785 led Austria to move away from France, but the alliance actually came to end following the domestic troubles of one of its members. The ultimate paradox of an often paradoxical story was that this domestic crisis was partly due to the 1756 treaty. According to Leopold von Ranke, in fact, the alliance with Austria was one of the underlying causes of the French Revolution, since it contributed to a cooling off in relations between the crown and the nation that "noticed only what others conquered and not what she had kept. She looked with resentment on such strong, well-established powers, for which she was no longer a match."[39]

We have seen how control over an ally can be exercised by rejecting its overtures, concessions, and offers of expansion; perhaps, as Vergennes claimed, France no longer had any territorial ambitions, satisfied as it was with the status quo (Labourdette 1990, 74–77), or perhaps those offers were never sufficiently appealing. Be that as it may, this attitude was a great hindrance to any real cooperation with Austria, and it was certainly one of the reasons France failed to achieve any tangible results during this period. All of this was a further source of serious discredit for the government, accused (among other things) of having clearly reduced France's international ranking. It was no surprise, therefore, that from the very beginning French revolutionary energies were directed toward other countries, in particular Austria, in a veritable rediscovery of geopolitical vocations and tendencies that were totally in keeping with France's traditions.

The heterogeneity and symmetry that characterized Austro-French relations led to a unique situation from the very start: the two countries' respective positions meant that neutrality between them was impossible. Either they were allies or they were at war (Hardman and Price 1998, 145). This was true of the France of the Ancien Régime and of its revolutionary successor; on at least two occasions—in 1783, in the name of protecting the Ottoman Empire, and in 1785, in the name of protecting the Germanic empire—France was on the point of moving from its alliance with Austria to war against Austria. Then in the tumultuous month of January 1792 the Girondists asked provocatively whether the guarantee that the emperor had granted to the territories of the elector of Trier—one of the émigrés' refuges—was compatible with the 1756 alliance or not, because if it was not then this would mean not only the end of the Austro-French alliance but also an immediate state of war between the two countries—a war which was to be declared just three months later.

Conclusions

A REAPPRAISAL OF THE ALLIANCE DILEMMAS

The case studies examined in this book were chosen to illustrate the most salient characteristics of the four types of alliance submitted in the first part of the present study. They were thus selected because they reflect those traits and dynamics we emphasized in the theoretical section. At the same time, the attributes of the four types have been established by a process of theoretical deduction, often taking the implications of each characteristic to the extreme in order to differentiate it as much as possible from the others, and drawing clear borders around each type. As usually happens in such cases, these borders become hazier as we move from the theoretical to the historical-empirical level, or in other words, as the relations between certain variables, expressed in as stylized and simple a form as possible, are juxtaposed to a complex and at times contradictory reality. If, despite this, we can observe some correspondence between the historical reconstruction and what our framework led us to expect, we can proceed with our research in these directions in order to perform a real test of our hypotheses; however, even those discrepancies that inevitably emerge may be of use, because they can give us suggestions as to how to review and redraft the ideas drawn up here.

If alliances are to be seen, first and foremost, as a means by which one ally tries to obtain the other's conformity, then it would be fair to expect what we have called the alliance power dilemma to play a major role. Our fear that an ally is going to become too powerful clearly reflects the need to control that ally's movements, and to see that it does not free itself of our control. Equally, the opposing fear that the same ally could become too weak is the result of the need we have of its "services," whatever they may be; an excessively weak ally is not going to be able to help us and indeed will force us to take responsibility for it. Such trends can be seen in both symmetrical and asymmetrical alliances. Where power relations are even, each party will do its utmost to prevent the other from upsetting this balance and moving into a commanding position from which it can exercise power unilaterally; where there is a power imbalance, the stronger ally will benefit from the continued presence of the weaker ally, while the latter will try to circumscribe its dependence in various ways. The general rule, let us not forget, is that an ally should be strong enough to provide those "services" deemed necessary, but not so strong as to refuse its conformity. The two asymmetrical alliances we examined have often revealed this trend: Great Britain, which was the major ally in both cases, constantly maneuvered to keep the United Provinces and France in a subordinate position that would have rendered the two countries susceptible to British pressure. Similarly, the two minor allies regularly attempted to limit their dependence on Britain, by trying to differentiate their own diplomatic contacts, making themselves indispensable to British policy, or getting involved in lengthy negotiations and complex processes of mediation. The struggle for power that characterizes both types of asymmetrical alliance with such essential traits does, however, differ to a certain extent from one case to the other. In the Anglo-Dutch alliance, for example, the parties concerned were often prepared to settle their differences, whereas in the Anglo-French alliance, each tried to impose its will on the other by forcing through a solution that would have benefited one to the detriment of the other. This is immediately confirmed by the characteristic results of such forms of interaction; despite the United Provinces being in a position of subordination in relation to their stronger ally, they nevertheless benefited from the alliance, whereas France was often penalized by its alliance with Great Britain. In the two symmetrical alliances, by contrast, the alliance power dilemma appeared in a very different form; in the case of Anglo-Prussian relations, neither of the two allies showed any concern about its ally's successes, and both were capable of cooperating in a feasible, mutually beneficial manner. In the case of the Austro-French alliance, the two nations closely controlled one another, using their powers to block the other's movements. Indeed, the most important thing was to ensure that the distribution of power within the alliance was not upset, even if this meant there was to be no significant cooperation between the parties.

These differences within the same classes of alliance have been linked to a further dimension of inter-ally relations, their homogeneity or heterogeneity. It was logical to imagine that the fear of an ally growing too strong would be greater within heterogeneous alliances, where the members often find themselves in dissimilar positions, while the fear that one's ally may become weaker would be more commonly found in homogeneous alliances, where the presence of a common cause overrides concern about the strengthening of the other party. Such hypotheses may now be revised, if we consider that even in homogeneous alliances it is only under extreme conditions—that is, prior to, or during the course of, a war—that the fear of the excessive strengthening of the ally gives way to the opposing fear of excessive weakening of that same ally. The Anglo-Prussian alliance existed in its entirety during the course of a war, when Britain's major worry was the possible collapse of Prussia; but as soon as the war looked as if it were coming to an end, the collapse of Prussia proved to be, on the contrary, to Great Britain's advantage, because it seemed to enable Britain to force Frederick to accept peace terms essentially based on British interests. As far as the Anglo-Dutch alliance is concerned, this saw Britain pushing for the strengthening of the ally's army, particularly in view of a possible new war with France. It is true that the United Provinces had already entered a phase of decline some time earlier, and so their strengthening could never have constituted grounds for concern from the British point of view; but it is also true that when peace seemed sufficiently solid, the British government did all kinds of things to hinder any Dutch diplomatic or trade measures that could have enabled them to get free of British control. The two heterogeneous alliances, for their part, clearly highlight the importance played by the fear of an ally's strengthening. This was the case with the Austro-French alliance, when France never seconded Austrian plans in the Balkans, in Bavaria, and in the Low Countries, and it even rejected the offer of a series of reciprocal territorial acquisitions, convinced as it was that such acquisitions would have benefited Austria even further. The Anglo-French alliance was constantly characterized by Britain's determined undermining of its ally's political and diplomatic weight, by forcing it to abandon previously consolidated positions and increasingly compromising it, so as to strictly bind it to British policy.

This constant struggle for power between allies constitutes the broad context within which some manifestations of Snyder's alliance security dilemma become more precise. According to Snyder, allies often have to deal with two opposite fears, of being abandoned and of becoming entrapped; the measures taken to avoid one outcome render the other outcome more likely. Having noted that this dilemma arises in particular in situations in which there is a real risk of war, and thus generally only during certain phases of an alliance, we then developed one of Snyder's own points and hypothesized that this dilemma is more acute in symmetrical alliances as a result of each ally's awareness of its need of the other's support, whereas in asymmetrical alliances it is the more dependent member that is particularly affected. Indeed the minor ally, fearing abandonment, tends to hold on so tightly to the stronger member that it then runs the risk of entrapment; the less dependent member has to be particularly careful not to become entrapped. In practice, in the two asymmetrical alliances we have examined here, Great Britain (the less dependent member in both cases) never showed any concern about becoming entrapped; being the leader of the two alliances in question, it often took the initiative and was well aware of its superiority in relation to the other allies. If anything, Great Britain was not worried about being abandoned in the strict sense of the word (that is, in the face of an enemy), but rather was concerned that it might have lost control over its weaker allies, which were important not only (and not so much) for the common cause but also for its foreign policy as a whole. In other words, the true risk for the more powerful ally is that it may not be able to obtain the conformity of its weaker partner; this risk is associated more with the broader power dilemma than with the security dilemma. As far as the minor allies are concerned, the risk of being abandoned is indeed more palpable; nevertheless, it should not be exaggerated. Given that the major ally benefits from exercising power over the minor allies, its threats of dumping them if they do not conform to its requirements are not entirely credible. In practice, the major ally has a series of other weapons at its disposal; one has only to think of the number of times Britain implicitly blackmailed (in trading terms) the United Provinces, or of the clever way in which British diplomacy managed to play off one nation against another during the period of the Anglo-French alliance, in a complex European diplomatic system that afforded France increasingly less room for maneuver. The regent not only had to be careful that France was not abandoned, he also had little alternative to a close relationship with Britain. As regards the two symmetrical alliances, the abandonment-entrapment dilemma was more evident in the case of Austro-French relations than in the Anglo-Prussian alliance, which means power relations alone cannot explain the various forms taken by the alliance security dilemma.

Once again, therefore, the further distinction between homogeneous and heterogeneous types of alliance has helped us get a better understanding of the conditions under which Snyder's hypotheses hold true or not. We have seen how the risk of entrapment is particularly high in heterogeneous alliances where the existence of several particular causes encourages every member to try to get its partner to conform to its own will. France paid the price for this in its alliance with Great Britain, when it was forced to declare war on Spain, and it did so once again in its alliance with Austria, during the initial stages of the Seven Years' War. In homogeneous alliances, by contrast, and in particular in those cases where a common enemy is present, the risk of entrapment would seem to be lower. Such a risk was almost nonexistent in the case of the Anglo-Prussian alliance, where neither ally ever found itself fighting for the other's benefit, or even running the risk of doing so. However, in the case of the Anglo-Dutch alliance, things were a little more complex. After the Peace of Utrecht, the United Provinces were always extremely reluctant when faced with the prospect of being involved in new wars. It is true that Dutch policy was easily influenced by French conduct; the United Provinces either held on tightly to Britain or tried to move away from it, depending on how threatening or conciliatory France was at the time—that is, to use our terms, depending on the degree of homogeneity that French conduct gave the alliance. However, this behavior, which was in keeping with our hypotheses, coexisted with another basic tendency of Dutch policy after 1713, its constant propensity toward neutrality. This was nothing more than the logical consequence of the Republic's inexorable decline, as historical studies have clearly shown, but it would suggest that even in homogeneous alliances one member may feel the risk of entrapment more than is normally expected, if its foreign policy is affected by its own weakness; on several occasions the United Provinces tried to reach an agreement with France *despite* the protection they were offered by Britain.

According to Snyder, the fear of abandonment and the fear of entrapment are closely interwoven. The measures taken to prevent the former make the latter more likely, and vice versa. This relationship is very convincing from a logical point of view, but it is less so from a historical perspective, since in those cases examined here the fear of abandonment is, to a certain extent independent of any fear of entrapment. Both Prussia and Great Britain were worried that their respective allies might have made a separate peace agreement with other nations; however, this fear did not contribute to their entrapment, since neither found itself fighting another nation's war. The United Provinces were abandoned by Britain during the final stages of the War of the Spanish Succession, despite their having supported British policy all along; in other words, the Dutch were first entrapped and then abandoned. Furthermore, although during the decades that followed there was less risk of being abandoned by Britain again, this was not matched by an equal reduction in the Dutch Republic's fear of entrapment. In the case of Austria and France, the risk of abandonment entailed the worrying prospect of the other party forming an alliance with the enemy—France with Prussia, and Austria with Britain—and this undoubtedly helped keep the Austro-French alliance going despite reciprocal recriminations. However, the two countries never got to the point where they risked entrapment. Perhaps the Anglo-French alliance was the only one (of those examined here) in which the correspondence suggested by Snyder held true: France complied to the point where it became entrapped (in the war against Spain), or more generally speaking to the point where it compromised itself in the eyes of the other states (both existing and future allies), for its fear of abandonment by Britain. Therefore it is only in the case of the asymmetrical, heterogeneous alliance—the hegemonic alliance—that the unfortunate consequences of each of the two options (getting closer to or moving away from one's ally) seem to be mutually connected in the manner Snyder indicates, and only in the case of the weaker ally.

The policy adopted vis-à-vis the adversary does not necessarily have the implications for inter-ally relations that Snyder suggests it does, either. According to Snyder, a firm stand with regard to the enemy would have two effects: on the one hand, it would reassure the ally and as a result lessen the risk of its abandoning us, and on the other hand it would reduce our bargaining power in relation to that ally and put it in a position to entrap us. A conciliatory approach to the enemy also has two effects: it enables us to block an impetuous ally, reducing the likelihood of its entrapping us, but at the same time such an approach will also displease the ally and give it cause to contemplate abandoning us. The cases examined here, however, tend to point to the existence of less linear relations in such circumstances. In heterogeneous alliances, where each ally has its own enemy, one ally has no reason to adopt a strict approach to the principal enemy of the other ally; neither France nor Austria reached such a point in their respective relations with Prussia and Great Britain. On the contrary, they always took great care to leave a door open for their traditional allies, as a means of exercising pressure on their current allies. When power relations are skewed in favor of one ally, as in the case of the Anglo-French alliance, the determination displayed by the more powerful ally with regard to its own enemy was obviously a concern for the weaker ally, because it perceived the risk of being dragged into a war that did not concern it, or in any case finding itself in a difficult position. Nevertheless, France had no choice and was obliged to conform to Britain's decisions, regardless of their nature. In other words, France often found itself entrapped by Britain's intransigence toward its enemies, which is the opposite outcome to the one envisaged by Snyder. A conciliatory approach to the ally's main enemy is a characteristic feature of heterogeneous alliances. Such an approach certainly reduces the risk of entrapment, and it also worries the ally as well. However, this does not mean that the dissatisfied ally can actually leave the alliance. In symmetrical alliances, reciprocal needs tend to discourage abandonment. Even though the relationship between Austria and France was one of constant accusations and recriminations, and regardless of the fact that one of them impeded the other's movements, all other alliance options promised to be even less favorable. In asymmetrical alliances, if the more dependent member adopts a flexible policy toward the major ally's enemy, it will be exposed not so much to the risk of abandonment as to that of being placed in an even more difficult position by the continuous pressure exerted by the major ally. France frequently tried to mediate between Britain and its enemies, but such mediation was always conducted subject to the terms and conditions established in London.

In homogeneous alliances, the allies can be expected to agree on the position to be taken, whether one of firmness or of conciliation, with regard to their common enemy, and so the negative effects traditionally associated with the two policies are felt to a lesser degree. In the Anglo-Prussian alliance, a joint policy of firmness with regard to the shared enemies had a reassuring effect on both allies and correspondingly helped reduce the risk of abandonment without this having any serious effect on the risk of entrapment. When a conciliatory approach was adopted—as shown in the lengthy negotiations conducted by Great Britain with France on two occasions during the course of the war—such a policy was also agreed on and so did not upset Frederick or encourage him to abandon his ally. It was only when the alliance's homogeneity became strained during the final stages of the war that the two aspects of the dilemma fully emerged. Britain's conciliatory policy blocked Prussia and upset it to the point where it was induced to take immediate advantage of the situation that presented itself as a result of Russia's realignment; for its part, Frederick's determination towards Austria led the British to fear they might become entrapped in a European war that, from the British point of view, had nothing more to offer. As regards the Anglo-Dutch alliance, Britain's firm stand against France reassured the United Provinces at a time when France seemed to represent a serious threat once again; however, this did not mean that Britain ran any risk of entrapment. On the contrary, on several occasions the United Provinces themselves feared they were being "overprotected" by their ally—entrapped by it—and consequently tried to maintain acceptable bilateral relations with France. Here, as in the case of the other type of asymmetrical alliance, if the minor ally adopts a flexible approach to the enemy, this exposes it not so much to the risk of abandonment as to the discontent of its more powerful partner, and therefore to the due consequences of such a situation.

CLASSES, TYPES, AND POLARITY

The various forms taken by the two dilemmas depend on the relation of forces between the allies, and how their respective situational contexts cause them to regard each other. The symmetry or asymmetry of power relations gives us important clues as to how each ally pursues the conformity of the other, and it indicates the existence of a relationship based on "exchange" in the first case or "dominion and dependence" in the second. However, all of this may not be enough for us to account for a series of further, equally important differences between allies, which may be expressed this way: in certain cases, the allies closely cooperate and negotiate in an accommodative manner, with beneficial results for both, but in other cases each ally opposes the other's actions and so any negotiations tend to be of a coercive character, whereby the results benefit one party to the detriment of the other or leave both parties dissatisfied. The distinction between symmetrical and asymmetrical alliances has been flanked by the distinction between homogeneous and heterogeneous alliances, in order to account for such differences.

The interweaving of the two dimensions has revealed certain clear characteristics in the case of symmetrical alliances. We have witnessed one case of substantial, positive cooperation (the Anglo-Prussian aggregation alliance) centered on exchange relations, and another case in which both parties denied their services to the other, with each party proving incapable of convincing the other to follow it (the Austro-French deadlocked alliance). A comparison of the two symmetrical alliances has revealed radically different characteristics for which homogeneity on the one hand and heterogeneity on the other would seem to offer a certain explanation. However, when the distribution of power is asymmetrical, then homogeneity and heterogeneity may well have less clear implications than one would have expected in the abstract. In fact, the comparison between the guarantee alliance and the hegemonic alliance offers more unclear conclusions regarding the effects of homogeneity and heterogeneity, since when power relations are skewed in favor of one party, the less dependent party, be it a guarantor or a hegemon, is always going to be inherently inclined to make its bargaining power felt, while the more dependent party will have very little room for maneuver. At times, homogeneity is capable of concealing or attenuating the consequences of a power imbalance, but it cannot do much at decisive moments in time. It did not prevent Great Britain from agreeing to a separate peace at the end of the War of the Spanish Succession; nor did it prevent the same country from imposing peace terms on the United Provinces (in Utrecht) that were very different from those the Dutch had hoped to obtain; nor did it prevent Britain from frequently attempting to involve its ally in wars that had nothing to do with the two powers' joint defense against French aggression. Furthermore, the tone of negotiations between the two countries was not always accommodative, because it did not reflect only the costs of an agreement that was almost taken for granted; in certain cases, agreement was not reached, a clear sign of the fact that the underlying grounds of the dispute went well beyond mere distribution of costs and benefits. Finally, the reluctance with which the United Provinces at times followed their guarantor was not that different from France's reluctance to follow the hegemon.

The objection could be made that the Anglo-Dutch alliance was therefore not particularly representative, from the point of view of homogeneity. However, we have seen how the two allies remained close for decades, as a result of their mutual fear of France, of the importance they both gave to the protestant succession, of their interest in the joint economic exploitation of the Low Countries, and how all of this gave them a certain propensity toward cooperation, regardless of the existence of particular causes, such as their chronic trade rivalry and the Dutch Republic's neutralist tendencies. Let us limit ourselves to noting that during the various stages in the life of an alliance, its symmetrical or asymmetrical, homogeneous or heterogeneous nature emerges to a more or less marked degree. As we shall see, it is a change in one, or both, of these dimensions that leads to transformation of an alliance, if not to its demise. Generally speaking, it is understandable that any alliance lasting for decades, even if it is homogeneous like the Anglo-Dutch alliance, will experience certain moments of crisis during the course of which the particular causes forcibly emerge. If such moments are more than simply a period of adjustment and actually represent a true process of transformation of homogeneity into heterogeneity (from the 1730s onward, the two countries began to move away from each other) and the inexorable decline of one of the allies (the growing weakness of the Dutch Republic we have mentioned on more than one occasion), then it not surprising that the mere asymmetry in terms of power is felt to an increasingly greater degree. However, the case in hand also suggests another conclusion, which could be of importance for all guarantee alliances: if the alliance is asymmetrical, homogeneity is chiefly a reflection of how the lesser power stands in relation to its more powerful ally, that is, how the former *unilaterally* adapts to the latter's needs. If the stronger party is always, in the last analysis, tempted to make its negotiating power felt, and if the weaker ally has no real choice but to reconcile itself to the major ally's needs, the fact that the weaker ally is in the end "guaranteed" to a certain degree depends on a combination of circumstances whereby, by resigning itself to the major ally's demands, the weaker ally nevertheless sees some of its more important objectives satisfied.

The multitude of international alliances that characterized the 18th century included, in truth, but a few homogeneous alliances[1]; there were not several cases in which a common cause monopolized the allies' attention to the point where their particular causes were pushed into the background, unless a common enemy, or several common enemies, managed to perform this catalyzing function. This conclusion renders justice to traditional approaches, but it also demonstrates once again their limitations, which we may now formulate in more specific terms. If the theoretical focus is very much on the role played by the common enemy, not only can very little be said about heterogeneous alliances but we are forced to underestimate certain characteristics of homogeneous alliances as well. One only has to think of the rather ambiguous position often adopted by the United Provinces with regard to France. As was argued at the very beginning of the present work, traditional theory manages to grasp only one aspect of certain alliances (homogeneous alliances), which are indeed a rare occurrence.

In the case of 18th century alliances, this latter assertion needs further qualification. To this end, we should be reminded of one important structural variable that has been parameterized so far in order to make it easier to compare the four historical alliances examined here: the polarity of the international system. It has been pointed out that during the Cold War, the Atlantic Alliance represented an example of truly extraordinary homogeneity, given the number of allies in question and their respective geographical positions, and that this homogeneity can be traced back to the bipolar nature of the international system: "the definition of interests was to a large extent the result of the structure of the system" (Colombo 2001, 152). To tell the truth, not even this view should be absolutized; we are all well aware of the chronic differences within NATO during the Cold War, of the neutralist tendencies of some European allies, of the struggle for conformity aimed at establishing who should have taken on the greatest risks, and of the recurrent doubts about the trustworthiness of the American guarantee (Joffe 1987). In any case, an initial comparison between alliances in a bipolar system and those in a multipolar system would suggest that in the latter case homogeneity is truly a rare occurrence. Of course, as we have seen, systemic pressures can also be strong in a multipolar system, when the configuration of alignments leaves states little room for maneuver or a limited number of options—the unlikely, yet fortunate, Anglo-Prussian alliance being perhaps the best example of this. However, whereas in bipolar systems (if we admit a generalization based on the Cold War) the closing of spaces coincides with identification of a common enemy, in multipolar systems alliances often have a less specific function, that is, to avoid isolation. France found itself isolated in 1716 and in 1756, while Great Britain and Prussia were both isolated in 1756. Forming an alliance with whoever is willing to do so (there are some nations that are willing to do so almost by chance, and others that reach such a point following a process of patient, expert diplomacy) does not mean ipso facto sharing an enemy or enemies. As a rule, then, uncertainty and precariousness are common features of alliances in multipolar systems; things are even more complicated when, as in our case, the system in question is not only multipolar but also devoid of any one state with the strength and means to impose its own hegemonic will upon others. In other words, it is a system with no coagulating factor, any fixed point of reference that catalyzes the attention of the majority of states. The immediate result of this peculiar arrangement is that international relations are always extremely fluid, both between traditional enemies (the Austro-French alliance being the most sensational example of this) and, more important, between allies themselves. The very fact that the differences in power between the states in question are not so great means that each is prone to pay particular attention to the other's moves, be they enemies or allies, in order to defend one's relative position at the very least.

When there is a fairly even distribution of power among the members of an alliance, then this competitive logic is taken to the extreme. In fact, during the historical period examined here, within the class of homogeneous alliances there are far more guarantee alliances than aggregation alliances, which would seem to confirm that among equals shared interests are no more important than conflicting interests as a rule.[2] "Three-way" systems are not particularly representative of multipolarity; nevertheless, it is interesting to note that in his studies of "triads" Theodore Caplow (1959) reaches the conclusion that alliances among equals are more likely in a so-called terminal situation, which is explicitly compared to the case of hostile states contemplating the use of force. Such extreme circumstances require exceptional measures to be taken. The Anglo-Prussian alliance emerged in a terminal situation: the imminence, and then outbreak, of a war that temporarily rendered the relationship between the two powers homogeneous. Guarantee alliances, on the other hand, are slightly more common; thus there is a greater chance of finding a genuine common cause when the relationship between allies is of a hierarchical nature. If one may try and extrapolate a conclusion from this observation, one could say that homogeneity is a consequence not only of the minor ally's ability to adapt to the policy of its more powerful partner but also of the latter's ability to shape the former's milieu, and thus its interests. Without the guarantee offered by Great Britain, the United Provinces would inevitably have behaved differently toward France, and they would have been even more likely to pursue a settlement with the French. It was their alliance with Britain that contributed to preservation of the French threat over the course of the years following the Peace of Utrecht.

In light of all this, one can understand the specific meaning of the term *balance of power* when referred to the 18th century. It was not a case of preventing one state from becoming the hegemon of the system, since there was no one state capable of filling this role. Rivalries at that time were mainly bilateral: France-Great Britain, Austria-Prussia, France-Austria, Russia-Ottoman Empire. So it was not a case of maintaining the balance of power in Europe so much as preventing one's direct rival from damaging one's position. Thus the balance of power took the form of a system of alliances and counteralliances that were created and then broken up, over the course of the years. During the period of "British preponderance," the Anglo-French alliance (also involving the United Provinces) was countered at a certain point by the Austro-Spanish alliance; the War of Austrian Succession gave rise to the opposition of Britain and Austria on the one hand and France and Prussia on the other; and then after the Seven Years' War, the Austro-French alliance was countered by the Russo-Prussian alliance. All of these alliances, on which the European system of states was based, were characterized by a strong degree of heterogeneity; they never consisted in mere opposition to a common enemy but displayed all those competitive traits that we have highlighted in the present study.

THE TRANSFORMATION AND DEMISE OF ALLIANCES

It is, of course, a truism to say that the transformation and demise of alliances depends on changes in the circumstances that give rise to them, or inspire their creation, in the first place. What exactly is hidden behind this term *circumstances*—which is so frequently employed and which neither historians nor political scientists seem to be able to do without? According to our theoretical-conceptual framework, the term refers, first and foremost, to the two main dimensions so often cited, that is, the power relations between the two parties to an alliance, and the congruity of their positions. Our typology is an attempt to underline the essential features of a given alliance, establishing the ideal-type state of relations between its members. In this sense, there can be no doubt that the typology tends to be of a static nature. However, one can imagine shifts from one type to another in terms of the two dimensions; for example, power relations initially weighted heavily toward one member of an alliance could become more evenly balanced; likewise, relations that at the beginning are basically heterogeneous could become homogeneous, thereby lending the alliance greater cohesion and rendering it more effective; or initially homogeneous relations that eventually become heterogeneous can create problems from the point of view of inter-ally cooperation (in the case of symmetrical alliances) or exacerbate the coercive nature of bargaining (in the case of asymmetrical alliances). Then when the bargaining space becomes so narrow as to virtually disappear altogether—that is, when even the constraint not to break up the alliance (so characteristic of heterogeneous alliances) becomes weakened sufficiently to no longer constitute a deterrent, the alliance collapses; this means the downward movement along the homogeneity-heterogeneity axis has eventually pushed relations between the two allies outside of the typology. This is just another way of saying that the alliance no longer exists.

The four historical cases help illustrate such dynamics, albeit as a first approximation. The Anglo-Dutch alliance started as an aggregation alliance, before being transformed into a guarantee alliance during the course of the War of the Spanish Succession. Nevertheless, it remained a homogeneous alliance, although the power relations between Britain and the United Provinces had changed. The two allies continued to cooperate for many years on the basis of this transformed arrangement; however, over the course of time a marked heterogeneity began to emerge. The United Provinces' extreme weakness, and France's conciliatory approach, meant that those obligations undertaken by the Dutch in relation to Great Britain became increasingly burdensome, while the protection offered by Britain became almost counterproductive. For its part, British policy designed to involve the ally in anti-French actions was gradually meant almost exclusively to control overseas trade, rather than provide the two allies with necessary security and protection. In other words, it would be true to say that during their final years Anglo-Dutch relations resembled those of a hegemonic alliance more than a guarantee alliance, given the prevalence of coercive tactics developed by Britain and the clear difference in the systemic positions of the two nations.

The other homogeneous alignment—the Anglo-Prussian alliance—developed in a very different manner and according to its own timescale. Britain and Prussia suddenly found themselves united by war, and they separated just as quickly toward the end of that war following changes affecting both dimensions of the alliance. Prussia's increasing problems were countered by Britain's successes, and this altered the initial symmetry of their alliance, seeming to place Frederick in a subordinate, dependent position in relation to his ally. The very same situation meant that Britain was prepared to quickly come to a peace agreement if necessary, to the detriment of Prussia. In our terms, there was a short-lived transformation of an aggregation alliance into a hegemonic alliance. Russia's withdrawal, however, gave Prussia renewed bargaining force compared with its ally; for an equally brief period, the two countries were involved in a serious trial of strength, in an incipient deadlocked alliance that almost immediately came to an end.

The Anglo-French alliance changed and came to an end when its heterogeneity became so pronounced that Britain decided to come to an agreement with France's traditional enemy, Austria. Given the choice between continuing with a relationship that strongly penalized it or breaking off that relationship, France chose the second course of action. However, we should bear in mind that France could afford to withdraw from a hegemonic relationship that had become increasingly burdensome because in the meantime the distribution of power between the allies evened out.

Finally, another case was that of the Austro-French alliance. For its entire duration, it remained a deadlocked alliance, with the very brief exception of the period between the second and third treaties of Versailles, when the aggregational aspects perhaps prevailed to a certain degree. However, from the end of the Seven Years' War until the French Revolution, relations between the two allies remained basically symmetrical within a constantly heterogeneous context. The alliance lost any real significance once France gradually withdrew from the international scene, as a result of its serious domestic crisis.

It should go without saying: one cannot validly extrapolate generalizing conclusions from analysis of four cases chosen ad hoc. Yet one cannot help noticing that of the four cases, only one faithfully mirrors the "law" so often referred to in academic literature, according to which once the threat leading allies to come together in the first place no longer exists, an alliance will come to an end. As we previously pointed out, the aggregation alliance, more than all the other types, is the one best presenting what traditional theory usually deems to be universal: the union of forces (equal or otherwise) against a common enemy. It is thus no surprise that this type of alliance best conforms to the most widely held generalization regarding the end of alliances. The other three cases, by contrast, followed very different paths. The Anglo-Dutch alliance survived—indeed, it took on the form of a guarantee alliance—following the War of the Spanish Succession, when the French threat appeared less serious than in previous years. The Austro-French alliance went through a similar evolution, without the two allies sharing a common enemy, however. In the case of the Anglo-French alliance, the two allies briefly fought side-by-side against

Spain, a few years after stipulation of the treaty, although their relationship continued thereafter. Furthermore, the final collapse of the alliance was never associated with the mere disappearance of a threat in any of these cases, since the three alliances in question always served further functions, or even differing functions altogether. This does not mean, however, that the common enemy did not play any part in the transformation and demise of the alliances in question. Clearly, the behavior of the enemy deeply affected the nature of inter-ally relations, especially when this very enemy itself conferred homogeneity on the alliance. The conciliatory, reassuring approach adopted by France in relation to the United Provinces rendered the Anglo-Dutch alliance less homogeneous and less asymmetric, given that a less immediate threat from France meant the United Provinces felt less need for British support; and Russia's withdrawal from the Seven Years' War, together with its getting closer to Prussia at the same time, played a similar role with regard to the Anglo-Prussian alliance. Once again, the existence of a common enemy, or more generally speaking of some form of threat, is only one of the numerous factors in play, and it is not always the decisive one.

Consequently, some of the directions taken by the process of transformation of alliances may be interpreted as movement from one type to another. As far as concerns the breakdown of an alliance, this always comes about, by definition, in a highly heterogeneous context, a situation where the heterogeneity is so strong that in the end it eliminates any possible bargaining range between the parties, to the point where one or the other, or even both, find it more convenient to break, rather than keep, the alliance. Such preferences may be seen as "efficient causes," as grounds underlying action, and as such they throw some light on the reasons one state is led to free itself from another: the changed relation of forces, the clear incompatibility of the adopted policies. However, we know that such preferences are not enough in themselves to explain any specific behavior, and even less so the consequences of such behavior, since each decision taken by an individual player arises within a broader context indicating the available opportunities and establishing the limits of what is possible. Thus efficient causes should be accompanied by "permissive causes,"[3] which are to be found in the incessantly moving diplomatic constellations within which the spaces available to each state open up and close in an alternate, and sometimes overlapping, series of thrusts and counterthrusts, incentives and disincentives, that condition each state's propensity to act.

One may be led to believe that heterogeneous alliances are necessarily short-lived; however, the two alliances we have discussed were, on the contrary, rather long-lasting. It may come as no surprise that a homogeneous alliance such as the Anglo-Dutch alliance lasted for decades but the other homogeneous alliance examined here—between Britain and Prussia—lasted no more than a few years. Even if we consider only power relations, a certain basic indeterminateness emerges. In one case, a symmetrical alliance lasted just a few years, while in another case it lasted roughly 30 years; furthermore, if we look at the two asymmetrical alliances examined here, one was characterized by decades-long cooperation, while the other consisted in a relatively brief period of collaboration between two traditional rivals. Anyone deciding to put an end to an alliance (either officially or in practice) does so by being in a position to reverse the foreign policy adopted up to the moment in time; and whoever renounces trying to obtain the conformity of one state normally possesses the means with which to obtain the conformity of another—and, more important, has another state with which to interact. At this point, the type of international system in question comes back into play. In bipolar systems, it is generally argued that the realignment options are usually limited, whereas in multipolar systems there are, in theory, many more such alternatives. Nevertheless, this fact is belied by the cases presented here, which tend to suggest that even a multipolar system like the one present in 18th century Europe may be blocked, in the sense that often a nation has little choice about who its allies are to be.[4] Furthermore, although in multipolar systems one would logically expect spaces to open up more often than in bipolar systems, this does not preclude a state in a multipolar system from remaining tied up in a relationship that conditions and substantially constrains it for much longer than it would deem desirable.

Neither the class nor the type offers us any real clues as to the duration of a given alliance. Following the Peace of Utrecht, the Anglo-Dutch alliance survived a change in the power relations between the two allies, whereas the Anglo-French alliance did not. In the first case, symmetry was replaced by asymmetry within the context of a relationship that remained homogeneous, whereas in the second case there was a change in the opposite direction within the context of a relationship that was heterogeneous from the very start. In other words, the member of an alliance that is penalized by its own ally will abandon the ally as soon as it can, which is exactly what happened in the case of the Anglo-Prussian alliance as well. As soon as Prussia managed to get back on equal standing with Britain, within the context of a strong heterogeneous relationship, the tie between the two allies was broken. We also have the case of a heterogeneous, symmetrical alliance, the Austro-French alliance, which survived for decades despite the one state constantly hindering the other's actions. In the preceding cases, recovery of a position of equality with an ally coincided with the end of a heterogeneous relationship; in this particular case preservation of parity in a heterogeneous context coincided with the persistence of the alliance. Neither the relation of forces nor heterogeneity is therefore capable on its own of accounting for the end of alliances, unless they are accompanied by such an alteration in the situational context of at least one of the allies that this change offers one ally the opportunity to find elsewhere the services hitherto afforded by the other ally (this was the case of Prussia, and of Great Britain at the end of its alliance with France), or enables it to do without such services, at the very least (the case of the United Provinces). In other words, the end of an alliance directly reflects the alternative options available to the parties. Austria and France maintained their deadlocked alliance, despite their both being unsatisfied with it, because the alternatives were judged to be even worse; but Prussia in 1763, and Britain in 1731, were both able to rely on other partners when they each left their respective allies; as for the United Provinces, France had offered it the most attractive alternative at a very difficult moment in time, namely neutrality.

In short, the various phases in the transformation and demise of an alliance are also characterized by those concerns we have focused on in this present study: the rather ambiguous nature of conflicting and cooperative relations among states, which are hardly ever absolute foes or friends; the central importance of the position held by one state in relation to the other states; the forms taken by the struggle for conformity among allies; the important, albeit not always decisive, role played by the common enemy; and the conceptualization of alliances not so much as unions of forces as instruments of control, by means of which each state tries to render another state's behavior foreseeable, thus circumscribing the uncertainty permeating such an anarchical context as the international system. The typology of alliances outlined here has tried to illustrate how such dynamics develop and interact, and to offer a preliminary explanation of such differences.

Notes

Notes to Chapter One

1. *Il principe*, Chap. XXI (Engl. trans. G. Bull, *The Prince*, New York: Penguin, 1980, 123). Incidentally, Machiavelli is aware of the risks inherent in choosing sides; however, "this is the way things are: whenever one tries to escape one danger one runs into another" (ibidem). Machiavelli's condemnation of neutrality echoes the views of important figures of classical antiquity, including Livy (IX, 3, 12, and XXXII, 21, 34) and Tacitus (*Germania*, XXXVI).

2. *Della ragion di Stato*, 1589 (Engl. trans. P. J. and D. P. Waley, *The Reason of State*, London: Routledge & Kegan, 1956, Book VIII, Chap. 13, 162).

3. Boutros-Ghali (1963, 15–17). The text of the treaty is available in Langdon and Gardiner (1920).

4. The theoretical literature on alliances is extremely rich, as we will see. There are a few reviews available—Burgess and Moore (1972); Bueno de Mesquita and Singer (1973); Holsti, Hopmann, and Sullivan (1973, 1–47); Sullivan (1974); Job (1981): and Ward (1982)—but they are dated. Other introductory works include Fedder (1968), Jervis (1979), and Donelan (1990).

5. As for the liberal tradition, its critical attitude with regard to power politics has inevitably affected alliances as well. Throughout the second half of the 18th century, the *philosophes* constantly contrasted the "true policy" (i.e., a policy aimed at stimulating trade and economic activity) with the "false policy" (power politics leading invariably to war). Figures such as V. Mirabeau, D'Argenson, Mercier de la Rivière, Gaillard, Condillac, Le Trosne, Raynal, and Mably looked at a balance of power as a main threat to peace and at alliances as "temporary armistices," "preparations for treason," schemes that are always offensive in nature, whose secrecy is evidence in itself of double dealing and intrigue (Gilbert 1951). Jeremy Bentham, John Stuart Mill, and Richard Cobden gave those ideas their classical formulation. All this, however, should not lead to the conclusion that the liberal tradition rejects any forms of association among states, provided those states share some internal features: Immanuel Kant's *foedus pacificum*, as described in the "Second Definitive Article," was indeed a league; but this league must be made of states that share a same "republican constitution" (I. Kant, *Zum ewigen Frieden. Ein philosophischer*

Entwurf, 1795, Engl. trans. L. White Beck, *Perpetual Peace*, Indianapolis: Bobbs-Merrill, 1957); likewise, Woodrow Wilson deeply believed that a broad association of nations was necessary to go beyond the deadly logic of alliances and the balance of power; at the same time, institutional agreements, to him, would be best pursued among democracies.

6. Smith (1986) still offers the most comprehensive historical and intellectual profile of representative realist figures of the 20th century. Haslam (2002) is a fine reconstruction, organized around key issues, of the evolution of realist thought since the beginning of the modern age.

7. An alliance is "a formal agreement among a limited number of countries concerning the conditions under which they will or will not employ military force" (Russett 1971, 262–63); "a collaborative agreement between two or more states to join together, for a stipulated period, to pursue common political economic or security interests" (Bercovitch 1988, 8); "a written, formal agreement among two or more states which is designed to serve, for a specified term, the interests of those states [. . .] in regard to national security" (Dingman 1979, 249); "a formal agreement that pledges states to cooperate in using their military resources against a specific state or states and usually obligates one or more signatories to use force, or to consider [. . .] the use of force, in specified circumstances" (Osgood 1968, 17); "formal associations of states for the use (or nonuse) of military force, in specified circumstances, against states outside their own membership" (Snyder 1997, 4). On the differences among alignment, coalition, entente, and alliance, see Dingman (1979) and Modelski (1963); for a discussion of the strengths and weaknesses of entente *vis-à-vis* alliance, see Kann (1976) and Berridge (1989).

8. William Riker's coalition theory might be mentioned here as a further example of the "aggregational" conception of alliances (Riker 1962); however, as has been persuasively pointed out, Riker's coalitions can hardly be seen as similar to international alliances (Holsti, Hopmann, and Sullivan 1973, 6–10; Russett 1970; Zinnes 1970, 356–62; Rosen 1970; Nicholson 1989, 125–29).

9. The bibliography on the balance of power is extraordinarily abundant and variegated. A comprehensive historical and theoretical summary is in Sheehan (1996); for a recent assessment and interpretation, see Little (2007). Two useful collections of excerpts ranging from classical antiquity to the 20th century are in Seabury, ed. (1965) and Wright, ed. (1975).

10. *La storia d'Italia*, 1561 (Engl. trans. S. Alexander, *The History of Italy*, New York: Phaidon, 1969, Book I, Chap. 1, now in Wright, ed., 1975, 10).

11. *Relatione della Republica Venetiana*, Venezia: Varisco, 1605 (Engl. trans. J. Warrington, "On the Counterpoise of Princes' Forces," in Wright, ed., 1975, 22).

12. *Directions pour la conscience d'un roi—Supplement*, ca. 1700 (Engl. trans. W. Grant, "On the Necessity of Forming Alliances . . . ," now in Wright, ed. (1975, 42).

13. *A Review of the State of the English Nation*, 1706, now in Wright, ed. (1975, 48–49).

14. *Le droit des gens*, 1758 (Engl. trans. C. Fenwick, *The Law of Nations*, Wash-

ington, DC: Carnegie Institution, 1916, Book III, Chap. 3, par. 47, now in Wright, ed., 1975, 72).

15. *Fragmente aus der neusten Geschichte des Politischen Gleichgewichts in Europa*, 1806 (Engl. trans. *Fragments upon the Balance of Power in Europe*, London: Peltier, 1806, now in Forsyth, Keens-Soper, and Savigear, eds., 1970, 290).

16. Quoted in Holbraad (1971, 138).

17. "Die grossen Mächte," *Historisch-Politische Zeitschrift*, II, 1, 1833 (Engl. trans. R. Wines, "The Great Powers," in L. von Ranke, *The Secret of World History: Selected Writings on the Art and Science of History*, New York: Fordham University Press, 1981, 128–29).

18. For example, Paolo Paruta, reflecting on Venice's policy during the struggle between Charles V and Francis I, pointed out that the Venetian Senate would often shift sides, "being still constant in their aim, which was to keep their Forces as equally balanced as they could, and that they should both be weakened by their contention one with another" (*Discorsi Politici*, 1599, Engl. trans. H. Carey, *Politick Discourses*, London: Moseley, 1657, Book II, Discourse 9, p. 184). The most celebrated case, however, is Britain's traditional foreign policy, characterized at the beginning of the 20th century in these terms by Eyre Crowe: "it has become almost an historical truism to identify England's secular policy with the maintenance of this balance by throwing her weight now in this scale and now in that, but ever on the side, opposed to the political dictatorship of the strongest single, State or group at a given time" (*Memorandum on the Present State of British Relations with France and Germany*, 1907, now in Morgenthau and Thompson 1950, 249).

19. It is worth mentioning another set of studies that address the question of when alliances are formed from a quantitative-statistical perspective. Most of those works are based on the data gathered by Singer and Small (1968; Small and Singer 1969) and test some of the hypotheses available in the literature, especially those derived from Morton Kaplan's Balance of Power model (Kaplan 1957). Thus McGowan and Rood (1975) have studied formation of alliances as a stochastic process, prompting the critiques of Lawson (1976) and Chatterjee (1977), and offering a rejoinder in McGowan and Rood (1977). In a similar vein are Job (1976), Siverson and Duncan (1976), Li and Thompson (1978), and Duncan and Siverson (1982). Two general assessments of this literature are in Siverson and McCarty (1982) and Thies (1991).

20. Walt tests his hypotheses on the origins of alliances, drawing on the international relations of the Middle East from 1955 to 1979. Priess (1996) applies Walt's "balance of threat" theory to yet another case in the same region, the Gulf Cooperation Council. For a critique of Walt, see Vasquez (1997 and 1998)—but see also Walt's rejoinder (1997a)—and Frieden (1999), especially 50–51.

21. The importance of security considerations is stressed also in other works centered on formal models and statistical data, addressing the issue of the origins of alliances (Lalman and Newman 1991; Chiu 2003) as well as the policies to be adopted when one's ally is threatened (Scarborough and Bueno de Mesquita 1988).

22. Taking inspiration from the theory of finance, Conybeare (1992) adds another benefit: the greater return and lower risk produced by some alliances.

23. See the long list of scholars who share this view in Holsti, Hopmann, and Sullivan (1973, 17 and 254–55). Holsti and colleagues themselves come to similar conclusions at the end of their study of NATO and the Warsaw Pact (ibidem, 88–148). On analogous positions, see Bercovitch (1988, 17–19) and Liska (1962, 86–103). It is no coincidence, therefore, that even the theoretical debate on the future of NATO after the Cold War has focused on the disappearance of the Soviet threat (Walt 1989 and 1997b; Hellmann and Wolf 1993; McCalla 1996; Skålnes 1998; Joffe 1995; Wallender and Keohane 1999; Waltz 2000; Rafferty 2003).

24. This is yet another frequent observation in the literature; see the list of authors and loci in Bueno de Mesquita and Singer (1973, 263–64). Walt (1997b, 158–61) mentions two sets of security-related causes of the end of alliances: a "changing perception of threat" and a "declining credibility." Finally, less frequently invoked reasons for the demise of alliances include size (Gulick 1955, 78; Horvath and Foster 1963; Bueno de Mesquita and Singer 1973, 266–67), domestic politics (Walt 1997b, 161–63; Gaubatz 1996), the alliance's offensive or defensive nature (Liska 1962, 39–40), the character of the interests it serves (Morgenthau 1973, 192–93), and its symmetrical or asymmetrical structure (Morrow 1991). An assessment of those hypotheses is in Bennett (1997).

25. For example, Gulick (1955, 77–89); Osgood (1968); Singer, Bremer, and Stuckey (1972); Morgenthau (1973, 188); Holsti, Hopmann, and Sullivan (1973, 31–32); Siverson and Tennefoss (1984); Saperstein (1992); and Kegley and Raymond (1990b, 180–217).

26. Highly influential, in this regard, have been Karl W. Deutsch and J. David Singer (1964), according to whom alliances lead to instability in multipolar systems (a view challenged by Kegley and Raymond 1994a, 1994b). Empirical analysis of the relationship between alliances and war has been conducted mostly in a statistical-quantitative vein and has often led to contradictory findings. Those works can be divided into three groups (Oren 1990), according to their analytical focus: aggregate-systemic studies (Singer and Small 1968; Wallace 1973; Ostrom and Hoole 1978; Sabrosky 1985; Siverson and Tennefoss 1984; Kim 1989, 1991); works that adopt the war, or the alliance, or both as their focal unit (Sabrosky 1980; Levy 1981; Smith 1995; Wayman 1990; Gibler 1996, 1997; Gibler and Vasquez 1998); and studies that concentrate on the member state (Siverson and King 1979; Siverson and King 1980; Most, Schrodt, Siverson, and Starr 1990; Bueno de Mesquita 1981; Wayman 1990; Oren 1990). This literature is surveyed by Siverson and Sullivan (1994).

27. The reasons for bandwagoning put forward by Walt are shared, at least partially, by Rothstein (1968, 11, 26–27), Handel (1990, 186) and Mearsheimer (2001, 162–64).

28. For example, from a structural angle bandwagoning seems more likely in multipolar systems than in bipolar systems; under multipolarity, balancing may be hampered by the typical logic of collective action (Snyder 1991). That states, as a general rule, tend to adopt a balancing policy is called into question by a number of studies covering both the modern and the contemporary age (Levy and Thompson, 2005), or more limited periods, including the 18th century (Schroeder 1994b),

the Napoleonic age (Rosecrance and Lo 1996; but see also the reply by Whiteneck 2001), the 20th century (Rosecrance and Stein, 1993), the post–Cold War international system (Kapstein and Mastanduno, 1999). Quantitative studies have tried to find out which behavior—balancing or bandwagoning—is more likely, with dubious results; see Healy and Stein (1973), McDonald and Rosecrance (1985), Cusack and Stoll (1991), and Jones (1994). For a critique of this scholarship, see Schroeder (1977). Finally, even in Powell's sophisticated model (1999, 149–96) balancing and bandwagoning occur more or less with the same likelihood.

29. See Brand (1994a, 1994b), Barnett and Levy (1991), Levy and Barnett (1992), Cooper (2003–2004), and Gause (2003–2004).

30. See David (1991a, 1991b) and Harknett and Van Dan Berg (1997).

31. The work of Deborah W. Larson (1991) is in part an exception. Larson's thesis is that a policy of bandwagoning reflects the precarious domestic position of the ruling elite. Since elites are mostly interested in preserving their rule, those elites who feel threatened internally do not hesitate to accept the support of a foreign power and share the latter's expansionist policy, if necessary. One is left wondering, however, why the external support a weak elite is looking for can be provided by an expansionist state only. The historical cases examined by Larson, i.e., the policies adopted by several European states vis-à-vis revisionist Germany in the 1930s, have been revisited by other scholars as well; indeed some interpret those events as evidence of bandwagoning (Groth and Randall 1991; Kaufman 1992a, 1992b), but others point out elements of balancing (Walt 1992; Resende-Santos 1992). Perhaps the most convincing position, in this context, is Randall L. Schweller's (2004, 2006), that domestic politics is responsible for what he calls "underbalancing," or a paltry and imprudent response—or even lack of response—to an external threat.

32. On the choice between arms and allies, see Altfeld (1984), Most and Siverson (1987), Morrow (1993), Sorokin (1994b), and Conybeare (1994a).

33. One example is the rise of the Athenian empire as described by Thucydides (I, 89–117).

34. After all, the relationship between ideology and alliances has always been considered rather weak. To Liska, (1962, 15) conflicts with third parties are more important than ideological affinity in bringing states together; Wolfers (1968) claims that ideology does not constitute a prerequisite for alliances and lists a number of alliances between ideologically differing states; and Schwarzenberger (1941, 114) expresses himself in a very similar vein. Quantitative studies come to analogous conclusions; Holsti, Hopmann, and Sullivan (1973, 64) find that, for the period 1815–1939, "whether ideology does or does not play a role in alliance formation seems not to be important for alliance performance." It is only after 1945 that, to some, the relevance of ideology seems to increase (Siverson and Emmons 1991; Lai and Reiter 2000). Yet not even a work on NATO as an association of democratic nations goes so far as to claim that alliances among democracies are "special" (Risse-Kappen 1995, 195). Among those who, on the contrary, stress the importance of ideology, see Haas (2003) and Owen (2005).

35. Quotations are from Rex Warner's English translation, *History of the Peloponnesian War*, London: Penguin, 1972.

36. *Les six livres de la République*, 1576 (Engl. trans. R. Knolles, *The six bookes of a Common-weale*, London: Bishop, 1606, Book V, Chap. 5, p. 611.

37. Ibidem, 612.

38. Paruta, op. cit., p. 154.

39. Botero, *The Reason of State*, op. cit., p. 163.

40. Two celebrated accusations, obviously biased, are Jonathan Swift, *The Conduct of the Allies and of the Late Ministry, in Beginning and Carrying on the Present War*, London: Morphew, 1711; and David Hume, "Of the Balance of Power," in *Political Discourses*, Edinburgh: Kincaid and Donaldson, 1752, pp. 101–14.

41. Fénelon, op. cit., p. 42.

42. For example, Liska (1962, 30–39; 1968, 23–43) states that alliances reflect at least two further interests, other than that of protection from an enemy, namely the desire to maintain a certain international order by controlling an imprudent ally (as Bismarck's Germany did for many years in relation to Austria) and the need to consolidate a political regime and its institutions by means of international recognition (Italy's membership in the Triple Alliance helped give the country the status of great power). Furthermore, Liska (1962, 103–15) focuses on the specific aims of allies, and on how such aims may clash, thus compromising the internal cohesion and effectiveness of the alliance. This may happen, for example, if one state is prevalently concerned with military security, while another has joined the alliance in order to consolidate internal stability or promote a certain kind of economic growth. Robert E. Osgood (1968, 17–31) and Robert L. Rothstein (1968, 49–53) also made similar observations in enumerating the various functions of alliances. Rothstein distinguished between "military alliances" (related to the power aggregation model) and "political alliances." The latter, according to Rothstein, are created in the hope of influencing an unstable ally, and of checking its movements to a certain extent. Military alliances derive from the perception of a threat that cannot be dealt with alone, but political alliances emerge from the perception of a situation that can be exploited by means of the alliance itself. However, observations of this kind very rarely go any further than this. Hence what is offered is little more than a series of promising ideas.

43. William B. Moul (1983) is the first scholar, to my knowledge, who has tried to develop Schroeder's important insight. The theme of inter-ally control has been touched on also by Skålnes (1998) with regard to NATO, and by Gelpi (1999) in a quantitative study on the 1918–1988 period. However, it is Patricia A. Weitsman (1997, and especially 2004) who has offered the most important contribution. To Weitsman, (2004, 17–29), states may adopt four coalitional behaviors, according to the perceived level of threat: *hedging*, a flexible and limited commitment, at a low level of threat; *tethering*, an attempt to manage relations with one's rival "by drawing closer to it via agreement" (ibidem, 21), as the threat posed by the rival grows; *balancing*, the classical response to a threat, as the latter becomes even more serious; and *bandwagoning*, at an extreme level of threat. In other words, Weitsman suggests

a curvilinear—as opposed to a linear—relationship between threat and propensity to ally. In doing so, she has the merit of showing that the desire to aggregate power is not the only plausible explanation of alliances. At the same time, however, her framework and argument are not entirely convincing. To begin with, Weitsman's complete reliance on the notion of threat makes it difficult to account for those alliances in which security is not the uppermost concern—unless one is willing to overstretch the meaning of threat, with dubious results. Second, the relationship between threat and propensity to ally deserved some more thought; it looks likely that the choice of coalitional strategy depends not only on the level of threat but on other variables as well, including the available alternatives in terms of potential allies. Third, the four strategies are national strategies, which is to say policies, or attitudes, adopted by individual states. They identify *types of ally*, not *types of alliance*; as such, one cannot expect too much from them when it comes to examining the functioning of a given alliance. Weitsman does combine the various types of ally, ending up with eight types of alliance (2004, 27–30). Yet the profile of the types of alliance remains very general.

44. Along a similar line, Robert Jervis (1997, 210–52) talks of "consistent" international systems, i.e., systems divided into two camps and characterized by certain conditions: "each actor has friendly relations with every other actor in its camp, each actor has hostile relations with every other actor in the other camp, and there are no actors outside either camp—i.e., no neutrals" (ibidem, 210). The most powerful force pushing toward consistency is, to Jervis too, a common enemy.

45. Aron (1962/1967, 44–45), in any case, had already seen the problem. In addition, other scholars (Russett 1968, 299; Liska 1968; Bueno de Mesquita and Singer 1973, 261; Rosen 1970, 232–33; Haas and Whiting 1956, 162–67) have noted various "redistributive" effects.

46. The debate on the economic theory of alliances can be followed through the works of Burgess and Robinson (1969), Russett (1970), Simowitz (1976), Väyrynen (1976), Jones (1988), Oppenheimer (1979 and 1980), Conybeare (1994b), and Palmer (1990, 1991). A comprehensive critical review and assessment is in Sandler (1993).

47. Such a conclusion is less compatible with Olson and Zeckhauser's original thesis than with the "joint production" model. The latter refers to a situation in which private and public goods are produced simultaneously. In this case, the allies may have strong incentives to contribute significantly to the collective effort (Sandler 1975, 1977; Sandler and Cauley 1975; Sandler, Cauley, and Forbes 1980; Murdock and Sandler 1982, 1984, 1991; but see also Shaffer 1978). The joint production model, in turn, has sparked a lively debate, leading to extensions (Boyer 1989; Gates and Terasawa 1992), comparisons to the theory of Olson and Zeckhauser (Oneal 1990a, 1990b) and to the theory of hegemonic stability (Oneal and Elrod 1989; Murdock and Sandler 1991), and further empirical research (Conybeare and Sandler 1990; Sandler and Hartley 1999).

48. The concepts of "chain-ganging" and "buck-passing" as national security strategies have been developed by Christensen and Snyder (1990). They argue

that the choice between the two options depends on the beliefs held by national elites, at a given historical time, about the advantages and disadvantages of an offensive strategy relative to a defensive one. If national leaders believe that a defensive strategy will lead to a favorable outcome, they will pass the buck to other states; if they believe that an offensive strategy holds the promise of success, they will chain themselves to their allies. Christensen (1997) has further developed this argument by stressing the importance of the leaders' perceptions about the distribution of power.

49. This is one of the reasons Waltz (1979, 163–70) rejects the argument that multipolar systems are more stable than bipolar systems. Although the former are characterized by flexible alliances, such flexibility may be offset by rigid national strategies aimed at preserving the existing alliances; precisely because realignment is a credible option, no one can risk losing a partner. Conversely, although a bipolar system is characterized by rigid alliances, such a rigidity is coupled with flexible strategies on the part of the two bloc leaders; precisely because realignment is not a real option, the two superpowers can restrain their respective allies and exercise some control. Similar views are expressed also by Dinerstein (1965) and Beres (1972). For further analysis of inter-ally relations in bipolarity and multipolarity, see Aron (1962/1967, 125–49).

Notes to Chapter Two

1. Wolfers (1962, 147–65) and Baldwin (1997) are two fine works on the concept of security.

2. But see also the rejoinders of those criticized by Vasquez, i.e., Christensen and Snyder (1997), Schweller (1997), Walt (1997a), and Waltz (1997).

3. Consistent with his own theoretical stand, Waltz (1996) denies this possibility.

4. We cannot possibly do justice here to those variants of realist theory. In short, to offensive realism (Mearsheimer 1994–95, 2001; Labs 1997), security is by definition a scarce commodity in anarchy; this induces states to take initiatives and measures that fatally make conflict more likely (a logic very similar to the old notion of "security dilemma"); to defensive realism (Walt 1987; J. Snyder 1991; Glaser 1996), by contrast, states tend to become aggressive mostly when facing a danger. Aggressive foreign policies that cannot be explained as a reaction to an external threat are then traced back to domestic variables. Finally, neoclassical realism tries to combine systematically structural and domestic variables (Rose 1998). Unlike offensive and defensive realism, neoclassical realism is above all a theory of foreign policy.

5. Three-way relations should not be confused with triads (Portinaro 1986, 67–75). The former take place in systems made of several units, some of which try not to be absorbed by the friend-foe polarization. The latter are systems exclusively made of three units. Triads, and their coalitional dynamics, have been studied extensively in social psychology (Caplow 1956, 1959, and 1968; Gamson (1961a, 1961b, and 1964). For a comprehensive assessment, see Chertkoff (1967, 1970).

6. A useful selection of Simmel's writing on three-way relations is in Nooteboom (2006).

7. However, it goes without saying that a small power has a narrower margin of maneuver relative to a great power. As soon as it chooses a side, it automatically loses its blackmail potential and begins to transform itself into a satellite.

8. Snyder's basic insights can be traced back to his previous work (Snyder and Diesing 1977, 471–80). Other scholars have tried to develop a similar conceptual framework (Buzan, Jones, and Little 1993). Still others emphasize the importance of a systemic approach that does not limit itself to analysis of structural causes; Robert Jervis (1997, 5), for example, argues that any explanation of state behavior "should start with how the actors are positioned."

9. The interaction among opportunities, constraints, and preferences in international relations is amply debated in Lake and Powell (1999), Frieden (1999), Morrow (1999), and Stein (1999).

10. This is why, according to Mario Stoppino (2001, 225–67), the ideal-typical goal of political action is "stabilized and generalized power," i.e. "guaranteed conformity."

11. For an introductory, yet useful, discussion of the concept of power in international relations, see Barnett and Duvall (2005).

12. The attempts to contrast Waltzian neorealism and offensive realism are not always convincing. Eric J. Labs (1997), for example, takes the states' defensive attitude, as postulated by neorealism, as sheer defense of the status quo. Yet, to be a "defensive positionalist"—Joseph M. Grieco's memorable characterization of states (1988)—necessarily implies a constant assessment of the relation of forces. Facing a rising power, those who intend to defend their own position will be induced to take action, including offensive action, to contain it. In addition, there are other reasons neorealism cannot be described in strictly defensive terms. The competitive nature of international relations entails not only some threat of military attack; first, one cannot be sure that today's friend will not turn into tomorrow's foe, and second, states are concerned not just about survival but about independence and autonomy as well, i.e., about their bargaining power.

13. Mearsheimer's "offensive" realism, just like Waltz's neorealism, does not seem able to capture much of the complexity of alliance politics. The conditions under which balancing is more or less likely than buck passing, for example, are essentially descriptive and can hardly constitute a conceptual definition of the context in which state action takes place. In addition, after classifying great powers strategies as either offensive or defensive, Mearsheimer acknowledges that buck passing can be both offensive and defensive, which deprives the basic distinction of some meaning. Finally, looking at war as the optimal strategy to increase power, Mearsheimer underestimates the importance of diplomatic pressures, of alignments, of those political and economic maneuvers and initiatives that are paramount in achieving and maintaining a prominent position in the international system. The cost entailed by such a view is immediately evident when it comes to alliances: that a balancing strategy is associated with alliances is hardly a surprise, and as for buck passing, it is seen as a strategy of independence. Yet passing the buck is a significant policy *between allies* as well.

14. On commitment and its role in bargaining, the *locus classicus* is the work of Thomas Schelling (1960, 84–161; and 1966, 35–91).

15. Those who focus on security as an explanation of alliances simply skip this crucial step. Inevitably, their perspective is limited. This is also the case with Snyder (1997, 10) who, along with a number of other scholars, mentions two "ideal-type motives" for creating an alliance: the "guarantee motive" (a strong interest in defending another state) and the "get help motive" (the promise to help in order to get help in turn).

16. The difference between the traditional conception of alliances and the conception presented here is reminiscent of the difference in organizational theory between two approaches to the study of organizations, i.e. the "organismic model" and the "social contract model" (Keeley 1980). The former assumes the existence of organizational goals (in our case, this would correspond to opposition to the common enemy), whereas the latter focuses on the pursuit of individual interests (in our case, national interests), that can be achieved thanks to conformity of other individuals (in our case, states). In addition, just like the organismic model, the "aggregational" conception of alliances does not contemplate the possibility of a struggle for power among the partners, despite the fact that such a struggle affects all alliances (as well as all organizations; Crozier and Friedberg 1977/1980). "By rejecting common ends as necessary bases of cooperation, a contractual approach not only escapes the severe problem of defining these ends but avoids the overly harmonious description of organizational life that is characteristic of organismic views. Participants are allowed to behave in a self-interested manner, as they often seem to do, and conflicts among their purposes, instead of being wished away, are acknowledged as probable facts of organization, as they appear to be" (Keeley 1980, 352). In short, the perspective adopted here sheds light on the various ways in which the allies (just like the individual members of any organization) act strategically, pursuing multiple and occasionally contradictory goals, and are sensitive to the constraints and the opportunities that derive from their partnership, their relationships, and the structure of the international system.

17. There are several statistical-quantitative works that focus on the propensity of allies to support, ignore, or even fight one another: Singer and Small (1966); Holsti, Hopmann, and Sullivan (1973, 48–87); Altfeld and Bueno de Mesquita (1979); Sabrosky (1980); Siverson and King (1980); Bueno de Mesquita (1981, 73–83); and Wayman (1990). Unfortunately, besides presenting uncertain results, many of those works show a modest interest in conceptual issues, absorbed as they are in their effort to gather data and find correlations. Even the more sophisticated models (e.g., Bueno de Mesquita's) are based on questionable premises. For example, assuming that two allies have, by definition, a similar foreign policy is a gross oversimplification that cannot be justified even by the desire to be theoretically parsimonious. For a critique of Bueno de Mesquita, see Ray (1990). Finally, Leeds (2003) sees an association between the reliability of the allies, their status, and their domestic political institutions; great powers, as well as nondemocratic states, are seen as the most likely allies to break their pledge in case of war.

18. For a work that stresses the importance of reputation in alliance politics, see Miller (2003).

19. Morrow (1994) focuses on the role of alliances in international crises. However, very few studies deal specifically with wartime alliances. Among those, see Weitsman (2003).

20. Institutional theory has addressed the general issue of cooperation among allies from at least two perspectives, a "sociological" approach (Kegley and Raymond 1982, 1990a, 1990b) and a "functional" approach (Stein 1990; Keohane 1988; Wallender and Keohane 1999). According to this last work, alliances are "security institutions" whose main function is to provide information about the interests, preferences, strategies, and intentions of the various players through a set of rules, norms, and procedures that diminish uncertainty and make cooperation likely. But see the important critique of Stephen Krasner (1991), according to whom functional institutional theory neglects power considerations—a view that we cannot but share.

21. To some (Leeds, Long, and McLaughin Mitchell 2000), if one considers the specific obligations included in alliance treaties and the terms adopted, alliance reliability is much higher than is commonly believed.

22. In general terms, political relations are "economic" or "coercive," according to the nature of the sanctions that can be applied. The actor that refuses to comply is sanctioned with "diminishing benefits," in the case of economic relations, and with "emerging costs," involving use of violence, in the case of coercive relations (Stoppino 2001, 175). This further differentiates relations among allied states from relations among nonallied states. Among the former, exchange and power dynamics are based on the threat of diminishing benefits; among the latter, the threat of emerging costs is made as well.

23. This is why inter-ally relations lend themselves to be studied with what Thomas Schelling calls a "strategic approach." Such relations can easily be seen as "situations involving two or more participants, each trying to influence, to outguess, or to adapt to the decisions or lines of behavior that others have just adopted or are expected to adopt" (Schelling 1984, 198).

24. Two memorable definitions may be useful here: "the power of A over B is equal to, and based upon, the dependence of B upon A" (Emerson 1962, 33); and "power is conceptualized [...] as resting on the net ability of a person to withhold rewards from and apply punishment to others [...]. Its source is one-sided dependence" (Blau 1964, 117–18).

25. A model formulated by James Morrow (1991) does contemplate the possibility that costs and benefits may be expressed in terms of *both* security *and* autonomy. Yet this promising idea is not fully developed. To Morrow, small powers are, by definition, less secure than great powers, and his security-autonomy trade-off refers, on closer investigation, to a highly specific case of alliance only, the "asymmetrical alliance" *in presence of a threat.*

Notes to Chapter Three

1. Two early formulations of the "alliance security dilemma" are in Snyder (1984, 1990). As Snyder himself acknowledges, the basic idea behind the dilemma was first put forward by Michael Mandelbaum (1981, 151–52). Among the few systematic

applications of the alliance security dilemma, see Victor D. Cha's study (2000) on the relations among the United States, Japan, and South Korea in the last three decades of the 20th century.

2. Joanne Gowa (1994) makes a similar point with regard to trade relations. To her, "security externalities" induce states to impose tariffs on adversaries more often than on allies.

3. This combination of alliance and adversary relations is called by Snyder (1997, 194–98) the "composite security dilemma."

4. See, for example, Aron (1962/1967, 25–30), Boutros-Ghali (1963, 20–28), Holsti (1977, 121–25), Liska (1962, 75–78), Morgenthau (1959 and 1973, 188–200), Morrow (1991), Mueller (1995), Russett (1971), Singer and Small (1966), and Snyder (1997, 11–16).

5. The classical partition here is between "permanent" and "temporary" or "occasional" alliances (Aron 1962/1967, 25–30; Boutros-Ghali 1963; and Morgenthau 1959 and 1973, 192–93).

6. Morgenthau (1959 and 1973, 193) differentiates between "operative" and "inoperative" alliances.

7. Another classical division is between offensive and defensive alliances, as well as possible combinations of the two (Boutros-Ghali 1963; Snyder 1997, 11–16).

8. Holsti (1977, 121–22) talks of "vague" and "precise" alliances, in this regard.

9. The integration of forces constitutes, to Holsti, (1977, 121–24), one of the most visible differences between pre-1945 and post-1945 alliances (NATO being of course the best example of highly integrated alliance).

10. Morgenthau (1959 and 1973, 190–93) differentiates, in this case, among alliances serving "identical interests," "complementary interests," and "ideological interests." In addition, alliances can be "limited" or "general." The latter embrace the total interests of their members, while the former address only a fraction of the objectives of the signatories. Wartime alliances tend to be general; peacetime alliances tend to be limited (on wartime versus peacetime alliances, see also Liska 1962, 75–78). Yet another classification based on the interests of the allies is Morrow's (1991): if the partners receive different benefits—one in terms of security, the other in terms of autonomy—the alliance is asymmetric; if each partner receives the same type of benefit, on the other hand, the alliance is symmetric.

11. Karl Mueller (1995) associates various types of alliance with the geographical position of the allies and their rivals and ends up identifying five main configurations: "satellite belts," "buffer zones," "checkboards," "independent aggregations," and "alignment balances." Regional great powers, in addition, can be aligned with each other according to two main patterns, i.e., a "condominium" or a "consociation." Another attempt to apply a geopolitical logic to alliances is in Starr and Siverson (1990).

12. Holsti (1977, 122–23) distinguishes between "mutual" and "one-sided" alliances, depending on how responsibilities are distributed among the parties.

13. The basic partition, here, is between "equal" and "unequal" alliances (Boutros-

Ghali 1963; Snyder 1997, 11–16). To our purposes, this point is extremely important, and we will get back to it shortly.

14. Morgenthau (1959 and 1973, 191–92) mentions here "mutual" and "one-sided" alliances. In the former case, the services performed by the partners are commensurate with the benefits received; in the latter case, one ally receives the lion's share of gains and the other bears the main bulk of costs.

15. *Discorsi Politici*, 1599 (Engl. trans. H. Carey, *Politick Discourses*, London: Moseley, 1657, Book II, Discourse 5, p. 150).

16. Ibidem.

17. Ibidem, 153.

18. *Della ragion di Stato*, 1589, (Engl. trans. P. J. and D. P. Waley, *The Reason of State*, London: Routledge & Kegan, 1956, Book VIII, Chap. 13, p. 163).

19. *Les six livres de la République*, 1576 (Engl. trans. R. Knolles, *The six bookes of a Common-weale*, London: Bishop, 1606, Book V, Chap. 5, p. 614).

20. Ibidem, Chap. 6, p. 618. Another significant observation, in this regard, is that "oftentimes a pension is payed to the protector, not so much to warrant him from his enemies, as from the protector himselfe" (ibidem, 616–617).

21. *Il Principe* (English trans. G. Bull, *The Prince*, New York: Penguin, 1980, Chap. XXI, p. 123). Yet neutrality may entail serious risks too: "The conqueror does not want doubtful friends who do not help him when he is in difficulties; the loser repudiates you because you were unwilling to go, arms in hand, and throw in your lot with him" (ibidem, p. 121). The dangers associated with offensive alliances are pointed out by Paruta (op. cit., 303) and Botero (*The Reason of State*, cit., 264) as well.

22. *The Prince*, cit., 122 (emphasis added). Francesco Guicciardini expresses a slightly different view on the subject. Although he agrees that the weak can hardly afford neutrality ("for the neutral party remains the prey of both victor and vanquished"), for the strong not choosing sides may be a wise thing to do ("for the strong man can maintain himself without trouble, and he can hope to gain from the disorders of the others" (*Ricordi*, C 68, Engl. trans. M. Domandi, *Maxims and Reflections*, Philadelphia: University of Pennsylvania Press, 1965, p. 59).

23. *Discorsi sopra la prima deca di Tito Livio* (Engl. trans. L. Walker, *The Discourses*, London: Penguin, 1983, Book II, Discourse 4, p. 284).

24. Ibidem, 285. This view is shared by others; for Botero (*The Reason of State*, cit., 163), "the Romans truly showed a wonderful judgment in this, for in the name of friendship and alliance they won by the combined forces of many dominion over the whole world for themselves alone"; to Bodin (cit., 620) "by that meanes [the Romans] conquered the greatest empire that ever was," and "what equall league soever the Romans made, they were still the stronger, and held their allies as it were in subiection." One often quotes the bitter words that Livy attributes to a Latin praetor, Lucius Annius: "*sub umbra foederis aequi servitutem pati possumus*" (VIII, 4, 2; "we are capable of submitting to servitude under the shadowy pretext of a treaty on equal terms").

25. *La storia d'Italia*, 1561 (Engl. trans. S. Alexander, *The History of Italy*, New

York: Phaidon, 1969, Book I, Chap. 1, now in Wright, ed., 1975, 11). Francis Bacon offers a strikingly similar interpretation of this alliance (*Considerations Touching a War with Spain*, 1623, now in Wolfers and Martin, eds., 1956, 16).

26. A sharp comparison of small powers and great powers is in Rothstein (1968, 11–45). On small powers, alliances, and war, see Krause and Singer (2001).

27. It might be useful to mention here the debate on the coalitional options of small, or weak, powers. To some (Rothstein 1968; Handel 1990, 175–95), nonalignment is the first choice of small powers; other scholars—as we have seen—argue that bandwagoning is the general tendency, mostly for domestic reasons; and still others (Labs 1992) claim that although it is true that small powers would prefer neutrality, when forced to choose sides they tend to balance, for structural reasons—although free riding remains a possibility under certain circumstances, such as a favorable geopolitical position. Dan Reiter (1994, 1996) has offered a different explanation of the alignment behavior of small powers, according to which previous experiences play a crucial role in shaping decisions. Such a view sounds reasonable in general terms, but the attempt to leave out any systemic effect is far less convincing. To Reiter, for example, Finland "opted" for neutrality after World War II because its previous alliance experience had been a failure—as if Soviet preferences had no impact on Finnish policy. Similarly, Reiter claims that his "learning" hypothesis explains the alignment decisions of other Scandinavian states better than realist arguments, to which one can reply that Swedish neutrality was not simply the continuation of a traditional policy that had served Swedish interests well but also an effect of Finnish neutrality. Had Finland been incorporated into the Soviet bloc, it is quite likely that Sweden in turn would have joined NATO. On the alliance policies of small powers in Europe during and after the Cold War, see Erich Reiter and Gärtner (2001).

28. Two of the cases that will be examined below illustrate this point quite nicely. On the grounds of sheer material capabilities, one might be tempted to conclude that the relation of forces between France and Britain, after the War of the Spanish Succession, was approximately even. Yet their interdependence was asymmetrical, and this allowed Britain to systematically exert power on France. By the opposite token, despite the gap in material resources between the two partners, the alliance of Britain and Prussia in 1756 was characterized by a symmetrical dependence. The two parties exchanged services, and neither was able to impose its views on the other.

29. According to Thomas C. Schelling (1960, 37) there are "cases in which bargaining 'strength' inheres in what is weakness by other standards. When a person—or a country—has lost the power to help himself [...] the other interested party has no choice but to assume the cost or responsibility."

30. If A risks being (or is actually) exploited by B, one might wonder why A remains in alliance with B. Although such a question is a legitimate one, it suffers from a bias deriving from traditional theory that overemphasizes the "interests in common" and neglects that state choices are often severely constrained. The two heterogeneous alliances examined below—both of which, incidentally, lasted for quite some time—illustrate how states can remain allies even if one does little or nothing for the other, or one is damaged by the other, if there are no serious re-

alignment options—that is, if the cost of breaking up would be higher than the cost entailed in continuing the alliance.

31. The work by Snyder and Diesing (1977, especially 183–281) has inspired the second part of this section.

32. In game theory, a pure coercive strategy is characterized by player A's attempt to impose on player B a solution that results from A's defection and B's cooperation, under the constraint of avoiding mutual defection. In accommodative strategy, both players aim not so much at "winning" but at "settling," i.e., they aim at a cooperative solution. At the same time, each player would like settling to be as close to winning as possible; hence, neither is inclined to make excessive concessions.

33. The Anglo-Prussian alliance in the Seven Years' War is the case that we have selected to illustrate the aggregation alliance in detail. Other alliances that can be interpreted along similar lines include the Italo-Prussian alliance of April 1866 (a sheer war tool against Austria) and the Balkan League of 1912, in which Bulgaria, Serbia, and Greece, having joined forces, expanded at the expense of the Ottoman Empire (Schroeder 1976, 241, 248).

34. Besides the 18th century Anglo-Dutch alliance, which will be examined below, other examples of the same type can be found in Bismarck's alliances with Bavaria, Württemberg, and Baden in 1866 and 1867. Here the minor German states are promised security, above all against France; Prussia, in turn, besides making sure that its new allies will not fall under the influence of another great power (France itself, or Austria), finds those alliances helpful in promoting unification of Germany (Schroeder 1976, 241). Similarly, the Franco-Belgian alliance of 1920 and the Franco-Polish alliance of 1921 are guarantee alliances; the two minor powers are offered security vis-à-vis Germany and become clients of France, following French leadership on a number of international issues (Carr 1963, 25–38).

35. This is analogous to the "influence effect" discussed by Albert O. Hirschman (1980) with regard to foreign trade as a source of power among nations.

36. The Austro-French alliance of 1756 may be seen as a representative example of the deadlocked alliance. As such, it will be examined in depth below. Other illustrations of similar dynamics can be found in the Holy Alliance of 1815 and the Franco-Russian alliance of 1894. To be sure, the former is, to Austria, Prussia, and Russia, a union of forces against revolution and revision of the status quo. But the Holy Alliance performs above all a different function, i.e., prevention of unilateral initiatives by its own signatories in Germany, Italy, and Poland; Austria relies on it to keep an eye on Russia (Schroeder 1976, 231–32). As for the latter, although the allies do share a common fear of isolation against a hostile coalition, they also have divergent interests (France on the Rhine, Russia on the Straits) that neither is willing to support, which prevents destabilizing unilateral initiatives (ibidem, 244–45).

37. Guicciardini, *The History of Italy*, 11.

38. It is Liska (1962, 89) who suggests that a minor ally is concerned about the further strengthening of its partner because it fears that the latter may lose interest in the alliance.

39. This is the case with the Anglo-French alliance, 1716–1731, as will be shown

below. Another example is the Austro-German alliance of 1879. Although both parties are concerned about Russia, Austria has more reasons than Germany to fear the eastern neighbor. Germany, in addition, uses the alliance to tie the hands of Austria, in a twofold sense, by discouraging those domestic reforms that might predispose Austria to closer cooperation with the Slavic world and, more in general, by preventing Austria from pursuing an independent foreign policy (Taylor 1954, 255–80). After Bismarck's fall, Austria will try to escape from German control, to avoid entrapment in the incipient Anglo-German rivalry, to find an understanding with Russia (Schroeder 1976, 245–46). Yet another case is the Germano-Italian alliance of 1939. After the *Anschluss*, Italy sees its freedom of action seriously constrained; and after the occupation of Prague, Mussolini begins to think about an alliance with Hitler. In light of the lukewarm signals coming from London, Italy fears above all isolation. In addition, Mussolini hopes that the alliance will enable him to influence German policy and make Hitler move along predictable lines. Germany, in turn, ties the ally tightly to itself and blocks any Italian attempt to resume the previous "determinant weight" policy (Di Nolfo 1994, 280–306).

40. According to Hirschman, those who are dissatisfied with the performance of an organization or the quality of a product can resort to two strategies: *exit* and *voice*. The former implies defection (one leaves that organization, one stops buying that product); the latter is defined as "any attempt at all to change, rather than to escape from, an objectionable state of affairs, whether through individual or collective petition to the management directly in charge, through appeal to a higher authority with the intention of forcing a change in management, or through various types of actions and protests, including those that are meant to mobilize public opinion" (1970, 30). Hirschman refers to consumers and members of organizations; thus any analogy with states and international affairs should be taken with a grain of salt. Having said that, I find Hirschman's basic insight indeed useful in our context as well.

41. This does not mean, of course, that such a strategy will succeed. One of the reasons for failure can be extrapolated from Hirschman (1970, 83): "the *effectiveness* of the voice mechanism is strengthened by the possibility of exit."

42. On the theory and practice of the balance of power in the 18th century, see Kaeber (1907), Quazza (1968), Kluxen (1978), and Anderson (1970)—and the response of Black (1983)—as well as Anderson (1993, 163–80), a revisitation of his own previous work. Sheehan (1996) is a comprehensive study on the balance of power throughout the modern and contemporary age; one chapter is devoted to the 18th century. The same goes for the classical works of Donnadieu (1900) and Dupuis (1909), which are still quite useful.

43. One of the most incisive reconstructions of the international "political habits" of the time is Albert Sorel's (1885–1904/1946, especially 7–71); for a briefer, and yet exhaustive, discussion, see Gilbert (1961, 89–104). Meinecke (1924/1962, chaps. 11–12) offers a lucid and telling portrait of two representative figures of the time, Jean Rousset and Frederick the Great. For general textbooks on 18th century diplomatic history, see Black (1990) and McKay and Scott (1983). Older, and yet very

useful, are Muret (1949), Zeller (1955), Roberts (1947), Dorn (1940), and Gershoy (1944).

44. In the second half of the century, balance of power means, from a British perspective, containment of France on the continent and free hand on the oceans; to France, though, the same balance requires a counterweight to British naval power. The balance of power in the Germanic world means, from a Prussian perspective, parity between Vienna and Berlin and the preservation of the status quo in the empire; but to Austria, the same balance implies some primacy both over Prussia and the empire. Similar considerations can be applied to Austrian and Russian designs over Eastern and South Eastern Europe, to Prussian and Russian conceptions of the Nordic balance, and to British, French, Russian, and Ottoman interests in the Mediterranean.

Notes to Chapter Four

1. Dunthorne (1986, 9–12). For a general overview of Anglo-Dutch political and military relations in the first half of the century, see Lodge (1930), Horn (1967), Eyck (1990), Rodger (1990), and Zwitzer (1990). On commercial and financial relations, see Wilson (1941).

2. It is perhaps useful to remind the reader that the Low Countries roughly corresponded to the territory of contemporary Belgium.

3. "The Netherlands line up with England, as a sloop in the wake of a warship to which it is attached." *Mémoires, Introduction* (quoted in Sorel 1885–1904, 279).

4. Grand Pensionary of Holland from 1727 to 1736.

5. "Our situation and our dependence [...] will force us always to follow the stream."

6. See the text of the treaty in Miller (1970, 118–19).

7. See the text of the treaty in ibidem, 116–17.

8. See the text of the convention in Powley (1972, 368–69).

9. The "Protestant cause" was another central theme of the inter-allied public debate; however, confessional considerations did not prevent William III from allying with Austria and Spain as well.

10. This analogy is attributed to the Duke of Bedford (Rodger 1990, 23).

11. For most of the period under investigation—more precisely, from the death of William III in 1702 to the Orangist restoration in 1747—no stadtholder existed. The regents of the seven provinces, where sovereignty lay, conducted foreign policy. The provinces in turn sent representatives to the States General, at the Hague; here, foreign affairs were collectively discussed in the Committee for Foreign Affairs, whose membership included one representative from each province, the president of the States General (*greffier*), and the pensionary of the Province of Holland (usually known as "grand pensionary"). If the committee expressed unanimous views, debate would move on to the States General. But in case of disagreement, matters were referred back to the provinces. This was very often the case since representatives frequently arrived at the Hague with no instructions. In one word, it was a completely decentralized, slow, and uncertain decision-making procedure. The most effective way to get things done in a reasonable amount of time was to secure

the support, on a given issue, of the grand pensionary, Holland being the richest and most influential of the seven provinces. This is why foreign governments and their envoys looked at the grand pensionary as an informal foreign minister of the United Provinces. A brief yet detailed analysis of the Dutch institutional machinery is in Hatton (1950, 21–29).

12. Still, as a general rule, the two maritime powers found it easier to join forces to thwart French trade than to agree on sharing mercantile profits (Horn 1967, 91). On inter-allied relations in the first part of the war, see Haute (1932).

13. For a detailed analysis of the negotiations and the treaty of 1709, see Geikie and Montgomery (1930, 99–164).

14. "The Conduct of the Allies" was published in November 1711. The quote comes from Coombs (1958, 280). According to Swift, the Dutch had never committed themselves seriously to the war effort, their only concern being their own commerce. Another pamphlet claimed to offer a precise estimate of the economic gains achieved by the Dutch at the expense of the British during the war, and it came to the conclusion that "No Nation, no, not a petty Conquer'd Province, was ever treated with more Contempt, or more infamously Bubbl'd and Amus'd, than Great-Britain has been by its Al—s, especially the D—h" (quoted in Coombs 1958, 292). It should be pointed out, however, that this press campaign had a clear domestic target, the Whig government, blamed by the Tories precisely for having accepted Dutch demands for so long. For a thorough reconstruction and analysis of those issues, see Coombs (1958, 277–336).

15. On Anglo-Dutch relations from 1714 to 1721, see Hatton (1950); for the following period, see Dunthorne (1986); a short, yet incisive, survey from 1715 to 1789 is in Lodge (1930).

16. As early as 1717, Stanhope suggested to seize all ships—including Dutch vessels—going into or coming out of Swedish ports, on the grounds that the king "can neither in good Policy or Honour, allow the Subjects of the States to build their Fortune on the Loss and Ruin of his, and to the Strengthening at the same time of his Enemies" (Stanhope to Leathes, March 22, 1717, O.S., quoted in Hatton 1950, 154).

17. The Dutch sent troops during the revolt in Ireland; also, during the first years of the war, they advanced some money to the British troops (Hatton 1950, 20–21). Those debts would be settled only after Stanhope's death.

18. An English journalist of the time writes that the United Provinces act "like a prudent Mistress, insist[ing] upon their own Terms: Whereas a Nation that comes in plumb at once [to a treaty], is like a foolish Girl that first goes to Bed, and afterwards begins to ask for a Marriage or a Settlement" (quoted in Dunthorne 1986, 235).

19. The maritime powers jointly attempted, and jointly failed, to mediate between Spain and Portugal (1735–1737) and between Russia and the Ottoman Empire (1736–1739) as well (Dunthorne 1986, 307–10).

20. This shows, once more, how difficult it is to tell the security motive from the profit motive in state action; the policy adopted by the Dutch reflects the dual need to minimize the risk of aggression and maximize commercial gains.

21. What was at stake was not the principle *free ships, free goods* but whether

those caught in contraband would forfeit not only their cargo—as the 1674 treaty contemplated—but their ships as well, as was now threatened. Privateers usually carried out British retaliatory activities, and the courts would often condemn Dutch property, despite the treaty (Pares 1938, 231–35).

22. This is what Robert Trevor writes to Carteret in April 1744: "I am clearly convinced, it is essentially necessary to the welfare of England, that she [the Dutch Republic] should take a part in the quarrel, were it only to deprive France of the advantages, which that nation is indisputably entitled to, by treaty, in point of trade and navigation, in this country, as long as this country can be only deemed neuter; not to speak of the counter-advantages of a like nature, which the Dutch might reap during this war, in France" (quoted in Pares 1938, 237).

23. As Britain entered war against France in April 1744, the United Provinces did dispatch 20 ships in support. However, by the end of 1745 all those ships had been recalled; according to the regents, they were indispensable for the protection of convoys, many of which were going into French ports (Rodger 1990, 20–21).

24. According to Newcastle, thanks to the restoration of the stadtholder "the republic of Holland will recover its ancient weight and strength, and England will have a useful friend and ally instead of a jealous, timid, and burthensome neighbor" (quoted in Anderson 1995, 173).

25. "The great point, either in peace or war, is to preserve the concert, and union between the allies: with that, nothing very bad can be done; and without that, it is impossible to do any good" (quoted in Black 1991, 203).

26. Lord Holdernesse, secretary of state for the Northern Department, to Yorke, September 1755 (quoted in Carter 1971, 44).

27. It was in the final stages of the War of the Austrian Succession that Britain, exasperated by the Dutch refusal to declare war on France, began to think about establishing an explicit linkage between British conformity with the 1674 trade treaty and Dutch conformity with the 1678 defensive treaty. Since the United Provinces had proved so unreliable, Britain came to the decision to deny the Dutch any commercial gain by putting them in the position of not keeping their defensive pledge. In 1753 Newcastle, traditionally one of the firmest supporters of the Old System, informed Yorke that the next time Britain would find itself at war with France it "will begin by insisting that pursuant to the treaty of 1678, the Republic should immediately send the succours there stipulated; and, within two months, declare war against France also; and in case of refusal on the part of Holland, will declare that that part of the Marine Treaty, which stipulates *Free ships, free goods*, will not and cannot be observed" (quoted in Pares 1938, 241).

28. This view is expressed by Horn (1967), Rodger (1990), Smit (1968), and Lodge (1930).

29. As Newcastle told Bentinck, in July, "We cannot suffer without ruin to ourselves that the whole trade of France should be carried on for them" (quoted in Lodge 1923, 89, n. 3). After a few months, what would become known as the Rule of 1756 would forbid a neutral nation to conduct in wartime a trade it was not permitted to carry on in peacetime.

Notes to Chapter Five

1. See, for example, McKay and Scott (1983, 94–137), Muret (1949, 65–189), Langford (1976, 71–103), Horn (1967, 22–52), Bourgeois (1909), and Lodge (1935).

2. See Oakley (1994, especially 235–42), Murray (1942–1943), and Black (1988a).

3. The abbé le Blanc described British "francophobia" at the beginning of the 18th century in these terms: "they [the British] seem to believe that we are in regard to them what the Persians were to the Athenians; that the king of France is the great King; hence their invincible aversion to the people who obey him, whom they suppose that they alone prevent from giving laws to the rest of Europe" (quoted in Horn 1967, 25).

4. This is, for example, the general thesis that permeates the works of Bourgeois (1909, 1910).

5. To which one can add that the attempt to simultaneously compete with Austria on the continent and with Britain on the oceans will end in a French defeat on both fronts in the following decades (Sorel 1885–1904, 223–24).

6. On the first years of the foreign policy of George I, see the classic work of Hatton (1978, 147–210). The complex relations between Hanover and Britain are examined in Simms and Riotte (2007), Birke and Kluxen (1986), Dann (1991), and Hatton (1982, 1986).

7. Detailed analyses of the negotiations can be found in Shennan (1979, 53–60), Muret (1949, 75–79), and Bourgeois (1909, 97–122).

8. In the case of the Anglo-Dutch treaty, the United Provinces pledged to provide financial and possibly military support against the Jacobites, but they declined to restore the Grand Alliance. For an overview of Anglo-Dutch relations in this period, see Carter (1975, 35–72), Smit (1968), and Raven and Rodger (1990). The Anglo-Austrian treaty was slightly more than a façade agreement. For Austria, now that war with the Ottoman Empire was imminent, its main function was to complicate whatever plans Spain might have; for Britain, the treaty was useful mostly to intimidate France. On Anglo-Austrian relations in this period, see McKay (1986). Finally, the deal with Spain entailed trade concessions that were highly advantageous for the British. However, in this case too some ambiguity was there; Spain's conciliatory attitude was an attempt to decouple Britain from Austria and win British support in Italy, and for its part Britain found it convenient to cultivate Spain's illusions (Muret 1949, 68–69).

9. With regard to this, Dubois writes: "Mon sentiment secret est que l'affaire de Mardick leur tenait à coeur plus qu'aucune autre, plus que l'expulsion du chavalier Saint-George même" (quoted in Bourgeois 1909, 108).

10. Historians seem split here along national lines. British scholars usually emphasize that the alliance was advantageous to France as well (see, for example, Shennan 1979, 51–75, and Black 1985a); French historians often express negative views (see Bourgeois 1909, 1910; and Muret 1949, 65–189).

11. To Frederick Wilhelm, "Cette cour se regarde comme le centre où les intérêts de l'Europe doivent aboutir" (quoted in Bourgeois 1909, 209–10).

12. "Spain's conduct will lead the regent to settle with the emperor to the exclu-

sion of Spain, and to pursue firmly the plan business." Robethon (private secretary to George I) to Dubois, August 2, 1717 (quoted in Bourgeois 1909, 202).

13. The deal contemplated (1) Charles's renunciation of the Spanish throne; (2) Spain's renunciation of Sardinia, to the advantage of the emperor, who in turn would cede it to the Kingdom of Sicily in exchange for Sicily; (3) the future cession of the Duchies of Parma and Tuscany to Isabella Farnese's son, Don Carlos; and (4) Anglo-French concerted action to enforce conformity on those who might reject any of the terms.

14. Emile Bourgeois (1909, 202) defines it as "la plus impolitique et [...] la plus fâcheuse des guerres, une guerre contre l'Espagne, au profit de l'Angleterre." However, the war was accepted by people such as Torcy, Louis XIV's former minister, who could not be suspected of pro-Austrian or pro-British sentiments (Shennan 1979, 68); this seems to suggest that the French decision did not simply reflect the regent's dynastic interests.

15. "Montrons dans toutes les occasions que ce n'est pas au roi catholique ni à la nation espagnole qu'on fait la guerre, mais à ce ministre turbolent, faisons-lui personnellement tout le mal que l'on pourrai," Dubois writes on this occasion (quoted in Bourgeois 1910, 46).

16. "We were chained to England in the lowest servitude." Saint-Simon too expressed a similar view: "L'Angleterre nous rendit sourds aux invitations du Tsar" (XIV, June 20, 1717). Stanhope, for his part, was delighted; the Regent "faisait non seulement tout ce qui pouvait convenir à Sa Majesté Britannique, mais encore bien au delà de ce qu'elle pouvait en désirer" (quoted in Bourgeois 1910, 110).

17. A change in the order of dynastic succession that would allow the daughter of Charles VI, Maria Theresa, to inherit the Austrian throne and the Habsburg lands.

18. Saint-Simon observed that "on avait mis le couteau à la gorge de l'Espagne pour l'entière et énorme satisfaction des Anglais" (XVII, 241).

19. The standard reference on the alliance of Hanover is still Chance (1927).

20. In supporting the United Provinces in their struggle against the Ostend Company, the French clearly hoped to improve bilateral relations. In fact, France had been trying to win Dutch confidence since the last years of Louis XIV, knowing that, if reassured, the United Provinces would be less inclined to follow Britain. The latter, as we have seen, was always reluctant to enter a war without the Dutch, so France was able to affect British policy indirectly by adopting a conciliatory attitude with the United Provinces. Such a strategy was implemented several times in an attempt to restrain or immobilize Britain (Wilson 1936, 133–34).

21. From the British perspective, the alliance of Hanover had less a practical function than coercive: what Britain had in mind, from the very beginning, was to scare Austria into accepting British terms without resorting to a general war (Gibbs 1958, 415–16). Such an attitude is nicely grasped by Albert Sorel (1885–1904, 264), as he points out the "intermittent" character of British foreign policy. As a general rule, Britain makes war for trade-related reasons, yet war disrupts trade; its wealth allows it to take out debts, yet precisely because it is wealthy it feels all the weight of those debts.

22. Although the alliance, as a general rule, suffered from frequent attacks from various quarters, British ministers could rely on solid parliamentary majorities on foreign policy issues from 1716 to 1729. On those matters, in addition, the king's views were quite influential. In other words, the role of Parliament and public opinion must not be exaggerated; they were only one of the forces at play, and not the decisive one (Black 1985a, 306–10; 1985b, 75–92; 1989a). On Parliament and foreign policy in those years, see also Turner (1919) and Gibbs (1962, 1967, 1970).

23. British terms included the end of the siege of Gibraltar, the return of a confiscated ship, and full restoration of the *indulto* (trade privileges) in exchange for the withdrawal of British ships from Spanish and American waters and a general availability to negotiate on all the issues that were still open at a forthcoming congress at Soissons.

24. A detailed list was provided of British obligations in terms of troops, ships, and money, according to different contingencies (e.g., whether the emperor would or would not attack Hanover; Muret 1949, 183).

25. "One of those forced commitments that result much less from natural interests than from necessity."

26. Even if Britain had acted more tactfully, there is little indication that France would have ever accepted joining in the Anglo-Austrian deal. Fleury intended to play the succession card to weaken Austria and was not at all inclined to offer guarantees for free. France was willing to recognize the Pragmatic Sanction in exchange for Lorraine, which would have prevented the wedding of Maria Theresa and Francis of Lorraine from resulting in the dynastic union of Austria and Lorraine. Once informed about the signing of the second Treaty of Vienna, Fleury limited himself to remark that this amounted to a violation of the Treaty of Hanover, with all that this entailed. In June 1731 he wrote to the French ambassador to Spain that "we desire nothing which binds us, directly or indirectly, with people who have failed us so explicitly"; the instructions to the minister plenipotentiary to England, in December, read: "there is no further occasion for negotiation between His Majesty and the King of England; and their reciprocal interests are separated by a distance so considerable that it is no longer a question of deliberating together upon the affairs of Europe" (quoted in Wilson 1936, 230–31).

Notes to Chapter Six

1. In light of all this, one might be tempted to see the Anglo-Prussian alliance as the counterpart of the Austro-French alliance, i.e., as another case of heterogeneous alliance. Such a conclusion, though, would neglect two important differences between the two cases. What keeps Austria and France apart, from the very beginning of their relationship, is not so much the diverse identity of their respective adversaries as the policies to be adopted. Britain and Prussia are united both in preserving peace in Europe, in early 1756, and in waging war, once hostilities have broken out, later in the same year. The first Treaty of Versailles is seen in contradictory terms by the signatories; to France, it is a way of keeping the European front quiet, but to Austria it is the first step toward getting France involved in a war against Prussia. In addition,

although Britain is more interested in the naval war, military operations in Germany will always be quite important to Pitt; France finds itself almost trapped in a continental war that is costly and scarcely relevant in strategic terms, so much so that it will eventually negotiate redefinition of its commitment in 1759 (third Treaty of Versailles).

2. "A naval force, tho' carried never so high, unsupported by even the appearance of a force upon the continent, will be of little use [...] France will outdo us at sea, when they have nothing to fear by land [...]. I have always maintained that our marine should protect our alliances upon the continent; and they, by diverting the expense of France, enable us to maintain our superiority at sea" (quoted in Rodger 1992, 42).

3. Although uttered under different circumstances (the naval mobilization of 1775), Horace Walpole's sarcastic words are quite revealing of this chronic dilemma of British policy: the fleet "being so formidable will, I suppose, be towed overland to Warsaw and restore the Polish Constitution and their King to his full rights—how frightened the King of Prussia must be" (quoted in Rodger 1992, 54).

4. In 1742, James Hyndford, British envoy to Berlin, informs his government that Frederick "seems to apprehend that sooner or later the house of Austria will endeavour to reconquer Silesia, and for that purpose they would hereafter leave the maritime powers and join with France"; and in 1748, the King of Prussia tells Henry Legge, the new British envoy, that "dès que la paix générale serait faite, la cour de Vienne commencerait à chipoter avec celle de Versailles, et qu'alors l'Angleterre pourrait compter sur moi comme sur son allié le plus fidèle" (both quotations in Lodge 1923, 76).

5. In revising the English text, Frederick substituted "Germany" for "the Empire" and added the "passing" of foreign troops to their "entering." Both alterations reflected his desire not to antagonize France; the Low Countries (a traditional target of French expansionism) were formally part of the Empire (but not of Germany); as such, they were not guaranteed by Prussia. In addition, the commitment to prevent the passing of foreign armies was probably designed to show Louis XV that Prussia had taken into account the possibility of a Russian attack on France (Doran 1986, 27).

6. "France will never misjudge her interests so much as to work for the aggrandizement of the new House of Austria."

7. He is the secretary of state for the Northern Department until March 1761; as such, he is the minister in charge of relations with Prussia.

8. Both demands could not be met for solid reasons: Prussia was fighting on two fronts, and the British navy had been fully engaged since the outbreak of war (Black 1988c, 103).

9. Although the *risk* of abandonment was indeed low, for systemic reasons, the *fear* of abandonment was at times acutely felt. Prussia's precarious position would occasionally lead Frederick to suppose that Britain might come to terms with his enemies, at his expense. This was a recurrent concern of his during the Anglo-French talks of 1760 and 1761, as well as in the last months of 1761. His fears, however, proved largely groundless.

10. "If the King of Prussia is not successful and we have no means at hand the King [George II] is undone in Germany, if he is and can force the Empress to a separate peace how will our ends be served unless we engage him in some measure against France [?]" (Holdernesse to Newcastle, September 9, 1756, quoted in Doran 1986, 101).

11. Holdernesse to Newcastle: "Enfin La Bombe a crevé [...] il ne nous reste plus qu'à souhaiter de success à notre allié"; Newcastle to Holdernesse: "As the King of Prussia has by This Time begun the Dance, I must wish Him Success; we have had no Hand in it, and yet possibly we may get some advantage from it" (both quotations in Doran 1986, 99).

12. On the Seven Years' War, Robson (1957) offers a brief yet exhaustive presentation, while Waddington's (1899–1914) is still the most detailed (albeit incomplete) work. On military operations, see also, for the British, Charteris (1925) and Corbett (1907) and for the Prussians Duffy (1974) and Showalter (1996).

13. According to the report Mitchell sent to Holdernesse on July 11, 1757, Frederick lamented his "misfortune to have allied himself with England in her decadence and to have been used as no ally of England ever was" (quoted in Schweizer 1989, 50).

14. Frederick was widely celebrated in poems, songs, and illustrated articles (Schweizer 1989, 57); one year after Rossbach, an old and notorious prussophile, Horace Walpole, wrote: "It is incredible how popular he is here; except a few who take him for the same person as Mr. Pitt, the lowest of the people are perfectly acquainted with him: as I was walking by the river the other night, a bargeman asked me for something to drink the King of Prussia's health" (quoted in Tunstall 1938, 206).

15. The British army, at the time, numbered about 70,000, while the French and the Prussian armies were roughly twice as much each (Middleton 1985, 25 and 29; Ritter 1954/1968, 96).

16. Mitchell to Holdernesse, February 9, 1758 (quoted in Doran 1986, 166).

17. Mitchell to Holdernesse, February 8, 1758 (quoted in ibidem, 164).

18. Holdernesse to Mitchell, February 25, 1758 (quoted in Eldon 1938, 160).

19. This is what Mitchell writes in his memoirs (quoted in ibidem). The strategy of raids along the French coasts, in addition, was useful on the domestic front as well; the incursions were carried out with the means that were already available, and they contributed to defuse the controversy—both in Parliament and in the press—over the dispatch of British troops to Germany.

20. On receiving the news of the Prussian victory over the Russians at Zorndorf (August 1758), Pitt celebrated the "King of Kings, whose last glories transcend all the pasts. The modesty of His Prussian Majesty's relation, his silence of himself, and entire attribution of victory to General Seidlitz, are of a mind, as truely heroick, as His Majesty's taking a colours in his own hand, when exhortations failed, and forcing a disordered infantry to follow him or see him perish. More glory cannot be won, but more decisive, final consequences we still hope to hear, and languish for farther letters from the Prussian army" (quoted in Black 1992, 183).

21. On the Hague negotiations, see Waddington (1899–1914, vol. III, 503–41).

22. "Je n'avais connu aucun de sa droiture et sa probité d'honnête homme" (quoted in Doran 1986, 241).

23. Frederick's initial request was simply that Prussia be given back all the territories held in 1756. He now submitted further demands: Britain's allies must all be included in the peace agreement with France, the latter must deny any support whatsoever to those powers that wanted to continue the war, French subsidies to Sweden and other states must cease, and France must withdraw its armed forces from Prussian territory at the signing of the preliminaries with Britain (Waddington 1899–1914, vol. III, 536).

24. "As you possess," whereby territory and other property remains with its possessor at the end of a conflict.

25. On those negotiations, see Waddington (1899–1914, vol. IV, 511–600).

26. On the origins and development of the historiographical controversy, see Dorn (1929, 529, n. 1). It is not surprising that the betrayal thesis was usually supported by German scholars; yet such a view was shared also by Waddington (1899–1914, vol. V, 278ff.) and even by Lodge (1923, 113), who considered the entire affair as "one of the least creditable in the history of English diplomacy." Dorn's article was one of the first attempts to offer a more balanced interpretation; a similar path was then followed by Spencer (1956) and, more recently, by Schweizer (1989, 97–120; and 1991, 142ff.).

27. Israel Mauduit authored the leaflet. On its contents and impact, see Peters (1980, 182–86).

28. "To keep the English court, should its negotiation with France be renewed, from making any decisions detrimental to his interests." The Prussian minister, Count von Finckenstein, to the envoy to London, Baron von Knyphausen, December 12, 1761 (quoted in Schweizer 1991, 150–51).

29. "The King [George III] cannot but suppose, that His Prussian Majesty must have begun to turn his thoughts to the way of accommodation, and must be convinced of the necessity of suiting the terms of peace on which he may resolve ultimately to insist, to the means, that may be in his power, of enforcing his demands by the sword." Bute to Mitchell, January 6, 1762 (quoted in Dorn 1929, 539).

30. Galitzin's letter to the tsar has been the source of yet another historiographical dispute centered on its authenticity. To Waddington (1899–1914, vol. 5, 315–17), Lodge (1923, 122–24), and Doran (1986, 315–17), the letter genuinely reflected Bute's words; Dorn (1929) and Spencer (1956), on the other hand, express different views.

31. In March, Frederick suggested to Peter III that the trade weapon might induce Britain to take part in the war against Denmark; the instructions for the Russian envoy to London show that Peter was quite receptive to such advice (Spencer 1956, 109–10).

Notes to Chapter Seven

1. Among the works of diplomatic history that focus on the second half of the 18th century, see Dorn (1940), on the 1740–1765 period; Muret (1949, 465–574), who stops at 1763; Gershoy (1944), on the years between 1763 and 1789; and, more

in general, Zeller (1955, 222–346); Schroeder (1994b, 3–52); and McKay and Scott (1983, 159–271). A brief yet incisive overview from the end of the Seven Years' War to the French Revolution is in Anderson (1965); for a powerful assessment of the whole century, see the classic work by Sorel (1885–1904).

2. As a result of such reforms, for example, in 1756 the crown could rely on twice as many resources for military spending as in 1740. On those issues, see the solid work by Dickinson (1987).

3. "Of its duplicity and its desire to harm."

4. "Horrible, contradictory, outrageous."

5. "The alliance, family ties, friendship only to deceive and insult."

6. On the "reversal of alliances" of 1756, see Waddington (1896); for a briefer analysis, see Horn (1957). For a detailed reconstruction of the events leading to the Austro-French alliance, see Broglie (1897); on the role of Russia, see Kaplan (1968); on Anglo-Prussian relations, see Schweizer (1989, 1991).

7. On the evolution of Kaunitz's views, see McGill (1968, 1971) and Szabo (1979). A broader portrait of the Austrian chancellor is in Szabo (1994) and Schilling (1994).

8. Broglie (1897, 178–283) and Waddington (1896, 294–332) offer two exhaustive discussions of the period between August and December 1755.

9. Paradoxically, Frederick had been misled by a similar consideration. Although informed of the Austro-French negotiations, he thought it unlikely that Louis XV would ever reach an agreement with France's traditional Habsburg rival (Broglie 1897, 304–6; Ritter 1954/1968, 103).

10. Choiseul tells Louis XV that Britain is "l'ennemie déclarée de votre Etat. Elle le sera toujours" (quoted in Bourgeois 1911, 523); and Vergennes writes to Louis XVI that England is "incontestablement et héréditairement l'ennemie de la France" (quoted in Labourdette 1990, 90), "l'ennemie invéterée de cette monarchie" (memorandum of April 12, 1777, in Hardman and Price 1998, 247). Choiseul, who has inherited a diplomatically compromised situation, bitterly observes that "cette nouvelle alliance fit négliger la guerre de mer et d'Amérique qui était la véritable guerre" (quoted in Scott 1979, 18); and Vergennes is determined to prevent any further similar distortion of an alliance that, if correctly used, "peut paraître utile en ce que faisant une sûreté de plus à la conservation de la paix sur le continent elle lui [Louis XVI] donne plus de moyens de veiller et de se mettre en mesure contre l'Angleterre" (memorandum of April 12, 1777, in Hardman and Price 1998, 248).

11. This is Choiseul's nightmare as early as 1759: "Nous sentons qu'après cette guerre [...] la maison d'Autriche pourrait reprendre ses liaisons avec l'Angleterre" (quoted in Hardman and Price 1998, 110). Fifteen years later, Vergennes expresses a similar concern: "le jour que la cour de Vienne se séparera de la France, elle aura pour alliée l'Angleterre. L'une et l'autre se tiennent en mesure de se relier au moment où un intérêt quelconque les y conviera. L'Angleterre réunie à la maison d'Autriche et partageant ses projets et ses vues, la France ne pourra plus avoir de guerre qui ne soit sur mer comme sur terre" (quoted in Labourdette 1990, 85).

12. "His Majesty [...] may get involved in a number of wars to defend his ally,

but the latter may never be in a position to reciprocate." Memorandum of April 12, 1777, in Hardman and Price (1998, 248).

13. "We know only too well that the king of Prussia has been lowered enough and that it is not in our interest to see him completely abated." Quoted in Hardman and Price (1998, 110).

14. "[Frederick] being placed on the flank of Austrian territories, it is the fear that this instills in the court of Vienna that makes [Austria] get closer to France. This same fear holds the Austrians still in our relationship and will hold them as long as its motive remains."

15. "If we destroy the power of the king of Prussia, no dam will be left to contain Austrian ambition; Germany will be forced to bend under Austrian rule and will easily pave for Austria the way to our frontiers." Memorandum of April 12, 1777, in Hardman and Price (1998, 249).

16. On those negotiations and the second Treaty of Versailles, see Waddington (1899–1914, vol. I, 145–56).

17. The classic reference is still Waddington (1899–1914).

18. On the negotiations leading to the Peace of Paris, see Rashed (1951).

19. In a memorandum written on September 27, 1764, Kaunitz explained why Austria should stick to the alliance with France; unable to find a single positive reason, he came to the conclusion that what truly mattered was to prevent France from resorting to its traditional hostility toward Austria (Beer 1872, 63–74).

20. Louis XV's system of secret diplomacy (the *secret*) was established in 1746, mainly to manage Polish affairs. After the diplomatic revolution, it became the gathering point for all those who opposed the new alliance and intended to revive a traditional foreign policy based on diffidence toward Austria and open hostility toward Russia. Vergennes took part in the *secret*; his appointment to minister, in 1774, entailed the confluence of the *secret* and official diplomacy, and the end of the former. An important collection of documents is in Broglie (1878).

21. He was Choiseul's cousin. In 1761, Choiseul was appointed minister for war and the navy, while Choiseul-Praslin took over as minister for foreign affairs.

22. The March 1777 instructions for the French ambassador to Vienna, the Baron of Breteuil, reveal that Vergennes was perfectly aware of Austria's expansionist intentions. In Vergennes's view, Vienna was not really satisfied with the terms of the partition of Poland and was likely to aim at a new partition, this time of the Ottoman Empire. Therefore, Vergennes expected that Austria would try to get France involved in this design by using the pretext of actually defending the Turks against the Russians. But France should not fall into this trap; it should interpose itself between Prussia and Austria on the one hand and between Russia and Austria on the other, and make the Austrian ally understand the risks inherent in its unscrupulous policy, for France could not tolerate any further weakening of the Ottoman Empire (Fagniez 1922, 19–20; and Sorel 1881).

23. "Catherine would realize only too well that I would be completely at her command, which might be very convenient for her but not really suitable for me." Joseph to Leopold, quoted in Anderson (1958, 29).

24. "Egypt! We would not want those marabouts even if one offered them to us."

25. The project contemplated creation of a "Greek empire" ruled by Catherine's nephew, and a kingdom of Dacia, that would probably be assigned to Prince Potemkin; the remaining Ottoman territory would be shared between Austria and Russia (Roider 1982, 162–63; and Madariaga 1981, 387–88).

26. "It could not but give the emperor just cause of offense."

27. It is the famous memorandum of April 12, 1777, so often mentioned. For the integral text of this document, see Hardman and Price (1998, 247–50).

28. "It is so easy to bring about war without being physically the aggressor that His Majesty would be driven against his interests whenever Austrian policy found war convenient." Ibidem, 248–49.

29. "There is no compensation that could offset the damage that any increase in power of the House of Austria would inflict on His Majesty." Ibidem, 249.

30. "A guarantee of the conduct of the House of Austria to His Majesty and a way to contain or repress it, depending on need." Ibidem.

31. Hardman and Price (1998, 64–66) notice here a curious coincidence of date: Louis XVI's sudden decision to intervene openly against Britain on the side of the American colonists was made the same day as news of the death of Maximilian III arrived at Versailles (January 6). Hence the two scholars put forward the suggestive hypothesis that France decided to fight Britain not to be trapped in a European war over Bavaria, rather than keeping neutrality in Europe in order to wage war against Britain on the oceans and in America. To which one has replied that Hardman and Price probably take the triggering event as real motivation; France's decision to intervene was above all the logical result of a process that can be traced back to Choiseul's years (Scott 1999, 943).

32. Not only did not the Habsburgs help France in its struggle against Britain but they damaged, albeit indirectly, their ally; although Leghorn, for example, was part of the Grand Duchy of Tuscany ruled by Leopold, the emperor's brother, it became a British port in those years. That France did not expect much from its ally is also revealed by the quick dismissal of Austria's offer to mediate, in 1781; to Louis XVI, such an offer reflected nothing but "leur grand désir [...] de se mêler de l'affaire; je crois que s'ils pourront procurer quelques adoucissements à l'Angleterre ils s'y jeteront sans le paraître trop" (Louis to Vergennes, February 19, in Hardman and Price 1998, letter 168, 295–96). The British, for their part, entertained the opposite fear, i.e. that Kaunitz's mediation would be to France's advantage (Scott 1990, 314–16).

33. For a detailed reconstruction of the negotiations leading to the peace treaty, see Fagniez (1922, 178–98) and Oursel (1921).

34. "The king will be forced to deploy troops along his borders, since in no case could he be indifferent to the fate of the United Provinces." See the integral text of the statement in Hardman and Price (1998, 346–47). The various documents prepared by the king's ministers on that occasion reflected a unanimous anti-Austrian stand. In some cases, such an attitude ran very deep indeed; Breteuil and Castries,

for example, talked about the 1756 alliance as "cet aveuglement funeste, cet oubli des nos intérêts" and argued that it was a "droit et devoir de la monarchie française" to put an end to it (quoted in Tratchevsky 1880, 1881, 8).

35. According to Grosjean (1925, 110) and Bernard (1965, 194), in his conversation with Vergennes Mercy took the initiative—without being authorized by Vienna—of offering the provinces of Luxembourg and Namur to France. His purpose was allegedly to get the ally to quickly agree and force the hand of his own government with a fait accompli. France might have been tempted by the perspective of substantial territorial gains, and this would explain why Vergennes did not reject the Austrian plan outright. However, there is no trace of this offer in the document that Mercy was to submit to Louis XVI a few days later—which might explain the harsh tone of France's final response in the following weeks—or in any other document for that matter. Be that as it may, what we do know for sure is that Joseph's letter to Louis XVI in which the emperor stated that the two provinces were not included in the exchange plan irritated Vergennes quite a bit. Why support Vienna's scheme if France would not even get rid of the Austrian presence on its own borders? (Hardman and Price 1998, 348).

36. The only voice supporting the Austrian proposal was, of all ministers, Vergennes himself, possibly an attempt to appease the queen, whose hostility had placed him in an embarrassing position more than once (Murphy 1982, 415–16). The views of the French ministers are familiar, by now. French support for the exchange plan would entail paving the way for Austro-Russian expansionism, placing the Habsburgs in control of Germany and giving up whatever French influence was left over the empire, as well as altering the balance between Prussia and Austria (Tratchevsky 1881, 29–30).

37. "If only we could have bartered the Low Countries, then we would be out of their claws, and we could someday maybe make them regret it, if they had a new war with the English." Joseph to Leopold, December 3 and 24, 1784 (quoted in Sorel 1885–1904, 352).

38. "Si la France aura bien des affaires sur les bras et manquera d'argent et des ressources, le roi de Prusse seul n'osera rien entreprendre et pourra être contenu par les deux cours impériales. *On pourra faire ce que l'on voudra*, et les Turcs sont perdus." Joseph to Leopold, December 16, 1782 (quoted in Sorel 1885–1904, 353).

39. "Die grossen Mächte," *Historich-Politische Zeitschrift*, II, 1, 1833 (Engl. trans. R. Wines, "The Great Powers," in L. von Ranke, *The Secret of World History: Selected Writings on the Art and Science of History*, New York: Fordham University Press, 1981, 144. In a later work, Ranke draws a direct connection between the Austrian alliance and the French Revolution: "Man darf mit Grund behaupten, daß die österreichisch-französische Allianz eines der wesentlichsten Motive der Revolution ausgemacht hat" (*Ursprung und Beginn der Revolutionskriege 1791 und 1792*, Leipzig: Duncker & Humblot, 1875, 152). More recently, Hochedlinger (1997) has showed how anti-Austrian feelings, clearly reflected in the general hostility toward the queen, were an instrument employed by all those who intended to attack the monarchy.

Notes to Conclusions

1. This seems to be the common trait of the most important alliances of the 18th century, in addition to those under investigation here. Heterogeneity marked the alliances between Austria and Britain from 1713 to 1756. The treaty of Westminster (1716) was a surface agreement that Austria tried to use against the Ottoman Empire and that Britain found useful to intimidate France (Muret 1949, 69). Despite the second Treaty of Vienna (1731), Britain kept a low profile at the outbreak of the wars of Polish and Austrian succession. In the latter case, in addition, when Britain did intervene, its policy was aimed less at supporting Austria than at damaging France, and as a result the British did not help Austria retake Silesia. In the end, they forced their ally to accept a disadvantageous peace (Black 1991, 183–215). Heterogeneity also marked the Austro-Russian alliances that from 1726 onward became almost a constant feature of European diplomacy. Although the allies fought against a common enemy (the Ottoman Empire), Austria was always concerned about Russian territorial gains, and Russia did not help the ally reconquer Silesia but defected in the last phase of the Seven Years' War. After 1763, finally, Austria increasingly valued the alliance as an anti-Prussian device, yet Prussia was an ally of Russia too, and while following Russia in its expansion at the expense of the Ottoman Empire Austria systematically tried to contain its ally (Roider 1982). Heterogeneity is further seen in the Russo-Prussian alliance in the aftermath of the Seven Years' War. Russia was interested in preventing French initiatives in Sweden and Poland, while Frederick used the alliance to restrain Russia itself and kept the ally from taking full advantage of its victories against the Turks (Sorel 1902). Finally, we find heterogeneity even in the alliance between the two major revisionist powers in the aftermath of the Peace of Utrecht, Austria and Spain (first Treaty of Vienna, 1725); the former adopted a fundamentally defensive attitude and did not support at all the latter's territorial ambitions (Wilson 1936, 91–214).

2. In the period between the Peace of Utrecht and the French Revolution, the only significant aggregation alliance is the Anglo-Prussian alliance. Guarantee alliances, on the other hand, are more numerous; in addition to the Anglo-Dutch alliance, one should mention at least the three Franco-Spanish "family compacts" (1733, 1743, 1761) that afforded both signatories a broad framework for anti-British cooperation (Sorel 1885–1904, 227–29, 286–89).

3. In international relations theory, the distinction between efficient causes and permissive causes can be traced back to Waltz (1959, 230–34); here, the same distinction is adopted, although in a sense that is slightly different from the original one.

4. At the end of his historical analysis of the formation of three alliances in a multipolar system, Snyder comes to a similar conclusion: he notices that "there was no indeterminacy about which alliance, if any, would form; the only indeterminacy lay in how the benefits and the costs of a single alliance would be divided," and that "this scarcity of alternatives throws into question the conventional notion of the flexibility of alliances in a multipolar system" (Snyder 1997, 148).

References

Aalbers, Johan (1977), "Holland's financial problems (1713–1733) and the wars against Louis XIV," in A. C. Duke and C. A. Tamse, eds., *Britain and the Netherlands*, the Hague: Nijhoff, vol. VI, pp. 79–93.

Altfeld, Michael F. (1984), "The decision to ally: a theory and test," *Western Political Quarterly*, 38:4, 523–44.

Altfeld, Michael F., and Bruce Bueno de Mesquita (1979), "Choosing sides in wars," *International Studies Quarterly*, 23:1, 87–112.

Anderson, Matthew S. (1958), "The great powers and the Russian annexation of the Crimea, 1783–1784," *Slavonic and East European Review*, 37:88, 17–41.

Anderson, Matthew S. (1965), "European diplomatic relations, 1763–1790," in *New Cambridge Modern History*, Cambridge: Cambridge University Press, vol. VIII, pp. 252–78.

Anderson, Matthew S. (1970), "Eighteenth-century theories of the balance of power," in R. Hatton and M. S. Anderson, eds., *Studies in Diplomatic History*, London: Longman, pp. 183–98.

Anderson, Matthew S. (1993), *The Rise of Modern Diplomacy, 1450–1919*, London: Longman.

Anderson, Matthew S. (1995), *The War of the Austrian Succession, 1740–1748*, London: Longman.

Aron, Raymond (1962/1967), *Paix et guerre entre les nations*, Paris: Calmann-Lévy (Engl. trans. R. Howard and A. Baker Fox, *Peace and War: A Theory of International Relations*, New York: Praeger).

Baldwin, David A. (1997), "The concept of security," *Review of International Studies*, 23:1, 5–26.

Barnett, Michael, and Raymond Duvall (2005), "Power in international politics," *International Organization*, 59:1, 39–75.

Barnett, Michael N., and Jack S. Levy (1991), "Domestic sources of alliances and alignments: the case of Egypt, 1962–1973," *International Organization*, 55:3, 369–95.

Beer, Adolf (1872), "Denkschriften des Fürsten Wenzel Kaunitz-Rittberg," *Archiv für österreichische Geschichte*, 48, 3–162.

Bennett, D. Scott (1997), "Testing alternative models of alliance duration, 1816–1984," *American Journal of Political Science*, 41:3, 846–78.
Bercovitch, Jacob, ed. (1988), *ANZUS in Crisis: Alliance Management in International Affairs*, New York: St. Martin's Press.
Bérenger, Jean (1997), *A History of the Habsburg Empire, 1700–1918*, London: Longman.
Beres, Louis R. (1972), "Bipolarity, multipolarity, and the reliability of alliance commitments," *Western Political Quarterly*, 25:4, 702–10.
Bernard, Paul P. (1965), *Joseph II and Bavaria: Two Eighteenth Century Attempts at German Unification*, the Hague: Nijhoff.
Berridge, Geoff R. (1989), "Ententes and alliances," *Review of International Studies*, 15:3, 251–60.
Birke, Adolf M., and Kurt Kluxen, eds. (1986), *England and Hanover*, München: Saur.
Black, Jeremy (1983), "The theory of the balance of power in the first half of the eighteenth century," *Review of International Studies*, 9:1, 55–61.
Black, Jeremy (1985a), "The Anglo-French alliance, 1716–1731: a study in eighteenth century international relations," *Francia*, 13, 295–310.
Black, Jeremy (1985b), *British Foreign Policy in the Age of Walpole*, Edinburgh: Donald.
Black, Jeremy (1986), *Natural and Necessary Enemies: Anglo-French Relations in the Eighteenth Century*, Athens: University of Georgia Press.
Black, Jeremy (1987), *The Collapse of the Anglo-French Alliance, 1727–1731*, New York: St. Martin's Press.
Black, Jeremy (1988a), "Anglo-Baltic relations, 1714–1748," in W. Minchinton, ed., *Britain and the Northern Seas*, Pontefract: Lofthouse, pp. 67–74.
Black, Jeremy (1988b), "French foreign policy in the age of Fleury reassessed," *English Historical Review*, 103:407, 359–84.
Black, Jeremy (1988c), "Naval power and British foreign policy in the age of Pitt the Elder," in J. Black and P. S. Woodfine, eds., *The British Navy and the Use of Naval Power in the Eighteenth Century*, Leicester: Leicester University Press, pp. 91–107.
Black, Jeremy (1989a), "England's foreign alliances in the eighteenth century," *Albion*, 20:4, 573–602.
Black, Jeremy, ed. (1989b), *Knights Errant and True Englishmen: British Foreign Policy, 1660–1800*, Edinburgh: Donald.
Black, Jeremy (1990), *The Rise of the European Powers, 1679–1793*, London: Arnold.
Black, Jeremy (1991), *A System of Ambition? British Foreign Policy, 1660–1793*, London: Longman.
Black, Jeremy (1992), *Pitt the Elder*, Cambridge: Cambridge University Press.
Bladen, Cristopher (1970), "Alliance and integration," in J. Friedman, C. Bladen, and S. Rosen, eds., *Alliance in International Politics*, Boston: Allyn & Bacon, pp. 121–26.
Blau, Peter M. (1964), *Exchange and Power in Social Life*, New York: Wiley.

Bourgeois, Emile (1909), *Le secret du Régent et la politique de l'Abbé Dubois*, Paris: Colin.

Bourgeois, Emile (1910), *Le secret du Dubois, cardinal et premier ministre*, Paris: Colin.

Bourgeois, Emile (1911), *Manuel historique de politique étrangère*, Paris: Belin, T. vol. 1: *Les Origines (1610–1789)*, 5th ed.

Boutros-Ghali, Boutros (1963), *Contribution a une théorie générale des alliances*, Paris: Pedone.

Boyer, Mark A. (1989), "Trading public goods in the western alliance system," *Journal of Conflict Resolution*, 33:4, 700–727.

Brand, Laurie A. (1994a), "Economics and shifting alliances: Jordan's relations with Syria and Iraq, 1975–81," *International Journal of Middle East Studies*, 26:3, 393–413.

Brand, Laurie A. (1994b), *Jordan's Inter-Arab Relations: The Political Economy of Alliance Making*, New York: Columbia University Press.

Broglie, J. V. Albert (1878), *Le secret du Roi. Correspondance secrète de Louis XV avec ses agents diplomatiques, 1752–1774*, Paris: Lévy, 2nd ed., 2 vols.

Broglie, J. V. Albert (1897), *L'alliance autrichienne*, Paris: Calmann Lévy.

Browning, Reed (1975), *The Duke of Newcastle*, New Haven: Yale University Press.

Bueno de Mesquita, Bruce (1981), *The War Trap*, New Haven: Yale University Press.

Bueno de Mesquita, Bruce, and J. David Singer (1973), "Alliance, capabilities, and war: a review and synthesis," in C. Cotter, ed., *Political Science Annual*, Indianapolis: Bobbs-Merrill, vol. 4, pp. 237–80.

Burgess, Philip M., and David W. Moore (1972), "Inter-nation alliances: an inventory and appraisal of propositions," in J. A. Robinson, ed., *Political Science Annual*, Indianapolis: Bobbs-Merrill, vol. 3, pp. 339–83.

Burgess, Philip M., and James A. Robinson (1969), "Alliances and the theory of collective action: a simulation of coalition processes," *Midwest Journal of Political Science*, 13:2, 194–218.

Buzan, Barry, Charles Jones, and Richard Little (1993), *The Logic of Anarchy: Neorealism to Structural Realism*, New York: Columbia University Press.

Caplow, Theodore (1956), "A theory of coalitions in the triad," *American Sociological Review*, 21:4, 489–93.

Caplow, Theodore (1959), "Further development of a theory of coalitions in the triad," *American Journal of Sociology*, 64:5, 488–93.

Caplow, Theodore (1968), *Two Against One: Coalitions in Triads*, Englewood Cliffs: Prentice Hall.

Carr, Edward H. (1946), *The Twenty Years' Crisis 1919–1939: An Introduction to the Study of International Relations*, London: Macmillan, 2nd ed.

Carr, Edward H. (1963), *International Relations Between the Two World Wars (1919–1939)*, London: Macmillan.

Carter, Alice C. (1971), *The Dutch Republic in Europe in the Seven Years War*, London: Macmillan.

Carter, Alice C. (1975), *Neutrality or Commitment: The Evolution of Dutch Foreign Policy, 1667–1795*, London: Arnold.

Cha, Victor D. (2000), "Abandonment, entrapment, and neoclassical realism in Asia: the United States, Japan, and Korea," *International Studies Quarterly*, 44:2, 261–91.

Chance, James F. (1927), *The Alliance of Hanover: A Study of British Foreign Policy in the Last Years of George I*, London: Murray.

Charteris, Evan (1925), *William Augustus Duke of Cumberland and the Seven Years' War*, London: Hutchinson & Co.

Chatterjee, Partha (1977), "Alliance behavior in balance-of-power systems," *American Political Science Review*, 71:3, 1047–49.

Chertkoff, Jerome M. (1967), "A revision of Caplow's coalition theory," *Journal of Experimental Social Psychology*, 3, 172–77.

Chertkoff, Jerome M. (1970), "Sociopsychological theories and research on coalition formation," in S. Groennings, E. W. Kelley, and M. Leiserson, eds., *The Study of Coalition Behavior. Theoretical Perspectives and Cases from Four Continents*, New York: Holt, Rinehart & Winston, pp. 297–322.

Chiu, Daniel Y. (2003), "International alliances in the power cycle theory of state behavior," *International Political Science Review*, 24:1, 123–36.

Christensen, Thomas J. (1997), "Perceptions and alliances in Europe, 1865–1940," *International Organization*, 51:1, 65–97.

Christensen, Thomas J., and Jack Snyder (1990), "Chain gangs and passed bucks: predicting alliance patterns in multipolarity," *International Organization*, 44:2, 137–68.

Christensen, Thomas J., and Jack Snyder (1997), "Progressive research on degenerate alliances," *American Political Science Review*, 91:4, 919–22.

Colombo, Alessandro (1994), *Solitudine dell'Occidente*, Milano: il Saggiatore.

Colombo, Alessandro (2001), *La lunga alleanza. La NATO tra consolidamento, supremazia e crisi*, Milano: Angeli.

Conybeare, John A. C. (1992), "A portfolio diversification model of alliances: the triple alliance and triple entente, 1879–1914," *Journal of Conflict Resolution*, 36:1, 53–85.

Conybeare, John. A. C. (1994a), "Arms versus alliances: the capital structure of military enterprise," *Journal of Conflict Resolution*, 38:2, 215–35.

Conybeare, John A. C. (1994b), "The portfolio benefits of free riding in military alliances," *International Studies Quarterly*, 38:3, 405–20.

Conybeare, John A. C., and Todd Sandler (1990), "The triple entente and the triple alliance, 1880–1914: a collective goods approach," *American Political Science Review*, 84:4, 1197–1206.

Coombs, Douglas S. (1957), "The augmentation of 1709: a study in the workings of the Anglo-Dutch alliance," *English Historical Review*, 72:285, 642–61.

Coombs, Douglas S. (1958), *The Conduct of the Dutch. British Opinion and the Dutch Alliance During the War of the Spanish Succession*, the Hague: Nijhoff.

Cooper, Scott (2003–2004), "State-centric balance-of-threat theory: explaining the misunderstood Gulf Cooperation Council," *Security Studies*, 13:2, 306–349.

Coquelle, Pierre (1902), *L'alliance franco-hollandaise contre l'Angleterre, 1735–1788*, Paris: Plon.
Corbett, Julian S. (1907), *England in the Seven Years' War: A Study in Combined Strategy*, London: Longmans, Green and Co., 2 vols.
Crozier, Michel, and Erhard Friedberg (1977/1980), *L'acteur et le système. Les contraintes de l'action collective*, Paris: Sevil (Engl. trans. A. Goldhammer, *Actors and Systems. The Politics of Collective Action*, Chicago: University of Chicago Press).
Cusack, Thomas R., and Richard Stoll (1991), "Balancing behavior in the interstate system, 1816–1976," *International Interactions*, 16:4, 255–70.
Dann, Uriel (1991), *Hanover and Great Britain, 1740–1760. Diplomacy and Survival*, Leicester: Leicester University Press.
David, Steven R. (1991a), *Choosing Sides: Alignment and Realignment in the Third World*, Baltimore: Johns Hopkins University Press.
David, Steven R. (1991b), "Explaining Third World alignment," *World Politics*, 43:2, 233–56.
Deutsch, Karl W., and J. David Singer (1964), "Multipolar power systems and international stability," *World Politics*, 16:3, 390–406.
Di Nolfo, Ennio (1994), *Storia delle relazioni internazionali, 1918–1992*, Roma-Bari: Laterza.
Dickinson, Peter G. M. (1987), *Finance and Government Under Maria Theresa, 1740–1780*, Oxford: Oxford University Press, 2 vols.
Dinerstein, Herbert S. (1965), "The transformation of alliance systems," *American Political Science Review*, 59:3, 589–601.
Dingman, Roger V. (1979), "Theories of, and approaches to, alliance politics," in P. G. Lauren, ed., *Diplomacy: New Approaches in Theory, History, and Policy*, New York: Free Press, pp. 245–66.
Donelan, Michael (1990), *Elements of International Political Theory*, Oxford: Clarendon, pp. 121–36.
Donnadieu, Louis (1900), *Essai sur la théorie de l'équilibre*, Paris: Rousseau.
Doran, Patrick F. (1986), *Andrew Mitchell and Anglo-Prussian Diplomatic Relations During the Seven Years War*, London: Garland.
Dorn, Walter L. (1929), "Frederic the Great and Lord Bute," *Journal of Modern History*, 1:4, 529–60.
Dorn, Walter L. (1940), *Competition for Empire, 1740–1765*, New York: Harper & Row.
Duffy, Christopher (1974), *The Army of Frederick the Great*, New York: Hippocrene Books.
Duncan, George T., and Randolph M. Siverson (1982), "Flexibility of alliance partner choice in a multipolar system: models and tests," *International Studies Quarterly*, 26:4, 511–38.
Dunthorne, Hugh (1986), *The Maritime Powers, 1721–1740: A Study of Anglo-Dutch Relations in the Age of Walpole*, London: Garland.

Dupuis, Charles (1909), *Le principe d'équilibre et le concert européen de la paix de Westphalie à l'Act d'Algesiras*, Paris: Perrin.
Eckstein, Harry (1975), "Case study and theory in political science," in F. I. Greenstein and N. W. Polsby, eds., *Handbook of Political Science*, Reading: Addison-Wesley, vol. 7, pp. 79–137.
Eldon, Carl W. (1938), *England's Subsidy Policy Towards the Continent During the Seven Years' War*, Philadelphia: University of Pennsylvania Press.
Elman, Colin (1996a), "Cause, effect, and consistency: a response to Kenneth Waltz," *Security Studies*, 6:1, 58–61.
Elman, Colin (1996b), "Horses for courses: why not neorealist theories of foreign policy?" *Security Studies*, 6:1, 7–53.
Elster, Jon (1989), *Nuts and Bolts for the Social Sciences*, Cambridge: Cambridge University Press.
Emerson, Richard M. (1962), "Power-dependence relations," *American Sociological Review*, 27:1, 31–40.
Eyck van Heslinga, E. S. van (1990), "A competitive ally: the delicate balance of naval alliance and maritime competition between Great Britain and the Dutch republic, 1674–1795," in G.J.A Raven and N.A.M. Rodger, eds., *Navies and Armies: The Anglo-Dutch Relationship in War and Peace, 1688–1988*, Edinburgh: Donald, pp. 1–11.
Fagniez, Gustave (1922), "La politique de Vergennes et la diplomatie de Breteuil (1774–1787)," *Revue historique*, t. CXL, mai–juin, 1–25, and juillet–août, 161–207.
Fedder, Edwin H. (1968), "The concept of alliance," *International Studies Quarterly*, 12:1, 65–86.
Forsyth, Murray, Maurice Keens-Soper, and Peter Savigear, eds. (1970), *The Theory of International Relations. Selected Texts from Gentili to Treitschke*, New York: Atherton.
Freund, Julien (1983), *Sociologie du conflit*, Paris: Presses Universitaires de France.
Frieden, Jeffry A. (1999), "Actors and preferences in international relations," in D. A. Lake and R. Powell, eds., *Strategic Choice and International Relations*, Princeton: Princeton University Press, pp. 39–76.
Gamson, William A. (1961a), "An experimental test of a theory of coalition formation," *American Sociological Review*, 26:4, 565–73.
Gamson, William A. (1961b), "A theory of coalition formation," *American Sociological Review*, 26:3, 373–82.
Gamson, William A. (1964), "Experimental studies of coalition formation," in L. Berkowitz, ed., *Advances in Experimental Social Psychology*, New York: Academic Press, vol. 1, pp. 81–110.
Gates, William R., and Katsvaki L. Terasawa (1992), "Commitment, threat perceptions, and expenditures in a defense alliance," *International Studies Quarterly*, 36:1, 101–18.
Gaubatz, Kurt (1996), "Democratic states and commitment in international relations," *International Organization*, 50:1, 577–92.

Gause, Gregory F. (2003–2004), "Balancing what? threat perception and alliance choice in the Gulf," *Security Studies*, 13:2, 273–305.

Geikie, Roderick, and Isabel A. Montgomery (1930), *The Dutch Barrier, 1705–1719*, Cambridge: Cambridge University Press.

Gelpi, Christopher (1999), "Alliances as instruments of intra-allied control," in H. Haftendorn, R. O. Keohane, and C. Wallender, eds., *Imperfect Unions: Security Institutions over Time and Space*, Oxford: Oxford University Press, pp. 107–39.

Gershoy, Leo (1944), *From Despotism to Revolution, 1763–1789*, New York: Harper & Bros.

Geyl, Pieter (1925–26), "Holland and England during the war of the Austrian succession," *History*, 10, 47–51.

Geyl, Pieter (1964), *The Netherlands in the Seventeenth Century, Part Two: 1648–1715*, London: Benn.

Gibbs, Graham C. (1958), "Britain and the alliance of Hanover, April 1725–February 1726," *English Historical Review*, 73:288, 404–30.

Gibbs, Graham C. (1962), "Parliament and foreign policy in the age of Stanhope and Walpole," *English Historical Review*, 77:302, 18–37.

Gibbs, Graham C. (1967), "Parliament and the treaty of Quadruple Alliance," in R. M. Hatton and J. S. Bromley, eds., *William III and Louis XIV*, Liverpool: Liverpool University Press, pp. 287–305.

Gibbs, Graham C. (1970), "Laying treaties before Parliament in the eighteenth century," in R. M. Hatton and M. S. Anderson, eds., *Studies in Diplomatic History*, London: Longman, pp. 116–37.

Gibler, Douglas M. (1996), "Alliances that never balance: the territorial settlement treaty," *Conflict Management and Peace Studies*, 15:1, 75–97.

Gibler, Douglas M. (1997), "Control the issues, control the conflict: the effects of alliances that settle territorial issues on interstate rivalries," *International Interactions*, 22:4, 341–68.

Gibler, Douglas M., and John A. Vasquez (1998), "Uncovering the dangerous alliances, 1495–1980," *International Studies Quarterly*, 42:4, 785–807.

Gilbert, Felix (1951), "The 'New Diplomacy' of the eighteenth century," *World Politics*, 4:1, 1–38.

Gilbert, Felix (1961), *To the Farewell Address: Ideas of Early American Foreign Policy*, Princeton: Princeton University Press.

Glaser, Charles L. (1996), "Realists as optimists: cooperation as self-help," *Security Studies*, 5:3, 122–63.

Goldstein, Avery (1995), "Discounting the free ride: alliances and security in the postwar world," *International Organization*, 49:1, 39–71.

Gowa, Joanne (1994), *Allies, Adversaries, and International Trade*, Princeton: Princeton University Press.

Gowa, Joanne, and Edward D. Mansfield (1993), "Power politics and international trade," *American Political Science Review*, 87:2, 408–20.

Gowa, Joanne, and Edward D. Mansfield (2004), "Alliances, imperfect markets, and major power trade," *International Organization*, 58:4, 775–805.

Grieco, Joseph M. (1988), "Anarchy and the limits of cooperation: a realist critique of the newest liberal institutionalism," *International Organization*, 42:3, 485–508.

Grieco, Joseph M. (1993), "Understanding the problem of international cooperation: the limits of neoliberal institutionalism and the future of realist theory," in D. Baldwin, ed., *Neorealism and Neoliberalism: The Contemporary Debate*, New York: Columbia University Press, pp. 301–38.

Grieco, Joseph M. (1995), "The Maastricht treaty, Economic Monetary Union, and the neorealist research programme," *Review of International Studies*, 21:1, 21–40.

Grieco, Joseph M. (1996), "State interests and international rule trajectories: a neorealist interpretation of the Maastricht Treaty and Economic and Monetary Union in Europe," *Security Studies*, 5:3, 261–306.

Grosjean, Georges (1925), *La politique Rhénane de Vergennes*, Paris: Les Belles Lettres.

Groth, Alexander J., and Richard G. Randall (1991), "Alliance pathology: institutional lessons of the 1930s," *Political Science Quarterly*, 106:1, 109–21.

Gulick, Edward V. (1955), *Europe's Classical Balance of Power: A Case History of the Theory and Practice of One of the Great Concepts of European Statecraft*, Ithaca: Cornell University Press.

Haas, Ernst B., and Allen S. Whiting (1956), *Dynamics of International Relations*, New York: McGraw-Hill.

Haas, Mark L. (2003), "Ideology and alliances: British and French external balancing decisions in the 1930s," *Security Studies*, 12:4, 34–79.

Haley, Kenneth H. D. (1958), "The Anglo-Dutch rapprochement of 1677," *English Historical Review*, 73:289, 614–48.

Handel, Michael (1990), *Weak States in the International System*, London: Cass.

Hardman, John, and Munro Price, eds. (1998), *Louis XVI and the Comte de Vergennes: Correspondence, 1774–1787*, Oxford: Voltaire Foundation.

Harknett, Richard, and Jeffrey A. Van Dan Berg (1997), "Alignment theory and interrelated threats: Jordan and the Gulf crisis," *Security Studies*, 6:3, 112–53.

Haslam, Jonathan (2002), *No Virtue Like Necessity: Realist Thought in International Relations Since Machiavelli*, New Haven: Yale University Press.

Hatton, Ragnhild M. (1950), *Diplomatic Relations Between Great Britain and the Dutch Republic, 1714–1721*, London: East and West.

Hatton, Ragnhild M. (1978), *George I: Elector and King*, London: Thames and Hudson.

Hatton, Ragnhild M. (1982), *The Anglo-Hanoverian Connection, 1714–1760*, London: University of London.

Hatton, Ragnhild M. (1986), *England and Hanover 1714–1837*, in A. M. Birke and K. Kluxen, eds., *England and Hanover*, München: Saur, pp. 17–31.

Haute, Gabryelle van den (1932), *Les relations anglo-hollandaises au début du XVIIIe siècle d'après la correspondance d'Alexandre Stanhope, 1700–1706*, Louvain: Uystpruyst.

Healy, Brian, and Arthur Stein (1973), "The balance of power in international history: theory and reality," *Journal of Conflict Resolution*, 17:1, 33–62.

Hellmann, Gunther, and Reinhard Wolf (1993), "Neorealism, institutionalism, and the future of NATO," *Security Studies*, 3:1, 23–48.

Hertz, Gerald B. (1906), "England and the Ostend Company," *English Historical Review*, 12:86, 255–79.

Hirschman, Albert O. (1970), *Exit, Voice and Loyalty. Responses to Decline in Firms, Organizations, and States*, Cambridge: Harvard University Press.

Hirschman, Albert O. (1980), *National Power and the Structure of Foreign Trade*, Berkeley: University of California Press, expanded edition.

Hochedlinger, Michael (1997), "'La cause de tous les maux de la France'. Die 'Austrophobie' im revolutionären Frankreich und der Sturz des Königtums, 1789–1792," *Francia*, 24:2, 73–120.

Holbraad, Carsten (1971), *The Concert of Europe: A Study in German and British International Theory, 1815–1915*, New York: Barnes & Noble.

Holsti, Kalevi J. (1977), *International Politics: A Framework for Analysis*, Englewood Cliffs: Prentice-Hall, 3rd ed.

Holsti, Ole R., P. Terrence Hopmann, and John D. Sullivan (1973), *Unity and Disintegration in International Alliances: Comparative Studies*, New York: Wiley.

Horn, David B. (1957), "The diplomatic revolution," in *New Cambridge Modern History*, Cambridge: Cambridge University Press, vol. 7, pp. 440–64.

Horn, David B. (1967), *Great Britain and Europe in the Eighteenth Century*, Oxford: Clarendon.

Horvath, William J., and Caxton G. Foster (1963), "Stochastic models of war alliances," *Journal of Conflict Resolution*, 7:2, 110–16.

Huth, Paul K., and Bruce M. Russett (1993), "General deterrence between enduring rivals: testing three competing models," *American Political Science Review*, 87:1, 61–73.

Jervis, Robert (1976), *Perception and Misperception in International Politics*, Princeton: Princeton University Press.

Jervis, Robert (1979), "Systems theories and diplomatic history," in P. G. Lauren, ed., *Diplomacy: New Approaches in Theory, History, and Policy*, New York: Free Press, pp. 212–44.

Jervis, Robert (1997), *System Effects: Complexity in Political and Social Life*, Princeton: Princeton University Press.

Job, Brian L. (1976), "Membership in inter-nation alliances: 1815–1865," in D. A. Zinnes and J. V. Gillespie, eds., *Mathematical Models in International Relations*, New York: Praeger, pp. 74–109.

Job, Brian L. (1981), "Grins without cats: in pursuit of knowledge of inter-nation alliances," in P. T. Hopmann, D. A. Zinnes, and J. D. Singer, eds., *Cumulation in International Relations Research*, Denver: University of Denver Graduate School of International Studies, pp. 39–63.

Joffe, Josef (1987), *The Limited Partnership: Europe, the United States, and the Burdens of Alliance*, Cambridge: Ballinger.

Joffe, Josef (1995), "'Bismarck' or 'Britain'? Toward an American grand strategy after bipolarity," *International Security*, 19:4, 94–117.

Jones, Daniel M. (1994), "Balancing and bandwagoning in militarized interstate disputes," in F. W. Wayman and P. F. Diehl, eds., *Reconstructing Realpolitik*, Ann Arbor: University of Michigan Press, pp. 227–44.

Jones, Philip R. (1988), "Defense alliances and international trade," *Journal of Conflict Resolution*, 32:1, 123–40.

Kaeber, Ernst (1907), *Die Idee des europäischen Gleichgewichts in der publizistischen Literatur vom 16. bis zur Mitte des 18. Jahrhunderts*, Berlin: Duncker.

Kann, Robert E. (1976), "Alliances vs. ententes," *World Politics*, 28:4, 611–21.

Kaplan, Herbert H. (1968), *Russia and the Outbreak of the Seven Years War*, Berkeley: University of California Press.

Kaplan, Morton A. (1957), *System and Process in International Politics*, New York: Wiley.

Kapstein, Ethan B., and Michael Mastanduno, eds. (1999), *Unipolar Politics: Realism and State Strategies After the Cold War*, New York: Columbia University Press.

Kaufman, Robert G. (1992a), "To balance or to bandwagon? Alignment decisions in 1930s Europe," *Security Studies*, 1:3, 417–47.

Kaufman, Robert G. (1992b), "The lessons of the 1930s, alliance theory, and US grand strategy: a reply to Stephen Walt," *Security Studies*, 1:4, 690–96.

Keeley, Michael (1980), "Organizational analogy: a comparison of organismic and social contract models," *Administrative Science Quarterly*, 25:2, 337–62.

Kegley, Charles W., and Gregory A. Raymond (1982), "Alliance norms and war: a new piece in an old puzzle," *International Studies Quarterly*, 26:4, 572–95.

Kegley, Charles W., and Gregory A. Raymond, (1990a), "Forging ties that bind: the impact of war termination on alliance norms," in C. Gochman and A. Sabrosky, eds., *Prisoners of War? Nation-States in the Modern Era*, Lexington: Lexington Books, 271–84.

Kegley, Charles W., and Gregory A. Raymond (1990b), *When Trust Breaks Down: Alliance Norms and World Politics*, Columbia: University of South Carolina Press.

Kegley, Charles W., and Gregory A. Raymond (1994a), *A Multipolar Peace? Great Power Politics in the Twenty-First Century*, New York: St. Martin's Press, 89–120.

Kegley, Charles W., and Gregory A. Raymond (1994b), "Networks of intrigue? Realpolitik, alliances, and international security," in F. W. Wayman and P. F. Diehl, eds., *Reconstructing Realpolitik*, Ann Arbor: University of Michigan Press, 185–203.

Kennedy, Paul (1987), *The Rise and Fall of the Great Powers*, New York: Random House.

Keohane, Robert O. (1988), "Alliances, threats, and the uses of neorealism," *International Security*, 13:1, 169–76.

Kim, Woosang (1989), "Power, alliance, and major wars, 1816–1975," *Journal of Conflict Resolution*, 33:2, 255–73.

Kim, Woosang (1991), "Alliance transition and great power war," *American Journal of Political Science*, 35:4, 833–50.

Kluxen, Kurt (1978), "Zur Balanceidee in 18. Jahrhundert," in *Vom Staat des*

Ancien Régime zum modernen Parteienstaat, Festschrift für Theodor Schieder, München-Wien: Oldenbourg, pp. 41–58.

Krasner, Stephen D. (1991), "Global communications and national power: life on the Pareto frontier," *World Politics*, 43:3, 336–66.

Krause, Volker, and J. David Singer (2001), "Minor powers, alliances, and armed conflict: some preliminary remarks," in E. Reiter and H. Gärtner, eds., *Small States and Alliances*, Heidelberg: Physica, pp. 15–23.

Labourdette, Jean-François (1990), *Vergennes. Ministre Principal de Louis XVI*, Paris: Desjonquères.

Labs, Eric J. (1992), "Do weak states bandwagon?" *Security Studies*, 1:3, 383–416.

Labs, Eric J. (1997), "Beyond victory: offensive realism and the expansion of war aims," *Security Studies*, 6:4, 1–49.

Lai, Brian, and Dan Reiter (2000), "Democracy, political similarity, and international alliances, 1816–1992," *Journal of Conflict Resolution*, 44:2, 203–27.

Lake, David A., and Robert Powell (1999), "International relations: a strategic-choice approach," in D. A. Lake and R. Powell, eds., *Strategic Choice and International Relations*, Princeton: Princeton University Press, pp. 3–38.

Lalman, David, and David Newman (1991), "Alliance Formation and National Security," *International Interactions*, 16:4, 239–253.

Langdon, Stephen, and Alan H. Gardiner (1920), "The treaty of alliance between Hattusili, king of the Hittites, and the pharaoh Ramesses II of Egypt," *Journal of Egyptian Archeology*, 6:3, 179–205.

Langford, Paul (1976), *Modern British Foreign Policy: The Eighteenth Century, 1688–1815*, London: Black.

Larson, Deborah W. (1991), "Bandwagon images in American foreign policy: myth or reality?" in R. Jervis and J. Snyder, eds., *Dominoes and Bandwagons: Strategic Beliefs and Great Power Competition in the Eurasian Rimland*, Oxford: Oxford University Press, pp. 85–111.

Lawson, Fred H. (1976), "Alliance behavior in nineteenth-century Europe," *American Political Science Review*, 70:3, 932–34.

Leeds, Brett A. (2003), "Alliance reliability in times of war: explaining state decisions to violate treaties," *International Organization*, 57:4, 801–27.

Leeds, Brett A., Andrew G. Long, and Sara McLaughlin Mitchell (2000), "Reevaluating alliance reliability: specific threats, specific promises," *Journal of Conflict Resolution*, 44:5, 686–99.

Levy, Jack S. (1981), "Alliance formation and war behavior: an analysis of the great powers, 1495–1975," *Journal of Conflict Resolution*, 25:4, 581–613.

Levy, Jack S., and Michael N. Barnett (1992), "Alliance formation, domestic political economy, and third world security," *Jerusalem Journal of International Relations*, 14:4, 19–40.

Levy, Jack S., and William R. Thompson (2005), "Hegemonic threats and great power balancing in Europe, 1495–1999," *Security Studies*, 14:1, 1–33.

Li, Richard P., and William R. Thompson (1978), "The stochastic process of alliance formation behavior," *American Political Science Review*, 72:4, 1288–1303.

Liska, George (1962), *Nations in Alliance: The Limits of Interdependence*, Baltimore: Johns Hopkins University Press.

Liska, George (1968), *Alliances and the Third World*, Baltimore: Johns Hopkins University Press.

Little, Richard (2007), *The Balance of Power in International Relations: Metaphors, Myths and Models*, Cambridge: Cambridge University Press.

Lodge, Richard (1923), *Great Britain and Prussia in the Eighteenth Century*, Oxford: Clarendon.

Lodge, Richard (1930), "The maritime powers in the eighteenth century," *History*, 15, 246–51.

Lodge, Richard (1935), "The Anglo-French alliance, 1716–1731," in A. Coville and H. W. Temperley, eds., *Studies in Anglo-French History During the Eighteenth, Nineteenth and Twentieth Centuries*, Cambridge: Cambridge University Press, pp. 1–18.

Long, Andrew G. (2003), "Defense pacts and international trade," *Journal of Peace Research*, 40:5, 537–52.

Madariaga, Isabel de (1959), "The secret Austro-Russian Treaty of 1781," *Slavonic and East European Review*, 38:90, 114–45.

Madariaga, Isabel de (1981), *Russia in the Age of Catherine the Great*, New Haven: Yale University Press.

Mandelbaum, Michael (1981), *The Nuclear Revolution: International Politics Before and After Hiroshima*, Cambridge: Cambridge University Press.

Mansfield, Edward D., and Rachel Bronson (1997), "Alliances, preferential trade arrangements, and international trade," *American Political Science Review*, 91:1, 94–107.

McCalla, Robert B. (1996), "NATO's persistence after the cold war," *International Organization*, 50:3, 445–75.

McDonald, H. Brooke, and Richard Rosecrance (1985), "Alliance and structural balance in the international system: a reinterpretation," *Journal of Conflict Resolution*, 29:1, 57–82.

McGill, William I. (1968), "The roots of policy: Kaunitz in Italy and the Netherlands, 1742–46," *Central European History*, 1:2, 131–49.

McGill, William I. (1971), "The roots of policy: Kaunitz in Vienna and Versailles," *Journal of Modern History*, 42:2, 228–44.

McGowan, Patrick J., and Robert M. Rood (1975), "Alliance behavior in balance of power systems: applying a Poisson Model to nineteenth-century Europe," *American Political Science Review*, 69:3, 859–70.

McGowan, Patrick J., and Robert M. Rood (1977), "Letter to the editor," *American Political Science Review*, 71:3, 1049–50.

McKay, Derek (1986), *Allies of Convenience: Diplomatic Relations Between Great Britain and Austria, 1714–1719*, London: Garland.

McKay, Derek, and Hamish M. Scott (1983), *The Rise of the Great Powers, 1648–1815*, London: Longman.

Mearsheimer, John J. (1994–95), "The false promise of international institutions," *International Security*, 19:3, 5–49.

Mearsheimer, John J. (2001), *The Tragedy of Great Power Politics*, New York: Norton.

Meinecke, Friedrich (1924/1962), *Die Idee der Staaträson in der neueren Geschichte*, München-Berlin: Oldenbourg (Engl. trans. D. Scott, *Machiavellism: The Doctrine of raison d'état and Its Place in Modern History*, New Haven: Yale University Press).

Middleton, Richard (1985), *The Bells of Victory: The Pitt-Newcastle Ministry and the Conduct of the Seven Years' War, 1757–62*, Cambridge: Cambridge University Press.

Miller, Daniel A. (1970), *Sir Joseph Yorke and Anglo-Dutch Relations, 1774–1780*, the Hague: Mouton.

Miller, Eric A., and Arkady Toritsyn (2005), "Bringing the leader back in: internal threats and alignment theory in the Commonwealth of Independent States," *Security Studies*, 14:2, 325–63.

Miller, Gregory D. (2003), "Hypotheses on reputation: alliance choices and the shadow of the past," *Security Studies*, 12:3, 40–78.

Modelski, George (1963), "The study of alliances: a review," *Journal of Conflict Resolution*, 7:4, 769–76.

Morgenthau, Hans J. (1959), "Alliances in theory and practice," in A. Wolfers, ed., *Alliance Policy in the Cold War*, Baltimore: Johns Hopkins University Press, pp. 184–212.

Morgenthau, Hans J. (1973), *Politics Among Nations: The Struggle for Power and Peace*, New York: Knopf, 5th ed. rev.

Morgenthau Hans J., and Kenneth W. Thompson, eds. (1950), *Principles and Problems of International Politics*, New York: Knopf.

Morrow, James D. (1991), "Alliances and asymmetry: an alternative to the capability aggregation model of alliances," *American Journal of Political Science*, 35:4, 904–33.

Morrow, James D. (1993), "Arms versus allies: trade-offs in the search for security," *International Organization*, 47:2, 207–33.

Morrow, James D. (1994), "Alliances, credibility, and peacetime costs," *Journal of Conflict Resolution*, 38:2, 270–97.

Morrow, James D. (1999), "The strategic setting of choices: signaling, commitment, and negotiation in international politics," in D. A. Lake and R. Powell, eds., *Strategic Choice and International Relations*, Princeton: Princeton University Press, pp. 77–114.

Most, Benjamin A., and Randolph M. Siverson (1987), "Substituting arms and alliances, 1870–1914: an exploration in comparative foreign policy," in C. F. Hermann, C. W. Kegley, and J. N. Rosenau, eds., *New Directions in the Study of Foreign Policy*, Boston: Allen & Unwin, pp. 131–60.

Most, Benjamin A., Philip Schrodt, Randolph M. Siverson, and Harvey Starr (1990), "Border and alliance effects in the diffusion of major power conflict, 1815–1965," in C. Gochman and A. Sabrosky, eds., *Prisoners of War? Nation-States in the Modern Era*, Lexington: Lexington Books, pp. 209–29.

Moul, William B. (1983), "European great power pacta de contrahendo and interstate imperial war, 1815–1939: suggestions of pattern," *Canadian Journal of Political Science*, 16:1, 81–102.

Mueller, Karl (1995), "Patterns of alliance: alignment balancing and stability in eastern Europe," *Security Studies*, 5:1, 38–76.

Murdock, James C., and Todd Sandler (1982), "A theoretical and empirical analysis of NATO," *Journal of Conflict Resolution*, 26:2, 237–63.

Murdock, James C., and Todd Sandler (1984), "Complementarity, free riding, and the military expenditures of NATO allies," *Journal of Public Economics*, 25, 83–101.

Murdock, James C., and Todd Sandler (1991), "NATO burden sharing and the forces of change: further observations," *International Studies Quarterly*, 35:1, 109–14.

Muret, Pierre (1949), *La prépondérance anglaise, 1715–1763*, Paris: Presses Universitaires de France, 3rd ed.

Murphy, Orville T. (1982), *Charles Gravier, Comte de Vergennes: French Diplomacy in the Age of Revolution, 1719–1787*, Albany: State University of New York Press.

Murray, John L. (1942–43), "Baltic commerce and power politics in the early eighteenth century," *Huntington Library Quarterly*, 6, 293–312.

Nicholson, Michael (1989), *Formal Theories in International Relations*, Cambridge: Cambridge University Press, pp. 116–46.

Niebuhr, Reinhold (1932), *Moral Man and Immoral Society: A Study in Ethics and Politics*, New York: Scribner's.

Nooteboom, Bart (2006), "Simmel's treatise on the triad (1908)," *Journal of Institutional Economics*, 2:3, 365–83.

Oakley, Stewart P. (1994), "Trade, peace and the balance of power: Britain in the Baltic, 1603–1802," in G. Rystad, K. R. Böhme, and W. M. Carlgren, eds., *In Quest of Power and Security: The Baltic in Power Politics, 1500–1900*, Stockholm: Probus, vol. 1, pp. 221–56.

Oliva, Lawrence J. (1964), *Misalliance: French Policy in Russia During the Seven Years' War*, New York: New York University Press.

Olson, Mancur, and Richard Zeckhauser (1966), "An economic theory of alliances," *Review of Economics and Statistics*, 48:3, 266–79.

Olson, Mancur, and Richard Zeckhauser (1967), "Collective goods, comparative advantage, and alliance efficiency," in R. N. McKean, ed., *Issues in Defense Economics*, New York: Columbia University Press, pp. 25–48.

Oneal, John R. (1990a), "Testing the theory of collective action: NATO defense burdens, 1950–1984," *Journal of Conflict Resolution*, 34:3, 426–48.

Oneal, John R. (1990b), "The theory of collective action and burden sharing in NATO," *International Organization*, 44:3, 379–402.

Oneal, John R., and Mark A. Elrod (1989), "NATO Burden Sharing and the Forces of Change," *International Studies Quarterly*, 33:4, 435–56.

Oppenheimer, Joe (1979), "Collective goods and alliances: a reassessment," *Journal of Conflict Resolution*, 23:3, 387–407.

Oppenheimer, Joe (1980), "Some reflections on clubs and alliances: an extension and rejoinder," *Journal of Conflict Resolution*, 24:3, 549–57.

Oren, Ido (1990), "The war proneness of alliances," *Journal of Conflict Resolution*, 34:2, 208–33.

Osgood, Robert E. (1968), *Alliances and American Foreign Policy*, Baltimore: Johns Hopkins University Press.

Ostrom, Charles W., and Francis W. Hoole (1978), "Alliances and wars revisited: a research note," *International Studies Quarterly*, 22:2, 215–36.

Oursel, Paul (1921), *La diplomatie de la France sous Louis XVI: succession de Bavière et paix de Teschen*, Paris: Plon-Nourrit.

Owen, John M. (2005), "When do ideologies produce alliances? the Holy Roman Empire, 1517–1555," *International Studies Quarterly*, 49:1, 73–99.

Palmer, Glenn (1990), "Alliance politics and issue-areas: determinants of defense spending," *American Journal of Political Science*, 34:1, 190–211.

Palmer, Glenn (1991), "Corralling the free rider: deterrence and the western alliance," *International Studies Quarterly*, 34:2, 147–64.

Pares, Richard (1936), "American versus continental warfare, 1739–1763," *English Historical Review*, 51:203, 429–65.

Pares, Richard (1938), *Colonial Blockade and Neutral Rights, 1739–1763*, Oxford: Oxford University Press.

Peters, Marie (1980), *Pitt and Popularity: The Patriot Minister and London Opinion During the Seven Years' War*, Oxford: Clarendon.

Portinaro, Pier Paolo (1986), *Il Terzo. Una figura del politico*, Milano: Angeli.

Powell, Robert (1999), *In the Shadow of Power: States and Strategies in International Politics*, Princeton: Princeton University Press.

Powley, Edward B. (1972), *The Naval Side of King William's War*, London: Baker.

Priess, David (1996), "Balance-of-threat theory and the genesis of the Gulf Cooperation Council: an interpretative case study," *Security Studies*, 5:4, 143–71.

Quazza, Guido (1968), "La politica dell'equilibrio nel secolo XVIII," in *Nuove Questioni di Storia Moderna*, Milano: Marzorati, vol. 2, pp. 1181–1215.

Rafferty, Kirsten (2003), "An institutional reinterpretation of cold war alliance systems: insights for alliance theory," *Canadian Journal of Political Science*, 36:2, 341–62.

Rain, Pierre (1945), *La diplomatie française*, Paris: Plon, vol. 1: *D'Henry IV à Vergennes*.

Rashed, Zenab E. (1951), *The Peace of Paris, 1763*, Liverpool: Liverpool University Press.

Raven, G.J.A., and N.A.M. Rodger, eds. (1990), *Navies and Armies: The Anglo-Dutch Relationship in War and Peace, 1688–1988*, Edinburgh: Donald.

Ray, James L. (1990), "Friends as foes: international conflict and war between formal allies," in C. Gochman and A. Sabrosky, eds., *Prisoners of War? Nation-States in the Modern Era*, Lexington: Lexington Books, pp. 73–91.

Reiter, Dan (1994), "Learning, realism, and alliances: the weight of the shadow of the past," *World Politics*, 46:4, 490–526.

Reiter, Dan (1996), *Crucible of Beliefs: Learning, Alliances, and World Wars*, Ithaca: Cornell University Press.

Reiter, Erich, and Heinz Gärtner, eds. (2001), *Small States and Alliances*, Heidelberg: Physica.

Resende-Santos, Joao (1992), "System and agent: comments on Labs and Kaufman," *Security Studies*, 1:4, 697–702.

Riker, William H. (1962), *The Theory of Political Coalitions*, New Haven: Yale University Press.

Risse-Kappen, Thomas (1995), *Cooperation Among Democracies: The European Influence on U.S. Foreign Policy*, Princeton: Princeton University Press.

Ritter, Gerhard (1954/1968), *Friedrich der Grosse*, Heidelberg: Quelle und Meyer (Engl. trans. P. Paret, *Frederick the Great*, Berkeley: University of California Press).

Ritter, Gerhard (1954/1969), *Staatskunst und Kriegshandwerk. Das Problem des "Militarismus" in Deutschland*, München: Oldenbourg (Engl. trans. H. Norden, *The Sword and the Scepter: The Problem of Militarism in Germany*, Coral Gables: University of Miami Press, vol. 1).

Roberts, Penfield (1947), *The Quest for Security, 1715–1740*, New York: Harper & Row.

Robson, Eric (1957), "The seven years war," in *New Cambridge Modern History*, Cambridge: Cambridge University Press, vol. 7, pp. 465–86.

Rodger, N.A.M. (1990), "The British view of the functioning of the Anglo-Dutch alliance, 1688–1795," in G.J.A. Raven and N.A.M. Rodger, eds., *Navies and Armies: The Anglo-Dutch Relationship in War and Peace, 1688–1988*, Edinburgh: Donald, pp. 12–32.

Rodger, N.A.M. (1992), "The continental commitment in the eighteenth century," in L. Freedman, P. Hayes, and R. O'Neill, eds., *War, Strategy, and International Politics*, Oxford: Clarendon, pp. 39–55.

Roider, Karl A. (1982), *Austria's Eastern Question, 1700–1790*, Princeton: Princeton University Press.

Rose, Gideon (1998), "Neoclassical realism and theories of foreign policy," *World Politics*, 51:1, 144–72.

Rose, J. Holland (1914), "Frederick the Great and England, 1756–1763," *English Historical Review*, 29:113, 79–93 and 29:114, 257–75.

Rosecrance, Richard, and Chih-Cheng Lo (1996), "Balancing, stability and war: the mysterious case of the Napoleonic international system," *International Studies Quarterly*, 40:4, 479–500.

Rosecrance, Richard, and Arthur A. Stein, eds. (1993), *The Domestic Bases of Grand Strategy*, Ithaca: Cornell University Press.

Rosen, Steven (1970), "A model of war and alliances," in J. Friedman, C. Bladen, and S. Rosen, eds., *Alliance in International Politics*, Boston: Allyn & Bacon, pp. 215–37.

Rothstein, Robert L. (1968), *Alliances and Small Powers*, New York: Columbia University Press.

Russett, Bruce M. (1968), "Components of an operational theory of international alliance formation," *Journal of Conflict Resolution*, 12:3, 285–301.

Russett, Bruce M. (1970), *What Price Vigilance?* New Haven: Yale University Press.

Russett, Bruce M. (1971), "An empirical typology of international military alliances," *Midwest Journal of Political Science*, 15:2, 262–89.

Sabrosky, Alan N. (1980), "Interstate alliances: their reliability and the expansion of war," in J. D. Singer, ed., *The Correlates of War II: Testing Some Realpolitik Models*, New York: Free Press, pp. 161–98.

Sabrosky, Alan N. (1985), "Alliance aggregation, capability distribution, and the expansion of interstate war," in A. N. Sabrosky, ed., *Polarity and War: The Changing Structure of International Conflict*, Boulder: Westview, pp. 145–89.

Salomon, Robert (1935), *La politique orientale de Vergennes (1780–1784)*, Paris: Les Presses Modernes.

Sandler, Todd (1975), "The economic theory of alliances: realigned," in C. Liske, W. Loehr, and J. McCamant, eds., *Comparative Public Policy: Issues, Theories, and Methods*, New York: Wiley, pp. 223–39.

Sandler, Todd (1977), "Impurity of defense: an application to the economics of alliances," *Kyklos*, 30, 443–60.

Sandler, Todd (1993), "The economic theory of alliances: a survey," *Journal of Conflict Resolution*, 37:3, 446–83.

Sandler, Todd, and Jon Cauley (1975), "On the economic theory of alliances," *Journal of Conflict Resolution*, 19:2, 330–48.

Sandler, Todd, Jon Cauley, and John F. Forbes (1980), "In defense of a collective goods theory of alliances," *Journal of Conflict Resolution*, 24:3, 537–47.

Sandler, Todd, and Keith Hartley (1999), *The Political Economy of NATO: Past, Present, and into the 21st Century*, Cambridge: Cambridge University Press.

Saperstein, Alwin M. (1992), "Alliance building versus independent action: a nonlinear modeling approach to comparative international stability," *Journal of Conflict Resolution*, 36:3, 518–45.

Savory, Reginald A. (1966), *His Britannic Majesty's Army in Germany During the Seven Years War*, Oxford: Clarendon.

Scarborough, Grace I., and Bruce Bueno de Mesquita (1988), *Threat and Alignment Behavior*, International Interactions, 14:1, 85–93.

Schelling, Thomas (1960), *The Strategy of Conflict*, Cambridge: Harvard University Press.

Schelling, Thomas (1966), *Arms and Influence*, New Haven: Yale University Press.

Schelling, Thomas (1984), "Strategic analysis and social problems," in *Choice and Consequence*, Cambridge: Harvard University Press, pp. 195–212.

Schilling, Lothar (1994), *Kaunitz und das Renversement des alliances. Studien zur aussenpolitischen Konzeption Wenzel Antons von Kaunitz*, Berlin: Duncker und Humblot.

Schroeder, Paul W. (1976), "Alliances, 1815–1945: weapons of power and tools of management," in K. Knorr, ed., *Historical Dimensions of National Security Problems*, Lawrence: Allen, pp. 227–62.

Schroeder, Paul W. (1977), "Quantitative studies in the balance of power: an historian's reaction," *Journal of Conflict Resolution*, 21:1, 3–22.

Schroeder, Paul W. (1993), "The Transformation of Political Thinking, 1787–1848," in J. Snyder and R. Jervis, eds., *Coping with Complexity in the International System*, Boulder: Westview, pp. 47–70.

Schroeder, Paul W. (1994a), "Historical reality vs. neo-realist theory," *International Security*, 19:1, 108–48.

Schroeder, Paul W. (1994b), *The Transformation of European Politics, 1763–1848*, Oxford: Clarendon.

Schuman, Frederick (1948), *International Politics*, New York: McGraw-Hill, 4th ed.

Schwarzenberger, Georg (1941), *Power Politics*, London: Cape.

Schweizer, Karl W. (1989), *England, Prussia, and the Seven Years War: Studies in Alliance Policy and Diplomacy*, Lewiston: Mellen Press.

Schweizer, Karl W. (1991), *Frederick the Great, William Pitt, and Lord Bute: The Anglo-Prussian Alliance, 1756–1763*, New York: Garland.

Schweller, Randall L. (1994), "Bandwagoning for profit: bringing the revisionist state back in," *International Security*, 19:1, 72–107.

Schweller, Randall L. (1997), "New realist research on alliances: refining, not refuting, Waltz's balancing proposition," *American Political Science Review*, 91:4, 927–30.

Schweller, Randall L. (1998), *Deadly Imbalances: Tripolarity and Hitler's Strategy of World Conquest*, New York: Columbia University Press.

Schweller, Randall L. (2004), "Unanswered threats: a neoclassical realist theory of underbalancing," *International Security*, 29:2, 159–201.

Schweller, Randall L. (2006), *Unanswered Threats: Political Constraints on the Balance of Power*, Princeton: Princeton University Press.

Scott, Hamish M. (1979), "The importance of Bourbon naval reconstruction to the strategy of Choiseul after the seven years war," *International History Review*, 1:1, 17–35.

Scott, Hamish M. (1989), " 'The true principles of the revolution': the duke of Newcastle and the idea of the Old System," in J. Black, ed., *Knights Errant and True Englishmen: British Foreign Policy, 1660–1800*, Edinburgh: Donald, pp. 55–91.

Scott, Hamish M. (1990), *British Foreign Policy in the Age of the American Revolution*, Oxford: Clarendon.

Scott, Hamish M. (1999), "Louis XVI and Vergennes," *International History Review*, 21:4, 941–44.

Seabury, Paul, ed. (1965), *Balance of Power*, San Francisco: Chandler.

Shaffer, Stephen M. (1978), "Alliance politics: a model based on divisibility of payoffs," in W. Loehr and T. Sandler, eds., *Public Goods and Public Policy*, Beverly Hills: Sage, pp. 145–76.

Sheehan, Michael (1996), *The Balance of Power: History and Theory*, London: Routledge.

Shennan, Joseph H. (1979), *Philippe Duke of Orléans: Regent of France, 1715–23*, London: Thames and Hudson.

Showalter, Dennis (1996), *The Wars of Frederick the Great*, London: Longman.
Simms, Brendan, and Torsten Riotte, eds. (2007), *The Hanoverian Dimension in British History, 1714–1837*, Cambridge: Cambridge University Press.
Simowitz, Roslyn L. (1976), "Alliances and the theory of collective goods: an evaluation," in D. A. Zinnes and J. V. Gillespie, eds., *Mathematical Models in International Relations*, New York: Praeger, pp. 333–47.
Singer, J. David, and Melvin Small (1966), "Formal alliances, 1815–1939: a quantitative description," *Journal of Peace Research*, 3:1, 1–32.
Singer, J. David, and Melvin Small (1968), "Alliance aggregation and the onset of war, 1815–1945," in J. D. Singer, ed., *Quantitative International Politics*, New York: Free Press, pp. 247–86.
Singer, J. David, Stuart A. Bremer, and John Stuckey (1972), "Capability distribution, uncertainty, and major power war, 1820–1965," in B. M. Russett, ed., *Peace, War, and Numbers*, Beverly Hills: Sage, pp. 19–48.
Siverson, Randolph M., and George T. Duncan (1976), "Stochastic models of international alliance initiation: 1885–1965," in D. A. Zinnes and J. V. Gillespie, eds., *Mathematical Models in International Relations*, New York: Praeger, pp. 110–31.
Siverson, Randolph M., and Juliann Emmons (1991), "Birds of a feather: democratic political systems and alliance choices in the twentieth century," *Journal of Conflict Resolution*, 35:2, 285–306.
Siverson, Randolph M., and Joel King (1979), "Alliances and the expansion of war," in J. D. Singer and M. D. Wallace, eds., *To Augur Well: Early Warning Indicators in World Politics*, Beverly Hills: Sage, pp. 37–49.
Siverson, Randolph M., and Joel King (1980), "Attributes of national alliance membership and war participation, 1815–1965," *American Journal of Political Science*, 24:1, 1–15.
Siverson, Randolph M., and Charles McCarty (1982), "Alliances in the interwar era, 1919–1939: a re-examination," *Western Political Quarterly*, 35:1, 24–32.
Siverson, Randolph M., and Harvey Starr (1994), "Regime change and the restructuring of alliances," *American Journal of Political Science*, 38:1, 145–61.
Siverson, Randolph M., and Michael Sullivan (1994), "Alliances and war: a new examination of an old problem," *Conflict Management and Peace Science*, 8:1, 1–15.
Siverson, Randolph M., and Michael R. Tennefoss (1984), "Power, alliance, and the escalation of international conflict," *American Political Science Review*, 78:4, 1057–69.
Skålnes, Lars S. (1998), "From the outside in, from the inside out: NATO expansion and international relations theory," *Security Studies*, 7:4, 44–87.
Small, Melvin, and J. David Singer (1969), "Formal alliances, 1816–1965: an extension of the basic data," *Journal of Peace Research*, 6:3, 257–82.
Smit, J. W. (1968), "The Netherlands and Europe in the seventeenth and eighteenth centuries," in J. S. Bromley and E. H. Kossman, eds., *Britain and the Netherlands in Europe and Asia*, London: Macmillan, pp. 13–36.

Smith, Alastair (1995), "Alliance formation and war," *International Studies Quarterly*, 49:4, 405–25.
Smith, Alastair (1998), "Extended deterrence and alliance formation," *International Interactions*, 24:4, 315–43.
Smith, Michael J. (1986), *Realist Thought from Weber to Kissinger*, Baton Rouge: Louisiana State University Press.
Snyder, Glenn H. (1984), "The security dilemma in alliance politics," *World Politics*, 36:4, 461–95.
Snyder, Glenn H. (1990), "Alliance theory: a neorealist first cut," *Journal of International Affairs*, 44:1, 103–25.
Snyder, Glenn H. (1991), "Alliances, balance, and stability," *International Organization*, 45:1, 121–42.
Snyder, Glenn H. (1996), "Process variables in neorealist theory," *Security Studies*, 5:3, 167–92.
Snyder, Glenn H. (1997), *Alliance Politics*, Ithaca: Cornell University Press.
Snyder, Glenn H., and Paul Diesing (1977), *Conflict Among Nations: Bargaining, Decision-Making, and System Structure in International Crises*, Princeton: Princeton University Press.
Snyder, Jack (1991), *Myths of Empire: Domestic Politics and International Ambition*, Ithaca: Cornell University Press.
Sorel, Albert (1881), "Vergennes et sa politique," *Revue historique*, t. 15, 273–82.
Sorel, Albert (1885–1904), *L'Europe et la Révolution Française*, Paris: Plon, 8 vols., vol 1: *Les moeurs politiques et les traditions*, reprinted 1946.
Sorel, Albert (1902), *La Question d'Orient au XVIIIe siècle. La partage de la Pologne et le traité de Kaïnardji*, Paris: Plon, 3rd ed.
Sorokin, Gerald L. (1994a), "Alliance formation and general deterrence: a game-theoretic model and the case of Israel," *Journal of Conflict Resolution*, 38:2, 298–325.
Sorokin, Gerald L. (1994b), "Arms, alliances, and security tradeoffs in enduring rivalries," *International Studies Quarterly*, 38:3, 421–46.
Spencer, Frank (1956), The Anglo-Prussian breach of 1762: an historical revision," *History*, 41, February–October, 100–112.
Spykman, Nicholas J. (1942), *America's Strategy in World Politics: The United States and the Balance of Power*, New York: Harcourt, Brace & World.
Starr, Harvey, and Randolph M. Siverson (1990), "Alliances and geopolitics," *Political Geography Quarterly*, 9:3, 232–48.
Stein, Arthur A. (1983), "Coordination and collaboration: regimes in an anarchic world," in S. D. Krasner, ed., *International Regimes*, Ithaca: Cornell University Press, pp. 115–40.
Stein, Arthur A. (1990), *Why Nations Cooperate: Circumstance and Choice in International Relations*, Ithaca: Cornell University Press, pp. 151–71.
Stein, Arthur A. (1999), "The limits of strategic choice: constrained rationality and incomplete explanation," in D. A. Lake and R. Powell, eds., *Strategic Choice and International Relations*, Princeton: Princeton University Press, pp. 197–228.

Stoppino, Mario (2001), *Potere e teoria politica*, Milano: Giuffré, 2nd ed.

Sullivan, John D. (1974), "International alliances," in M. Haas, ed., *International Systems: A Behavioral Approach*, New York: Chandler, pp. 99–122.

Szabo, Franz A. J. (1979), "Prince Kaunitz and the balance of power," *International History Review*, 1:3, 399–408.

Szabo, Franz A. J. (1994), *Kaunitz and Enlightened Absolutism, 1753–1780*, Cambridge: Cambridge University Press.

Taylor, Alan J. P. (1954), *The Struggle for Mastery in Europe, 1848–1918*, Oxford: Clarendon.

Thies, Wallace J. (1987), "Alliances and collective goods: a reappraisal," *Journal of Conflict Resolution*, 31:2, 298–332.

Thies, Wallace J. (1991), "Randomness, contagion and heterogeneity in the formation of interstate alliances: a reconsideration," *International Interactions*, 16:4, 335–54.

Tratchevsky, Alexandre (1880 and 1881), "La France et l'Allemagne sous Louis XVI," *Revue historique*, t. 14, 241–85 and t. 15, 1–46.

Tunstall, W. C. Brian (1938), *William Pitt Earl of Chatham*, London: Hodder and Stoughton.

Turner, Edward R. (1919), "Parliament and foreign affairs, 1630–1760," *English Historical Review*, 34: April, 172–97.

Vasquez, John A. (1997), "The realist paradigm and degenerative versus progressive research programs: an appraisal of neotraditional research on Waltz's balancing proposition," *American Political Science Review*, 91:4, 899–912.

Vasquez, John A. (1998), *The Power of Power Politics: From Classical Realism to Neotraditionalism*, Cambridge: Cambridge University Press.

Väyrynen, Raino (1976), "The theory of collective goods, military alliances, and international security," *International Social Science Journal*, 28:2, 288–305.

Waddington, Richard P. (1896), *Louis XV et le renversement des alliances, 1754–56. Préliminaires de la Guerre de Sept Ans*, Paris: Firmin-Didot.

Waddington, Richard P. (1899–1914), *La guerre de sept ans*, Paris: Firmin-Didot, 5 vols.

Wallace, Michael D. (1973), "Alliance polarization, cross-cutting, and international war, 1815–1964: a measurement procedure and some preliminary evidence," *Journal of Conflict Resolution*, 17:4, 575–604.

Wallender, Celeste A., and Robert O. Keohane (1999), "Risk, threat, and security institutions," in H. Haftendorn, R. O. Keohane, and C. Wallender, eds., *Imperfect Unions. Security Institutions over Time and Space*, Oxford: Oxford University Press, pp. 21–47.

Walt, Stephen M. (1985), "Alliance formation and the balance of world power," *International Security*, 9:4, 3–43.

Walt, Stephen M. (1987), *The Origins of Alliances*, Ithaca: Cornell University Press.

Walt, Stephen M. (1988), "Testing theories of alliance formation: the case of southeast Asia," *International Organization*, 42:2, 275–316.

Walt, Stephen M. (1989), "Alliances in theory and practice: what lies ahead?" *Journal of International Affairs*, 43:1, 1–17.

Walt, Stephen M. (1992), "Alliance, threats, and US grand strategy: a reply to Kaufman and Labs," *Security Studies*, 1:3, 448–82.

Walt, Stephen M. (1997a), "The progressive power of realism," *American Political Science Review*, 91:4, 931–35.

Walt, Stephen M. (1997b), "Why alliances endure or collapse," *Survival*, 39:1, 156–79.

Waltz, Kenneth N. (1959), *Man, the State and War: A Theoretical Analysis*, New York: Columbia University Press.

Waltz, Kenneth N. (1979), *Theory of International Politics*, Reading: Addison-Wesley.

Waltz, Kenneth N. (1986), "Reflections on *Theory of International Politics*: a response to my critics," in R. O. Keohane, ed., *Neorealism and Its Critics*, New York: Columbia University Press, 1986, pp. 322–45.

Waltz, Kenneth N. (1996), "International politics is not foreign policy," *Security Studies*, 6:1, 54–57.

Waltz, Kenneth N. (1997), "Evaluating theories," *American Political Science Review*, 91:4, 913–17.

Waltz, Kenneth N. (2000), "Structural realism after the cold war," *International Security*, 25:1, 5–41.

Ward, Michael D. (1982), *Research Gaps in Alliance Dynamics*, Denver: University of Denver Graduate School of International Studies.

Wayman, Frank W. (1990), "Alliances and war: a time-series analysis," in C. Gochman and A. Sabrosky, eds., *Prisoners of War? Nation-States in the Modern Era*, Lexington: Lexington Books, pp. 93–113.

Weitsman, Patricia A. (1997), "Intimate enemies: the politics of peacetime alliances," *Security Studies*, 7:1, 156–92.

Weitsman, Patricia A. (2003), "Alliance cohesion and coalition warfare: the Central Powers and Triple Entente," *Security Studies*, 12:3, 79–113.

Weitsman, Patricia A. (2004), *Dangerous Alliances: Proponents of Peace, Weapons of War*, Stanford: Stanford University Press.

Whiteneck, Daniel J. (2001), "Long-term bandwagoning and short-term balancing: the lessons of coalition behavior from 1792 to 1815," *Review of International Studies*, 27:2, 151–68.

Wight, Martin (1978), *Power Politics* (edited by H. Bull and C. Holbraad), New York: Holmes & Meier, pp. 122–35.

Wilson, Arthur M. (1936), *French Foreign Policy During the Administration of Cardinal Fleury, 1726–1743*, Cambridge: Harvard University Press.

Wilson, Charles H. (1941), *Anglo-Dutch Commerce and Finance in the Eighteenth Century*, Cambridge: Cambridge University Press.

Wolfers, Arnold (1962), *Discord and Collaboration. Essays on International Politics*, Baltimore: Johns Hopkins University Press.

Wolfers, Arnold (1968), "Alliances," in *International Encyclopaedia of the Social Sciences*, London: Macmillan, vol. 1, pp. 268–71.

Wolfers, Arnold, and Laurence W. Martin, eds. (1956), *The Anglo-American Tradition in Foreign Affairs: Readings from Thomas Moore to Woodrow Wilson*, New Haven: Yale University Press.

Wright, Moorhead, ed. (1975), *Theory and Practice of the Balance of Power, 1486–1914*, London: Dent.

Zakaria, Fareed (1992), "Realism and domestic politics," *International Security*, 17:1, 177–98.

Zeller, Gaston (1955), *Les temps modernes*, Paris: Hachette, vol. 2: *De Louis XIV à 1789*.

Zeller, Gaston (1956), "Le principe d'équilibre dans la politique internationale avant 1789," *Revue historique*, t. 215, 25–37.

Zinnes, Dina A. (1970), "Coalition theories and the balance of power," in S. Groennings, E. W. Kelley, and M. Leiserson, eds., *The Study of Coalition Behavior: Theoretical Perspectives and Cases from Four Continents*, New York: Holt, Rinehart & Winston, pp. 351–69.

Zwitzer, H. L. (1990), "The British and Netherlands armies in relation to the Anglo-Dutch alliance, 1688–1795," in G.J.A Raven and N.A.M. Rodger, eds., *Navies and Armies: The Anglo-Dutch Relationship in War and Peace, 1688–1988*, Edinburgh: Donald, pp. 33–48.

Index